THE AMERICAN ALPINE JOURNAL

2024

COVER: Morning at 7,300 meters on the north face of Jannu. Matt Cornell (helmet) contemplates a cold start to day five. See story on p.10. [A rope below the bivouac was digitally removed from this image.] *Jackson Marvell*

THIS PAGE: Elisabeth Lardschneider and Markus Ranalter on the northwest face of Little Jamyang Ri in India. See p.289. *Stefan Plank*

CONTENTS

10   **JANNU'S NORTH FACE** BY JACKSON MARVELL
A new route in alpine style, after three years of effort.

24   **THE SECRET LINE** BY KENRO NAKAJIMA
Climbing the enigmatic north face of Tirich Mir in Pakistan.

34   **DICKEY DOUBLE** BY MATT CORNELL
A new route and a second ascent on the 5,000-foot east face of
Mt. Dickey—in the same month.

44   **A DREAM FULFILLED** BY ORIOL BARÓ
The 3,000-meter north spur of Monte San Valentín.

50   **RENAISSANCE** BY SILVAN SCHÜPBACH
A new route up the Eiger Nordwand in pure traditional style.

58   **TOMORROW IS ANOTHER DAY** BY MATTHIAS GRIBI
The north face of Flat Top in Kishtwar, India.

66   **BRILLIANT BLUE** BY CHRISTIAN BLACK
A new route up White Sapphire in the Kishtwar Himalaya.

74   **THE LOST WORLD** BY ALEXANDER PARFYONOV
A big wall at altitude in the Tien Shan.

80   **RECON: GRAND DESCENTS**
BY JASON ALBERT AND ADAM FABRIKANT
A half-century of ski alpinism in the Tetons.

PHOTO: During the first ascent of Super Thuraya on a 5,400-meter pillar in India's Miyar Valley. See story on p.294. *Alessandro Baù*

CLIMBS + EXPEDITIONS

94	UNITED STATES
160	CANADA
174	GREENLAND
186	MEXICO
190	PERU
198	BOLIVIA
202	BRAZIL
205	ARGENTINA & CHILE
222	ANTARCTICA
224	NORWAY
230	GREECE
232	MIDDLE EAST
234	AFRICA
239	GEORGIA
243	UZBEKISTAN
245	TAJIKISTAN
246	KYRGYZSTAN
259	KAZAKHSTAN
260	RUSSIA
262	PAKISTAN
282	INDIA
301	NEPAL
328	CHINA
338	NEW ZEALAND
340	IN MEMORIAM
353	BOOK REVIEWS
360	INDEX
384	INTERNATIONAL GRADE CHART

The American Alpine Club
710 10th St., Suite 100
Golden, Colorado, 80401
E-mail: aaj@americanalpineclub.org
publications.americanalpineclub.org
ISBN (paperback): 979-8-9874576-4-1
ISBN (hardcover): 979-8-9874576-5-8

PHOTO: Sebastian Pelletti leading the summit block of
Serra 4 in the Waddington Range of British Columbia.
See p.161. *Ethan Berman*

2023 GREAT RANGES FELLOWSHIP

A-B

Anonymous Supporters
Payam Abbassian
Lisa Abbott
Peter David Ackroyd
Russell Adams
Alpenglow Foundation
and the John Hobby Catto
Family
Mark L. Andreasen
Conrad and Jenni Lowe-
Anker
Michael Edward Ashley
Michael A Barker
George Basch
Maureen Beck
Gordon A. Benner MD
John M. Berry
John Q Bird
Ronald H. Bixby
Brian Block
Jim Bodenhamer
Stephen J. Bonowski
Steve Bott
Ryan M Bouldin
Tanya Bradby and Martin
Slovacek
Dr. Michael T. Brandt
Zachary Brannan
David Brewster
Samuel Britton
Virginia Brown
Jennifer Bruursema
R Scot Buell
Will Butcher

C-D

Edmund and Betsy Cabot
Foundation
Brandon Cambio
Mitch Campbell
Stephen Carroll
John Carter
The Cherry Family
Ward Chewning
Dan and Ilene Cohen
Colby Colegate
Kevin Cooney
Dr. Joshua Corsa
William G. Cox
Lori Coyner
Christopher Croft
Rupert S. Dance
Joseph K. Davidson
Scott E. Davis
Laura Dawson
Rob DeConto
Ed Diffendal
Jeff Dozier
Richard Draves
The Duckworth Family

E-F

James Edwards and
Michele Mass
Justin Egdorf
Stuart H. Ellison
Dan Emmett
Philip Erard
Carla Firey
Keith Martin Fleischman
James A. Frank
Bruce Franks
Alexander S. Friedman
Jim Frush
Tricia Fusco

G-H

Pete Gallagher
Michael Gibbons
David V. Goeddel
Trish Goodwin
Jonathan Gopel
Former Vice President Al
Gore
Matt Gowie
Leah Graham and Eddie
Espinosa
Marc Gravatt
Russell Gray
Dylan Greenberg
Allyson Gunsallus
Vivek Gurudutt
Robert B. Hall
Joan E. Hansen
Dr. Travis Hays
Rocky Henderson
Janette Heung Memorial
Foundation Limited
Scot T. Hillman
Michael Hodges
Jennifer and Marley
Hodgson
Richard E. Hoffman MD
Holdfast Collective
Thomas F. Hornbein MD
Raymond B. Huey
Aimee Hunt
Rob Hutchinson
Minh Huynh

I-K

Alex Intermill and Lisa
McKinney
Zhen Jian
Dylan and Jenna Johnson
Cody Kaemmerlen
Adam Kilgus
Mark and Samskriti King
Karl S. F. Kirchner
Kendall Krause
Gary A. Kuehn

L-M

Phil Lakin Jr.
David Landman and
Marian Hawley
Tom Lannamann
The Lasky-Barajas Family
Fund
Ryan Lauth
Brody Leven
Dave N. Lonack
George H. Lowe III
Howard Lukens
Randy Luskey
Chris Lynch
Liam Mac Sharry
Bridget Martin
Troy Martin
Katie Massey
Edward E. Matthews
Thomas McCarthy
Heidi McDowell
Craig McKibben and Sarah
Merner
Lisa McKinney
Brad and Melissa
McQueen
Andrew C. Mergen
Richard A. Merritt
George Mesires
Paul H. Morrow

N-P

Alan F. Nagel
Anne Nelson
Hilaree J. Nelson Gift Fund
John Nicholson
Sean O'Brien
Peter O'Neil and Kim
Reynolds
Bob Palais
Joyce Palmese
John Parsons
Charles Peck
Dale Allen Peery
Richard Perlman
Jeff Phillips
Michael Plunkett
Mark Powers

R-S

John Raaf
Dr. John D. Reppy
Jodi Richard
Scott Richards
Mark and Teresa Richey
Michael Riley
Carey Roberts
Joel P. Robinson
Rebecca Robinson
Jesse Rubenstein

Peter Sachs
Naoe Sakashita
Jacob Salcone
Anne Sandman
Janet Schlindwein
Raymond VJ Schrag
Steve and Paula Mae
Schwartz
Stephen Scofield
Ellen Sebastian
Karsang Sherpa
Will Shillito
Samuel Silverstein MD
Susan Skagen
Anne Smith
Cody J Smith
James Sneeringer
Steven Sorkin
Katelyn Stahley
Brian Steers
John Brink Stenderup
Barbara Straka
Theodore "Sam" Streibert
Bob and Janette Strode
Brandon Strope
Duncan Stuart
Pavan Surapaneni
Steven J. Swenson
Emerson Stewart and Parisa
Tabriz

T-V

Jack E. and Pat Tackle
John Taladay
Eddie Taylor
Keith Thomajan
Greg Thomsen
Andrew Tomko
Lawrence True and Linda
Brown
Jay Underwood
Alexander R. Uy
Nick Ray Valencia

W-Z

Robert J. Weggel
Steve Whitaker and Sheila
Walsh
Ryan Whitted
Russell Wilcox
Mark D. Wilford
Nathan Cain Wilhelm
Emily Williams
Nina Williams
Grant Winthrop
Dr. Mark Woodard
Bonnie Zhang
Graham Zimmerman
Jane and Jeff Zimmerman

FRIENDS OF THE AAJ

Peter Ackroyd
Gordon A. Benner
Max Buchsbaum
Carla Firey
Richard Hoffman
Holdfast Collective
Dougald MacDonald
Mark Richey
Samuel Silverstein
Theodore "Sam" Streibert

Ossy Freire nearing the
summit of Dragpoche
(6,575m) in Nepal. See
p310. *Joshua Jarrin*

THE AMERICAN ALPINE JOURNAL

EDITOR
Dougald MacDonald

ART DIRECTOR
Randall Levensaler

SENIOR EDITOR
Lindsay Griffin

ASSOCIATE EDITORS
Whitney Clark, Damien Gildea, Michael Levy,
Matt Samet, David Stevenson (Books)

CONTRIBUTING EDITORS
Owen Clarke, Pete Takeda,
Maarten van Haeren

PROOFREADERS
Laura Larson, Bruce Normand, Katie Sauter

TRANSLATORS
Omar Gaytán, Kim Dong-soo, Heikki Ruuska,
Kat Tancock, Xia Zhongming

INDEXERS
Ralph Ferrara, Eve Tallman

CORRESPONDENTS
Steve Gruhn, Mark Westman, *Alaska*; Ian
Welsted, *Canada*; Sevi Bohorquez, Nathan
Heald, Sergio Ramírez Carrascal, *Peru*; Luis
Pardo, *Colombia*; Damien Gildea, *Antarctica*;
Rolando Garibotti, Camilo Rada, Marcelo
Scanu, *Argentina and Chile*; Alex von Ungern,
Bolivia; Harish Kapadia, Nandini Purandare,
India; Rodolphe Popier, Richard Salisbury, *Nepal*;
Hiroshi Hagiwara, Tamotsu Nakamura, Kaoru
Wada, *Japan*; Peter Jensen-Choi, Oh Young-
hoon, *Korea*; Anna Piunova, *Russia, Tajikistan,
and Kyrgyzstan*; Xia Zhongming, Zhu Leibo,
China; Ben Dare, *New Zealand*

ADVISORY BOARD
Chantel Astorga, Kelly Cordes, Brody Leven
(ski alpinism), Colin Haley, Mark Jenkins, Simon
Richardson, Graham Zimmerman

SPECIAL THANKS TO...
Jenny Abegg, Christine Blackmon, Alex Buisse,
Ryan Cooper, Elizabeth Cromwell, Jeff Deikis,
Foster Denney, Chris Kalman, Carter Ley, Sierra
McGivney, Anna Piunova, Erik Rieger, members
of the American Alpine Club, and our hundreds
of authors, photographers, and donors

United
WE
Climb.

As an AAC member, you are linked to a Club of passionate climbers focused on connecting with each other, protecting climbing landscapes, and equipping ourselves with expert climbing knowledge and inspiring stories from the cutting edge.

Leverage your membership—and feed your passion for climbing—by applying to our adventure grants, snagging those discounts, reading up on your Rescue and Medical Expense Benefit, and finding events to connect with your community.

Not a member and feel like you're missing out? Learn more at americanalpineclub.org

 **American
Alpine Club**

AAC member Jeremiah Watt

JANNU'S NORTH FACE

A NEW ROUTE IN ALPINE STYLE, AFTER THREE YEARS OF EFFORT AND INNOVATION

JACKSON MARVELL

On **an especially hot and dusty day in 2020,** Alan Rousseau and I were working construction, building decks together in Utah. Voicing the thoughts in my daydreaming brain, I threw out the idea of joining forces for a Himalayan expedition. At that moment, I'm sure the high peaks and frigid north faces of the Himalaya sounded extremely pleasant.

Living in Utah, Alan and I both were drawn to steep ice and mixed climbing in the hills near our homes. Our very first expedition together, in the spring of 2019, resulted in a new line up the east face of Mt. Dickey in the central Alaska Range. Our shared interest in such routes had sent both of us searching the globe for steep alpine walls, and our research soon led us to Jannu.

At 7,710 meters, Jannu (known in Nepal as Kumbhakarna) stands just ten kilometers west of Kangchenjunga (8,586m), the third-highest peak in the world. These days, many mountaineers who travel to this region are chasing only the 8,000-meter summits, and they'd look past Jannu with barely a second glance. However, the altitude was never a factor in our desire to stand below this peak and, hopefully, have the opportunity to climb it. The north face of Jannu is the stuff of alpinists' dreams: about 2,000 meters of challenging alpine terrain leading to a stunning 700-meter headwall that is spiderwebbed with crack systems and plastered with sheets of ice, so steep that a hanging rope rarely touches it. We had to go there and see it for ourselves.

The awe-inspiring view of Kumbhakarna (Jannu) from base camp below the north face. The 7,710-meter summit rises about 2,700 meters above the rock glacier running below camp. *Matt Cornell*

Pieces of the legacy from past attempts. *Alan Rousseau*

JANNU: CLIMBS AND ATTEMPTS FROM THE NORTH

PREPARED BY CARTER LEY AND RYAN COOPER

1975
ATTEMPT: Climbing siege style, a team of ten from New Zealand forges a line up the left side of the north face, joining the northeast ridge. They call the face the Wall of Shadows. The team retreats from 7,300m in high wind.

1976
SUMMIT: Following the same line as the Kiwis, a 21-strong team from Japan completes Jannu's first ascent from the north on May 11, fixing 6,750m of rope.

1982
ATTEMPT: A team of six led by Pierre Beghin (France) tries a line to the right of the 1976 route, aiming to join the northeast ridge at 7,400m. They reach 7,100m twice.

1987
SUMMIT: A team of six from the Netherlands repeats the 1976 Japanese route, fixing ropes to 6,100m before continuing in alpine style. Two of the summiters perish during the descent.

(Continued on p.14)

Jannu was first climbed from the north by a Japanese team in 1976, following a route on the far left side of the face that had been pioneered to 7,300 meters by New Zealanders the year before. The Kiwis dubbed the face the Wall of Shadows. In 2004, after an attempt the previous year, a large and powerful team of Russian climbers claimed the first ascent of the direct north face, straight up that steep headwall. That expedition, led by Alexander Odintsov, climbed in a classic siege style, fixing thousands of meters of rope leading nearly to the summit. They spent more than 50 days working on the route. Our dream was to climb the north face headwall in alpine style.

The Wall of Shadows route was first climbed in partial alpine style in 1987 by a Dutch team (using some fixed ropes low on the route) and has been repeated in this style a couple of times. Tomo Cesen from Yugoslavia claimed to have soloed a very steep new route to the left of the Russian line in 1989, but this ascent has been widely disputed. In 2007, Valery Babanov and Sergey Kofanov started up the far right side of the north face and climbed alpine style to the summit by the northwest ridge (a.k.a. West Pillar). "Perhaps someday," Kofanov wrote in *Alpinist*, "a pair will climb a direct route on the north face in alpine style, but they'll need to accept the likelihood that they're buying themselves a one-way ticket."

In preparation for our first expedition to Jannu in the fall of 2021, Alan and I planned a trip to Alaska where we hoped to climb several routes in continuous-push style. The routes we had earmarked were the Bibler-Klewin (Moonflower Buttress) on Mt. Hunter, the Infinite Spur on Mt. Foraker, and the Slovak Direct on Denali. The aim for this trip (besides having a great time hanging around on a cold, snowy glacier) was to use these climbs as a litmus test for our plans on Jannu. We figured if we could climb three of Alaska's biggest testpieces in non-stop pushes in a single season, then our hopes of

climbing the direct north face of Jannu in alpine style might not be ridiculous.

We ended up climbing the Bibler-Klewin to the top of the buttress and back in 25 hours, and we climbed the Infinite Spur, round-trip from Kahiltna base camp, in a 65-hour push. Poor weather foiled our plans for the Slovak Direct, but we did summit Denali via the West Buttress route in 21 hours round-trip from Kahiltna base, while retrieving a cache we'd left at the 14,000-foot camp.

Alan and I departed for Nepal early in September, feeling excited and nervous. From Kathmandu, we drove for two days to the town of Taplejung, then transferred to a jeep for 18 hours of bumpy, wet driving. The road ended at a comfortable little guesthouse next to the Ghunsa River. Getting out of the jeep and feeling the cool night air was a great relief after three days of driving through the steaming lowlands.

For five days we trekked along the Ghunsa River. The canyon walls towered above us on both sides, and it wasn't until the last day of walking that we started to catch glimpses of snow-covered mountains. When at last we turned a corner and lay eyes on Jannu, I remember the distinct impression of never having felt so small.

Base camp was in an idyllic meadow hanging above a rock glacier. Whenever Jannu wasn't shrouded in clouds, we had a direct view from the doors of our tents. This did nothing to help with the feelings of trepidation we both had been carrying the entire trip.

As we saw it, the north face consisted of three sections. The first was a 300-meter rock buttress capped by a 300-meter icefall; the second was a ramp feature that gained about 1,100 meters, mostly

Jannu (Kumbhakarna, 7,710m) from the north, showing approximate lines of (1) Tosas attempt to 6,900 meters (2007); (2) Japanese route to northeast ridge and summit (1976, climbed to 7,300 meters in 1975 by New Zealand team); (3) Russian direct north face route (2004); (4) Round Trip Ticket (2023); and (5) West Pillar (2007). Not shown: the 1989 line claimed by Tomo Cesen. *Expedition Photo*

1987

SUMMIT: A French-Spanish quartet attempts a new route right of the Japanese line in alpine style, reaching 6,800m. Pierre Beghin and Erik Decamp then repeat the Japanese route, using the Dutch fixed lines to 5,600m, then continuing in alpine style.

1989

ATTEMPT: Tomo Cesen (Yugoslavia) claims a solo ascent of a direct new route in a single push from April 27–29, navigating the left side of the upper north face headwall. The claim is generally not accepted.

1994

ATTEMPT: Xavier Cret, Robin Molinatti, Pierre Rizzardo, and Paul Robach (France) make an alpine-style attempt on the northwest spur in autumn, after finding inadequate conditions on Beghin's line. They fix ropes up an 800m face to reach the ridge, then continue in alpine style to a high point of 6,900m.

1997

ATTEMPT: A team of nine led by Damian Benegas (USA) attempts a direct line up the north face.

1998

ATTEMPT: Four French climbers attempt the 1994 line, aiming for the northwest spur, but retreat before the ridge.

1999

ATTEMPT: A team led by Oleg Grigoriev (Uzbekistan) attempts a direct line in siege style, reaching 6,800m.

2000

SUMMIT: Climbing in the spring, Athol Whimp (New Zealand) and Andy Lindblade (Australia) attempt a new line twice in alpine style. The duo then repeats the 1976 route, climbing alpine style above 5,600m.

2000

ATTEMPT: Jared Ogden, Mark Synnott (USA), and Kevin Thaw (U.K.) attempt a new line in the autumn.

on steep névé, and the third was the headwall. The first piece of the puzzle to unlock was the route up the rock buttress, and the day after we arrived in base camp, we made that our mission.

After several hours of wandering around the hanging meadow, we found a way to descend through the moraine wall to the rock glacier: a steep, sketchy gully with vertical dirt at the bottom. We traveled this section countless times, and it always had us on our toes. After climbing up the moraine wall on the far side of the rock glacier, we tied in and started piecing together a route through vertical, blocky terrain. As we meandered up the rock, artifacts from prior ascents served as occasional guideposts. At the exit from the buttress, we took our first good look at the icefall and then went down to base camp.

Poor weather descended on us, and we used this time to scramble around on nearby Mera Peak. By the time the weather cleared, we had completed a couple of rounds of acclimatization to 5,500 meters. We packed the bags and headed back up, with the aim of figuring out our route through the icefall and bivying in the bergschrund below the ramp.

Back on top of the rock section, we donned our double boots for the first time of the trip and began plodding up the seam

Climbing through the icefall above the initial rock buttress, en route to the glacial plateau at the foot of the north wall. *Jackson Marvell*

between the main icefall and the side of the upper rock buttress. This section was a bit intimidating—the sun was shining and enormous gendarmes of ice hung out over our heads. When we stood on the glacial plateau above the icefall, about 2,100 meters of the north face of Jannu still rose above us. We sat on our packs and gawked at what finally felt like our very real future.

Once in the 'schrund below the ramp, we set about experimenting with our new bivy system. Alan and I had brought the newly released G7 Pods, but neither of us had used them, outside of setting them up in our homes. Our hope was that these inflatable hanging sleeping pads—like one-person portaledges—would be the key to successfully climbing the headwall, with its limited bivy sites, in alpine style. We built an anchor out of ice screws, inflated the Pods, hung the fly over both of them, and crawled in to sleep.

That night was spooky, with so much terrain still above us and the ramp feature acting as a funnel for constant spindrift. After a fitful night of sleep, we packed our bags and descended to base camp, feeling good about the progress but knowing we had a long way to go.

2002
ATTEMPT: Erhard Loretan and Ueli Steck (Switzerland) try for a new line in capsule style. Fixing lines to 6,600m, they retreat in early October after several close calls with avalanches.

2003
ATTEMPT: Erhard Loretan, Frédéric Roux, Ueli Steck, and Stefan Siegrist (Switzerland), climbing in capsule style, climb to 7,200m in the center of the north face in the spring.

2003
ATTEMPT: A team of nine from Russia, led by Alexander Odintsov, sieges a direct route up the headwall in the autumn. Five climbers push the route to 7,200m before retreating.

2004
SUMMIT: Odintsov's team returns in the spring and fixes 3,375m of rope to complete the north face headwall. Five climbers summit in two parties, grading their route VII 5.10d A3+ M6.

2007
ATTEMPT: Jordi Tosas from Catalunya attempts to solo the 1976 route, with a major variation to the left of the original line. In September, he reaches 6,900m in two days before descending.

2007
SUMMIT: Valery Babanov and Sergei Kofanov (Russia) complete the northwest ridge, starting on the lower north face, over eight days in autumn, climbing alpine style.

2021–2023
ATTEMPTS AND SUMMIT: After two attempts in two years, Matt Cornell, Jackson Marvell, and Alan Rousseau (USA) succeed with an alpine-style new route on the north face, described in this article.

SOURCES: *Himalayan Database, AAJ, Alpinist, and (U.K.) Alpine Journal. See the AAJ website for additional attempts, more info on these climbs, and links to online reports.*

With more bad weather on the way, Alan and I took the opportunity to descend to the village of Ghunsa for some recovery. Sitting in a teahouse drinking *tongba* next to a woodburning stove seemed to be what the doctor had ordered. After a few days of this, and with good weather inbound, we walked the ten miles back to base camp with thoughts of the headwall rattling around our brains.

We speculated that we would need a forecast for at least seven days of good weather to make an all-in attempt, however this forecast called for five good days. With this in mind, we packed for what we expected to be an exploratory mission up the ramp to the base of the headwall, where we would hopefully be able to gauge its seriousness.

After the initial ramp, we started up a block of technical, steep mixed climbing. This section was wonderful, with thin runnels of ice and short rock sections. After about 300 meters, we found ourselves climbing steep snow flutings on the edge of the lowest of the hanging seracs guarding the upper ramp. With daylight starting to disappear and no visible spots to bivy, we kept climbing, hoping to reach the top of the serac. At times, the flutings were very insecure, including one spot where we had to jump across a void and stick the landing to a near vertical snow wall. In the 'schrund on top of the serac, we chopped a small, uncomfortable ledge to set up the Pods.

Breaking down the Pods in the early hours was cold and difficult—trying to roll them tight enough to fit in a pack

WITH THE WEATHER WINDOW NOT BEING AS OPEN AS WE WOULD HAVE LIKED, WE PUT THE HAMMER DOWN AND MOVED AS QUICKLY AS WE COULD.

We had come to Jannu with the intention of repeating the 2004 Russian route in alpine style, but while studying their line through a spotting scope, we'd noticed another system branching to the right and slashing up the headwall to reach the west ridge at a little over 7,500 meters. We had decided to put our efforts toward climbing this new line, in part because we would've run into large amounts of old fixed rope and hardware on the Russian route, which not only would have been unpleasant but also would have added a significant asterisk to our ascent.

Back at the 'schrund below the ramp, we spent a more comfortable night on a chopped ledge away from all the spindrift. We woke at 4 a.m., broke camp, and began moving up. The first 600 meters of the ramp consisted of nice névé with occasional vertical steps. With the weather window not being as open as we would have liked, we put the hammer down and moved as quickly as we could.

took time. But by 7 a.m. we were moving again, every step bringing us closer to our planned exit onto the headwall. The feeling of excitement was tangible. To this point, Alan and I had been simul-climbing, using Micro Traxions between us to protect the leader.

As the headwall reared up, we climbed three pitches into the steepness, then found ourselves dead-ended, with daylight quickly slipping away. We rappelled a rope length and set up the Pods for our first full hanging bivy of the climb. We were somewhere near 7,200 meters, and it felt like the summit might only be one long day of climbing away. But we also reminded ourselves that this had been planned as another exploratory and acclimatization mission. We decided to sleep on it. When morning came, we quickly made the decision to descend and wait for a more appropriate window.

Back at camp, we spent the next seven days in a nuclear snowstorm. Four feet of

snow piled up in the lush green meadow. When the storm subsided, the jet stream was over the summit of Jannu and we decided to throw in the towel for this season. With all the pieces of the puzzle we had put in place, we were eager to come back.

Even before decompressing at home, we were already scheming for our return in 2022. We had previously talked about enlisting a third climber to lighten the pack loads and create a bigger safety net. With our first season in the rearview, it seemed like a good call to bring someone else on.

TOP: Heading up toward the north face headwall and new terrain. *Alan Rousseau*

BOTTOM: Jackson Marvell, Matt Cornell, and Alan Rousseau (left to right) relax in the Pods in base camp. The nights on the wall would not be as comfortable. *Expedition Photo*

I had been climbing with Matt Cornell as one of my main partners since 2019 and thought he would be a perfect fit. Alan agreed but wanted to test our systems for climbing as a team of three before committing. We decided to go back to Alaska and try to finish our business on the Slovak Direct.

On the 2,750-meter route up Denali's south face, we refined two climbing systems we'd later use on Jannu. When the terrain was such that that simul-climbing would be more efficient than pitching out single rope lengths, we climbed with two followers at the end of the rope, about three meters apart, with the leader placing Micro Traxions along the way as protection. When the climbing became too technical for simul-climbing, we used the fix-and-follow method, where the leader would climb around half a rope length, pull in all the slack, and fix the rope to an anchor. As the second climbed to the belay, protected by Micro Traxions, the leader would rest and haul the packs. When the second arrived at the anchor, the leader would start up again, belayed with the remaining rope, while the third continued to follow the pitch below.

These techniques helped Alan, Matt, and me climb the Slovak in less than 24 hours in May 2022. Once out of the Alaska Range, all three of us booked tickets to Kathmandu.

On September 4, we arrived back in Kathmandu, excited but once again all feeling a sense of trepidation. At the Hotel Shanker, we were sitting down for dinner one hour after arriving when I got a phone call from my girlfriend's co-workers. Brenna had been in a serious climbing accident in the Alps and was being life-flighted to a hospital. I booked a ticket to Switzerland that would leave Nepal in three hours. Alan, Matt, and I sorted our

Emily, who both would accompany us to base camp. We also were joined by Michael Gardner and Sam Hennessey, who planned to share camp with us and tackle their own objective in the area. [*These two climbers were unsuccessful with their attempt but plan to return.*] The journey to the base camp meadow we had called home for the last two autumns was incredible, with lots of laughter and hardly any feelings of trepidation or fear.

After two rounds of acclimatizing up to 6,000 meters on Mera Peak, we got the news that the window we had all been awaiting was approaching: seven days of splitter weather. We started packing

THE JOURNEY TO THE BASE CAMP MEADOW WE HAD CALLED HOME FOR TWO AUTUMNS WAS INCREDIBLE, WITH LOTS OF LAUGHTER AND HARDLY ANY FEELINGS OF FEAR.

group gear, and I left them with my best wishes for a successful climb and headed out into an uncertain future.

Matt and Alan had poor weather throughout their trip that season, with high winds and brutally cold temperatures. They made several attempts on the face but were only able to get to around 6,500 meters.

Two months later, while they were traveling home and I was sitting in a hospital in Chicago with Brenna (who has experienced a long but very positive recovery), we again started talking about our return to Jannu.

The three of us did one more big climb together in the spring of 2023: a new route up the east face of Mt. Dickey in Alaska (*see p.34*). Apart from using the fix-and-follow technique more often, we didn't make any major updates to our systems. But climbing a 5,000-foot first ascent as a team bolstered our confidence.

On September 4, 2023, we once again returned to Kathmandu, this time with Matt's and Alan's partners, Whitney and

bags and fine-tuning our gear choices. In addition to food and hardware, we packed a single 60-meter, 9mm lead rope and a 60-meter, 6mm hyperstatic tagline. We did not pack a bolt kit.

Nathan Kukathas of Grade VII Climbing Equipment, maker of the G7 Pods, had made the journey from Squamish, arriving in base camp a week before the weather window. He hand-delivered some custom equipment for us that he'd been building while we were walking in and acclimatizing. The three-man sleeping system we took up the route weighed around 11 pounds (5kg), including two G7 Pods, a burly custom tent that enveloped the Pods, and a custom elephant's foot sleeping bag that the three of us would share. We also had figured out a way to lash together the two Pods, making it easier to set them up and to pack them for climbing.

On October 7, after two days of waiting for the face to shed new snow, we woke early and started following the now familiar

terrain across the rock glacier and up the lower buttress. We made fast time and soon found ourselves building a nice, flat bivouac site in the 'schrund at about 5,800 meters. We thought we'd chosen a spot that would be protected from the nightly deluge of spindrift, but at midnight the walls of the bivy started to collapse inward. We put on our boots and tried to divert the stream of snow that was pouring onto us.

After a few more hours, we woke at 4 a.m. to start brewing water for coffee. The plan was to climb the ramp feature and hopefully bivy on the first serac, where Alan and I had slept in 2021. We crossed the 'schrund at around 7 a.m. and found good névé and snow throughout much of the day. When we reached the start of the steeper mixed climbing, about 300 meters below the serac, we decided to cut hard left and see if we could skirt some of the difficult terrain. This ended up being a mistake: About 60 meters below the lip of the serac, it became too dangerous to continue. Fortunately, this mistake provided an excellent bivy, as we discovered an ice cave beneath the serac at 6,800 meters.

In the morning we rappelled two rope lengths diagonally to the right to regain the point where Alan and I had climbed two years earlier. Matt then led us through all this terrain in a long block and landed us at the bottom of the headwall at 7,000 meters.

TOP: Jackson Marvell on day four of the final ascent, moving up the massively exposed headwall on the north face. *Matt Cornell*

BOTTOM: High camp at 7,500 meters, one pitch below the top of the headwall. *Alan Rousseau*

Here, I took the sharp end and started up broken granite, aiming for our 2021 high point. I ended my block on a sharp fin of snow about 60 meters below the hanging bivy we'd used in 2021. We spent several hours chopping a stance as wide as possible before bottoming out on rock. When we set up the Pods, both edges hung over the abyss by six to eight inches.

This day was super memorable, as the energy of our group really started to blend into a feeling of group flow. We had continued to get weather updates every morning and evening, and no major changes were on the horizon. It was starting to feel like the moment we had all dreamt about for years. That night was stressful, though, as falling ice shelled the bivy and tore open the fly over our Pods. We clamped the fabric

Matt and I watched him throw an overhead heel hook. The move was stylely, but back at the belay, we commented that this probably wasn't the best beta, just Alan being Alan. His block finished in the dark and led us to the hole left by the mushroom that had hit us earlier in the day, now a well-protected bivy site at 7,300 meters.

This was our first fully hanging bivy in the Pods. Matt and Alan sat on the wall-side ledge, with their legs draped over me as I lay on the outside ledge. We had tested this configuration in base camp and had higher hopes for it than we actually experienced on the wall. It was an uncomfortable and sleepless night.

After another early alarm, we spent a good bit of time drinking hot coffee, trying to warm up before packing up in the bitter

THE NIGHT WAS STRESSFUL, AS FALLING ICE SHELLED THE BIVY AND TORE OPEN THE FLY OVER OUR PODS.

together with two screw-gate carabiners and hoped for the best.

From our high point of 2021, we moved right into a system we had scoped the first year. The next two pitches were phenomenal, with perfect cracks for gear and tool placements, and steeper than anything we had climbed so far. I ended my block and started handing the rack to Alan, and as Matt climbed toward the two of us, a large snow mushroom far above gave way. Alan and I took a direct hit from the snow; Matt was traversing in from the left and escaped most of the carnage. The impact split the hood of my belay parka in half, but other than losing some insulation and having clouds of feathers floating around us for the next few days, we came away unscathed.

Several more mushrooms loomed directly above us, so we opted to follow a more wandering line to the right to get out from under them. Alan's block had two difficult leads back to back—at one point,

cold. During our time on the wall, the face only got sun for about ten minutes each evening. Eventually we crawled out of the ledge to face another day of hard climbing. We were hoping to finish the headwall that day and bivy on the shoulder of the mountain.

Matt started off his first block by tension traversing ten meters out from the belay, then climbing what we later deemed to be the crux of the route. A vertical smear of ice was followed by cryptic mixed climbing, with perfect pick-sized and crystal-lined pockets leading him through an improbable slab. After two more pitches, we could see the top of the wall. I led three more pitches, often encountering dead-end terrain that required lateral movement to find another upward option. When the sun set, we were at 7,500 meters, just below the top.

Although we had fallen short of the shoulder, we were elated to be so close. We set up another hanging bivy and crawled in

Matt Cornell fully engaged with the crux pitch on day five: a smear of ice leading to a line of crystal-filled pockets in the rock at about 7,300 meters. *Jackson Marvell*

for another hard night. Once above 7,000 meters, we wore all of our layers every night, only adding down mittens and fresh socks. We didn't sleep much in any of the hanging bivys, but none of us had expected to sleep well on Jannu's headwall. This time we decided we'd all sit on the wall-side Pod, arranged tallest to shortest to match the taper of the Pods. This configuration was definitely better than our previous nights had been, but it's possible it contributed to the cold injuries that Alan and I later suffered, as we were both sitting on the outside of the lineup and I eventually got frostbite on my right hand, Alan got it on his left, and Matt had none.

On the morning of October 12, we felt exhausted but excited to see where day six of the climb would take us. We had made the decision to go light to the summit, so we left the Pods, sleeping bag, and other gear at the bivy. Matt led us up the last pitch and then started breaking trail up the west ridge to the beginning of the technical climbing on the summit pyramid. We were in the sun for the first time in five days—the warmth from the galactic heater was a very welcome source of energy.

As Alan started a block of rambling mixed pitches, we were all feeling the effects of multiple days of hard climbing, a low-calorie diet, and lack of sleep—and the high altitude wasn't helping. We moved much slower than we had hoped.

At the end of Alan's block, I felt motivated to keep pushing the rope upward on the last bit of the southwest spur route, climbed in 1983. Below the final technical pitch of the route, I took off my gloves to reference a photo of the terrain above and noticed that the tip of one pinkie had turned purple. When Matt and Alan arrived at my stance, we took a moment to discuss the situation and made the decision to keep moving up. We were only 100 meters below the top and felt we would be able to get up and down without it making a significant difference in the outcome for my finger. After the final pitch—a roof with an offwidth that didn't

end up being as difficult as it had looked—Matt took over and broke trail to the top.

We arrived at the summit at 4:20 p.m. on the dot. We had worked three years for this moment, but at the moment it didn't feel all that important. We spent less than five minutes on top—we took a group photo and a panoramic video, and that was it. We knew we needed to make tracks with it being so late in the day.

We downclimbed for a few hundred feet and then began a series of slow rappels. It was well into the night—probably 10 or 11 p.m.—before we made it back to our high bivy at 7,500 meters. The best option was to spend another night there and descend to base camp the next morning. We set up the Pods once again and crawled in for what ended up being a brutal night. The Pods were deflating, and I had to wrap my right arm around one of the suspension straps to hold myself in. The night felt never-ending. In the morning, I discovered my frostbite had gotten significantly worse, and I was now struggling to use my right hand.

We spent the entire seventh day descending, mostly rappelling from clean threads on ice and occasionally leaving gear anchors. At midnight, we were finally back in base camp.

Once there, we discovered that Alan had frozen the tips of the fingers on his left hand. We warmed our fingers in water and discussed our next moves, but quickly realized we needed to sleep before we could make good decisions. With clearer heads in the morning, we concluded that walking through the jungle for five days and then driving for three more days to reach Kathmandu would present a significant risk of infection to our frostbitten fingers. We also learned from friends back home that a clinic in Kathmandu could administer an intravenous treatment called iloprost, which, if administered within 72 hours, might reverse some of the damage to our fingers. We opted to call for a helicopter

ride back to Kathmandu.

Alan and I spent five days in the hospital receiving the iloprost treatment. Matt often would spend time with us, bringing us ice cream to cheer us up during painful infusions. We'd each lost around 20 to 25 pounds during our seven-day round trip on Jannu. Months later, Alan would lose the tip of his left pinkie, and I may also lose a bit of my little finger. We learned a lot from the injuries on Jannu, and we don't expect them to slow us down.

The three-year effort to climb Jannu's north face taught us what might be possible with steady determination, through many ups and downs. The journey didn't end up being about standing on the summit; instead, it proved to be about growing closer as a team and learning what we are capable of accomplishing together. During those days in the hospital in Kathmandu, we all felt fulfilled, yet also shared a seemingly contradictory desire to be back in the mountains. It was then that Alan, Matt, and I started enthusiastically scheming for our next expedition.

TOP: Moving toward the summit tower on day six of the climb. The route wound around to the right on rock and mixed terrain, finishing on the 1983 route up the southwest spur, climbed by a team from France. *Expedition Photo*

BOTTOM: Cornell, Rousseau, and Marvell (left to right) on top. The tip of Marvell's pinkie is purple with frostbite. The descent to high camp would last long into the night. *Jackson Marvell*

SUMMARY: New route climbed in alpine style up the north face of Jannu (Kumbhakarna, 7,710m) in Nepal, by Matt Cornell, Jackson Marvell, and Alan Rousseau (all USA), October 7–12, 2023. The route is called Round Trip Ticket (2,700m, M7 AI5+ A0). The trio descended from high camp at 7,500 meters on October 13, mostly following their ascent route.

ABOUT THE AUTHOR: Born in 1996, Jackson Marvell grew up in Utah and learned to climb on that state's red sandstone and water ice; he lives in the town of Heber, Utah, with his partner and dog, and supplements his career as a professional climber by working as a welder.

THE SECRET LINE

CLIMBING THE ENIGMATIC NORTH FACE OF TIRICH MIR

KENRO NAKAJIMA

With **an elevation of 7,708 meters,** Tirich Mir is the highest peak of the Hindu Kush mountains, which straddle Afghanistan and northwest Pakistan. Although the peak was first climbed in 1950 and was relatively popular among mountaineers in the 1960s and '70s, officials in Pakistan had not permitted mountaineering or tourism in the area since September 11, 2001, due to its proximity to the Afghan border. A French party got permission to climb the mountain in 2016, but after that it was closed again.

In 2019, a local agent informed Kazuya Hiraide and me that tourists could re-enter the area, leading us to head to Pakistan. Unfortunately, we did not get permission to attempt Tirich Mir that year, and we ended up climbing Rakaposhi instead (*see AAJ 2020*). We left some gear in Pakistan with the intention of returning for Tirich Mir the following summer, but the coronavirus pandemic intervened. Only in the summer of 2023 could we finally head to the mountain.

Tirich Mir is visible from the large foothills town of Chitral, just 30 kilometers to the south. The locals, appreciating the resources flowing down from the mountain, have many legends about it. One tells that there is a castle of fairies on the top. They are guarded by a huge frog that lives in the crevasses of the glacier and eats all who try to climb the mountain. This story is told with

Four days out from base camp, Kazuya Hiraide leads the way at about 6,500 meters on the north face of Tirich Mir. With careful route-finding, the climbers were able to weave a path mostly up steep snow and moderate ice on the enormous face. *Kenro Nakajima | Ishii Sports*

tongue in cheek, but it illustrates the deep connection between the mountain and the lives of the townspeople.

It was hard to believe there was still unexplored territory on such a famous mountain, but the north face, our objective, had never even been attempted. During a 2002 solo trip in Pakistan, Hiraide had seen the mountain from Chitral. After returning home, he did some research and found the north face to be a carte blanche. At the time, he felt himself too inexperienced to attempt such unknown terrain, but he stashed Tirich Mir's north face into a corner of his mind for the future.

The reason the north face remained unexplored is simple: The access is anything but easy. The Lower Tirich

once-a-week direct flight from Islamabad in a propeller plane. The flight takes only about an hour, a vast improvement over eight hours in a truck on Pakistani roads. Meeting us at the airport was our old friend and local guide Sahib Alam, who had joined us on the Rakaposhi expedition in 2019—we were very happy to see him again after so many years.

Chitral lies at 1,500 meters, but under the harsh sun it feels as hot as Islamabad during the day. The local men wear the Afghan pakol hat and subsist on naan bread. The closest big city is Jalalabad in Afghanistan, causing strong cultural influence. What made us especially happy about this was access to delicious Afghan barbecue for dirt cheap. There would be little chance of eating fresh meat—fresh

ALTHOUGH THE GLACIER PRESENTS A GATE INTO THIS CASTLE, IT IS NEARLY IMPOSSIBLE TO PASS, BLOCKED BY A DANGEROUS ICEFALL ALMOST 1,000 METERS HIGH.

Glacier, directly below the face, is ringed by a horseshoe of steep-walled 6,000- and 7,000-meter peaks, like the walls of a mighty castle. Although the glacier presents a gate into this castle, it is nearly impossible to pass, blocked by a dangerous icefall almost 1,000 meters high. A Czech party had been through the gate in 1967, but they did not get onto the north face; instead, they followed the Upper Tirich Glacier to access the mountain from the northwest, completing what became the normal route up the mountain. There is no record of anyone passing through the Lower Tirich icefall ever since. We were stoked about the prospect of genuinely unexplored territory in this day and age. There was nothing to do but go see what was hiding in there.

On June 22, we landed in Chitral, fortunate that conditions had been good for the

anything, really—after reaching base camp, so we made sure to fill our stomachs here.

After gathering and packing supplies in 25-kilogram loads for the porters, we started our acclimatization by hiring a 4WD to drive us to Zani An (Zani Pass, 3,840 meters), where we spent two nights and hiked above the pass to 4,300 meters. Then we hiked down to the valley at Shagrom, where the trek to base camp would begin.

On the 30th of June, the 27 porters and their leader assembled in the early morning light. In these parts, there are no full-time porters; instead, load carrying offers an enticing occasional source of income for local people, who were assisted early in our walk by donkeys and children. We followed the Tirich Gol (valley) to the west on a pleasant trek and reached Sherniak in five hours. This would be the last campsite with trees. Next to the raging campfire, our

cook made us a delicious curry from a sheep the locals had sacrificed earlier in a ritual for our safety and success.

The next day saw us arrive at the edge of the Lower Tirich Glacier, on which we and the porters alike maneuvered around crevasses in trekking shoes without difficulty. When the crevasses became more frequent, we moved to the right-hand bank, arriving after five and a half hours at Shoghor Biasun.

From our camp, we could finally see the dreaded Lower Tirich icefall. Though the debris from countless broken seracs seemed like it might form a possible path, I had never seen an icefall with that much widespread destruction. Great boulders of ice, shining blue and white in the sun, were everywhere. The two of us discussed the matter and determined that ascending the icefall was a no-go. It would be the fastest route to Tirich Mir's north face, but the risks were too great. Thus, we decided on plan B. As the saying goes, "When you're in a rush, go around."

TOP: Tirich Mir, in back, rises above a stronghold of 6,500-meter peaks guarding the north face. *Ishii Sports*

BOTTOM: The icefall of the Lower Tirich Glacier gains nearly 1,000 meters and is only known to have been breached once, in 1967. The highest summit in back is Bindu Gul Zom West (6,340m). Tirich Mir is out of view to the right. *Ishii Sports*

On the 2nd of July, we trekked along the gentle moraine to the right of the Upper Tirich Glacier, which parallels the Lower Tirich to the north. In three and a half hours, we reached the base camp for Istor-o-Nal (7,403m, first climbed in 1955 by an American expedition), and in another hour and a half we arrived at the so-called Lower Babu Camp, at 4,600 meters. The site was narrow but sheltered and would be fine for our little party. In the whole Hindu Kush that season, there were only two other climbing parties: a Hungarian team on Istor-o-Nal and a Spanish one on Saraghrar.

From base camp, the north side of Tirich Mir was still mostly hidden by the long row of high peaks in front. [*These mountains form a line defining the north side of the Lower Tirich Glacier, ranging from Barun-Gul Zom (6,164m) at the east end, past Baipash Zom, to a high point at Tirich Mir North (6,732 meters).*] Most of the north face remained shrouded in mystery. Still, even seeing the top of our planned route got our spirits up.

Our next step was to acclimatize and do some reconnaissance. Using satellite imagery, we had come up with a plan to circle around to the west side of the mountains surrounding our objective and climb to the lowest col between Tirich Mir North and the towering massif of Tirich Mir West. From there, we hoped to descend to the glacier on the far side. This would be our back gate to the Lower Tirich Glacier. We didn't expect it to be trivial to cross this 6,200-meter col. No one had ever been there, so there was no information and no pictures.

From the great bend in the Upper Tirich Glacier, we moved between glacier and moraines until we reached the highest moraine and found a good site for Camp 1 at 5,400 meters. The next day, we climbed up the steep valley leading toward the col. Near the top was a wall of hard-packed snow, where falling was not an option. Finally we reached the col and at last could see the whole north face. We were relieved and very happy to see that the face looked just as we had imagined from the satellite

fortress and ventured down toward the Lower Tirich Glacier for the first time, we noticed it was a lot warmer, due to the lack of wind. The snow was wet and water was flowing. With a lot of loose rock everywhere, we took care to protect the ropes. The descent from the col to the glacier would total several hundred meters, and we had only four 50-meter ropes to fix, but we verified that this approach should work.

Next, we needed to scout our descent route along the normal route and the Upper Tirich Glacier. Although there are no technical difficulties on this route below 6,600 meters, the glacier has many hidden crevasses and we expected to be completely exhausted after summiting.

AT THAT MOMENT, DULL RUMBLING REVERBERATED ABOVE, ACCOMPANIED BY A SCREAM OF "ROCK!" I LOOKED UP AND A MASS OF ICE AND ROCK FILLED MY VISION, SEEMING TO FALL IN SLOW MOTION.

imagery. A cornice blocked our view of the route down the far side of the col, but one thing was clear: The descent would be even steeper than the approach had been.

We left for our second acclimatization trip on July 10, aiming to do a recon of the far side of the col, and also to figure out our route back to base camp after summiting. Although our acclimatization was proceeding, we moved slowly up the steep valley to the col, carrying the extra weight of ropes for fixing. We hadn't ever used fixed ropes on our recent expeditions—we hadn't even brought any to base camp—but this time we had come prepared for the potential rappel approach. Our plan was to leave some ropes in place in case we couldn't finish the north face of Tirich Mir and we had to return the way we'd come, back over the col.

As we crossed into the mountain

So, to mitigate the risk, we thoroughly recorded the descent route on a GPS, enabling a blind descent if necessary. We camped at 6,300 meters on the upper glacier, watching the sun set on the dry mountains in Afghanistan. It was our first camp at this altitude, and we felt surprisingly good. The rest of our acclimatization would need to happen during the climb.

On July 13 we returned to base camp to prepare for the climb. Using an inReach, we were receiving one-week forecasts from Japan. The Hindu Kush tends to have better summer weather than other mountains in Pakistan, and we hadn't had any bad weather so far. It was warm, however, and under the strong sunshine we could see the glaciers melting. Crevasses we had been able to step across would widen, and

The complex route to reach the north face of Tirich Mir. From Camp 1 on the Upper Tirich Glacier, the climbers gained a 6,200-meter col and descended to Camp 2 at 5,500 meters on the Lower Tirich Glacier. Three bivouacs on the north face (Camp 3 is hidden) brought them to the col between Tirich Mir West and the main peak. After summiting, they descended the 1967 route to the west and returned to base camp by the Upper Tirich Glacier. *Photo scanned from Himalaya, No. 287, courtesy of Ishii Sports*

on the next crossing we would need to jump, and then would be unable to cross at all. Now we got a forecast for heavy snowfall. We had intended to rest during these days anyway, but we worried our departure would be delayed.

It started raining before dawn on the 16th, and the weather remained icky the whole day. Around midnight, people at camp were woken by the sound of a river—the river that was supposed to be ten minutes away. Suddenly some of the tents were afloat, as the campsite had become the site of a new stream. Although the rain had stopped by now, dike digging and moving of tents commenced in the middle of the night. My own tent was 30 meters higher than the main campsite, and I slept like a baby through all the commotion.

In the end, fortunately, there was no big snowstorm, and we were able to keep to our planned departure after four days of rest. After supper on the last rest day, however, I had sudden stomach pain. I shivered through the night and had a sore throat. In the morning, the fever had come down, but my throat was still hurting. We departed regardless on the 18th of July, hoping the illness would pass during the two days of approach to reach the north face.

We moved back up the Tirich Glacier to Camp 1, being careful not to be eaten by the great frog protecting the mountain fairies. That night, nasal congestion made it difficult for me to breathe, and even worse, my snoring prevented Hiraide awake from getting much sleep. In the morning it was -6°C—about 7° warmer than the last time we'd been at Camp 1—which made us worry about the conditions for our traverse of the col.

Looking down from the col during our recon, Hiraide had said this would be "the crux before the climb." Now it was midmorning and the gully below the col was running with slush and meltwater. As I rappelled, a rope length below Hiraide, I thought about filling my water bottle in the stream. At that moment, dull rumbling reverberated above, accompanied by a scream of "Rock!" I looked up and a mass of ice and rock filled my vision, seeming to fall in slow motion.

The barrage continued for more than 30 seconds. I clung to a rock overhang, but there was no way to avoid all the debris. Luckily, I was only hit by a small rock on my shin, and the ropes weren't cut. We gave up on quenching our thirst, even though my sore throat could have used it, and moved as quickly as we could to safer terrain.

After eight rappels and scrambling, we stood at the western end of the Lower Tirich Glacier, a place no one had ever been. From here, the safest way home would be to climb to the summit of Tirich Mir and descend the other side. We melted snow, had a drink, and started toward the north face. Inside the fortress, there was no wind, and the only sound was us post-holing through unbroken snow. We pitched our tent near the bottom of the wall, at 5,500 meters, and prepared to start up the face.

On July 20, the sound of thunder woke us before dawn. It was not close, but the roaring reverberated through the valley. Possibly the ground had warmed during these past few days, causing the atmospheric conditions to become unstable. Engulfed by clouds, we began the ascent of the north face. At first, we made quick progress by simul-climbing up the ice and snow wall, but as the wall steepened, we switched to leading and jumaring. Since this is a north face, we were expecting to find hard blue ice, but it seemed like this was a north face hit by the sun during the day. Our tools penetrated the ice nicely, without bouncing back.

After three hours, we hit a rock band. Going straight up would be very steep and time-consuming, so we traversed to the right, looking for a way around. The visibility was very bad, making it hard to estimate where we were on the wall. The first attempt led to a dead-end cliff. Going back, we followed the next most promising route, traversing a band to the right across a stony ridge, and found a line connecting to a gully. There, we started ascending ice and snow again, and in three hours, we reached our planned bivy site, at 6,150 meters, near some seracs where the wall was a little less steep.

As we dug a platform into the snow, we soon struck ice, as expected, which

meant we finally got to use our new weapon: the ice hammock. Hanging the lightweight hammock from two ice screws and filling it with snow, we created a wonderful terrace in 30 minutes. If we had cut ice for a ledge, it would have taken two and a half hours, and even then a third of the tent would have hung free. A sitting bivy would, of course, have been an option, but getting decent rest feels more important the older you get. I had an altitude headache and my throat pain still hadn't gone away. Hiraide was kept up by my snoring again.

We started up again on a beautiful morning, the fourth of our climb, on top of a sea of clouds. Névé led us into a rocky gully. Directly above, the way was steep and protection sparse, so we traversed right and hit a snow face. After a bit, we got to a second gully, and this one had ice in it. Soon it started snowing. We climbed up and right, hitting a small ridge. The top of the ridge, at 6,750 meters, had a flatter spot that, when enhanced with the ice hammock, provided a luxurious site for our tent, so we called it a day at 2 p.m. The sun setting over Afghanistan was beautiful, seeming to promise good weather for the next day.

A sea of clouds dispersed quickly the next morning, and we basked in the sun. This would be the day to pass through a large serac band near the top of the face that we had worried about but hadn't been able to see properly. If we could clear that obstacle, we knew we'd be able to summit. On the other hand, if we didn't, we would have a long, long exit back the way we'd come.

We traversed to the edge of the glacier and looked up. Though steep, it looked like there was a continuous icy couloir between the rock and the seracs. The shaded ice there was cold and hard

OPPOSITE PAGE: Rappelling from the 6,200-meter col toward the Lower Tirich Glacier. The climbers fixed four ropes in case they were forced to retreat. *Kenro Nakajima | Ishii Sports*

ABOVE: From Camp 2 on the Lower Tirich Glacier, the north face route gained about 2,200 meters to the summit. *Ishii Sports*

but took bomber ice screws. Relieved, we carefully climbed to the plateau on top of the seracs.

Only a final rock headwall remained, but it was too late in the day to try to summit. Also, since we were already above 7,000 meters, we didn't want to sleep much higher. Since it was still before noon, we decided to head for the col between Tirich Mir and Tirich Mir West, where we would join the normal route. At around 7,200 meters, in the windy col, we built a wall with snow blocks to protect the tent. We went to sleep with the sun rendering the summit crimson red.

We woke at 4:15 a.m. as usual. At -18°C, it was the coldest day so far, but it still felt warm compared with our previous expeditions at this altitude. My sore head and throat had hindered my sleep once again, but my altitude symptoms were better than before. We left the campsite in sunshine. Through deep snow, we traversed toward a gully leading right to the summit. There seem to be many ways to reach the top from high camp, and though we believe we were on the normal route, we didn't see any old pitons or ropes. A steep mixed wall took good pro, making for a pleasant 60-meter pitch. The ice wall above was also steep, but with our light packs, we were able to simul-climb to the summit ridge.

We had expected to encounter multiple false summits, but after climbing to the first top, we realized we had reached the highest peak of the Hindu Kush, at 9:35 in the morning; the second- and third-highest peaks, Noshaq and Istor-o-Nal, were in clear view. To the south, we could see all the way to the town of Chitral. Our objective of the last five years had finally been accomplished. We took pictures and radioed base camp, and for the next 40 minutes the time flew by.

On descent, we rappelled the two steep pitches and traversed back to our high camp. We had summited quickly, and it was only noon. Since we were feeling strong, we decided to descend as far as possible. We entered the rocky couloir of the normal route, finding discarded ropes and pitons here and there, testifying to the difficulty of the climbing. After roughly six rappels, we finally stood on the Upper Tirich Glacier. Continuing down as far as we could, we made it to the 6,300-meter camp we had used for acclimatization.

As we had already scouted the glacier, we had no problems with the 1,700 meters of descent the next day. (Unfortunately, there was no practical way to retrieve the four ropes we'd left below the 6,200-meter col.) We reached base camp at noon.

We weren't sure how the local people had found out, but the trek back to Shagrom

was a day filled with celebration. We had so many congratulatory necklaces hung on us that we couldn't move our heads.

The most delightful event of this day was at the local orphanage. We pointed back at Tirich Mir and showed a picture from the summit, telling the kids we had climbed it. They hadn't even thought of their local mountain as something people would climb, but after seeing the picture and the two of us with our sunburns, they seemed to accept it. One boy raised his hand and said, "I want to climb that mountain as well!" This made us very happy. At the end of our visit, the head of the orphanage asked us a question: "Were there fairies at the summit?"

Nakajima nearing the summit of Tirich Mir. Behind, across the Lower Tirich Glacier, is the Baipash Zom group. In the distance, the Noshaq Glacier leads up to Noshaq (7,492m), on the left. Istor-o-Nal (7,403m) is in the center. Kazuya Hiraide | Ishii Sports

SUMMARY: First ascent of the north face of Tirich Mir (The Secret Line, 2,200 meters from the Lower Tirich Glacier to the summit), July 18–24, 2023, by Kazuya Hiraide and Kenro Nakajima from Japan. The pair spent two days approaching the Lower Tirich Glacier from base camp and bivouacked three nights during the climb and once more during the descent to the west along the 1967 (normal) route.

ABOUT THE AUTHOR: Kenro Nakajima, age 38 at the time of the Tirich Mir ascent, is a professional climber and mountain cameraman, and also works with outdoor retailer ICI Ishii Sports. He lives in Chiba, Japan. His story about the first ascent of the northeast face of Shispare, also climbed with Hiraide, appeared in the 2018 AAJ. Hiraide and Nakajima discussed the climb of Tirich Mir on episode 61 of the Cutting Edge podcast.

This article was translated from Japanese by Heikki Ruuska, with additional assistance provided by Kaoru Wada.

DICKEY DOUBLE

A NEW ROUTE AND SECOND ASCENT ON THE 5,000-FOOT EAST FACE—IN THE SAME MONTH

MATT CORNELL

I kept my head down and stared into the 'schrund. I couldn't watch. Alan Rousseau, 150 feet above, was digging into an overhanging tube of powdery snow, as he had for the past hour and a half. Jackson Marvell, the third member of our party, was climbing up and down the 'schrund in various locations to keep occupied. He and I hadn't even left the ground, and already the route was demanding, stressful, and dangerous.

Alan kept peering down, as if preparing to aim for the bushes if he fell, à la Dwayne Johnson in *The Other Guys*. The two screws he'd placed below in rotten, patchy ice were only for his sanity. Another hour passed. Today had been meant as a quick recon for a potential first ascent up one of the many chimney systems on the 5,000-foot east face of Mt. Dickey, but it had turned into something else.

Matt Cornell low on Aim for the Bushes, a new testpiece of steep and insecure Alaskan snow climbing on Mt. Dickey's east face. *Alan Rousseau*

Mt. Dickey's 5,000-foot east face, showing (1) Aim for the Bushes (Cornell-Marvell-Rousseau, 2023) and (2) Blood from the Stone (Easton-Steck, 2002). Ruth Gorge Grinder (Marvell-Rousseau, 2019) takes the deep gash to the right of Blood from the Stone. Other routes not shown. *Matt Cornell*

Finally, with a cave excavated, Alan pulled through the lip of the overhang, his feet skating off granite and tools placed in soft névé. As the angle eased, he built an anchor and brought us up. Jackson ran 250 feet up the next pitch, a tight chimney filled with névé. I led more of the same, encountering an old anchor that the legendary alpinist Jack Tackle had left during an exploratory foray in 2007. (This had been the high point of previous attempts by several parties.) The chimney opened up. Snow and ice were plastered to the right wall, sprayed there by avalanches ripping down the gully and firing over a large mess of mushrooms that capped the slot. This feature had shut down all prior attempts. Jackson, always curious, wanted a closer look. He climbed to the end of our rope, level with the mushrooms, took some photos, then downclimbed vertical sn'ice back to the belay.

"It'll go—with some digging," Jackson murmured as he fiddled with a rap anchor.

Six hours after it had begun, our recon was over. We rappelled, pulled our ropes, and returned to camp.

Mt. Dickey (9,545') is a monster. When you look down the Ruth Gorge from any aspect, it captures the eye, especially its mile-high easterly wall, which destroys vertical perception in this gorge of giants. The east face's prominent buttress rounds to the south, where pillars of granite rise through an otherwise blank wall as the peak tapers down to 747 Pass. Above the granite walls, the summit slopes are capped with a final barrier of loose diorite and steep snow flutings.

These formidable features have long garnered attention from climbers. In 1974, David Roberts, Galen Rowell, and Ed Ward climbed the southeast face (NCCS VI F9 A3) big-wall style, fixing the first 900 feet and then climbing the rest in a three-day push. Since then, the buttresses and ridges have slowly been ticked off, but it wasn't until 2002 that climbers began to explore the deep clefts and chimneys that fracture the vertical granite. That year, Sean Easton and Ueli Steck, looking for an ice line up the center of the east face, established Blood from the Stone (5,000', WI6+ X M7+ A1), arguably one of the most striking ice-choked chimneys in the world. Two years later, in 2004, Sam Chinnery and Andy Sharpe again followed an ice chimney—this one to the right of the 1974 southeast face route—to establish Snowpatrol (1,600m, VI WI5+).

These ascents highlighted the shift in how Dickey was being approached, from big-wall tactics along protected ridges and pillars to fast-and-light alpinism that seeks out technical ice and mixed terrain deep within the mountain. In 2019, Jackson and Alan put up Ruth Gorge Grinder (5,000', AI6+ M7 A1) on the east face after finding their initial objective, Blood from the Stone, devoid of ice. It was on this trip that they saw the ongoing potential for new routes on Dickey's eastern aspect—Snowpatrol's bigger, badder brothers—especially a striking independent chimney system less than 400 feet to its right. On March 28, the three of us flew into the Ruth Gorge to attempt the unclimbed line.

On March 31—two days after that hairball recon—we skied out of camp, the Ruth's katabatic winds nibbling at any exposed skin as the sun lit the sky. We didn't say a word until we had crossed through a band of crevasses and arrived at the toe of Dickey's east face. We looked into the depths of the mountain, gauging our prospective line. A massive chockstone, visible without magnification, seemed to guard the last of the difficulties, 4,000 feet above us.

Jackson took the first block, firing through the pitch Alan had previously excavated. We were quickly back to our high point, 800 feet off the glacier. Alan and I hung from two screws on near-vertical terrain, directly below the billowing mushrooms. Jackson worked upward, digging underneath one mushroom while traversing on top of another—his tools hitting the rock below, his progress protected by beaks—and depositing all of the debris he removed straight onto the belay. Our minds wandered toward disaster. Alan had lost nearly all of the vision in his left eye in 2019 while attempting a new route with Jackson on nearby Mt. Bradley's north face, after Jackson kicked off ice that hit Alan in the face, forcing a retreat. Today, we kept our heads down and took our beating.

Four hours later, Jackson pulled through the final bit of overhanging snow by thrusting his arms deep and manteling out of the mushroom tunnel. We followed, admiring the effort it had taken to lead through such questionable terrain. Thin clouds

TOP: Approaching the base of Aim for the Bushes, which starts up the obvious long chimney system above and left of the skiers. The rock buttress directly above them was climbed big-wall style by Tomas Gross and Vera Komarkova in May–June 1977. *Jackson Marvell*

BOTTOM: Three men squeezed into a two-person bivy tent on Mt. Dickey. *Alan Rousseau*

hung high, the sun hidden as snow worked its way deep into our layers. Our gloves, soaked from digging, froze stiff with our hands inside. We shivered.

I took the rack. The chimney opened up, revealing vertical snow stepped with easier névé. We simul-climbed to stay warm, letting the rhythm of our progress consume us. I stopped below an intimidating wall of overhanging snow and mushrooms, then moved slowly and cautiously, placing a single picket as I committed to the shell of snow. The pitch ended with easier terrain above, where I belayed.

By late afternoon, we had rambled onto a snowfield and easier terrain. Cold, tired, and wet, we stomped out our first

Down at the belay, Jackson and I debated retreating into Snowpatrol, just to our left. However, after another hour of digging, Alan had masterfully pulled through the steepest snow climbing of the entire route. He continued to lead, squeezing and excavating. The rope was fixed; we followed.

Up at the belay, we found Alan unroped and shivering just above the anchor, attempting to catch the last bit of sun. It still felt like winter in the central Alaska Range. Almost everything exposed to water—like the snow that had penetrated Alan's outer layers and melted—would freeze instantly. We weighed our options. A potential bivy at this stance to dry out? Rappel back to a spot where we could link

UP AT THE BELAY, WE FOUND ALAN UNROPED AND SHIVERING JUST ABOVE THE ANCHOR, ATTEMPTING TO CATCH THE LAST BIT OF SUN.

bivy site underneath a protruding boulder. We brewed as the light faded, watching the raunchy buddy comedy *The Hangover* on my phone. The movie provided a great distraction from thoughts of the next day's obstacles, in particular the looming chockstone. We hardly said a word to each other—or during the entire climb, for that matter—as it was just too cold to do much more than shiver.

Ice feathered the inside of the tent in the morning. Everything was soaked, from base layers to sleeping bags. It was past 9 a.m. by the time we were packed, a much later start than anticipated; the sun was already high but cloaked by clouds, delivering little warmth.

Immediately, we encountered a narrow tube of sugar snow with more mushrooms guarding the exit. It was Alan's block, and he wiggled and stemmed, looking for gear. There was next to none. He dug into the sugar, tunneling behind the plastered snow and then re-emerging below the mushrooms. Two hours went by.

into Snowpatrol? Or just keep climbing? We looked above—the third option seemed like the best. A flake jutted out of the main chimney with a thin strip of ice behind. It looked reasonable. We continued.

Jackson took the lead, stemming and squeezing within the frozen maw—the quality of the ice was improving. Another steep pitch and we were below the chockstone. We stared into a deep cave capped by mushrooms that would have to be cleared, the cracks on either side of the chockstone looking way too wide for our cams. The pitch would *have* to go free.

Jackson climbed underneath, sizing up the crux, ready to go to war. Then he noticed light in the back of the cave. Moving up and behind the chockstone, he climbed a corkscrew of pure ice through a tunnel—the key to the route. We were filled with relief, fortunate to have had easy passage through what could have been an insurmountable obstacle. I led one more mixed pitch, and we exited the 4,000-foot tube that had enclosed us and

Matt Cornell (right) and Alan Rousseau following a hidden ice tunnel behind the enormous chockstone 4,000 feet up Aim for the Bushes. *Jackson Marvell*

dominated our lives for the last two days. As the pressure lifted from our chests, we howled with excitement.

A steep snow traverse leftward brought us into the upper drainage of Snowpatrol, where we encountered the first of the upper mountain's diorite bands. We simul-climbed up and right, out of the drainage and onto traversing snowfields that led to a flat cornice. It was nearly dark. Unwilling to push through the night, we set up the tent, crawled into our frozen down bags, ate the last of our food, and shivered until dawn.

Hazy clouds and falling snow kept us in the tent till midmorning. Summits occasionally poked through, parting the clouds to reveal the glacier a mile below. I broke trail in this dreamworld to the

out the Talkeetna Air Taxi bunkhouse and drinking beer at the Fairview.

Eventually, I was able to fly into the Tokositna Glacier below Mt. Huntington, with eyes set on soloing the West Face Couloir. I sat in poor weather for another week. During this time, Sam Hennessey, a friend and hardman alpinist, arrived on the Tok with a client. He had flown by Dickey's east face and noticed that Blood from the Stone was still holding ice. Together, we formulated a plan to attempt the second ascent of this spectacular feature after we left Huntington; eventually, we enlisted the alpine connoisseur and mountain guide Rob Smith, who, with Sam and Michael Gardner, had done the fastest-ever ascent of the Slovak Direct route on Denali

WE WERE FILLED WITH RELIEF, FORTUNATE TO HAVE HAD EASY PASSAGE THROUGH WHAT COULD HAVE BEEN AN INSURMOUNTABLE OBSTACLE.

summit plateau. The three of us stood on top at 10:52 a.m. on April 2. We felt empty, lucky to have survived. We'd found our threshold for risk on this ascent, and we also wondered if it had been worth it.

The descent by the west face took two hours and 45 minutes, completing the first ascent of Aim for the Bushes. This route embodies the "Alaska factor": The wall is foreshortened and steeper than it looks, and the route has many pitches of snow climbing and a high level of commitment.

After five stormy days at camp in the Ruth, the three of us parted ways. Jackson returned home to Salt Lake City, and Alan zipped down to Anchorage to meet a client whom he was to guide in the coming weeks. While I was back in Talkeetna on weather hold, it dumped three feet of snow in town and more in the range. I passed the time by digging

the previous year (*see AAJ 2023*). Good weather arrived on April 19, and Sam guided the Harvard Route as I soloed the West Face Couloir. Sam then returned to Talkeetna with his client, while I—too broke to afford another flight—festered on the Tok. Four days later, Rob, who had bought a last-minute ticket from Colorado, flew into the Tokositna with Sam in Paul Roderick's air taxi, so Paul could pick me up and ferry us all to the Ruth.

In the early afternoon of April 23, I stood below the massive east face of Mt. Dickey for the second time in a month. In a frenzy, Sam, Rob, and I sorted gear, pitched a single tent, and threw our duffels inside. Only an hour and a half after touching down, we were already booting to the base. The wall looked conspicuously dry, and we wondered if the ice in the lower chimneys had melted during the week since Sam had flown by.

At 3 p.m., we arrived at the broken

'schrund, shaded yet still warm. The snow was soft; conditions were changing quickly as the face melted. Sam, leading the first pitch, worked his way through a steep maze of crevasses. Suddenly, the snow gave way under his feet; tumbling downward, Sam disappeared into the 'schrund, his tools still in the snow where he'd fallen—an eerie sight and an inauspicious start, even though he immediately popped back out and finished the pitch.

We climbed snow to the first rock step, which accesses a hanging snowfield—this marks the start of Blood from the Stone. Here, we encountered a steep ice pitch where Ueli Steck had climbed hard mixed. The meat of the climbing was hidden just above, and we wondered if—as on Alan and Jackson's 2019 attempt—we'd find the lower chimney dry and unclimbable. Sam stomped out a bivy below the El Cap–sized headwall while Rob and I fixed the entrance pitch, a steep, broad curtain of thin névé where I found Jackson's bail nut. The ice barely clung to the chimney's water-polished granite. It would be just enough. We rapped back to the bivy and crawled into the tent, sharing a single sleeping bag.

We woke as the sun began to light the sky. I took the first block, squeezing up a six-to-12-inch-wide strip of ice in the tight slot for several rope lengths before entering a body-width chimney. The ice here was perfect. Less-than-vertical terrain allowed for simul blocks; I occasionally stopped to belay to avoid shelling my partners from high above. As the sun warmed the rock, the ice grew soft and wet. Then the wall steepened and the rock turned red; the was ice so soft it was melting in front of our eyes. This had been one of the M7+ crux pitches on the first ascent, and now it was fully covered in ice—though my tools were melting out as I led!

We climbed quickly and with elation, despite mounting concern over objective hazards, especially after watching a snow mushroom collapse over a pitch we had just climbed. Wondering how much more would fall, we sprinted for the top of the chimney system, eager to escape. Sam tiptoed through slabs sheathed in thin ice into a steep, left-facing corner. Above, vertical thin ice led into overhanging snow—the hardest pitch we'd encounter and where Sam's flawless technique got us to the deteriorating diorite

Matt Cornell (top photo) and Ueli Steck (bottom) in almost the exact same spot on Blood from the Stone in 2023 and 2002, respectively. During the first ascent, Steck found M7+ rock; Cornell found sticky (though rapidly melting) ice. *Rob Smith (top) and Sean Easton*

Sam Hennessey and Rob Smith following the deep chimney low on Blood from the Stone. *Matt Cornell*

bands below the summit ridge.

Rob took the sharp end on a pitch of steep black rock striped with white dikes and enclosed by flutings—the only mixed pitch we encountered. The way was cryptic, but he managed to link solid, juggy features on what looked to be utter garbage. One more short but intensely steep pitch of ice and we had surmounted the technicalities. We stood on the summit at 8:07 p.m. on April 24, full of disbelief. We'd climbed so quickly on such a serious route, yet it had felt almost casual. I was astonished to have climbed Dickey's east face for a second time so soon—I noticed my crampon impressions from weeks earlier still cast in the windblown snow, glowing red-orange in the fiery light of the setting sun. I owe these experiences, and success, to my partners who shared the rope and the vision.

After seven springs climbing around the Alaska Range, I have never seen a season so conducive to producing good conditions for such a prolonged period. When Alan, Jackson, and I arrived in the Ruth Gorge in late March, it was bitterly cold. The sun hid behind cirrostratus clouds, never raising the ambient temperature significantly, creating a very slow melt-freeze cycle at the lower elevations. There was also no significant warm front that melted all the snow and ice at once, which kept Dickey's garbage chutes fairly "safe" and free of falling debris. This cycle continued through the month, with only one significant snowstorm, between April 8 and 15. After the storm cycle, it remained cold and windy, which quickly cleared the mountains of fresh snow, plus the sun never poked out for more than a day or two before it hid behind clouds again. These were the perfect conditions to transform snow into ice.

As Sam, Rob, and I approached Blood from the Stone on April 23, it was the first truly warm day of the season—and clearly the last window to attempt a major route at lower elevations. The morning after returning from our ascent, we noticed that the route's bottom chimney pitches had fully melted out, one day after we climbed them. Given that we'd only encountered one pitch of mixed climbing and had placed mostly ice screws for gear, it was strange to know that Sean and Ueli had climbed M7+, with some bolts, on multiple pitches. For them, conditions had been drastically different.

I can quite easily say that Blood from the Stone is the best route I have had the opportunity to climb.

SUMMARY: First ascent of Aim for the Bushes (5,000', AI6 X M6) on the east face of Mt. Dickey in the Ruth Gorge of the Alaska Range, by Matt Cornell, Jackson Marvell, and Alan Rousseau, March 31–April 2, 2023. Second ascent of Blood from the Stone (5,000', WI6+ X M7+ A1, Easton-Steck, 2002) on Dickey's east face, by Matt Cornell, Sam Hennessey, and Rob Smith, April 23–24, 2023. Their ascent took about 29 hours.

ABOUT THE AUTHOR: Matt Cornell, 29, lives seasonally between Bozeman, Montana, and Yosemite, California. He made his first climbing trip to the central Alaska Range in 2016. Since then, he has been chasing new routes around the world.

Matt Cornell leading the thin ice pitch heading into the main chimney on Blood from the Stone. *Rob Smith*

A DREAM FULFILLED

THE 3,000-METER NORTH SPUR OF SAN VALENTÍN

BY ORIOL BARÓ
Prologue by Martín Elías

PROLOGUE

The Pyrenees and classic routes of the Alps, *where Oriol and I live and work, are experiencing a massive rise in popularity, a reflection of our society's apparent need for immediate success, results over experiences, and "likes" over emotions, feelings, or acceptance of any kind of failure. Unfortunately, alpinism has been impregnated with this societal rot, and ideas or values like exploration, the unknown, doubt, risk, and the thrill of uncertainty before an ascent have been lost to a pseudo-alpinism full of beautiful photos on peaks where the weather is always good and the climbers have bright, super-clean outfits and smiles that look like they've come straight from the dentist.*

Our mountains are becoming targets for commercial and consumerist exploitation, and, regrettably, we're allowing it. For this reason, our ascent of Monte San Valentín may have a certain value within the absurdity of the alpine, because it embodies the values of alpinism that are important to us: friendship, exploration, aesthetics, difficulty, and also, to some extent, a bit of failure, as you'll discover in the paragraphs that follow.

Oriol Baró on the morning of summit day on Monte San Valentín. After an arduous approach, the team climbed the massive route in just two days. *Team Photo*

THE ATTRACTION OF THE
THE ALLURE OF THE UNKNOWN

The first time I laid eyes on one of the Patagonian Icefields, an unusual sensation gripped me—I was standing at one of Earth's boundaries! From the summit of Aguja Standhardt, a cold desert stretched to the west, extending all the way to the Chilean fjords.

This striking image, coupled with the immediate sense that I felt of being at home the first time I set foot on Patagonian soil, fueled my annual escape from the Pyrenees to go and drink some maté in the southern reaches of the world. As I got to know the land's history, customs, and people, my friends transformed into an authentic family. I also began to grasp the huge scale of Patagonia. Just as I have mentally mapped the Pyrenees from east to west over two decades, I've spent 20 years attempting to navigate the north–south expanse of Patagonia. Exploring its summits, routes, and trails during the sporadic clear days, I've envisioned retracing the trails of the Tehuelche along the Andean mountains.

For many years, our discussions of Patagonian mountains have included the north face of Monte San Valentín, the highest summit in Patagonia, at the north end of the Northern Patagonian Icefield. [*Elevations given for San Valentín on maps and other sources range from 3,876m to 4,070m. It was measured with GPS at 4,032m in 2008; the most frequently cited elevation is 4,058m.*] Thanks to photos and the invaluable tool called Google Earth, I gained insight into the complex terrain of this mountain. In recent seasons, I've organized my annual pilgrimage to the southern Andes with the aim of attempting the prominent north spur, which separates the Grosse Glacier from the Exploradores Glacier, providing direct access to the mountain's northern summit.

BLAME IT ON PERE

My initial journeys to Chilean Patagonia were fueled by the stories shared by my friend Pere Vilarasau, who was originally from Catalunya but now is one of Chile's leading climbers and guides. His efforts in establishing new routes and exploring the vast Patagonian terrain are undeniable. Over the last 15 years, he has transformed Villa Cerro Castillo in Aysén into a place where boredom is nonexistent, offering sport climbing and multi-pitch routes near town, along with new access routes and climbs in the Castillo and Avellano massifs.

During my first season in the Aysén region, in 2022, I climbed Cerro Castillo with my friends Ferran and Juanjo, and waking up at the summit gave us an incredible view of the north side of San Valentín. After sipping many matés, driving many kilometers of gravel roads, and navigating the Valdivian jungle, we believed we had discovered the best way to access the massive wall. However, an eagerly anticipated weather window never arrived.

In mid-October 2023, I found myself back in Aysén, where a massive amount of snow left over from winter prevented us from spotting any signs of spring, let alone good weather. A couple of sunny but cold days in early November provided Lucía Guichot and me with an opportunity to follow in Pere's footsteps. We opened a beautiful ice route with two friends on Punta Miller (see p.210).

The following week saw the arrival of Martín Elías and Nieves Gil, followed by our friends Romi and Jonathan, completing the Iberian clan in Castillo. We enjoyed numerous sport climbs, asados, and parties while waiting for the good weather that just wasn't coming.

Finally, motivation prevailed over unfavorable conditions, and despite mechanical issues with our truck, Nieves, Lucía, and I set out to explore the approach to the Grosse Glacier. We left the road at 47 meters above sea level and spent five days hiking, getting soaked, and marveling at the dimensions of the place. We eventually set up a tent on the easternmost arm of the Grosse Glacier, a place we called Las Tripas

del Infierno ("The Bowels of Hell"). The northeast summit of San Valentín was still more than 3,000 meters above us.

Nieves, Lucía, and I reassured ourselves that the loud avalanches falling day and night wouldn't reach our small tent in the middle of the glacier. We seized a clear day to ascend a little peak of almost 2,000 meters that provided a perfect lookout. From there we could observe the conditions on the north spur of San Valentín, choose the best line to take, and plan the timetable we would need to follow for an ascent.

As we returned to civilization, Martín and our friend Romi met us a couple of hours before we reached the car and treated us to beers and empanadas. What a pair!

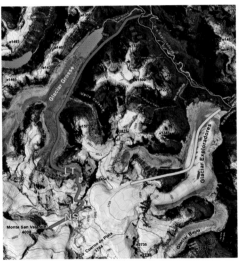

TOP: Approaching the headwall. *Team Photo*

BOTTOM: Red line is the 2023 route up San Valentin, starting from Glacier Grosse. LT: Las Tripas del Infierno camp. NS: northeast summit. Yellow line: attempts to approach from Glaciar Exploradores. *Base map by UNCHARTED Project (www.unchart.org)*

THE WINDOW ARRIVES

Initially, we doubted the usefulness of our exploration, as it seemed we might run out of time for an attempt on San Valentín. However, on our way back to Villa Cerro Castillo, Martín was already considering changing his plane ticket, delaying his return home by a week to take advantage of a long-awaited window of excellent weather that seemed be arriving.

Our rope party would be Martín, Nico Tapia, and me. We started on December 4, accompanied on the first day of the approach by Richi Mansilla and Felipe Romero, who wanted to get to know the

ABOVE: The upper ridge and headwall on San Valentín were reached in a long day of climbing from the cirque to the right. The bivouac is at approximately 2,500 meters, still about 1,500 meters below the top. The main summit lies two kilometers across a plateau beyond the northeast summit seen here. *Francisco Croxatto*

LEFT: Martín Elías and Nicolás Tapia savoring the sun's first caress on summit day. *Team Photo*

Grosse Glacier and offered to help carry some of the weight. Our hike started in the rain, which persisted into the night and the next morning. (After all, this is one of the rainiest places on Earth.) By the evening of the second day, the three of us found ourselves back on Las Tripas del Infierno, where we pitched our tent at 800 meters. That night was clear, and we could see the line ahead. However, we woke to light rain that didn't stop until we had surpassed the first 500 meters of the climb.

Above the bergschrund, on the west side of the spur, we climbed three mixed pitches up to M5/6a, followed by slopes up to 70° leading to a shoulder on the ridge, above 2,000 meters, that we called Collado del Mezzogiorno. (We named this simply because we arrived there at noon.) From here, we crossed over a hanging glacier to the steepest part of the ridge without any difficulties and bivouacked at around 2,500 meters.

The next day, five good mixed pitches of around M5 took us to ice slopes of 70° to 80° degrees and eventually an impressive 50-meter ice waterfall (WI5), the icing on the cake. We exited the face by an aesthetic 70° goulotte/ramp with an M5 shoulder.

Martín was eager to reach the main summit, so we had no choice but to walk

two kilometers across the plateau to San Valentín's highest point. It was all joy at the top, with hugs and views of the Northern Patagonian Icefield, although a cold wind didn't allow us to enjoy the show for long.

The walk back to the northern summit and rappels down the ridge proceeded with minimal delays, and soon we were back at the big shoulder of Collado del Mezzogiorno. The decision to keep going down from there, despite the afternoon heat, wasn't the best. Soon after we left the *collado*, a small wet snow avalanche dragged me down for more than 150 meters. I was a bit bruised up, but with the help of my friends, we continued down for a little while until we decided to bivouac again.

The more dangerous part of the descent was still to come in the morning: more than 800 meters of downclimbing and five rappels that would take us back to the Grosse Glacier. Painkillers and the tension that this place imposed pushed my pain into the background until we reached the middle of Las Tripas and felt safe at last.

Relieved, happy, and now more aware of my injuries—which included a moderately severe sprain in my left ankle and a cracked vertebra—we contacted Philippe Reuter from Puerto Guadal, about 55km away, and he promised to come and pick me up at 7 p.m. in his little helicopter.

With this arrangement in place, Martín and Nico left their gear with me and set out toward the road at a brisk pace. The helicopter flight that followed was exhilarating! Before 10 p.m., we all were enjoying our first beers together.

SUMMARY: First ascent of the Arista Norte (north spur) of Monte San Valentín (ca 4,058m), by Oriol Baró (Catalunya), Martín Elías (Spain), and Nicolás Tapia (Chile), December 4–8, 2023. After a two-day approach from just above sea level, their route (WI5 M5) gained 3,000 meters from the bergschrund to the summit. The trio descended by the same route.

HISTORICAL NOTES: Although several parties have tried to reach the north spur of San Valentín, none had attempted the actual climb before now. In 2008, Jim Donini and Thom

A 50-meter ice pitch was the key to breaching the final headwall on San Valentín. The northeast summit was soon reached. *Team Photo*

Engelbach explored the jungle approach from the Exploradores Glacier, to the northeast of the spur, reaching what Donini called Sound of Music Meadows, above the forest, and continuing to a glacier beyond. Donini returned the following year with Kelly Cordes and got a little farther. In 2016, Tad McCrea received an AAC grant for a plan to attempt this approach, climb the north ridge of San Valentín, descend the far side, and packraft out. Donini said this team got farther up the mountain than he had, but they were driven back by poor weather, again before starting the actual route.

The only other team known to have attempted San Valentín from the Grosse Glacier was a Chilean party in 1981. They climbed a long ridge to gain the head of the Reichert Glacier, which descends to the west from San Valentín, then reportedly climbed the steep west side of the peak to the top. One of the climbers died in a storm during the descent, and their climb has been disputed.

ABOUT THE AUTHOR: Born in Catalunya in 1979 and based in the Pyrenees, Oriol Baró is an IFMGA guide and prolific exploratory climber, with many new routes in South America and Asia. His story was translated from Spanish by Omar Gaytán.

RENAISSANCE

A NEW ROUTE UP THE EIGER NORDWAND IN PURE TRADITIONAL STYLE

SILVAN SCHÜPBACH

I'd been looking for something like this all these years, and it was right on my doorstep. I looked at it almost every day without seeing it—until August 2023.

A START WITH GLITCHES

Peter and I are sitting on the train from Thun, discussing the most important details of our climb, such as whether we've really brought enough mayonnaise and whether we need forks as well as spoons, when the announcement sounds: "Next stop, Lauterbrunnen." Oh no—we're on the wrong train!

Several hours later, back on track, we find ourselves at the Stollenloch. This renowned window onto the north face of the Eiger, accessible from the Jungfrau Railway, conveniently spares us from having to navigate the precarious, gently sloping initial 400 meters of the nordwand. We organize our bags—a total of 90 kilograms of material. I realize I've forgotten my helmet—not atypical for us. Real professionals!

Silvan Schüpbach leading pitch 18 (about 7c/5.12d) on Renaissance, following thin cracks that allowed just enough protection. *Peter von Känel*

The Eiger north face, showing the 2023 route Renaissance (2, red line), as well as (1) the classic 1938 route (first ascent of the face) and (3) the Ghilini-Piola Direttissima (1983). The new route shares three pitches with the Ghilini-Piola near the top of the face. (S) Stollenloch railway window. (A) Rote Fluh. (B) Czech Pillar. *Silvan Schüpbach*

A WALL STEEPED IN HISTORY

The north face of the Eiger is not only a huge chunk of limestone, standing 1,800 meters tall, but also an excellent marketing object for alpinists. The first ascent, in 1938, by the Austro-German team Anderl Heckmair, Heinrich Harrer, Fritz Kasparek, and Ludwig Vörg, perfectly fit with the propaganda of the Nazi regime and led to huge media hype. With a slew of deaths before and after the 1938 climb, the nordwand—sometimes called the "Mordwand" (or "murder wall")—is one of the most famous alpine faces in the world. Nowadays, even a charming bolted route of eight pitches on the far west side of the north face still sells well.

What the dazzled readers of these publications usually don't know: The rock on the Eiger is mostly excellent and has plenty of holds. What's more, thanks to global warming, the temperature here often is perfect for summer climbing. Consequently, the modern sport routes on the face have nothing in common with

the high-risk first ascent of 1938. Those climbers started their ascent without bolts, with little information, and with the certainty that they could not turn back from high on the icy wall.

THE IDEA

I think it's a shame that there are more bolts on the Eiger every year. A new line seemingly must be more difficult, more direct, or done faster—or at least with a high density of bolts so the route has as many repeat ascents as possible.

My dislike of how things are evolving on the Eiger (and on other mountains) is linked to my personal approach to the mountains: As a free spirit, I like to try projects off the beaten track. I am a trad climber and alpinist in the land of bolts and cable cars. My motivation has always been to experience real adventure—before starting to climb, I was into caving and other forms of remote exploration. The less information, the more interesting. And the less equipment left on a mountain, the more authentic the experience.

For a long time, I had been pursuing the idea of climbing the north face by a combination of existing routes without using any bolts—to find the most logical and appealing line for me personally. As I studied the route lines and topos, I realized there was still a 100-meter-wide swath of virgin rock to the right of the Ghilini-Piola Direttissima (1,400m, 6b A4; first climbed in 1983 and freed in 2013 at 7c). This part of the face, right of the nordwand's center, offers the Eiger's steepest features, such as the Rote Fluh, an overhanging wall 300 meters high. Above the Rote Fluh, a 400-meter pillar rises steeply and defiantly into the sky.

Due to its compact and crackless appearance, this proposed line didn't seem ideal for traditional climbing, but it motivated me nonetheless to try a first ascent instead of just combining existing routes.

TEAMWORK AND STRATEGY

When a one-week window of good weather opened up in August, it was easy to

Peter von Känel starting the first steep pitch on day one of the climb. A pocket provided a cam placement in just the right spot. *Silvan Schüpbach*

convince Peter von Känel to join the attempt. Peter and I share the same passion for adventure. Together, we've opened a couple of summer and winter routes on forgotten mountains. With Tradündition, an eight-pitch 8a (5.13b) we established in 2021 on the Dündenhorn in the Bernese Alps, we opened Switzerland's hardest pure-trad multi-pitch route.

We also complement each other well: Peter is mentally strong and fearless, while I'm a bit more hesitant but have greater physical reserves. Peter usually climbs the wildest pitches, and I take the hardest. We also share a sense of humor. We don't take each other too seriously, and the most heartfelt comments often come at the most stressful moments. This is always very funny and has a relaxing effect.

For the Eiger, in addition to our usual high-fat meals, we packed lots of pitons and Peckers, a portaledge, 200 meters of static rope, a set of nuts, and a double rack of Totem cams. We used the static rope to fix the pitches above the bivouacs, climbing in capsule style. At the bottom of our bags, we even packed a drill and some bolts for the worst case. But we never had to use them.

WE TAKE OFF

After a few phone calls, we find a solution to my helmet dilemma: Another Jungfrau railcar stops at the Stollenloch, and a mountain guide hands us a helmet. I must admit, it's not all bad having a train

incorporate laterally offset placements into the protection chain. Our years of experience trad climbing on limestone are coming in handy. To save time and energy, the second climber often ascends the rope to clean the pitches.

In the afternoon, we stand at the foot of the large ledges that separate the overhanging lower wall from the upper headwall. We have passed the entry test! We traverse back and forth on brittle ledges and look for a bivouac. We finally decide on a suitable site and dig a platform in the scree until it gets dark. Peter cooks us a feast: tortellini with gravy and plenty of butter. We're both firm believers in a high-fat diet, and we eat until we're full.

DECISION DAY

Sleeping is my greatest strength. Every morning, Peter must forcefully wake

MOST OF THE TIME, OUR ROUTE DOESN'T FOLLOW CRACKS BUT INSTEAD COMPACT WALLS. THUS, THE MENTAL WORKLOAD IS IMMENSE.

station inside the mountain. We finally start climbing. The first part of our route is pure Type 2 fun: hauling on slabs and traversing scree bands. But, as Peter says, "Keep smiling—we're on vacation here!"

At the end of the day, we are only six pitches higher but cautiously optimistic: We have found more protection than expected. A spacious bivouac site rounds out our first day.

THE ROTE FLUH

On the morning of the second day, we climb the steep right-hand section of the Rote Fluh, the first overhanging stronghold of our line. The initial pitches require the full range of protection techniques, which soon become routine: cam placements, nuts, short pitons, and lots and lots of Peckers—some good, some bad. Using double ropes helps us

me up; this morning, as usual, he runs out of patience at 8 o'clock. We are both nervous because today we'll be trying the huge overhanging pillar. This is clearly the hardest part of our route. We look somewhat enviously at the neighboring Piola route, which leads through logical cracks—we'll be on the compact overhangs to the right of it. Peter climbs three pitches confidently and efficiently. Now it's my turn.

I try different directions from the belay but can't find a way. My final option is to climb across a compact slab. I get farther and farther from the small Pecker I've hammered in, until I'm eight meters out. Close to the panic threshold, I place a good hook. I let the adrenaline subside and find two shallow Pecker placements. My psyche is exhausted by the time I reach easier terrain with a rappel traverse.

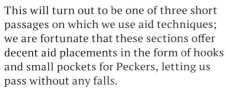

This will turn out to be one of three short passages on which we use aid techniques; we are fortunate that these sections offer decent aid placements in the form of hooks and small pockets for Peckers, letting us pass without any falls.

As I recover at the belay, I slowly come to appreciate the amazing quality of this rock. The gray limestone has perfect friction and beautiful *gouttes d'eau*, with shallow slots for cam placements. I'm seeing that I just need to keep climbing and the rock will offer its gifts. Gradually the fear subsides. We continue for the rest of the day, highly motivated and with great joy. As the evening sun reaches the north face, we rappel to our first bivouac site, the static line fixed to a ledge right at the top of the overhanging pillar. We are euphoric: Our chances of success are excellent. Peter unpacks a flask of delicious grappa, and we celebrate the successful third day in style.

ABOVE LEFT: A well-placed Pecker protecting the start of pitch 18. *Peter von Känel*

ABOVE RIGHT: Silvan Schüpbach hammers in a Pecker for the boulder problem at the start of pitch seven, rated approximately 7c/5.12d. *Peter von Känel*

THE TRAD GAME

For Peter and me, trad is the top league of climbing, combining risk assessment with protection of varying quality in unknown terrain: *Can I fall safely? Can I climb this passage without falling?* We must analyze the situation hundreds of times a day and find the answers to these questions. Then we must climb as the analysis suggests: either aggressively on the attack or defensively with maximum safety—or something in between.

Most of the time, our route doesn't follow cracks but instead compact walls. Thus, the mental workload is immense. It would be difficult to apply a commitment grade of R or X, since most of the protection is cams in limestone, which can be judged as "rather good" or "rather bad," but rarely "bombproof." I seldom

Schüpbach (left) and von Känel at the fourth and final bivouac on the wall. The next day, they topped out the north face and opted to enjoy another night there before heading to the summit. *Silvan Schüpbach*

feel the relief of thinking, "Now I can fall without any doubt." Route-finding is also more complex when trad climbing. To reach good placements for belay anchors, traverses and rappels are sometimes necessary. This enriches the range of movements and skills required. The actual climbing is only one aspect of the trad game; the intellectual work is just as important.

AN ALMOST PERFECT ENDING
The fourth and fifth days spoil us with wonderful climbing on the best rock—pockets, runnels, and nice, sharp holds. To increase the tension a little, Peter takes the liberty of throwing a helmet and a bunch of Peckers down the wall, but fortunately this doesn't change the outcome. The only flaw we encounter is that we must switch to the neighboring Piola route for three pitches because brittle overhangs block our planned direct exit.

When we reach the west flank of the Eiger on the fifth day, we sit atop the wall

and enjoy the moment. We both have tears in our eyes—the climb of a lifetime! We feel connected and deeply fulfilled. To savor these beautiful moments even longer, to maintain the best possible style, and to use up the last of the butter, we bivouac once more and summit the Eiger on the sixth day of our climb.

WHAT REMAINS
I have traveled by plane many times on expeditions in search of great adventures. I found the adventure, but increasingly I find it a contradiction to use expensive, motorized travel to measure myself against nature. With our Renaissance route on the Eiger, we want to inspire a rethink and show that there are high-quality adventures on our doorstep.

However, it is also important that we take care of our rocks and of nature. To ensure that future generations can find the same kinds of adventures, we should reduce the use of equipment to access the mountains. When we climb with

renunciation, the adventure increases: Without a plane, car, or bolts, you don't have to travel far to experience the wilderness.

Schüpbach searching for the line on the overhanging Rote Fluh.
Peter von Känel

EPILOGUE

During our ascent, we observed some rockfall in the central part of the wall. A week later, we learned that a huge flake had fallen from the Ghilini-Piola route, smashing into the wall below. Even though our route was probably not affected by this event, it did make me think about the risks in summer mountaineering these days. Though this rockfall was a clear warning signal, I still believe that steep, compact limestone walls pose fewer risks than classic mountain tours in glaciated terrain.

SUMMARY: First ascent of Renaissance (1,220m, 30 pitches of climbing), graded 7c (7a obl.), on the north face of the Eiger in the Bernese Alps, Switzerland, by Silvan Schüpbach and Peter von Känel, August 19–24. The route starts from the Stollenloch and ascends the right side of the Rote Fluh, then climbs to the right of the Czech Pillar between the Ghilini-Piola Direttissima (1983) and the Gelber Engel (1988); the new route shares three pitches with the Ghilini-Piola before finishing to the left.

ABOUT THE AUTHOR: Silvan Schüpbach lives in Thun, Switzerland, with his family and has done expeditions to Nepal, Pakistan, Greenland, and Patagonia. Originally a biotechnology engineer, he currently works for the Swiss Alpine Club and as a mountain guide.

TOMORROW IS ANOTHER DAY

THE NORTH FACE OF FLAT TOP IN KISHTWAR

MATTHIAS GRIBI

So, why not try Flat Top's north face next year?" I don't remember who said it first, but that's how it all started. My friend Hugo Béguin, an aspirant mountain guide, and I were leaving the mountains of Kishtwar, India, after a climb of Chomochior in 2022. The climb was the culmination of three years of training with the Expedition Team from the Swiss Alpine Club, a group of six young alpinists—including Hugo and me—selected from across the country.

To be honest, Chomochior (6,278m) wasn't our first goal. We had hoped to make one or more first ascents in the Nanth Nullah, a valley in Jammu and Kashmir that is surrounded by impressive peaks. We had read Tim Elson's 2019 *AAJ* article about his and Reg Measures' attempts on Flat Top and Kishtwar Eiger, and the photos of Flat Top's north face and other possibilities were very exciting. The Nanth Nullah seemed to have exactly what we were looking for: the opportunity to open mixed routes up virgin faces on rarely visited 6,000-meter peaks.

Unfortunately, we couldn't get the necessary permits in 2022. The Nanth Nullah is near the border with Pakistan, and there is a lot of tension here between the Indian Army and Pakistani armed groups. All of Kishtwar was closed to foreigners until 2012. Moreover, none of the Nanth Nullah peaks are on the Indian Mountaineering Foundation's Open Peaks list, detailing mountains for which it's easier to get permits. So we changed

Hugo Béguin starting day three on the north face of Flat Top. Soon after the climbers reached the prominent upper ridge on the face, an impassable step required a long detour over snow-covered slabs to regain the ridge, beyond the sharp rock tower. *Matthias Gribi*

Flat Top (6,100m) from the north. (1) Start of the 1980 first ascent by the northeast and east ridges; a hidden couloir led to a col, above which the team climbed the ridge and left flank. (2) Tomorrow Is Another Day, the first ascent of the 1,400-meter north face (2023). The climbers descended the west face, hidden beyond the right skyline, then crossed over the ridgeline at right to return to their starting point. (3) Attempt on north spur (2017). *Timothy Elson*

plans and went instead to the eastern Kishtwar, where, despite poor weather and conditions, we succeeded in repeating the southwest ridge of Chomochior, first climbed in 1988 by Roger Everett and Simon Richardson from the United Kingdom.

As Hugo and I hiked down from base camp, we started talking about a new project, and we quickly agreed that it would still be nice to get a closer look at Flat Top's north face. Tim Elson had sent additional pictures that showed the face was clearly a great objective. It was 1,400 meters high but had some weaknesses, so perhaps it was possible to find a line. The climbing seemed steep and technical, but not as much as on peaks like Jannu or other Himalayan monsters.

Back home, we started planning with our agency in India (IndMassif.com). The first goal was to find a third teammate. Hugo suggested Nathan Monard, a friend of his who works as a mountain guide and ski instructor in Zermatt. I didn't know

Nathan, but from the first time we met, I was sure we would form a good team. He is a strong alpinist, calm and determined— all the qualities we would need for this kind of project. He'd never been to the Himalaya, but he too was amazed by the photos of Flat Top's north face.

Now understanding the inherent delays with permits for mountains that aren't on India's Open Peaks list, we applied almost a year in advance. Our planning went perfectly, save for Nathan's visa, which was issued only one day before our departure.

We drove into the mountains by a similar route to the one we had taken in 2022, passing through Jammu and Kishtwar town. By September 18 we were trekking to base camp from the village of Sonder with our team: a cook, a helper, and our liaison officer, "Happy," with 17 ponies carrying our gear.

We reached base camp at 3,800 meters on September 20, three hours on foot from

the Hudh Mata temple, in a perfect sandy spot. From there, we hiked up to start acclimatizing and to survey our main objective. The first look at Flat Top's 1,400-meter face was not encouraging. It was full of fresh snow, bigger and steeper than expected, and the approach crossed a treacherous moraine. At that moment, we were more scared than happy.

After a day of rest, we set off to climb an easy 6,013-meter peak above camp. We spent a night at 5,000 meters, enduring headaches and nausea, and the next day, after I had puked from altitude sickness, we gave up 200 meters below the summit.

We rested for two days, then headed up to establish an advanced base camp (ABC) below Flat Top. We hiked for seven hours over sliding talus, sand, and tortured glacier to reach a flat stretch of ice near an enormous boulder and a small tarn at 4,500 meters. The face was directly above us, less than a kilometer distant, though still two hours away in this complex terrain.

Near the top of the face, the climbers faced four pitches on "a kind of steep, frozen soil that was neither rock nor ice, and was both tiring and hard to protect." Matthias Gribi

Now we could see that, while a few lines seemed possible, there was one that was most obvious. It followed a line of ice up the middle of the face for the first 600 meters, then traversed rightward on mixed terrain that was hard to inspect from below. That stretch seemed to be the crux, with steep rock and no visible weakness. But it would be the key to reach and then follow a 600-meter spur directly to the summit snow slopes. A descent via the west face seemed to be the best option—more direct and shorter than the east ridge, up which Flat Top's British first ascensionists had climbed in 1980 (*see p.65*).

We left a tent and climbing gear at ABC and returned to base camp. For a few days we rested, waiting for a weather window and stuffing ourselves with chapatis, dal, and rice. When a good forecast arrived from our weather connection, Yann Giezendanner (a famous Météo-France forecaster who has been connected to many expeditions), we set off for ABC. That night, however, 30 centimeters of snow fell, and so we descended again.

A few days later, Yann messaged us that a four-day weather window was headed our way. To take full advantage, we left base camp on October 2 under falling snow, then slept up at ABC for the third time on our expedition.

We woke at 4 a.m. on October 3. The weather was perfect, and we started hiking toward the north face, hoping to reach the top of the ice wall, 600 meters up, in one day. However, first light revealed strong wind and enormous spindrift avalanches raking the wall. We were obliged to wait a few hours for the wind to calm and the sun to leave the face.

We sat on our backpacks, looking up at the impressive wall. Usually, people choose a vacation destination with warm water, sun, beaches, and palm trees. We had chosen a gloomy, shaded 1,400-meter face of rock, snow, and ice. What the hell! We were quite intimidated, actually. At noon, the avalanches stopped and we started climbing.

of the ice line. Well done!

Night was coming as I took the lead for the mystery traverse—which, as expected, turned out to be the route's crux, halfway up the wall. The first two mixed pitches were not so hard but loaded with fresh snow, making for slow going. Then, after passing a snow patch, I ground to a halt at a 30-meter rocky traverse that looked steep and unprotectable.

After a bit of reflection in the light of my headlamp, I decided to try aiding. I was able to find body-weight placements—cams, nuts, Peckers, and one piton we left fixed—though nothing seemed solid enough to hold a fall. It was surreal to fight so hard in the dark amid a sea of rock, gripped by fear, for an hour and a half,

WE WERE SURPRISED TO FIND PERFECT CONDITIONS ON THE INITIAL PITCHES. THE 70° ICE WAS SO WELL FORMED AND EASY TO CLIMB THAT WE DECIDED NOT TO USE THE ROPE.

We were surprised to find perfect conditions on the initial pitches. The 70° ice was so well formed and easy to climb that we decided not to use the rope, in order to move faster. We set up our first bivy at a snow patch 200 meters above the start, where we could excavate a perfect tent platform. The night was good—three people in a two-person tent means not having much space, but you also stay warm.

We started again early the next morning. Unfortunately, the ice now was thin and fragile, making it difficult for Nathan in the lead. Our progress was slow, and we considered giving up a few times. At one point, Hugo, now in the lead, got stuck on thin ice, so he downclimbed and tried out left—where the ice turned out to be only powder snow. He stopped a moment to reflect and then returned to try again in the same spot as before. Nathan and I encouraged him and prayed he'd make it, and he did, bringing us to the top

in the tiny world enclosed by the halo of my headlamp. Finally, I reached a snow slope, about 100 meters below the spur, exhausted but relieved. Nathan took the lead for the last few meters, and we set up the tent on another perfect platform.

On our third day on the wall—October 5—the weather was still great. We really hoped this day would be easier, letting us reach the summit snow slopes. From below, the spur seemed to be not so steep, and we figured we could climb quickly.

What a joke! Initially, the ridgeline was impossible to climb, so Hugo had to traverse left and then back up to regain the spur. These three pitches were sketchy, steep slabs covered by 50 centimeters of snow, the kind of terrain that's difficult to protect and on which you take one step back for every two steps forward. Down at our anchor, we could hear Hugo exclaim "What a hell!" now and then. We were once again very slow.

Back on the ridge crest, we hoped for easier progress. However, as Nathan took the lead, it became clear that we were once again mistaken, as a succession of steep, technical, sustained pitches followed. Nathan did an incredible job by leading almost ten difficult pitches in a row, but soon the sun was going down.

We were only halfway on the upper spur—perhaps 1,000 or 1,100 meters up the 1,400-meter face—and with nowhere to set up the tent. Even finding a place to sit was difficult. Hugo found a tiny ledge where he could scoop out a narrow platform that was just long enough for us to sit down next to each other. We put our feet in our sleeping bags and tried to sleep, toes dangling over the void. It was not our best night—but at least the air temperature wasn't too low.

We stood up on our little ledge at 4 a.m., got ready to go, and ascended the rope Nathan had fixed the evening before while he was searching for a bivy site. After a bad night, the sunshine felt so welcome. (The north face would get about an hour of morning sun, from 8 a.m. to 9 a.m.) I led a few pitches, and the terrain remained sustained and technical. Here and there, I took off my gloves to be faster and more precise on the small holds. The rock wasn't very good, but the protection was okay.

The summit snow slopes still seemed far away—and the spur even steeper. It was increasingly stressful, as we weren't sure if we would make it to the top, and retreat would have been very complicated. "It seems like we've reached the point of no return," Hugo said solemnly. On the last pitch that I led, at a sharp section

Matthias Gribi on the key traverse toward the upper spur. As night fell, he reached a 30-meter rocky section that proved to be the route's crux, with body-weight aid moves in the dark. The team spent their second night on the route bivouacked on the snow patch just before the ridge. Hugo Béguin

Gribi on the final stretch of the sharp upper spur, bare-handing the rock for precision on delicate moves. *Hugo Béguin*

of ridge, I tried on the right without success, so Hugo belayed me down a few meters on the other side, where I reached a good crack that brought us to the final headwall.

Hugo took the lead again and found a way up four pitches on a kind of steep, frozen soil that was neither rock nor ice, and was both tiring and hard to protect. Finally, we reached the snow slopes. Nathan brought us to the summit, in the dark, at 7 p.m. on October 6. What a feeling! No view, no lights, nothing but a sense of happiness we'd rarely—maybe never—experienced.

We took pictures and checked in with base camp via the radio. Then we started rappelling the steep (and unclimbed) west face. After 15 rappels from Abalakov ice anchors, we set up the tent on the glacier below the west face and collapsed into our sleeping bags at 2 a.m., exhausted but so happy.

The next day, we climbed easily to reach the long ridge that eventually connects with Brammah I and then made a few rappels to return to the north side of the mountain and our ABC, where we found Happy waiting.

Happy loves to party, and we told him how psyched we were to celebrate our ascent when we got back to Delhi. His answer? "No, first you have to climb the Kishtwar Eiger, then we can make a party." We had just come back from the hardest route of our lives, and climbing Kishtwar Eiger from here would have meant opening another new route on a 1,200-meter face. We just laughed and started hiking down to base camp.

We called our route Tomorrow Is Another Day, for two reasons. First, every day, Happy would sing a song with the lyrics "Tomorrow is another day," and this became our expedition anthem. Second, the name seemed to sum up the way we dealt with the route's deceptively difficult terrain: one day at a time. We thought about giving up many times, but thanks to our strength as a team and as individuals—and our stubbornness— we were able to keep going. Our dream became real. Thank you, life.

SUMMARY: First ascent of the north face of Flat Top (6,100m) by Tomorrow Is Another Day (1,400m, ED 5c A2 WI4 M6), Kishtwar Himalaya, India, by Hugo Béguin, Nathan Monard, and Matthias Gribi, all from Switzerland, October 2–7, 2023. The three descended by the west face. After this climb, the trio climbed the south face of an unnamed rock peak near base camp; details are at the *AAJ* website.

ABOUT THE AUTHOR: Matthias Gribi, 23, from Geneva, is studying to become a mountain guide and a helicopter pilot. He works as a helicopter flight assistant in the Swiss Alps, which helps him stay up to date on local climbing conditions.

FLAT TOP FIRST ASCENT

The East Ridge in 1980

BY PETE FINKLAIRE, *U.K.*

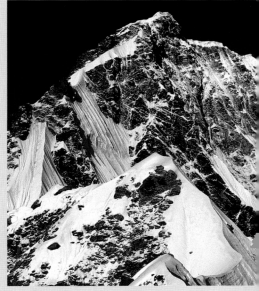

The first ascent of Flat Top was not reported in the AAJ, and other reports were unclear about the line. Here, a first-person description of the ascent.

In August 1980, Murray Hodgson, Roger Phillips, Rod Wilson, and I trekked into the Nanth Nullah and established base camp at Sattarchin, at the end of the Brammah Glacier. We made an advanced base on the south bank of the glacier, and from there, with the help of porters, we spent three days establishing a camp under the north face of Flat Top.

As it descends, the east ridge of Flat Top swings to the northeast, and we set about reaching a col low on the northeast ridge. The weather settled into a pattern of storms in the late afternoon and evening, so we were forced to sit out several bad days at this site. With time getting short, Rod went down to our glacier camp to retrieve more supplies and eventually returned to base camp to organize porters for the trek out.

We could see that the ridge above was heavily corniced, and as we gained height we were forced onto the southeast face, which made for time-consuming traversing. We made a camp just off the ridge, and Rod returned to bring supplies up to this point. It worried us seeing him soloing down in the late afternoon, but he got back to glacier camp just before dark.

TOP: The east ridge of Flat Top descends east and then northeast toward the camera, as seen from the first camp above the col on the ridge. See also photo p.60. *Pete Finklaire*

BOTTOM: Pete Finklaire (left) and Murray Hodgson on the summit in August 1980. *Roger Phillips*

As snow conditions were not good, we decided to stay on the southeast face, rather than climb back onto the crest. After descending a little, we climbed through a rock band and pitched the tent just below the final section of the ridge. The climbing had been continuously steep, with route-finding challenges.

Next morning dawned clear, and we made a lightweight push for the top. At this altitude snow conditions were good, but we found continuous difficulties. The weather worsened as we climbed the long and beautiful ridge to the large summit cornices, which we eventually negotiated by making a long traverse left. We then carefully crossed the final section of the alarmingly corniced summit ridge to the highest point.

We descended to the tent by a combination of many rappels and downclimbing. Fortunately, the next morning was clear, and we reached the initial tent site on the col late that evening. After yet another stormy night, we descended to the glacier. The mountain had given us a great climb, probably around AD/D. 🗒 📷

BRILLIANT BLUE

A NEW ROUTE IN THE KISHTWAR HIMALAYA

CHRISTIAN BLACK

In **early September,** Vitaliy Musiyenko, Hayden Wyatt, and I set off from the Salt Lake City airport with 400 pounds of gear and a crippling curiosity. I had forfeited my season of field-biology work for another international trip, an increasingly common event that continued to sabotage my personal finances. Vitaliy, shortly after his honeymoon, had packed his bags and taken time off from his job as an ER nurse to commence his second long expedition in one calendar year. And Hayden, having never even met Vitaliy, took a semester off law school in Portland to join us. These were all significant sacrifices, considering that our inspiration had been sparked solely by two blurry photos of an unclimbed line on a peak in India's Kishtwar region. The Himalaya was a place where Vitaliy had dabbled, but that Hayden and I had only dreamt of. As the plane took off from Vitaliy's and my home base in Salt Lake, I contemplated the absurdity of the events that had brought us here.

Approaching advanced base camp for White Sapphire (6,040m), the sharp peak in the center. The team had hoped to climb the big wall facing the camera, but an early winter storm prompted them to switch to the northwest couloir, left of the wall. From the prominent notch, they climbed the north face to the top. *Vitaliy Musiyenko*

A climbing trip to Mexico years ago had led to a fruitful connection with new friends, through whom I met Pete Takeda, an alpinist who was rediscovering his love of sport climbing. Pete and I linked up for another sport climbing trip to Spain the following year, during which he offhandedly probed my interest in a potential new route on a 6,040-meter (19,816-foot) Indian mountain called White Sapphire, a gem he'd been keeping in his back pocket for years. When prodded, Pete produced a few blurry photos of a diamond-shaped peak hosting a stunning, 2,700-foot unclimbed northwest face. Happy to pass the torch on this climb, Pete offered to mentor on logistics, and he helped with the ins and outs of submitting a proposal for the American Alpine Club's Cutting Edge Grant. Months later, I received notice that we'd been awarded $8,000, and I phoned Hayden to tell him to change his fall plans. Now we were buckling our seat belts to fly to India.

After a 28-hour blur of travel, we were at the Indian Mountaineering Foundation in chaotic Delhi, receiving our peak permit and meeting Anant Singh, our liaison officer. Only 21, he was bright-eyed and energetic, and he exuded an excitement for the mountains that resonated with us. Within five minutes of our meeting him, Anant was showing us photos of beautiful peaks from previous expeditions, his aspirations for the high alpine impossible to miss.

The following day, road-weary after another 18 hours of trains and taxis, we began our three-day trek to base camp from the town of Gulabgarh. As the valleys deepened and we distanced ourselves from the roadhead, so finally did our minds begin to settle. The roar of the river accompanied the soundscape of pack mules slowly ascending. Halfway through our day, the deep greens, blues, and grays of the valley were suddenly replaced by vibrant pinks, oranges, and yellows. We were at the famously colorful Chandi Mata temple in the village of Machail, where, each summer, thousands of Hindus come during the Machail Yatra holy pilgrimage. Following the lead of our logistics organizer, we too bowed before the temple to ask for blessings and safe passage.

The next morning, we reached a prominent split in the valley, demarcated by the towering peak of Kishtwar Shivling, named for the three rock spires on its shoulder resembling Lord Shiva's trident. The valley south of Shivling hosted the home village of one of our base camp cooks, Stenzing. The valley just north was our route to the Haptal Glacier and our base camp below White Sapphire. Farther north yet was a valley where the famously blue Kashmiri sapphires are mined.

We rounded a bend and came upon a skyline familiar to us from Pete's two blurred photos. The centerpiece, Cerro Kishtwar, looked like a dorsal fin penetrating the sky. Just to the south, at the farthest end of the valley, was White Sapphire, aptly named for its gemlike shape and angular features. The peak had only had two ascents to date. The first was in 2011 by Denis Burdet and Stefan Siegrist, who climbed the west face via La Virée des Contemporains (850m, WI6 M6 A2). The second ascent, in 2015, also by a Swiss team, accessed the southeastern aspect, climbing mostly moderate ice and mixed terrain along the south ridge to the summit. Our aspirations lay in the 2,700-foot unclimbed big wall on the northwest face, but we knew we would have to be flexible.

Fast-forward one week to mid-September. We were already conducting our first bit of alpinism—sitting stormbound in a bivy tent through 48 hours of rain at 14,500 feet, on our way to establish an advanced base camp (ABC). Our efforts of hiking loads had been put on pause, replaced by the softer skills of alpinism: reading, eating chocolate butter, and having horizontal dance parties to whatever music we'd downloaded on our phones. When we finally emerged from our nylon coffins, a quick look to the skyline jarred our vision. Winter had arrived, killing our dream of wearing rock shoes on a big-wall climb, a reality we accepted as we donned our ice boots and continued hiking loads up to ABC at 15,800 feet.

One of the few benefits of hiking heavy backpacks up large hills is the ample time for conversation and reflection. As we wobbled up loose talus and weaved through crevasse fields, we couldn't help but feel the juxtaposition of our current environment against each of our pasts.

The Himalaya is about as far as you can get from the flat ranchlands of my North Texas upbringing or the University of Texas rock gym where I'd begun my journey as a climber a decade earlier. Vitaliy was a city-raised immigrant to the United States from the Chernobyl area of Ukraine, and a former 300-pound high school linebacker and Domino's pizza delivery boy. He'd escaped the box of his childhood via a slow boil of increasingly epic feats in the mountains, including the solo first ascent of the 32-mile Goliath Traverse in the Sierra Nevada. Hayden, on the other hand, took joy in finally participating in the high-alpine lore of his own childhood. He had grown up to heroic tales told by his legendary, Tetons-based mountain-guide parents, Evelyn Lees and Rick Wyatt, who had ventured on expeditions to Nanga Parbat and the north face of Everest, to name a few. We reminisced about the absurdity of it all as we distracted our heaving lungs and anxious minds from the task at hand.

To be present in these mountains was a privilege not lost on any of us. With each memory we shared of our pasts and each concern we voiced about our near future, we cultivated the bonds between the members of a new team and the partnerships we'd need to rely on, high on the wall.

TOP: Kishtwar Shivling dominated the view during the approach to the Haptal Glacier. *Vitaliy Musiyenko*

BOTTOM: Blue-collar ice climbing en route to advanced base camp. *Vitaliy Musiyenko*

"I'm 9/10 fucked right now. I can't do it, Hayden. You gotta do it," I said, handing Hayden the rack as I turned on my headlamp at our hanging belay above 19,000 feet. We had left ABC early on September 21 on two hours of poor sleep and ascended the glacier to the start of the technical climbing at 17,200 feet. Due to the wintry conditions, we'd bailed on our original plan of climbing the northwest face's big wall. Instead, we'd picked a logical unclimbed line that followed a weakness of ever-steepening snow and ice cutting left of the main northwest face; after 2,000 feet, the ice and snow gully ended at a notch in a ridge, above which 650 feet of steep rock along the north face would lead to the summit.

While only 50 feet of mixed climbing remained until our prospective bivy spot at 19,200 feet in the notch, the previous 15 hours of simul-climbing and the huge jump in elevation had left me fatigued on a whole new level. Vitaliy, with his ultra-marathoner fitness, had set the pace for the day as he and Hayden swung leads through the first 1,500 feet of steep snow and ice, all of us frequently pausing to wait out torrents of spindrift. After fighting through fatigue, I had taken over for two tricky mixed pitches nearing the notch, but as the sun disappeared below the horizon, so did my remaining energy.

As 10:30 p.m. rolled around, we were finally sitting on a chopped-out snow bench at the notch. Our bivy site had turned out to be much smaller than we'd hoped—it was a tiny cornice just barely large enough for us to pitch our tent. With Vitaliy and me out of commission from semi-frozen hands and exhaustion, Hayden stepped in to start organizing our gear and melting water. As I sat there, almost useless, I recognized that my entire life's purpose had boiled down to a hilariously simple task—*hold the stove upright*—which I did for the next four hours as we ate and rehydrated. At 2:30 a.m., we settled into the tent, grateful to Hayden for keeping morale afloat throughout our evening.

Sunrise woke us five hours later from our cramped slumber, our splitting headaches softened by our first eye-level view of the high Himalaya. No longer were the surrounding peaks towering giants—

we had climbed up the beanstalk and were now among them. Cerro Kishtwar's shark fin of rock reared up to the north, now seeming larger than ever. To the west lay Dandagoporum, a similarly prominent peak with a razor-sharp northeast ridge ascending over 5,000 feet to its summit. And to the northwest were the 3,000-foot walls of Kishtwar Shivling's southeast face.

From our position in the notch, the only possibility of continuing up our giant was via the steep headwall of the north face. The rock here was not granite, as we'd previously thought, but instead very compact gneiss with few cracks. We looked up with uncertainty. A featureless slab blocked the way to the cracks above, which, while steep and sustained, appeared as if they would take good gear. This was more like a pure rock climb than we'd imagined, and would be difficult in boots and crampons. After a slow morning of good coffee and a concoction of altitude meds, my curiosity finally overcame my doubt and I volunteered to take the first lead.

In an effort to block out the crippling exposure, I let my childlike mind take over and began to tinker with the pointy bits of alpinism on the puzzle of rock in front me. I eventually found upward progress through a creative blend of aid and free climbing, linking shallow pins and thin edges. In that vein we proceeded upward, never certain of progress but never failing to find it either. By the end of the day, only 300 or so feet of headwall remained. As we fixed our ropes to descend to our bivy, we felt the tantalizing possibility of success.

The next morning, we awoke eager to complete our climb. Our daily coffee routine, however, was interrupted. *Chhhk, chhhk,*

OPPOSITE PAGE: Hayden Wyatt starting a simul-climbing block in the northwest couloir of White Sapphire. *Vitaliy Musiyenko*

ABOVE: Looking down the first pitch of the north face headwall on White Sapphire to the bivy site in the notch at the top of the couloir. Some aid was used during the first attempt, but all three climbers freed the headwall pitches during the final ascent. *Christian Black*

chhhk—Vitaliy flicked the lighter against the stove, but to no avail. The stove had slowly weakened during the climb, and now we could no longer even hear gas coming out, despite a full canister. We suspected it was related to the different fuel mix of canisters in India causing our stove to overheat and a safety mechanism to melt and block the fuel lines. All attempts at stove surgery were thwarted by not having the right tools, and inReach advice from the outside world proved fruitless as well. With less than one liter of melted water between us, we accepted the crushing conclusion that continuing would be irresponsible and unsafe. We retrieved our ropes and, frustrated, rappelled 2,000 feet back to the glacier.

out of the notch, a delicate, 50-meter M7+ through a slab and thin cracks to a small roof traverse up high. Vitaliy took over for the second pitch, another 50-meter M7+, this one consisting of delicate laybacking on poor feet and an improbable traverse to gain a section of ice.

We were now back at our high point. From our perspective in the middle of the face, the summit continued to seem far away, our perception of distances squashed by the magnitude of our surroundings. Pitch after pitch, the angle remained steep and the climbing proved harder than it looked. We wove through another five pitches of M4–M6, swapping out leaders naturally as our individual motivations waxed and waned. The hours were catching

IN THAT VEIN WE PROCEEDED UPWARD, NEVER CERTAIN OF PROGRESS BUT NEVER FAILING TO FIND IT EITHER.

After three days' rest in base camp, we hiked back up to ABC with more food—and a backup stove. We waited a full week at ABC for a weather window before finally starting back up the steep snow and ice toward the cornice bivy on October 5. It was much colder this time, and, despite the constant movement of simul-climbing, my layering failed to keep me warm. Fatigue and dehydration manifested as light nausea and uncontrollable shivering, forcing a pause midway through our day for hot fluids and forced calories. Back on the move, we continued at a good pace and arrived at our notch bivy just before sunset.

We awoke next morning to perfect weather, the cloudless skies blanketing the high peaks around us in rich blue. More acclimatized this time, we set off with the intent to free climb as a team and forgo any jumaring. We entered a high-alpine dance up the technical slabs and cracks, freeing sections we'd aided on the previous attempt. Once again, I led the first pitch

up to us, but there was no rush. The sky was clear, the air gentle, and our minds certain. We were going to the top.

Near the summit, the blanket of blue sky shifted to reveal a horizon of golden yellows and oranges, as if the setting sun itself were wishing us well. At 7:30 p.m., under the cover of night, I climbed a final five-inch crack to a starkly flat, 50-foot swath of horizontal ridge leading to the summit. There, on a perch the size of a compact car, Vitaliy, Hayden, and I smiled, embraced, and took a moment to reflect on our journey.

The previous three and a half weeks of labor had finally borne fruit. We had ferried hundreds of pounds of gear to ABC and climbed through the most fatigued moments of our lives only to retreat not far from the summit. Then we'd mustered up the energy to try again, and over two days had free climbed over 2,700 feet of technical terrain up to M7+, the most difficult pitches of which were above

19,000 feet. Had you told us that this would be the story of our climb, we all would have thought it impossible that we'd be the central characters in the narrative. From the countryside of Texas, the traumas of Ukraine and inner-city San Francisco, and an adventure-centered childhood in the Tetons, we'd each chosen to navigate our lives with synonymous purpose. What joined us on the summit was more than the climbing—it was a culmination of becoming who we'd each wanted to be.

We were certainly proud of our climb. More so, however, we were proud of each other. With each new difficulty, one of us stepped in to lead a hard pitch, volunteer for chores, or care for a tired teammate. The environmental stresses were only the final forging of our bonds as a team, bonds that were ultimately strong enough to bring us to the top of White Sapphire.

Sapphire, the second-hardest gem on Earth, is forged in a similar process. What begins as an unassuming bit of ancient seafloor is transformed into a resilient gem through the deep heat and pressure of a journey below the continents. Only when the gems are finally exhumed is their beauty evident. Much like those minerals, we'd endured our own metamorphic transformation, deep in the heart of the Indian Himalaya. The richness of our new friendship was now exhumed, emanating like the light through a Kashmiri sapphire: Brilliant Blue.

TOP: Vitaliy Musiyenko leads the delicate crack at the start of the second M7+ pitch on the north face. *Hayden Wyatt*

BOTTOM: Christian Black, Hayden Wyatt, and Vitaliy Musiyenko (left to right) celebrate a safe descent from White Sapphire. *Christian Black*

SUMMARY: New route and third ascent of White Sapphire (6,040m), above the Haptal Glacier in the Kishtwar Himalaya, by Christian Black, Vitaliy Musiyenko, and Hayden Wyatt (all USA), October 5–7, 2023. The trio climbed the northwest couloir and north face: Brilliant Blue (850m, AI3 M7+ 80°). They descended by the same route.

ABOUT THE AUTHOR: Christian Black, originally from northern Texas, began working for the National Park Service soon after college, eventually landing in Yosemite as a YOSAR member and climbing ranger. He now lives in Salt Lake City, funding new travels through his work as a field biologist and freelance writer.

THE LOST WORLD

A BIG WALL AT ALTITUDE
IN THE TIEN SHAN

ALEXANDER PARFYONOV

Voennyh Topografov (Peak of Military Topographers, 6,873m) is located near the border between Kyrgyzstan and China, east of giant Jengish Chokusu (Pik Pobeda). Base camp is on the South Inylchek Glacier, which can be reached by helicopter in 40 minutes and is at an altitude of 4,000 meters. The camp is relatively comfortable—there is a washroom, a canteen, Wi-Fi, and tents where you can stand up.

To reach the south side of Voennyh Topografov, it is necessary to trek up the South Inylchek Glacier, then branch south and east on the Zvyozdochka Glacier, which eventually reaches Chon-Toren Pass (5,400m) on the frontier. Once over the pass, the southwest face of Voennyh Topografov is not far away.

This face is composed of a big rock wall that is about 1,150 meters high, with a snow and ice face below it and alpine terrain leading to the summit. In all, our planned

Ratmir Mukhametzyanov arriving at the bivy ledge for the third night on the southwest face of Voennyh Topografov. In back is Chon-Toren Pass, which the team crossed during their two-day approach to the mountain. They would descend to the same pass at the end of the climb. *Alexander Parfyonov*

ABOVE: View from the south of (A) Khan Tengri and (B) Voennyh Topografov. (1) Northwest ridge (1965), descended to Chon-Teren Pass. The Zvyozdochka Glacier is hidden beyond. (2) The Lost World (2023). (3) Impromptu (2021). (4) South ridge (2006). *Chen Zhao | Wikimedia Commons*

RIGHT: Mukhametzyanov climbing the Zvyozdochka Glacier during the approach. *Alexander Parfyonov*

route would gain about 1,925 meters. Two prior routes climbed the south side of the mountain, farther to the right: the south ridge (Dzhuliy et al., 2006) and Impromptu (Golovchenko-Grigorev-Nilov, 2021).

Ratmir Mukhametzyanov, Aleksei Sukharev, and I had already done some difficult climbs together, including the second ascent of the Tukhvatullin Route on the north face of Ak-Su and a new route up the north face of Svarog, both in 2021, in Kyrgyzstan. In 2022, with Nadya Oleneva, Ratmir and I climbed a direct new route up the north face of Korolyova in the Western Kokshaal-too.

To acclimatize before attempting Voennyh Topografov, Ratmir guided on Pik Lenin, reaching 6,400 meters, and spent two nights at 6,100 meters. Aleksei and I each climbed Khan Tengri (ca 7,000m).

At the end of July, we started our approach, stopping for the night on the heavily crevassed Zvyozdochka Glacier. By noon the next day, we were at Chon-Toren Pass, where we flew a drone to find the best way through the cornices on the other side of the pass and photographed the wall on Voennyh Topografov in half profile; these photos ended up being our main way of orienting ourselves on the route. We left some gear on the pass and spent that night on the far side, without going any closer to the peak because of slushy snow.

On August 2, we started up the face at an elevation of 4,950 meters, and that day climbed 300 meters of ice and 240 meters of difficult rock. Aleksei led all day.

I took the lead the next day, on difficult rock climbing, including drilling holes for bat-hooks. As a whole, the climbing on the wall was about one-third aid and two-thirds free climbing. We covered only 120 meters that day and didn't make it to the ledge we'd hoped to reach for a bivouac; instead, we returned to the previous site for another night. We spent each night in a two-man tent, sharing a sleeping bag.

Day three on the route involved more difficult aid on a smooth, vertical wall, eventually moving to the right under a big

roof line. In all, during the big-wall climb, we placed about ten bolts and ten removable bolts. Temperatures on the face ranged from 5°C to -20°C. By the end of the day, we had made our way to a snowy ledge where, with the help of a hammock, we built a comfortable site for our small tent.

The terrain on the following day was more manageable, and before lunch we had made our way to a huge ledge that crosses the whole wall. The terrain above was overhanging. We decided to bivouac on the ledge, and Aleksei stayed there to dry our wet sleeping bag and tent while Ratmir led five more pitches along thin cracks. He used small cams and sometimes FiFis, a Russian invention that combines a modified ice-tool pick with a handle, used for both speed climbing on ice or aid on rock. High on the wall, our hand drill broke, but we fixed it with some tape; soon afterward, the drill and one of our hammers were dropped. The climbing remained difficult until lunchtime the next day, but by evening we had reached a large, snowy ledge that marked the exit from the wall onto the south ridge.

On day six of the climb (eight days out from base camp), we moved up the south ridge, with difficult climbing at times, alternating between snow and ice and rocky terrain. Toward evening, after climbing 300 meters, we gained the northwest ridge of Voennyh Topografov and spent a comfortable night under a rock roof at 6,700 meters.

The next morning, August 7, we started early and climbed to the western summit and then on to the main peak, in stormy weather, before starting our descent along the northwest ridge. The sky cleared during our descent, but we wished we had more than two ice axes for the three of us on the narrow, corniced ridge. Descending off the ridge, we hung up a rope on one of the rappels

ABOVE LEFT: Day four on the southwest face, with Mukhametzyanov leading the first pitch above the large ledge. *Alexander Parfyonov*

ABOVE RIGHT: The approximate line of The Lost World on the southwest face of Voennyh Topografov, as seen from Chon-Toren Pass. The height of the main rock wall is about 1,150 meters. *Alexander Parfyonov*

and had to abandon it. Nonetheless, we were back at Chon-Toren Pass by 5 p.m.

On the final day, we woke at 2 a.m., but there was no visibility, so we had to wait until dawn to start the long trek down. After 20 kilometers of hard work, we made it to base camp on the South Inylchek around midnight, where the staff had kindly left us dinner and two bottles of hot water.

SUMMARY: First ascent of the southwest wall of Voennyh Topografov (6,873m), by Ratmir Mukhametzyanov, Alexander Parfyonov, and Aleksei Sukharev, all from Russia. They descended by the northwest ridge. The trio spent six days climbing the rock wall, rated 6c A4 M4, and summited on August 7, 2023. The round trip from base camp took ten days. Their route was named The Lost World (Russian 6B).

ABOUT THE AUTHOR: Alexander Parfyonov lives in Novosibirsk in southern Russia, where he heads the quality-control office of a welding plant. He became a Master of Sport in the Russian system in 2016.

This story also relied on reports by the climbers published at Mountain.ru. Kat Tancock provided translation assistance.

TOP: Aleksei Sukharev low on the main wall, above the initial 300-meter ice slope. *Alexander Parfyonov*

BOTTOM: Sukharev and the tiny tent shared by the three climbers on the wall. The green hammock was filled with snow to expand the tent platform. *Alexander Parfyonov*

COUNTERCLOCKWISE FROM TOP: Descending the western ridge of Voennyh Topografov, with Jengish Chokusu (Pik Pobeda) across the valley; Mukhametzyanov leading steep rock on day five; Parfyonov takes a break during the trek back along the Zvyozdochka Glacier; Mukhametzyanov at base camp after ten days away. *Alexander Parfyonov and Aleksei Sukharev*

GRAND DESCENTS

A HALF CENTURY OF SKI ALPINISM IN THE TETONS

JASON ALBERT & ADAM FABRIKANT

Words **that might be blasphemy** in the *AAJ*: Climbing season is the shoulder season, at least for insatiable human-powered skiers and snowboarders in the Tetons. The summer and fall—with their slow pitching out of climbs and knee-pounding descents—are periods to endure until snow sticks to frozen ground and the mountainscape becomes a snow slider's paradise.

Although they are a magnet for North American alpinists, the Tetons offer a short climbing season—and ambitious alpinists don't like sitting around. Fortunately, the Tetons also are snow-draped sirens for alpinists who also like to ski or ride. The Grand Teton and the broader Teton Range have been focal points for ski mountaineers for decades, and remain so today for a cadre of locals, travelers, and dreamers. These mountains capture the imaginations of skiers gazing up from the valley floor the way El Capitan enthralls climbers entering Yosemite Valley for the first time.

Snow is a requirement for cutting-edge ski mountaineering, and the Tetons' gift of geography means there's plenty of it. Moist air flows unimpeded off the Pacific Ocean through a gap between the Sierra and the Cascades, then streams through the high desert's Snake River Plain, until the Tetons' orographic lift wrings heaps of snow from the sky. These mountains have sustained steepness, glacier-carved cirques, committing couloirs, and fine aesthetics. And the mountain gods blessed the region with another gift: Generally, access is relatively "easy."

This article isn't a guide to ski mountaineering in the Tetons, nor is it a comprehensive history. As with most things, there

Colby Stetson embracing the exposure and turns on Mt. Moran's upper east face (the CMC face), with the West Horn and frozen Jackson Lake far below. *Adam Fabrikant*

Bill Briggs during the 1968 first descent of the Skillet on Mt. Moran. *Fletcher Manley | Briggs Collection*

through heavily glaciated terrain, the nine-day forging of the line was proof of concept for Briggs' mountain skills and audacity, with which he'd eventually open up the Tetons as a ski mountaineering promised land.

Briggs ticked an early ski descent of Mt. Rainier in 1961 and eventually settled in as a climbing guide in Jackson Hole. In the mid-'60s, he purchased—and ran for decades—the ski school at Snow King, a steep hill that sits just above the town of Jackson. Any big-descent dreams Briggs harbored would have been provoked by Snow King's full south-to-north view of the Teton Range. In a 1995 article published in *Ski*, titled "The Man of First Descents," Briggs stated, "Skiing *mountains* is such an appropriate thing to do—it's part of the sport. If there was a feeling that a mountain or a run shouldn't or couldn't be skied, and I could eliminate that inhibition, *that's* what I really enjoyed."

Prior to Briggs' arrival in the range, there had been exploratory descents on some of the range's lesser, yet still formidable, peaks. In 1961, Corbet, Anna LaFarge, and Eliot Goss made the first descent of any of the Tetons' high peaks, the east face of Buck Mountain. Lore has Corbet skiing with his leather boots unfastened. However, into the late '60s, the Tetons' prominent skyline remained open for interpretation by skiers—the ethos of "shouldn't or couldn't" still reigned.

Briggs' first stamp on the high peaks ski scene came on Mt. Moran. When you gaze at the Teton Range from the northeast, Moran, at 12,610 feet, dominates the viewshed. A large massif with a plateau-like summit, Moran offers many walls and slabs to ascend, and an aesthetic skier's line called the Skillet that plunges from the summit—intimidating but alluring, with a dreamy, uninterrupted fall line.

In June 1968, a party of four—Briggs, Peter Koedt, Fletcher Manley, and Dick Pearson—skied the Skillet, Moran's most obvious line, top to bottom. The upper few hundred feet of this east-facing line pitch

were those who came before, and even before that. Teton Pass and some zones in the high peaks were explored on skis by the likes of Fred Brown, Jack Durrance, and Paul Petzoldt. Nor is this story all about the Grand Teton, the high point of the range at 13,770 feet (4,197m). It hopscotches around the range to capture some—again, not all—of the progression of Tetons ski alpinism.

In fact, the Grand is not even where our story begins. But it does start with the man who first skied the Grand: Bill Briggs.

Shouldn't or Couldn't?

As an apathetic East Coast college student in the 1950s, succumbing to the gravitational pull of wide-open spaces, Bill Briggs bolted west to find home. As a skier who climbed, Briggs had the ability to puzzle-piece mountain passes together. In 1958, Briggs, along with Barry Corbet, Bob French, and Sterling Neale, linked the now-storied Bugaboos to Rogers Pass ski traverse in British Columbia. Traveling

to nearly 50°, while the remaining slope backs off in difficulty and unfolds into 6,000 vertical feet of turns to Jackson Lake. The 1968 descent was notable for embracing Moran's wilderness—depending on the time of year, a mandatory six-mile ski or paddle across Jackson Lake guards the mountain from the east, and skinning and climbing the Skillet involves glaciated terrain.

Opening the Grand

As the tallest peak in the range, the Grand Teton was the prize for skiers, just as it was for early mountaineers in the West. Briggs set his eyes on a ski descent and began chasing the fleeting circumstances of snow stability and a band of willing partners. Describing his mindset at the time in a 2020 Wyoming PBS video interview, Briggs recalled with an emphatic sigh, "No one is going to do this unless I do this."

There were several false starts. In the spring of 1969, Briggs was unable to secure partners. A year later, during the 1969-70 season, insufficient snow coupled with snow instabilities snuffed plans. Three winters out from Briggs' Moran ski, the conditions and partners aligned. He was supported by John Bolton, Jorge Colon, and Robbie Garrett. On June 16, 1971, Briggs climbed the Stettner Couloir on the mountain's south face with Garrett, reached the Underhill Ridge, then ascended solo up the east face to the top.

"From the summit the skis were then used to descend to the top of the Underhill ridge," reads the 1972 *AAJ* entry (original language and punctuation retained). "A rappel over the rock pitch [climbed on the way up] permitted an uninterrupted ski descent of the mountain, first down the couloir to the Black Dike, then over to the Teepe Snowfield and down to within 1000 feet of the valley floor where the snow ended."

"Wonderful, fun skiing, for me," Briggs told *Live and Play Jackson Hole*, a local video program. "I cannot imagine having anything as varied in one ski run as [I] got in that."

Although Briggs had to convince locals he'd skied the Grand—it was verified the following day with aerial photos of his tracks taken by Virginia Huidekoper—his descent by the east face and Stettner Couloir, then down the Teepe Glacier, is considered by many to be the beginning of technical steep skiing outside of Europe. Skiers refer to this as the Briggs Route.

TOP: Alex Rienzie gazes at the Grand Teton from Middle Teton to the south, with the Ford Couloir dropping straight below the Grand's summit. The photo was taken during a Teton Trifecta, linking ski descents of the Grand, Middle, and South Tetons. *Connor Burkesmith*

BOTTOM: Mt. Moran from the northeast, showing approximate ski lines of (1) The Skillet, (2) the northeast ridge, (3) Sickle Couloir, and (4) Pika Buttress Couloir. *Beau Fredlund*

Briggs' gear—in particular, his skis—is worth a mention. He skied on long planks (30cm to 40cm longer than today's standard for steep skiing), equipped with the alpine bindings of the day, and he carried them up the mountain. In an interview with ski writer Lou Dawson, Briggs said of his ski choice for the Grand, "It was a K2 Elite. Very soft, light, 210cm, fiberglass ski. I added damping strips to both skis to reduce vibration, which worked very well, making it a very versatile (an all-conditions cheater) ski for its day."

A Grand Classic: The Ford

In July 1978, Pocatello, Idaho, locals Brad Peck and Jeff Rhoads cast their eyes in the direction of the Grand Teton's most elegant ski line, the Ford Couloir. This couloir is a fall-line descent dropping 1,000 feet directly off the Grand's summit. From a high camp, the duo ascended and then skied the Briggs Route on July 2, making the second ski descent of the peak. Then, on July 4, Rhoads and Peck climbed the Stettner to the Chevy Couloir (which usually has some ice climbing) to the Ford and onward to the summit.

On top, the team transitioned to skis, arced down the east face into the Ford's iconic fall line, and continued down into the Chevy. By downclimbing and rappelling, they eventually accessed their high camp near Glencoe Col. There, atop the Teepe Glacier, they clicked back into their skis and made turns down to the Platforms at roughly 9,000 feet. Nowadays, ski mountaineers regard the link-up of the Stettner, Chevy, and Ford couloirs as the standard ascent and descent path for skiing the Grand Teton.

Of note, Rick Wyatt made the second descent of the Ford-Chevy-Stettner route solo, in June 1982—and with his mind free, since he was descending on telemark skis.

This was also the line of the first female ski descent of the Grand, when Kristen Ulmer descended the Ford in June 1997. Ulmer was part of the day's "extreme" ski scene and already a ski film star. With a small group, she made an initial attempt on the Grand in May of 1997—the party pivoted after encountering snow instabilities while ascending. "I had heard a rumor that nobody's ever skied the Grand Teton on their first try," she said, "and the second I got up there, I realized why: Because you get up there and you're like, *What the actual heck is that?* It is so exposed."

Ulmer returned a few weeks later. "It wasn't on my radar that I'd be the first woman when I made my first attempt," added Ulmer. She just got motivated by the challenge. Her second attempt was successful, as she and her team navigated sluffing snow on the descent.

A decade later, in 2007, the first all-female team, consisting of Julia Niles and Lisa Van Sciver, onsighted their ascent and descent of the Grand.

Kit DesLauriers completed another women's first when she soloed the Grand Teton climb and ski in 2013. According to DesLauriers, "I did feel like it was a significant accomplishment and barrier breaking, though I did it only because I wondered if I could do it...without a rope yet with enough of a safety margin to ensure success. It was a mental exercise as much as a physical one."

Bigger and Bolder Lines

The Tetons truly shine when viewed from the north, with the sheer and imposing north face of the Grand and the picture-perfect skyline of the Cathedral Group. The skier's eye is drawn to the Hossack-MacGowan Couloir, an incut series of couloirs and ramps just to viewer's left of the mountain's iconic north face, instilling both inspiration and fear. The Hossack-MacGowan and its 100 percent don't-slip, no-fall skiing demanded a leap in commitment from Briggs' descent of the Grand. The Hossack combines challenging climbing with steep skiing—everything a proper ski alpinism adventure needs.

On several occasions in spring conditions—traditionally considered the safe and predictable season to ski steep, technical terrain—various local climbers and skiers were repelled by the route. In 1996, Hans Johnstone and Mark Newcomb, two local alpinists-skiers, tried a different strategy. Instead of waiting for the firm-then-soft snow of spring, they took advantage of a few weeks of midwinter high pressure and hit this king line in mid-February—the snow was very firm for their descent.

Johnstone and Newcomb carried mountaineering gear, including a rope and protection, but theirs was a fast-and-light affair. They made the approach on lighter touring skis, then swapped into more robust alpine ski gear for the climb and descent. After departing the trailhead at 3:30 a.m. and soloing up the entire route, Johnstone and Newcomb primed for some iconic steep turns just below the rocky summit at around 1:30 p.m.

"The descent back across the east face and down the upper couloir offered incomparable skiing amidst spectacular exposure," Newcomb recalled in the 1997 *AAJ*. "The steady 50- to 55-degree pitch of the couloir kept our attention, though its width and the perfect snow enabled us to link turns the entire distance to its termination above a 1,500-foot cliff. From there we traversed (skier's right) around two corners and across an apron of snow just about steep enough to keep our up-hill knee within biting distance of our chins."

By early evening, the understated Johnstone and Newcomb were homeward bound. Although this was over 25 years after Briggs' ski descent, it was the first one-day ascent and descent of the Grand Teton with skis. It was also the first winter ascent of the Hossack-MacGowan.

The north face of the Grand Teton. (1) The Hossack-MacGowan Couloir, which is reached by the upper east face of the Grand. (2) The north face ski route. The dashed lines indicate rappels to the Third Ledge, First Ledge, and the Grandstand. The arrows mark hikes up to the tops of First Ledge and the Grandstand. *Beau Fredlund*

The Otter Body

To looker's right of the Ford Couloir, positioned low on the Grand's precipitous east face, is the Otter Body, a hanging snowfield suspended on the underlying slabs, with somewhat of a resemblance to the mammal. A choke, often rappelled—but successfully skied twice—links the east face with the Otter Body's midsection. Enter the body, make some turns, maybe some sideslipping, then work toward the otter's tail, more rappels down the Otter Chimney and to the Teepe Glacier, where the turns continue.

Within the arcane world of visioning

bold ski lines, the idea of skiing the Otter Body route is attributed to local Jeff Zell. His vision was realized in June 1996, just a few months after the Hossack-MacGowan descent, again by Mark Newcomb, accompanied by legend-status skier Doug Coombs.

In looking over notes and correspondence about the Otter Body, this is clear: Repeat descents of the Otter Body are rare. The face is kissed by the sun at dawn and prone to large temperature fluctuations; signs of avalanches strafing the face, deep crowns, and hangfire are visible for miles—all evidence of gravity's wickedness.

The well-known Wasatch skier Andrew McLean, who made the second descent of the Hossack-MacGowan (with Hans Saari), had unsuccessful attempts on the Otter Body. He later summarized the conundrum posed by the Grand Teton: "I hadn't been back to ski on the Grand Teton for about ten years in part because I was still quaking in fear from my last descent...on the Hossack-MacGowan," he wrote. "Perhaps 'respect' is a better word than fear in this case, as after nine skiing trips to the Grand, it became apparent that picking a line, setting a date, and then traveling from out of state to try it was a dicey strategy. The Grand favors local knowledge over luck, and a combination of both is better yet."

Boldness is often premised on location-specific intimacy, not on throwing oneself at a problem over and over. Newcomb and Coombs, both Jackson Hole residents, eyed the Otter Body for years prior to their descent. Kim Havell, another Jackson Hole local, was the first woman to ski the Otter Body, in 2013, along with a strong team. Consider efforts like these tactical strikes.

The North Face

In 1949, 11 years after the first ascent of the Eiger Nordwand, the north face of the Grand was climbed by Ray Garner, Art Gilkey, and Dick Pownall. The route rises 3,000 feet off the Teton Glacier, ascending a combination

of rock pitches and snow ramps.

More than six decades later, in 2013, mountain guides Greg Collins and Brendan O'Neill skied the north face. O'Neill and Collins made this a top-down affair, after ascending the more straightforward Stettner-Ford to the summit.

To start the descent, the duo rappelled onto the north face's Third Ledge and clicked into skis. They linked the Third and Second Ledges on skis, then rappelled onto First Ledge. After 1,000 feet of skiable terrain, which terminated atop a rock climbing pitch (Guano Chimney), they pivoted, cramponed back up First Ledge, and rapped to a point partway down the Grandstand, at the head of the Teton Glacier. From there, they continued the steep skiing onto the glacier and completed their 7,000-foot descent back to the flatlands. In total, O'Neill and Collins made ten single-rope rappels, bracketed by relentless exposed skiing. The ascent and descent were completed trailhead-to trailhead-in 14 hours.

In a 2013 *Jackson Hole News & Guide* story on the north face descent, O'Neill is quoted as saying the line is as "technical a ski descent as there probably is."

The second descent of the north face was completed very recently, in March 2024, by Adam Fabrikant and Sam Hennessey. According to Hennessey, the team did not necessarily improve on the 2013 descent's style in any way, aside from ascending to the top of the Grandstand before skiing down it, rather than skiing that section from two-thirds height. Their day was ten hours car-to-car. Hennessey said, "Some people have dismissed this route as a contrived rappelling route. But, honestly, the north face has some amazing skiing in an outrageous position. We thought it was an excellent day of skiing."

OPPOSITE PAGE TOP: Hans Johnstone rips down the boot track during the first descent of the Hossack-MacGowan Couloir on the Grand Teton. *Mark Newcomb*

OPPOSITE PAGE BOTTOM: Doug Coombs contemplates his next turns during the first descent of the Otter Body. *Mark Newcomb*

ABOVE: Adam Fabrikant approaching the terminus of the First Ledge on the north face of the Grand. *Sam Hennessey*

Beyond the Grand

Mt. Owen is the second-highest peak in the range, at 12,933 feet, and was the last of the major Teton peaks summited, due to a complex approach and technical challenges. A few years after the Grand Teton's first descent, in 1974, Bill Briggs—that man again—climbed Mt. Owen and authored perhaps his most visionary line.

At a terse 91 words, let's allow the 1975 *AAJ* to do the documentation: "One more of the major Teton summits has been descended on skis, this time Mount Owen by Bill Briggs and Rob McClure on June 21. Putting on skis on the east ridge about 150 feet below the summit, they descended to the East Prong Col (a.k.a. Koven Col) and from there down the remaining part of the Northeast Snowfields. A rope and belay were used on the 60-foot pitch during this section. The snow finally gave out about 500 feet above Cascade Creek, about three hours and 5000 feet after they left the summit."

A few weeks before this descent, McClure skied from Mt. Owen's Koven Col, a precarious run that begins at just below 12,000 feet and descends the south-facing Koven Couloir. No doubt, this experience was of substantial benefit to his and Briggs' subsequent descent on Owen. Modern skiers refer to their line as The Diagonal.

Briggs and McClure's visionary project became a blueprint for progress in the range: Descents should aspire to making continuous turns toward the valley bottom, downclimbing or rappelling as little as possible. A May 1998 solo descent of Mt. Moran stands out as embracing this continuous-turns ethic. Stephen Koch made a 6,000-foot non-stop snowboard descent of Moran's northeast ridge. He wrote in the 1999 *AAJ* that he took a minimalist approach, leaving the axes and crampons at home. Perhaps as a result, Koch was able to move super efficiently: 14 hours car-to-car on this remote peak.

The ideals of style in the Tetons are complex, however. At the simplest level, rappelling is not skiing and downclimbing is not skiing, but the use of mountaineering skills allows skiers to make turns and have experiences in wild places. And on many Teton routes, there's an X factor that compounds the difficulties and complicates choices on which tactics to use. Those long rock slabs that make for enjoyable, moderate summer climbs in the Tetons can be the crux on ski descents, vastly different from the steep, firm snow or glacial ice that often presents as the crux in the central Alps. In the Tetons, ski descents require knowledge of the precise snow cover over rocks and/or the ability to descend safely regardless of how little snow blankets the granite slabs.

The slabby CMC Route on Moran's southeast face is a classic example, with a bit of fifth-class climbing and extensive third and fourth class in summer. The line has been skied twice, with the first descent in May 2002—involving some rappels—going to Doug Coombs, Bill Dyer, Hans Johnstone, and Kent McBride.

Given the craggy and unrelenting terrain of the Tetons, keeping the rope coiled and in the pack will only be aspirational for some lines. But it remains

the "in good style" ideal. Among the current vanguard of skiers helping to define these ideals is the co-author of this article, Adam Fabrikant. He and a close-knit group have been involved in so many interesting descents in recent years that, at this point, we'll switch to first person and let Adam tell the story directly.

OPPOSITE PAGE: Bill Dyer negotiating unskiable slabs during the first descent of Mt. Moran's east face (CMC Route). *Doug Coombs*

Modern Ski Alpinism

ABOVE: Brian Johnson descending into the depths of Mt. Owen's Run-Don't-Walk Couloir. *Adam Fabrikant*

"Without style and ethics in the mountains, what do we really have?" That's as basic a question as can be asked if you're an *AAJ* reader. And the basic answer to this perhaps rhetorical query is an unequivocal "not much."

I raised the question in an *AAJ 2021* report describing a few recent ski lines on Mt. Owen. In 2017, Beau Fredlund and I made a ten-meter rappel off the summit blocks, then continued all the way down the storied Northeast Snowfields on skis, making a variation (the Freddy-Fab) to bypass the traditional 60-meter rappel over the lower choke. The hour was later than we wanted, given the strong sun in May, and the threat of wet snow avalanches haunts me to this day.

In March 2019, Brian Johnson, Brendan O'Neill, I were able to safely descend Owen's Run-Don't-Walk Couloir, a line that skiers had discussed many a night as a potential descent. I was pretty apprehensive about giving it a go. First climbed in 1972, the couloir was an ice and mixed route rated WI4 M4. Our approach was to ski much of the Northeast Snowfields, pivot and climb with spikes up to the north ridge, transition again, then point skis down the Run-Don't-Walk. We made spicy jump turns, three rappels over the ice pitches, more jump turns, another ten-meter rappel, some "dry skiing" through a rock band (read Ptex on rock and no rope), and some fine powder turns. The technical sections of Run-Don't-Walk add up to about 2,000 feet of descent.

In 2021, Billy Haas joined Beau Fredlund and me in opening up

Mt. Owen (O), with the north face of the Grand Teton rising behind. (1) Original northeast face descent route, now known as The Diagonal. (2) Northeast Face. (3) Run-Don't-Walk Couloir. *Beau Fredlund*

the Pika Buttress Couloir on Mt. Moran. In Beau's elegant short film on the first descent, *Brother Crow*, I say, "The goal is not to just be risky, but to be in these wild, wild places, ideally with a pair of skis." A new line was born just across the six-mile frozen expanse of Jackson Lake: a fine position, close to where this all began in 1968 with Briggs' vision of the Skillet.

The Future Is Now

Let's think about climbing for a moment, specifically big link-ups in Yosemite Valley. There was the Nose in a Day, then El Cap and Half Dome in 24 hours. Add Mt. Watkins and there's a trifecta—the three biggest Yosemite walls, all scaled in a day. As with climbing in Yosemite, once the challenges are minimized by training, repetition, and familiarity, big and speedy Teton link-ups are possible, too.

The Tetons have a rich history of summer link-ups, most notably the Cloudveil, Cathedral, and Grand Traverses. It follows that Teton winter traverses, where gravity is optimized by skiing or boarding, are a natural extension of the summertime tradition—using a different set of tools for efficient movement through the mountains.

For Teton snow sliders, there's a tick similar to the Yosemite triple crown known as the Teton Trifecta: a single-push

effort ascending and skiing/riding the Grand, Middle, and South Tetons. In the 1990s, Koch and Newcomb completed the first in-a-day enchainment of the Teton Trifecta. The link-up has since become a seasonal tick for some, yet remains a cruxy, conditions-dependent fitness test.

Eventually, some in the community began talking about a ski link-up involving even more technical terrain. I first became aware of this vision in 2017, when I heard a talk where several prominent local skiers spoke about the history of ski mountaineering in the Tetons and where it all might be going. I recall Mark Newcomb offhandedly stating that one day it would be cool if somebody skied the Hossack-MacGowan on the Grand, then climbed Mt. Owen and skied the Northeast Snowfields, then climbed up to the summit of Teewinot and descended the east face to the valley floor. If you're a Teton climber, you know the link-up of these peaks as the Cathedral Traverse, moving north to south—Teewinot, Owen, and then the Grand. From the skier's point of view, it's more seamless to trend south to north.

Progress is usually the result of small steps rather than a quantum leap, and we embrace that ethos while imagining new Teton ski adventures. The incremental steps include repeating and becoming comfortable with ascent and descent routes. We closely follow weather and snow stability. We maintain sharp-end fitness and experiment with gear and nutrition. The end goal is to move fast and securely by removing the traditional challenges associated with moving through the mountains: things like route-finding, unknown sequences of moves, or how to protect certain pitches. We normalize the process by gaining intimate knowledge of a few mountains. As a result, attempting the link-up Newcomb imagined in 2017 becomes an endurance challenge. But, know this: The endeavor had our full attention.

In 2021, Sam Hennessey and I completed the Cathedral Traverse on skis—but by less committing lines, as

we didn't include the Hossack-MacGowan or the Northeast Snowfields.

By March 18, 2023, Brendan O'Neill, Hennessey, and I felt we had the skill set and the gathered knowledge to commit to and complete Newcomb's proposed link-up. After efficiently summiting the Grand Teton, we descended the east face and traversed into the Hossack-MacGowan, which went with three rappels. We then flowed toward the Koven Couloir on the south side of Mt. Owen and began booting up. The group topped out on Owen, downclimbed the summit pyramid, and clicked into skis roughly 100 feet below the top before skiing down the Northeast Snowfields. At roughly the 10,000-foot level, we contoured toward and into Teewinot's North Couloir, summited, and skied that peak's east face to the valley. The effort totaled roughly 13,500 feet of climbing (and descent) over 16 miles.

As in any famed and heavily climbed arena—again, think Yosemite Valley—things aren't necessarily as older generations think they are. The idea of someplace being climbed out can be considered nonsense. The same can be said of ski alpinism. Styles become more refined, skills more honed. Yes, the future is now, but it's also tomorrow for those who can vision a cleaner descent or imagine there's more light in a day and push even farther across the Tetons in good style, linking up classic lines.

In short, "skied out" isn't part of the vocabulary here.

ABOUT THE AUTHORS: Jason Albert lives in Bend, Oregon, and is the founder and editor of *the-high-route.com*. Adam Fabrikant lives in Kelly, Wyoming, and works full-time as an IFMGA climbing and skiing guide.

Sam Hennessey takes in the heady view from the north side of the Grand Teton, looking over Glacier Gulch to the Koven Couloir (leading to Mt. Owen) and Teewinot. The three peaks surrounding the Teton Glacier form the classic Cathedral Traverse as well as a hyper-modern ski link-up. *Adam Fabrikant*

CLIMBS + EXPEDITIONS

Climbs & Expeditions reports generally are arranged geographically, from north to south and from west to east, within a specific country or region. Unless noted, the reports cover climbs in 2023. The complete *AAJ* archive, from 1929 to the present, can be searched at *publications.americanalpineclub.org*. The online reports frequently contain additional text, photos, maps, and topos. Look for these symbols indicating additional online resources:

FULL-LENGTH REPORT

ADDITIONAL PHOTOS

MAPS OR TOPOS

VIDEO OR MULTIMEDIA

Elisabeth Lardschneider and Markus Ranalter return to their portaledge after a rest and some rain at base camp during the first ascent of the northwest face of Little Jamyang Ri in Zanskar. See p.289. *Stefan Plank*

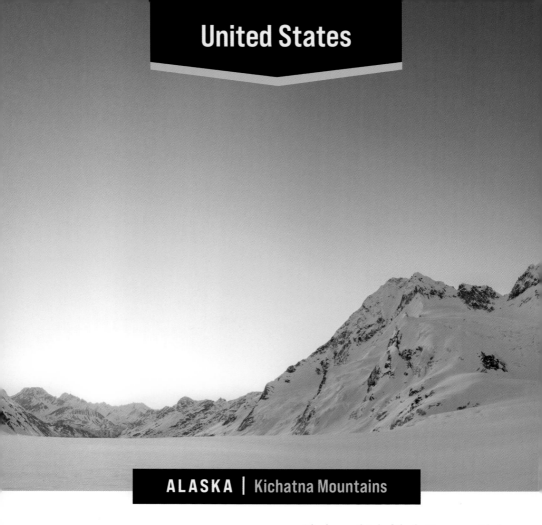

ALASKA | Kichatna Mountains

AUGUSTIN PEAK, NORTH BUTTRESS

On April 19, Kurt Ross, Nelson Neirinck, and I landed on the Trident Glacier with three weeks of food and one guaranteed day of good weather. We left our base camp the next morning at the comfortable time of 6 a.m., planning for two days on the north buttress of Augustin Peak (ca 8,600'), an attractive unclimbed feature I'd noticed while reading the *AAJ* report on the first ascent of the Erdmann-Roskelley Northeast Face (4,000', IV M3 70°) in 2014. Snow conditions were ideal after a month-long high-pressure system that had just ended, allowing for rather easy and safe snow travel on all aspects of the mountain.

The lower third of the buttress provided a long pitch of water ice followed by easy snow up to a rock band. Two long pitches of thin névé took us up a narrow groove in the rock, and thus through the route's biggest unknown, with little difficulty. After a short cornice crux, we unroped and climbed the remaining snow slopes to the top of the buttress, where we hydrated and soaked up the sun while we still could.

Instead of tackling the knife-edge ridge directly above, we chose the slightly less aesthetic option of traversing hard left across the northeast face, aiming for a col below the summit. (On top of the time constraints, we skipped the ridge because of deteriorating snow quality and a lack of obvious protection.) When we arrived

Kurt Ross and Michael Telstad crossing the Trident Glacier toward the north buttress of Augustin Peak (prominent at right). The 4,600-foot climb, with Nelson Neirinck, ran up the left side of the central buttress facing the camera and continued to the summit, which is beyond the rock tower at far right. The two other routes on Augustin—the West Face (Graber-Long-Schunk, 1977) and the Erdmann-Roskelley Northeast Face (4,000', IV M3 70°, 2014)—are hidden from view to the right and left, respectively. *Nelson Neirinck*

at the summit, 14 hours after crossing the bergschrund, the surrounding peaks glowed pink in the setting sunlight.

Though we had packed a bivy kit, we decided to push through the night to get down. We descended the east ridge to where we could downclimb the northeast face—no rappels needed. Our descent path roughly followed the same route that Ben Erdmann and Jess Roskelley climbed up in 2014, and that Michael Graber, Alan Long, and George Schunk descended in 1977 after their first ascent of the peak via its west face.

We arrived back at our skis well past midnight and made it back to camp shortly before sunrise. Hammering winds and subzero temps arrived later that day. We flew out after eight more days and several feet of fresh snow without having gotten the chance to climb anything else.

The North Buttress (4,600', Alaska Grade 5 AI4) is one of the longest routes in the Kichatna Mountains, starting lower than either of the prior routes up Augustin. Thanks to the AAC's Mountaineering Fellowship Fund for a grant that helped make this trip possible. 📷

—Michael Telstad

The line of Borealis Face (2,000', 85° ice), the probable first ascent of the northwest face of the Citadel, above the Shelf Glacier in the Kichatna Mountains. *Zach Lovell*

THE CITADEL, NORTHWEST FACE, AND RISE AND SHINE

Time is often an unhelpful metric when weighing the value of a trip in the mountains. Even a few days can gift the richest of experiences when partnership, conditions, and luck line up. In mid-April, Joseph Hobby and I were fortunate to do two new routes on back-to-back days in the Cathedral Spires of the Kichatnas, during a brief period of good weather amid a stormy spring.

Paul Roderick of Talkeetna Air Taxi deftly pioneered a new landing on the Shelf Glacier, with Joseph and me along as eager passengers. We hopped out and spent the rest of the day assessing conditions and enjoying as much sun as we could find in an otherwise shaded amphitheater.

The next day, we skied to the base of the Citadel (8,520'), aiming for the northwest face. In 1966, Arthur Davidson, David Johnston, Pete Meisler, Richard Millikan, and David Roberts would have gazed upon this face from their advanced base camp on the Shelf when they planned to try the Citadel. They experienced three days of poor weather and never made an attempt. After first seeing the Citadel's northwest face in 2021 from a neighboring ridge, I did a substantial amount of research; this face had very

likely remained unclimbed, despite holding an obvious line. I believe this was simply because of the difficult access—which, prior to Paul Roderick's opening of the Shelf Glacier landing, would have been from the Shadows Glacier or the Cul-de-sac Glacier.

Our route began with an overhanging bergschrund that gave way to snow climbing and ice runnels. These offered quick and secure soloing. Halfway up, we broke out the rope and simul-climbed through high-quality but thin alpine ice, with sections up to 85°. On the upper face, conditions were more variable, with steep, fluted snow and ice-covered rock slabs. Our line wandered slightly but had beautiful exposure. We reached the Citadel's breathtaking summit in four hours and switched into matching summit outfits—bright red tank tops emblazoned with unicorns—that we had discovered on a sale rack in an Anchorage Walmart.

Our three-hour descent had challenging anchor building in crackless rock. We generally reversed the ascent route, with several rappels and downclimbing. Borealis Face (2,000', 85° ice) is well worth a visit from parties seeking an off-the-beaten-track ice and snow route.

On April 20, we woke to the chirp of my satellite phone receiving the latest weather forecast. Our plans to take a rest day needed to change if we wanted to do another climb before flying out.

We headed to an easterly couloir on an unnamed formation immediately south of the Riesenstein. After skinning over the bergschrund, we donned crampons and simul-soloed until we reached an incredible 60m AI5 ice hose with a few mixed moves at the top. The crux of the route came on the following pitch: a snowy, overhanging chockstone that required extensive excavation, creative aid, and an exciting mixed exit. After reaching the col, we climbed a rope length to one of the formation's many subtle summits as the sun was setting, roughly seven hours after leaving camp. We descended our route

quickly, with bountiful options for rock-gear rappel anchors and secure downclimbing on lower-angle ice and snow.

Round-trip from camp, we climbed Superfly Couloir (1,700', AI5 M6 A2) in about 10 hours. There are no other reported routes on this formation (even from the Cul-de-sac Glacier), and we named it Rise and Shine. The formation has a plateau-esque top with a few summits that are at similar elevations, all between 7,300' and 7,400'.

The northern lights came out when we got back to camp, and an explosion of phosphorescent green illuminated the sky as we drank half-frozen beers. Despite the early morning hour, we were wide awake and briefly impervious to the cold tugging at our faces. When we finally fell asleep, it was only for a few precious hours before the sun came up again and we began packing up camp to fly out. 📷

An AI5 ice hose in the back of Superfly Couloir (1,700', AI5 M6 A2) on the previously unclimbed Rise and Shine formation in the Kichatna Mountains. Zach Lovell

—**Zach Lovell**

CEMETERY SPIRE, GOLD RUSH

Silvia Loreggian and I arrived in Alaska in mid-May for our first expedition to the Alaska Range, unsure what lay in store. At the first opportunity that weather allowed, we flew into the Kichatna Mountains and established a base camp on the Cul-de-sac Glacier.

For seven days, we were tentbound due to snowy nights followed by warm—and avalanche-prone—days. Our main goal had been Kichatna Spire, but its faces were full of snow. During our days in base camp, we used binoculars to scope nearby possibilities that we might be able to climb during a small weather

Gold Rush (600m, 5.12a A1+) on the southwest face of Cemetery Spire in the Kichatna Mountains. The couloir to the left was climbed to within 50 meters of the summit in 2006 by Katherine Fraser and Jen Olson. *Stefano Ragazzo*

window. Giacomo Poletti, our friend and meteorologist in Italy, texted us on our GPS device on June 4: "You have 30–33 hrs with no precipitation but high winds." Not a long window, but long enough. The southwest face of Cemetery Spire looked like the driest option.

We set off that same afternoon. The approach to Cemetery Spire's southwest face went fast: 20 minutes on flat glacier, 200 vertical meters of skinning up a snow couloir, and finally another 200m of easy terrain (UIAA III M3). At the end of this easy part, we came to a steep rock face with a big dihedral (which had been visible from our base camp). We climbed two pitches up beautiful rock, 5.11 and 5.10, with nice finger and hand cracks, then fixed ropes and returned to base camp.

The next day, we started at 6 a.m. and, after jugging up the fixed lines, started up new terrain.

The great rock continued for another three pitches. We free climbed as much as possible, swinging leads. Then the climbing and route-finding got more complicated.

The cold at the belays increased, too, forcing the follower to put on mountain boots and jumar. Two pitches with particularly grainy and crumbly rock were psychologically trying, but fortunately the rock improved. Next came another long, spectacular dihedral; a large roof in the corner forced us into aid-climbing mode, made trickier by ice stalactites clogging the cracks. When we came to a second roof, we found a way to exit the dihedral to the right. After three more moderate pitches, including some ice-choked offwidths, we were at the top of the wall.

About 200m below the summit, we came across an old, destroyed belay anchor, most likely from a previous attempt. We later spoke with other climbers, rangers, and Alaska climbing historian Steve Gruhn—no one had firm details on who might have left the anchor or when. [*The only known complete route up Cemetery Spire was the first ascent of the formation, in 1978, by Bryan Becker, Andrew Embick, Rob Milne, and Andy Tuthill, who climbed the north ridge, which they called Gargoyle Ridge. In 2006, Katherine Fraser and Jen Olson climbed 450m of a couloir on the west face, retreating 50m short of the summit.*]

We reached the top around 10 p.m. and immediately began the descent. The cold and wind were intense. At about 3 a.m., we bivouacked briefly, sitting in our sleeping bags on a small ledge. Three hours later, we were on the move again. Things got dicey as the rope snagged on the rough granite, and we had to chop off 30m. Thankfully, we were only around 200m above the ground. After six shorter rappels and some easy downclimbing, we were back at the base of the spire. During the descent, we left seven hand-drilled 8mm bolts, two pitons, and two nuts for rappel anchors; our descent route did not follow the exact line of ascent. We finally got back to our skis at 10 a.m.

Our new line is called Gold Rush (600m, 5.12a A1+). It was exactly the adventure that Silvia and I were looking for. 📷

—**Stefano Ragazzo,** *Italy*

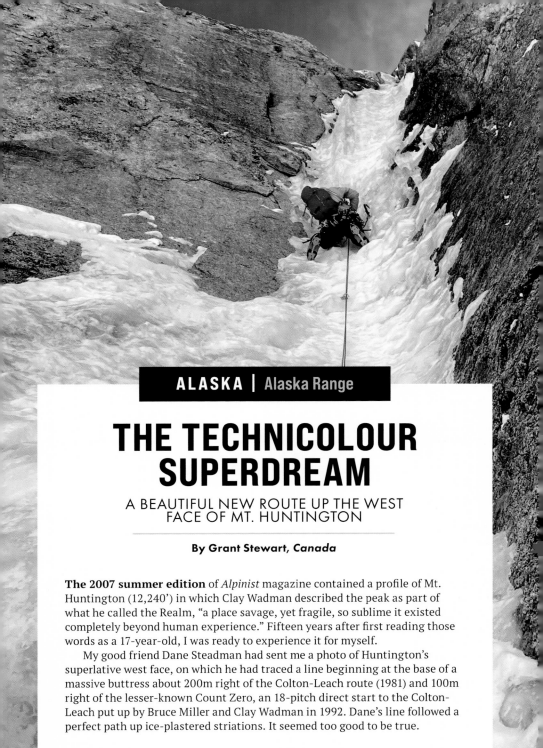

THE TECHNICOLOUR SUPERDREAM

A BEAUTIFUL NEW ROUTE UP THE WEST FACE OF MT. HUNTINGTON

By Grant Stewart, *Canada*

The 2007 summer edition of *Alpinist* magazine contained a profile of Mt. Huntington (12,240') in which Clay Wadman described the peak as part of what he called the Realm, "a place savage, yet fragile, so sublime it existed completely beyond human experience." Fifteen years after first reading those words as a 17-year-old, I was ready to experience it for myself.

My good friend Dane Steadman had sent me a photo of Huntington's superlative west face, on which he had traced a line beginning at the base of a massive buttress about 200m right of the Colton-Leach route (1981) and 100m right of the lesser-known Count Zero, an 18-pitch direct start to the Colton-Leach put up by Bruce Miller and Clay Wadman in 1992. Dane's line followed a perfect path up ice-plastered striations. It seemed too good to be true.

Zac Colbran climbing steep ice on the new route up Mt. Huntington's west face. The dreamy quality of this runnel inspired the route's name: The Technicolour Superdream. *Dane Steadman*

The west face of Mt. Huntington (12,240'), showing (1) Start of the Colton-Leach Route (1981); (2) Count Zero (Miller-Wadman, 1992); (3) The Technicolour Superdream (1,300m, VI AI5+ M6+ A2)—the route joins the Colton-Leach at the big horizontal snow band; (4) West Face Couloir; and (5) Community College Couloir (Thomas-Vance, 2009). (N) is the general location of the Nose on the Harvard Route. Other routes not shown. *Zac Colbran*

In mid-April 2023, Dane, Zac Colbran, and I bowed our heads in the abrasive wash of Paul Roderick's plane as the legendary pilot took off after dropping us on the Tokositna Glacier. We watched as the plane grew small, banked left, and vanished into the mountains. In the sudden silence, we turned our gaze to Huntington. Our hopeful eyes searched the west face, praying that our intended route hadn't been a photographic anomaly. And there it was—a thin line of gray ice soaring up the granite buttress.

After setting up camp, we set off to investigate the start of the route. Zac won rock-paper-scissors and carefully climbed 10m up a snice-filled corner before the ice disappeared and he hit overhanging snow mushrooms—the exact type of terrain we'd been worried about. After building a small nest of gear, Zac dry-tooled far to the right, delicately tiptoeing across the granite to a thin, barely there sheet of ice. He tapped his way slowly up the sheet, eventually sank his first screw, and shortly after built a good anchor to bring us up.

Dane took over and led a largely Pecker-protected pitch linking smatterings of ice and pick-torquing cracks up a steep wall to rejoin the corner system. At least for now, it looked like the route might go. We rapped down, stripping our ropes as we went.

Two days later, we left base camp at 5 a.m. Dane took the first block and cruised up the pitches we'd already done. Next, he excavated his way through a traversing snow pitch to reach great ice in the main corner system. A few pitches later, that ice petered out—and we were back to snow mushrooms. Zac and I watched as Dane put on a master class in mushroom dismantling, carefully slicing chunks away to access the steep rock behind.

The mushroom ordeal completed, Zac took over and led an incredible block of pitches up a massive ice hose we had seen from the ground. The hose ended with steep, wildly featured ice lasered into a corner that arced into the sky. With nowhere to shelter from falling ice, Dane and I erected a backpack force field above our heads and huddled beneath it.

Above us, a large swath of granite beckoned. From the ground, the only real feature we had been able to pick out at this spot was a roof; we were unsure whether it would go. This was my block, and I moved left across a slab and up into the overhang. Switching to aid and pulling through it, I found a perfect finger crack leading upward. Dane followed the pitch free at M7. Above this, I linked several chimneys and small snowfields. We had hoped to be done with the steep terrain and to have reached an obvious fin of snow by the end of the day, so that we could dig in and set up our tent. But with darkness lapping at our heels and more blank-looking granite ahead, we were forced to bivy sooner. Our only option was a small, triangular patch of 70° snow plastered to the rock. We hacked out a two-foot butt ledge in the ice before hitting rock and settled in for a cold night.

In the morning, we watched the sun explode over the south face of Mt. Hunter. My feelings of gratitude for the light after a long night were mixed with apprehension about the pitch to come—another blank-looking slab. Twenty meters above our bivy ledge, I placed a few pieces and set off to the right, uncertain what I'd find. Peeking around a corner, I saw that what had looked blank from the ground turned out to be a perfect, pick-torquing seam leading toward a ramp system above. Lucky again! I strung up a few more pitches, and then Dane took over to lead us up a series of ramps and chimneys peppered with steep ice bulges. Above these, our new route intersected with the Colton-Leach.

We had climbed 700m to this point. After a quick brew stop, we simul-climbed the amazing ramp system of the Colton-Leach. As the sun set, we kicked our way up the gold-washed summit icefield. To our surprise and relief, we found a perfect tent platform chopped into the snow. With a little excavation, we were able to pitch the tent for an all-time bivy, deeply appreciated by all after our prior evening's accommodations.

The next morning, we traced a line up the summit ridge to put the finishing touches on The Technicolour Superdream (1,300m, VI AI5+ M6+ A2). Standing on tiptoe atop Huntington, we could just catch the sun on our faces as it streamed over the cornice from the east. With the central Alaska Range spread out before me, it felt as if I had stumbled into the Realm that Wadman wrote of 16 years earlier. We descended the West Face Couloir and arrived back in camp around 2 p.m.

We would like to thank the John Lauchlan Award for their support to help make this trip possible. [*This climb is highlighted in episode 57 of the AAJ's Cutting Edge podcast.*] 📷 🔍

Zac Colbran about to begin a thin ice traverse to avoid snow mushrooms on the first pitch of The Technicolour Superdream. *Matt Cornell*

COMMUNITY COLLEGE COULOIR AND NOSE FREE: *On April 24, three days after returning to base camp, Dane Steadman and Grant Stewart went back for seconds on Huntington's west face, having spotted a right-angling ramp system between the West Face Couloir and the Harvard Route that they believed to be unclimbed. They later learned this line was first climbed in 2009 by Chris Thomas and Rick Vance, who named it the Community College Couloir. Steadman and Stewart followed that route to its intersection with the Harvard Route (Bernd-Hale-Jensen-Roberts, 1965) just below the 100' "Nose" pitch—an overhanging crack that was the only section of the route that had yet to go free. Steadman freed the pitch at M8. He and Stewart then traversed left and rappelled the West Face Couloir. An integral free ascent of the Harvard Route remains up for grabs.*

The Mini-Moonflower is a prominent buttress just to the northeast of the North Buttress of Mt. Hunter (Begguya). (1) North Couloir (Cordes-DeCapio, 1998). (2, yellow) Shadow People (Steadman-Stewart, 2023). (3) Kiss Me Where the Sun Don't Shine (Cool-Parnell, 2001; the first ascensionists stopped two pitches shy of the buttress' summit). (4) Dempster-Wilson, 2008. (5) Luna (Koch-Prezelj, 2001). *Grant Stewart*

MT. HUNTER, MINI-MOONFLOWER BUTTRESS, SHADOW PEOPLE

After climbing Mt. Huntington (*see previous story*), Dane Steadman and I bumped over to the Southeast Fork of the Kahiltna Glacier at the end of April. In ten days, we caught just one frigid day to climb between weather systems.

We left our tent at 4:30 a.m. on April 30. After crossing the 'schrund below the Mini-Moonflower Buttress on Mt. Hunter (Begguya), we climbed the ice apron at the start of the North Couloir (2,000', 85° ice, Cordes-DeCapio, 1998). Where the apron pinches down into the couloir proper, we traversed hard right on mixed ground to gain an ice runnel that leads

into the large icefield that cuts from left to right up the center of the buttress. After 100m of spine surfing, we reached the top of the icefield and found a perfect strip of blue ice that took us into a small basin below the upper headwall. From there, we climbed straight up on pitch after pitch of amazing ice, interspersed with high-quality mixed steps up to M5. We climbed directly up the final icefield and chopped through the cornice into sunshine around 3:30 p.m.

Despite wind-driven snow sluffs—a sign the bad weather was returning—the descent down the North Couloir went smoothly, and we reached the glacier around 6 p.m.

Over the last few years, the crux ice pitch of the North Couloir has been pretty anemic—when it forms at all—which makes for engaging dry-tooling but also a much harder route. Our new line, Shadow People (700m, IV AI4+ M5), offers an alternative for folks seeking excellent climbing at a surprisingly moderate grade.

—**Grant Stewart,** *Canada*

DENALI, WEST BUTTRESS, FASTEST KNOWN TIME

On June 5, Jack Kuenzle (USA) climbed and descended the West Buttress route on Denali (20,310'), using skis, in 10 hours, 14 minutes, 57 seconds. Kuenzle followed the Rescue Gully cutoff between the two highest camps on the route. The previous fastest round-trip time on the West Buttress was 11:44, set on foot by Karl Egloff (Ecuador) in 2019.

Kuenzle had an extraordinary year of speed records on U.S. mountains: Mt. Shasta in California, ascent in 1:28:58 on April 1 and round trip, using skis, in 2:30:48 on April 14; Mt. Rainier in Washington (round trip, using skis) in 3:04:31 on May 3; and the Presidential Traverse in New Hampshire (southbound) in 3:31:54 on September 15.

—**The Editors,** *with information from Fastestknowntime.com*

NENANA MOUNTAIN, INFLATION TOWER

The relative ease of access to Nenana Mountain, at the western margin of the Hayes Range, makes it well suited for smash-and-grab trips during short Alaskan high-pressure systems. On August 1, Tristan O'Donoghue and I returned to Nenana Mountain (7,881') for the third time, following trips in 2020 and 2021. We flew into the Hotel Glacier, on the south side of Nenana, with Temsco Helicopters.

We quickly got to work. After walking to the head of the glacier, we climbed two 70m pitches on the slabby flank of a previously unclimbed tower on the southeast side of Nenana. The granite was clean, the climbing engaging but never too difficult (up to 5.9). We resolved to return the next day.

Tristan O'Donoghue starting up Inflation Tower (1,200', IV 5.10a PG-13) on the southeast side of Nenana Mountain. Ethan Berkeland

Early the next morning, we re-led the first two pitches, then encountered the crux: run-out, difficult climbing that traversed up and right. The pitch finished on a striking arête that led to easier ground. The next two pitches went up and left over a chockstone, through a grovelly and poorly protected crux, then into a beautiful arching crack that was considerably easier than it looked. Wrapping around an arête to the left brought us to a brilliant corner, pitch six, that led onto the tower's south face. We climbed two pitches up the center of the face, finishing on the sharp summit of Inflation Tower (1,200', IV 5.10a PG-13). We rapped the route without issue.

The next day we attempted a striking feature near camp, but rappelled after five pitches. Rather than get scooped up by Temsco, we planned to hike and packraft out of the bush. Over two days, we hiked six hours and paddled 17 miles on the Yanert Fork and Nenana River (with class III whitewater in which I took a dramatic swim) to arrive back at the Temsco base. Soon we were clinking beers at 49th State Brewing in Healy. This trip was supported by a Mountaineering Fellowship Fund Grant from the AAC. 📷

—**Ethan Berkeland**

HEARTH MOUNTAIN, SOUTHWEST FACE

On April 7, Laron Thomas and I set out to explore a likely unclimbed 3,500'-plus couloir that slashes up the southwest face of Hearth Mountain. Standing at 6,182', Hearth is located up the

The southwest face of Hearth Mountain (6,182'), climbed by the prominent left-slanting couloir that starts on the right side of the face. *Joe Nyholm*

South Fork of the Snow River in the Kenai Mountains.

We set out on snowshoes at 5:30 p.m. from the snowmachine pullout across from the Meridian and Grayling Lakes trailhead. Despite a late start, there was a relatively good crust on the trails, and we made excellent time to a campsite seven miles up the riverbed.

We woke to overcast skies and set out at 6 a.m. There was increasingly heavy snowfall as we ascended the drainage to the bowl below the right side of the southwest face, and it seemed the day might turn into a reconnaissance mission. However, a fortuitous break in the clouds above Hearth's summit gave us hope. Roping up with a Petzl RAD Line and armed with three pickets, we left our snowshoes and started up a 1,000' avalanche-strewn slope before entering the narrow, rock-walled couloir.

Two bergschrunds proved to be the main challenge. One was at least five feet across and seemed like over 100' deep in places. Fortunately, we discovered a snow bridge that allowed us to tiptoe across. The conditions in the couloir alternated between firm snow and powder, with the final stretch being almost knee-deep. The steepest parts were a bit over 60°. Battling fatigue, we reached the summit at midday.

After a quick refuel, we started down the couloir amid deteriorating weather. Small sluff avalanches kept us on alert, and inside-the-ping-pong-ball whiteout conditions made navigation difficult. At camp, we took a longer break before embarking on the arduous trek through soft snow. Despite post-holing, we completed the hike out in roughly the same time as the approach, wrapping up a 14-hour summit day.

We believe ours to be the third ascent of Hearth Mountain. The first was by Willy Hersman, Rick Maron, Mike Miller, and Todd Miner in 1989, via the Fireside Glacier on the northwest side; the second was by Harold Faust, Tom Gillespie, Dano Michaud, and George Peck in 2008, going up the east side from the Billiken Glacier. Thanks are due to Michaud for suggesting this couloir climb.

— **Joe Nyholm**

ALASKA | Chugach Mountains

ABERCROMBIE MOUNTAIN, MOONLIGHT MILE

As Jed Brown observed in a report about his and Colin Haley's first ascent of the southwest face of Abercrombie Mountain (7,037') in 2007, good spring alpine conditions around Valdez are hard to come by. The mountains begin at sea level and rise to a mere 7,000', so spring usually comes on fast; alpine ice routes come into condition only briefly before melting out. In March, however, August Franzen phoned me to say conditions were shaping up favorably to give Abercrombie a go.

I drove from Palmer to August's house in Valdez on March 30, and the next day, August drove his snowmachine to the lake that sits at the toe of the Valdez Glacier, where I met him with our packs. I hopped on behind him and we puttered across the frozen lake and onto the glacier. We cruised about eight miles on windboard before running into heavily crevassed terrain. There, we parked the machine and hiked the last half mile to the base of Abercrombie, where we set up our tent in the early afternoon of March 31.

It was windy but sunny, and the entire southwest face was clattering with small rocks and ice chips. We took naps and ate dinner to wait for cooler conditions. Unable to sleep more, we left the tent at 11:30 p.m. under a nearly full moon. With the sun off the face, it was silent. After an hour of snow climbing, we reached an ice flow approximately 150m to the right of Jed and Colin's line and began climbing.

The bottom half of the route presented about 2,000' of sustained but straightforward WI3, with a couple of steeper pitches mixed in. A significant snow bench separates this lower part of the face from the upper half.

Moonlight Mile (5,280', WI4 M4), in red, on the southwest face of Abercrombie Mountain (7,037'). The route climbed by Jed Brown and Colin Haley in 2007, the first ascent of the southwest face, is shown in yellow. This photo, taken during a scouting mission in February, shows snowier conditions than those at the beginning of April, during the first ascent of Moonlight Mile. *August Franzen*

Above the bench, we took a gully to the left of where Jed and Colin climbed on the south ridge. (Based on Jed's report, I suspect they were attempting to climb the couloir feature we followed, but passed it in poor visibility while traversing the snow bench and ended up at the ridge.) The upper half of our route was another 2,000' of sustained, firm 40°–60° snow, punctuated by several 30m–60m headwalls that we climbed via small ice flows.

We simul-climbed much of the route, belayed a couple of pitches, and built approximately ten anchors in total. A few of those anchors were in rock and, as Jed observed in his report, the stone seemed unusually good for the Chugach. The crux of the lower half was a sunbaked WI4 pitch, and the upper crux was a run-out section of M4 involving very thin ice. Had we climbed the route a few days earlier, those two pitches likely would have had more ice.

Near the top, we wove between rime towers and reached the false summit at 10:30 a.m. on April 1, about 11 hours after beginning. We traversed over the true summit and started down the east ridge. We then downclimbed a gully into a large bowl on the southeast face, crossed a hanging valley, and downclimbed another gully below the south ridge to arrive back on the Valdez Glacier. We returned to camp at 3 p.m., making for a 15.5-hour round trip. After snacking and dozing, we drove the snowmachine back to August's house in time for dinner.

Ours was likely the second ascent of the face. The route is direct and has quality, sustained climbing—I would compare it favorably with other classic alpine ice climbs in Alaska, like Ham and Eggs on the Mooses Tooth. We calculated the vertical gain at 5,280', and we climbed the route almost entirely by moonlight, so we called it Moonlight Mile, after the classic Rolling Stones song. 📷 🔍 A grade of WI4 M4 seems consistent with the local standard.

—Simon Frez-Albrecht

GIRLS MOUNTAIN, SISTER SPIRE, EAST FACE, BING BONG BUTTRESS

Sister Spire, a detached gray tower protruding from the south shoulder of Girls Mountain (6,134'), rises to a modest 5,580'. However, the sheer, triangular east face towers about 1,000' above the Worthington Glacier, near Thompson Pass. Steep headwalls, dihedrals, and runnels are laced with snowy bands as the terrain gradually steepens from bergschrund to summit. While Sister Spire's summit has been reached via a sneak-around mountaineering route on the west ridge (1,000', M1 and steep snow, Brown, 2018), the east face had not seen any attention from climbers. This is likely because the face requires very particular early-season conditions: consistent freezing temps to "glue" the moss and rock together before the wall becomes covered with snow.

On October 16, Lauren Brand and I skied across the Worthington Glacier by headlamp, stashed our skis in the basin below Sister Spire, and crossed the bergschrund at 11 a.m. Simul-soloing the snow apron, we eventually funneled into a corner system we had eyed from the glacier. We climbed six long roped pitches up this central weakness, with (generally) moderate mixed climbing to connect corners. The line was devoid of ice and instead offered thoughtful hooking and stemming on delicate rock and frozen turf. Each pitch presented a distinct crux. Gear—mainly nuts and pins—was sparse throughout the entire climb.

The crux fifth pitch followed an exposed traverse to a steep, rocky pedestal with a bulge looming above. The key sequence on this pitch—a series of committing moves involving pick torquing, techy footwork, and swinging into frozen moss—went at M7 R/X. Another rope-stretching pitch of moderate mixed and steep snow put us on top of Sister Spire at 6 p.m. We descended the mountaineering route to our skis

Bing Bong Buttress (330m, IV M7 R/X) on the east face of Sister Spire, a prominent formation on the south side of Girls Mountain. *Lauren Brand*

and crossed the glacier once more by headlamp.

We named the route Bing Bong Buttress (330m, IV M7 R/X) as a tribute to Lauren's cat, Bings, whose legacy will now be cemented in Chugach alpinism for all time.

—**August Franzen**

ALASKA | Wrangell Mountains

CHITISTONE MOUNTAIN, HOT FRENCH GROTTO

In March 2023, Elias Antaya, Ethan Berkeland, Jonathan Koenig, and I were having a productive cabin-based trip climbing beautiful ice lines throughout the Chitistone Valley in Wrangell–St. Elias National Park. After repeating Broken Dreams (1,500', WI6, Comstock-Dial-Tobin, 1987), we were looking for a more leisurely day, which is what brought us to the base of Grotto Creek. Friends with whom we were sharing the National Park Service's Peavine Cabins had explored partway up the creek while awaiting good ski conditions and told us we had to check it out. The approach was a mere two miles along a flat, wind-scoured riverbed.

Ethan Berkeland leading the Spiral Pitch (WI4+) on the first attempt on Hot French Grotto (IV WI4+). *Jonathan Koenig*

Tristan O'Donoghue hikes up toward sunny ice pouring through one of the rock bands above the Grotto Creek canyon. *Ethan Berkeland*

the canyon's walls from the Alaskan sun, which was wreaking havoc on most other ice in the Chitistone Valley.

Now we were racing the oncoming darkness. "The ice ends here," Elias hollered down after he topped out the last of four ice steps, leading to a spot just below the canyon rim. *Thank god*, I said to myself. However, as we were preparing to rappel, Ethan untied and scrambled up for a better look at the cliffs above. To my chagrin, he yelled, "There's more ice up here!" Knowing we couldn't safely continue at that moment, we descended.

Once back at the cabins, we decided we had to return. Three days later, we regained our high point, much faster this time. Above, we found three sun-affected WI4 ice steps through a 350' band of rock. These brought us onto snow slopes, on which we wallowed higher and higher, eventually finding another rock band with four more WI4 ice steps that finished on the summit plateau of Chitistone Mountain (6,844'). We were now certain there could be no more technical climbing above.

We rappelled the line, content at having established Hot French Grotto (IV WI4+). The route has approximately 1,400' of technical climbing (12 pitches) and 3,500' of total gain. After the initial WI4+ pitch, nearly every pitch was solid and sustained WI4. The full round trip took us 14 hours. 📷

—**Tristan O'Donoghue**

What we found was one of the most aesthetically pleasing ice formations I've ever seen: a brittle and blob-filled staircase followed by spiraling WI4+ ice pillars. Climbing this 200' pitch brought us to the main canyon floor of Grotto Creek. With sheer 500' walls guarding access from above and previously unclimbed ice below, it is likely no one had ever set foot here before us. We post-holed with giddy anticipation of the ice that might wait ahead. A quarter mile up the canyon, after soloing past several easy ice steps, we found the Hippy Death Train Pitch. The ice burrowed into and out of the narrowing canyon walls, making the whole scenario more reminiscent of navigating a slot canyon in Utah than climbing an Alaskan peak.

By 4 p.m., we'd gotten more than we'd bargained for on our "rest day." I was ready to pull the plug on our exhausting slog up the canyon, but Elias, Ethan, and Jonathan were curious to explore "just a few more turns."

There was only one more turn, actually—and it revealed another spectacular ice flow. My enthusiasm reignited as I racked up for St. Patty's Pillar, a beautiful 60' WI4 sheltered by

ALASKA | Coast Mountains

THE SHARK'S TOOTH, FIRST WINTER ASCENT

The Shark's Tooth (ca 5,700', 58°43'4.45"N, 134°45'32.11"W) is a mountain that continues to lure me. Matt Callahan and I made its first ascent via the southeast ridge in 2018, and Evan Hartung, Mike Miller, Ben Still, and I opened the south rib in 2020, but the peak still hadn't been climbed in winter.

On March 12, with a casual 5 a.m. start, Seth Classen and I warmed up for the Shark's Tooth by skinning in from Glacier Highway to climb The Terminator, a four-pitch WI5 on the Main Wall in the Davies Creek valley. Then, starting around 6:30 p.m., we skinned farther up-valley, then clicked on our headlamps, stowed our skis on our packs, and pulled out ice tools and crampons for a 3,500' climb up a wind-packed couloir to a saddle. The night was moonless, eerily silent.

From the top of the saddle, we somehow nailed the roughly 2,000' descent into the opposite valley in total darkness, missing the myriad cliffbands and yawning crevasses. We arrived at the base of the Shark's Tooth around 12:30 a.m. and started up. A WI2 ramp took us to the southeast ridge, which goes at 5.7 in the summer. By this point we were out of water, so we stopped to brew up. The cold bit at our fingers and toes—subzero, for sure.

Most of the ridge went easily. Seth led us up snow and rime ramps, bypassing steeper rocky bits. Eventually we came to a 60' rock wall with no easy way around. We examined our options: the summer line, which is a steep 5.7, or a ledgy, snow-covered way to the left. We went left.

The Shark's Tooth (ca 5,700') was climbed by the southeast ridge (right skyline) in March 2023 for the first winter ascent. *Dylan Miller*

Instantly, the climbing proved harder than it had looked. I moved upward with frontpoints perched on granite nubs, my tools scraping desperately for anything to hook. I even threw a few gloveless finger jams. Protection was tricky; I used up our rack of three cams and three nuts too soon and ended up leaving both tools as pro, pounding the last one in with a snow picket. I punched handholds in the rime to climb the final 20' ramp and, using a rock, pounded the picket into a crack for a belay. The sun finally began to rise—and with it my fear and anxiety melted away.

We ate our last bar on the summit. By the time we reached our cars after a ten-hour return trip, we'd been on the move for 36 hours. 📷

—Dylan Miller

THIEL PEAK, FIRST RECORDED ASCENT: *On July 3, Matt Callahan made a solo ascent of Thiel Peak (5,910'), which is about 1.5 miles south of the Shark's Tooth at 58°41'49.0"N, 134°45'31.8"W. Callahan approached from the north end of the Juneau road system via the Davies Creek drainage, reached the saddle between Thiel and Dean Peak (Peak 5,883'), then scrambled the long west and southwest ridge to the summit (4th class and snow). The round trip was 22 miles and 7,700' of elevation gain. See more in the Scree, November 2023, published by the Mountaineering Club of Alaska.*

MENDENHALL TOWERS, MAIN TOWER, THE TRENCH CONNECTION

The Trench Connection (1,600', IV AI3 85°) on the south face of the Main Tower in the Mendenhall Towers massif. The line shares a start with the Mountaineer's Route, the original route up the Main Tower; that route continues to the saddle with the West Tower (left) and then up right along the west ridge to the summit. *Dylan Miller*

In early March, Seth Classen, Keagan Walker, and I made a rare winter ascent of the Main Tower (6,910') in the Mendenhall Towers massif, via the standard Mountaineer's Route (1,600', III 5.6 in summer). Prior to that, the last people to be up there in those conditions were my good friend Ryan Johnson and the renowned Marc-André Leclerc. They made the first ascent of the Main Tower's north face in March 2018, but died in an accident on the descent. While Keagan, Seth, and I were up there, we put our memories and respect for those two out into the universe.

Seth and I returned just a few weeks later, this time with Alex Burkhart and Cameron Jardell. On the afternoon of March 26, as we glided across frozen Mendenhall Lake on skis, we gazed up toward what we hoped would be our new route: a snaking line up the south face of the Main Tower, leading directly to the summit. This area of the face had not been climbed in either winter or summer, but a path looked possible.

The ten-mile, 5,400' approach went down in seven hours. We reached the base of the climb at nightfall, and instantly the temps plummeted. Taking turns holding the stove and kicking warmth into our toes proceeded for the next hour as we prepped for another nighttime winter alpine climb; we had opted for this strategy because, although it would have been below freezing during the day, the solar effect on the rime and snow would have translated to dangerous climbing conditions.

Seth and Cam started climbing while Alex and I finished up melting snow for water. Cam was in front, shovel in hand, and dug a trench through the waist-deep powder that had deposited at the base of the face. We did not rope up. Eventually the powder gave way to lovely smears of ice, and we picked up speed. We had started on the Mountaineer's Route,

slanting toward the peak's west ridge, but before long we headed straight up on brand-new terrain. An easy, 30' mixed section led to some more 70° ice and rime, followed by a long, exposed 75° traverse. We regrouped on a flat bench, halfway up the mountain; psych was high, everyone was doing well.

The next leg was a terrifyingly exposed hanging bowl, funneling down to a 500' cliff. We blasted up more AI2 névé and ice glazes, eventually reaching the back of the bowl, where we were forced into another long traverse. The névé turned to powder, and soon Seth was digging a deep cut through the snowfield with a five-foot snow wall on his left and exposure on the right.

Finally, we exited the bowl and gained the South Buttress (2,000', Clark-Svenson, 1973; FFA: 5.11a, Hayden-Johnson, 2011), a classic rock climb in the summer. We were only a few hundred feet from the top. Yet above us, all we saw was a near-vertical wall of rime. We broke out the rope for the first time on the climb, and Seth led a pitch of 85°, protection-less rime, trying not to disturb the ice too much, lest he be forced to deal with the featureless granite underneath. He brought us up one by one on a bomber anchor of ice screws and pickets. We crested the ridge and were greeted by a blood-red crescent moon, the summit just a short distance away.

After sharing the usual summit high-fives and stoke, we started down the west ridge. Nearly all of the rappel anchors from our ascent three weeks earlier were still findable, making the descent smooth and quick. We were back at our cars by 10 a.m. on March 27, happy with our effort on The Trench Connection (1,600', IV AI3 85°).

—Dylan Miller

MT. SWINEFORD, FIRST KNOWN ASCENT

The Taku River flows from British Columbia and eventually empties into a glacial fjord east of Juneau. Its environs are a landscape of 5,000' to 8,000' peaks that fall all the way to sea level. Mt. Swineford (58.43548, -133.72378) rises from the Taku's east side to a mighty 6,841'. Because it is much taller than the surrounding peaks, it's easily seen from the tops of mountains around Juneau, and it had been on my partners' and my radar for quite some time; in the summer of 2018, it was at the very top of our list.

On July 20, 2018, Mike Miller, Makaila Olson, Ben Still, and I flew in with Ward Air and landed on Swineford Lake, at an elevation of 1,000'. At 5:30 p.m., July's never-setting sun bathed the landscape in light; we wanted to make a high camp on the mountain, so we started climbing.

The lower third of the mountain was a laborious bushwhack through alder and sharp-needled brush. Three hours later, we broke into the alpine and made camp at just over 4,000', where we enjoyed evening colors on the Juneau Icefield. The next morning, we climbed through stunning alpine meadows and rocky terrain. Mike led the team up the glacier on the west face, which brought us to the north ridge at around 6,700'. From here, Makaila brought us to the top via about 100' of ice and snow on the ridge.

We descended our route back to high

Mt. Swineford (6,841') from the northwest. The first ascent was by the west face, partially hidden in clouds. *Dylan Miller*

camp and stayed another night, then descended to the lake. That evening we were back in Juneau. Though ours likely was the first climbing ascent (III 65°) of Swineford, it was probably not a virgin peak, as it had likely been "summited" by heli-skiers.

—Dylan Miller

DEVILS THUMB MASSIF, ONE-DAY TRAVERSE

Capping an extended bike-and-climb journey from Colorado to British Columbia and a sail up to Petersburg, Alaska, Tommy Caldwell and Alex Honnold made a one-day traverse of the Devils Thumb group. The Diablo Traverse, pioneered by Colin Haley and Mikey Schaefer in August 2010, ascends the two Witch's Tits spires, then crosses over the twin Cat's Ears to summit Devils Thumb by its west buttress. Haley and Schaefer completed the traverse over three days at 5.10 A2.

Honnold posted that he and Caldwell spent about 11.5 hours on the climbing portions of the traverse, simul-climbing most or all of the way, at maximum difficulty of about 5.11. Their round trip from high camp was about 17 hours.

—The Editors, *with information from the climbers' online reports*

HARD MOX, FIRST WINTER ASCENT

Hard Mox (8,504') is considered the most difficult of the Bulger List (Washington's 100 highest peaks) and was previously unclimbed in winter. [*Hard Mox is the southeastern of the two Mox Peaks and is less than four miles south of the Canadian border.*] Over the past three years, I've made six scouting trips and practice climbs to figure out the best winter route. Nick Roy and I previously made two unsuccessful attempts (in January and February 2023). On our third trip, the stars aligned.

On December 27, we double-carried my Zodiac boat, an outboard motor, and a week of supplies one mile to Ross Lake (which has no road access) in the North Cascades, then motored 15 miles up to the outlet of Little Beaver Creek, where we took out the boat and hiked in to Perry Creek. The bushwhack up Perry Creek the next day was challenging—I dislocated my shoulder in a fall and we broke all four snowshoes. It rained all day.

On the third day, we climbed up the Perry Glacier, then swung leads up the five-pitch WI2 M5 west ridge, which was plastered with rime ice. This route (5.5 in summer) was first climbed by brothers Fred and Helmy Beckey in 1941 for Hard Mox's first ascent. Nick led the cruxes. Our hexes were lifesavers; we pounded them into icy cracks that wouldn't hold cams. We topped out exactly at sunset, then rapped back in the dark for an 18-hour push.

We later climbed Mt. Spickard (8,980') and then bushwhacked back out. The boat motor wouldn't start, so we ended up paddling eight hours back down the lake, fixing a broken oarlock on the way. We then triple-carried the gear back to the trailhead.

—Eric Gilbertson

TOP: The ascent of Hard Mox followed the 1941 Beckey Route on the upper west ridge. The winter grade was WI2 M5, which fails to convey the full difficulties. *John Scurlock*

ABOVE: Eric Gilbertson starting pitch four. *Nick Roy*

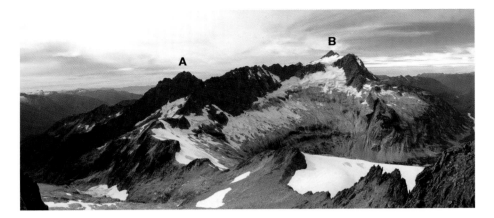

SEAHPO PEAK, TANUKI RIDGE

The southeast ridge of Seahpo Peak is one of the longest continuous ridges in the continental United States. Sprouting out of the Cascadian jungle, it rises more than 4,000' over 1.5 miles of horizontal travel before reaching the summit of 7,441' Seahpo (also known as Cloudcap Peak), east of Mt. Shuksan. The ridgeline continues on from there, becoming the Jagged Ridge (V 5.6), which leads directly west to Shuksan's ice cap. Considered together, the full ridge crosses roughly three miles of technical terrain and nearly 5,000' of vertical gain.

Despite its scale, this ridge—which is the southern of two distinct eastern ridges on Seahpo—is only visible from a couple of remote vantage points. I first saw it in 2022 on a trip into the Northern Pickets. I immediately made plans with my partner Lani Chapko to mount an attempt.

Our first try on what we came to call Tanuki Ridge was in September 2022. We approached via the Crystal Creek basin, where the underbrush had all been trampled as if dozens of bears had rolled through. This and the epic smoke that summer gave the valley a desolate feeling, reminding us of the animated film *Pom Poko*, which features the Japanese raccoon dogs called tanuki, known to be tricksters. It felt like the tanuki were messing with us. Foiled by a late-season heat wave and the intense wildfire smoke, we bailed after climbing around 800' of the lower ridge.

In July 2023, we tried again, this time from the north, via the Ruth Mountain–Icy Peak Traverse. Unprotectable slabs (which looked like 5.10 X) prevented us from reaching the toe of the ridge; instead, we tried to find a way up the north side, only to find more featureless and unprotectable rock. We bailed before even touching the ridge crest.

We set aside more time in late August for a third attempt. The Cascades had an extremely thin snowpack, so we were not expecting to find water or snow on the route. For this reason, we recruited a third climber to distribute the water load during the climb. We convinced Lani's friend Nick Gonzales to come with only a couple days of notice

View from Icy Peak showing the full Tanuki Ridge, starting with the southeast ridge of Seahpo Peak. Beginning in lower left, the ridge gains more than 4,000 feet to reach the 7,441-foot summit of Seapho (A). From there, the Jagged Ridge continues west to the ice slopes below 9,131-foot Mt. Shuksan (B). *Sam Boyce Collection*

ABOVE: Lani Chapko following one of the "Cascadian" 5.9 pitches on Tanuki Tower during the first attempt on the ridge in September 2022.

LEFT: Chapko following a knife-edge traverse on the upper Tanuki Ridge. *Sam Boyce (both photos)*

and once again set out.

Starting our approach from the south, we headed up the Baker River Trail to the fork with Crystal Creek. From here it was a mild cross-country bushwhack up into the Crystal Creek basin. We followed occasional remnants of an ancient, decommissioned trail—a huge help. Once in the basin, we quested uphill through thick undergrowth to a nice bivy immediately below the toe of the ridge.

The first 2,000' of the climb ascended a distinct tower, which we named Tanuki Tower. It was the definitive crux and most "Cascadian" part of the route. There was plenty of 5.9 R jungle climbing, reminiscent of nearby blue-collar classics such as the 1957 Northeast Rib of Johannesburg or the north face of North Index.

Beyond Tanuki Tower, the ridge backed off for a long section of scrambling with occasional steep pitches in and out of notches. This lower-angle section brought us to a large gendarme that marked the start of the more sustained upper ridge. We found a comfortable bivy that miraculously granted access to a glacier on the south flank of the ridge, providing a much-needed water source.

The upper route had sustained, moderate, and classic ridge climbing on clean rock. We made it to the summit of Seahpo around noon on our third day. We had a long debate about whether to continue along the Jagged Ridge or to descend Seahpo's standard east ridge route. Our biggest concern was icy glacier conditions, given our minimal snow equipment. We decided to continue, accepting that we might have to pitch out or rappel terrain that we would normally run across with the appropriate kit. That day we made it about halfway along the Jagged Ridge, stopping at an exposed bivy that was just big enough for the three of us.

On day four, the rest of the Jagged Ridge went smoothly, though the sections that are normally snow traverses were instead extremely loose gravel slopes. Once at the ridge's terminus, we decided it would be foolish to head to the top of Shuksan with our minimalist gear. The glaciers were almost entirely blue ice; even the Sulphide Glacier looked to be an ice climb. We traversed slabs below the Crystal and Sulphide glaciers to reach the Sulphide Glacier route and eventually the Shannon Ridge Trail, at the end of which Nick kindly offered to run the eight miles back to the Baker River trailhead to retrieve the car.

We climbed 30 pitches on Tanuki Ridge (V 5.9 R) to the summit of Seahpo, and another eight pitches on the Jagged Ridge traverse. Climbed together, they are a solid Grade VI. I feel it is one of the proudest lines in the Cascades and recommend it wholeheartedly for those in search of an adventure. 📷

—Sam Boyce

LAKE ANN BUTTRESS, CENTRAL PILLAR

With world-class alpine climbing right out the back door, my enduring curiosity about the Lake Ann Buttress struck friends as lunacy. The comments included "The rock is choss" and "Beckey said it's repulsive." But after staring up at the 1,000' buttress year after year during trips to guide the Fisher Chimneys route on Mt. Shuksan, I couldn't hold back—I had to check it out.

The south-facing Lake Ann Buttress on Shuksan Arm gets passed each summer by hundreds of climbers en route to the Fisher Chimneys and by thousands of hikers, yet there is little information about the few prior routes up it. The first recorded ascent, according to Fred Beckey's *Cascade Alpine Guide*, was by Les MacDonald and Elfrieda Pigou in 1960. MacDonald added a second line in "1964 or 1965" called the Yellow Slab Variation. Beckey and Tom Stewart put up the only other known line on the wall, Center Route (1,000', III 5.8 and some aid), in 1965.

After a couple of scouting hikes to identify potential lines, Timmy Rickert and I made an attempt in September 2021 on what I had taken to calling the Central Pillar. We scrambled up 4th-class terrain for 150' to reach the first pitch. From there, we free climbed six pitches up to 5.10a/b before rain forced us to retreat. I believe our first pitch followed the same "shallow open book" Beckey identified as the start of Center Route, after which we exited left and entered new territory.

My next attempt, with Matt Stahlberg, was in October 2021, but we retreated from the top of pitch three due to a preexisting joint injury Matt had sustained when he was a professional strongman competitor and bodybuilder.

Success finally came on October 4, 2022, in a single-day outing with Nate George. We completed the route by adding five additional pitches. Too tired to send the most difficult of these new pitches, we French-freed sections that felt like they would be about 5.10b. Relying on trad gear, pitons, and natural anchors, we rappelled the route to the top of pitch five and then continued rapping down climber's left of the original line to reach the ground.The Central Pillar (1,000', 10 pitches, IV 5.10b R A0) contains mostly good rock, washed clean by runoff down the cliff. There are some moderate runouts, but nothing death-defying.

—**Jere Burrell**

CUTTHROAT PEAK, EAST FACE, THE SWARM

On July 3, Alex Perz and I set out to climb a new route on the east face of Cutthroat Peak (8,050'), near Washington Pass. We hiked two miles from Highway 20, then cut right into the large basin to the east of the peak. Alex, having never climbed a new route, graciously offered to go into support mode for the day.

The first two pitches were low fifth class and ended at the large ledge system

The Swarm (850', 5.11c) on the east face of Cutthroat Peak. Two prior routes climbed the face farther to the right. Alex Perz

at the base of the main headwall. From here, the quality of the climbing improved drastically.

For the first 30' of the main wall, we climbed a shallow, left-facing dihedral. This was the only part of our route that shared terrain with the Southeast Corner (IV 5.11c), also known as Firefighter, a route put up by Bryan Burdo and Andy Cairns in 1985. [*Editor's Note: Dale Bard, Yvon Chouinard, and John Cunningham established an earlier route farther right on the face, in 1976, simply called the East Face (6 pitches, III 5.10).*] At the top of the dihedral, where the 1985 route continued up and right, I stepped down left to the base of a long, perfect splitter that was completely full of plants. I aided through the plants for 30', then cleaned them all out of the crack with a nut tool as Alex lowered me. From the stance at the base of the splitter, I then pulled the rope and freed this excellent pitch. It began with perfect finger locks and gradually widened; at a point where it suddenly pinched down, I reached right and transferred to yet another perfect splitter that took me to a small stance.

The climbing above this pitch was consistently difficult but on good rock with ample protection. The crux pitch was in a large dihedral. While leading it, I stepped out of the corner in desperation and couldn't get back in. Here, I placed the only protection bolt of the route, then climbed the dynamic crux moves with the heavy drill hanging from a sling around my shoulder. Subsequent parties reported that staying in the dihedral was easier and safer.

A couple easier, adventurous pitches took us to the top of the South Buttress. We tagged the summit of Cutthroat and then descended the South Buttress route.

Alex and I climbed The Swarm (850', 5.11c) in a single day, including placing bolted anchors on lead for every pitch above 5.9 and cleaning loose rock and vegetation. It is a high-quality route that avoids the crowds just south at the Liberty Bell group. 🔍

—**Justin Willis**

The Cascadian Route (2,000', 16 pitches, V 5.10+) climbs directly up the west face of the southwest summit of Bonanza Peak; each red dot represents about three pitches of the 16-pitch route. The yellow dot marks the top of the 8,700-foot pinnacle where the Soviet Route (1976) and the Oregonian Route (2,200', V 5.9+, Bonnett-Keena, 2013) meet before they continue up the northern aspect of the southwest summit. *Eric Wehrly*

BONANZA PEAK, WEST FACE OF SOUTHWEST SUMMIT, THE CASCADIAN ROUTE

In late August, Sam Boyce and I took a three-day weekend to climb a new route on the west face of Bonanza Peak's southwest summit (9,320'). The Cascadian Route (V 5.10+) gains over 2,000' in 16 pitches and 2,800' of climbing.

Our route is looker's right of its established neighbors to the north, the Soviet Route (1976) and the Oregonian Route (2,200', V 5.9+, Bonnett-Keena, 2013), both of which ascend the southwest peak's northwest buttress. (This has also been called the west buttress and, in the report on the Soviet Route, the north face.) The two older routes meet near an 8,700' pinnacle before continuing on mellower terrain up the northern aspect. Our route ascends the west face directly, with difficulties finally easing upon reaching the ridge just south of the true summit.

We did most of the time-consuming approach on August 25: a long drive, a ferry from Chelan to Lucerne, a bus to Holden Village, and finally more than 11 miles of hiking to a camp at 7,000' near the North

Star–Bonanza col. The next day, we finished the approach over talus and began climbing.

About 500' up the route, on our fourth pitch—after the first of several heinous choss bands but before the most technical climbing—we found a 2.5" Trango Flex Cam in a crack with a carabiner attached to it. This late 1990s or early 2000s cam was in a textbook placement and came out easily; its sling was weathered, having sat there for perhaps 10 to 20 years. A search for past attempts or climbs of this feature turned up no information. Finding no evidence of passage above this, we surmised that perhaps this cam had been used to bail.

While there were enjoyable stretches of climbing on our route, there also was plentiful choss. The technical highlights were five pitches of 5.10. Three of these—pitches eight, nine, and 13—sported steep, fun climbing, but the other two—pitches 11 and 12—were loose, run-out affairs. A full bag of tricks was necessary to find passable protection.

The rest of the route ranged up to 5.9 on varying rock quality; any given hold might be permanent or portable. We had been concerned about passage through roof systems near the top—bailing would have been fraught and difficult—but such worries proved unwarranted.

We descended back to camp via the Isella Glacier, scrambling and downclimbing a "walkway" of steep rock (low-fifth-class cruxes) and mellow moraine that horizontally splits the glacier at approximately two-thirds height. Shortly after exiting the glacier, we crossed westward through a notch in Bonanza's south ridge. The next day, we hiked out.

Climbing of the variety found on the Cascadian Route can be extremely engaging and stimulating (Sam and I certainly enjoyed it), but it might not be to others' tastes. [*A pitch-by-pitch route description and details on the descent are at the AAJ website.*]

—**Eric Wehrly**

Eric Wehrly climbs through a heinous choss band on pitch four of the Cascadian Route. *Sam Boyce*

ABOVE: Gabe Aeschliman brushing holds on the second pitch of Up in Arms on Concord Tower during work on the route. *Michael Telstad*

CONCORD TOWER, SOUTHWEST FACE, UP IN ARMS

On June 4, Michael Telstad and I ventured up the southwest face of Concord Tower in the Liberty Bell group. Our route, which is now perhaps the closest to the Blue Lake trailhead on the west side of Washington Pass, starts in the gully between Concord and Lexington towers, well to climber's left of the south face route.

Our initial ascent pieced together a line of corners and cracks, including a bit of easy aid to get through a narrow seam in an overhanging corner. Over two subsequent trips, an all-free route was cleaned and three protection bolts were added, along with one bolted anchor. The resulting six-pitch route, Up in Arms (700', 5.11), has fun, technical movement through a variety of features up a sunny wall, with the hardest climbing on the first pitch. 📷🔍

—**Gabe Aeschliman**

ABOVE: (1) The Merrill-Minton on the west face of Sloan Peak. The route joins with (2) Superalpine, likely the first winter-conditions route up Sloan's west face, after seven new pitches. *John Scurlock*

SLOAN PEAK, WEST FACE, MERRILL-MINTON

On January 29, 2023, Aaron Minton and I climbed a new ice route on the west face of Sloan Peak (7,835'), with seven new pitches up to WI4+, before continuing on the upper portion of Superalpine, a WI3/4 on the west face. [*Superalpine was attempted by Porter McMichael and Kyle McCrohan in 2020 and then climbed all the way to the summit by Fabien Le Gallo and Nick Roy in 2022, likely the first winter-conditions ascent of the west face of Sloan. Several other routes up the face have been climbed in summer.*] I had identified our line in photos and a scouting trip with Jeff McGowen earlier in the week. It looked like several intermittent ice flows to the left of Superalpine could be connected by traversing snowy ledges.

Aaron and I drove up to about 2,400' before getting stopped by snow, then camped there. We woke at 2:30 a.m. Conditions were prime for booting, so we left our skis at the cars and followed the trail that Jeff and I had put in. The approach followed the Bedal Creek drainage to an elevation of about 5,200'. From there we traversed about 150m to the mouth of a gully, which we climbed for an additional 100m to reach the base of the climb at about 7:20 a.m.

A snow gully with some low-angle ice led to the base of an amphitheater with several ice flows. Aaron led the first pitch at WI3 on hollow, aerated ice. A great way to wake up the nerves in the morning! When the ice ended, he crossed a snow slope to a rock belay. I took over and traversed 15m right to the base of a second steep ice pitch, another porous WI3 pillar.

Next, Aaron ran the ropes up a short ice step and across some snow to belay beneath a beautiful and intimidating hanging dagger. Both this and another flow about 50m to our right looked to be above our pay grade, so we decided to take a WI3 ramp even farther right. We romped up as quickly as we could to get away from the overhead hazard and then traversed right on a snowy ledge to the bottom of the money pitch. As I led up this 30m flow, I found solid WI4 ice and an engaging WI4+ bulge toward the top. From the top of this pitch, we joined the Superalpine route.

Aaron Minton romping up easy ice and bypassing an unclimbed overhanging dagger on the west face of Sloan Peak. *Tucker Merrill*

We found excellent snow conditions on the upper half of the route. At our high point 70m below Sloan's summit, we decided that it would be wise to turn around, with sunset approaching and an unfamiliar descent. We rappelled the Superalpine via seven or eight V-threads and a piton anchor. Spindrift chased us the entire way down. By the time we returned to our cars at 1:15 a.m., we had been on the move for 22 hours.

The Merrill-Minton Route (1,600', 10 pitches, IV WI4+) adds seven new pitches of climbing before joining up with Superalpine. An integral ascent to the summit via this new combination awaits. 🖹 📷

—Tucker Merrill

BLUEBELL: A CLIMB AND A TRIBUTE

FREEING ONE OF NORTH AMERICA'S STEEPEST WALLS

By Nathan Hadley

I didn't expect to feel so elated and relieved as I scrambled up the final stretch of Mt. Index's North Norwegian Buttress (NNB) for the first time on July 28. Although plenty of work lay ahead—days of cleaning, trundling, and bolting—the element of uncertainty had vanished. Navigating 2,000' of steep, sometimes treacherous rock with scarce reliable protection had demanded nearly all my mental fortitude.

The NNB has never been a popular climbing destination in spite of its prominent stature and location, plainly visible from busy Highway 2, just an hour east of Seattle. No one had made a serious effort to establish a free route since the 1980s, when Pete Doorish soloed the original aid line. In the years since, only two other routes had been climbed—both as aid routes: the Voodoo Proj (2002) and Jötnar (Boyce-Chapko-Willis, 2020). To my knowledge, none of these lines has been repeated. The NNB, shrouded in mystery due to rumors of loose gabbro rock and detached blocks, has mostly been left alone.

In spite of the rumors and the fear they instilled in me, the draw of the wall was irresistible. It's hard to pinpoint exactly when I began seriously considering a free route on the NNB— perhaps as far back as 2017 when I climbed Vanishing Point (1,400', 5.12b R), a creation of Bryan Burdo's on the Dolomite Tower of Mt. Baring, which is also in the Skykomish Valley and has

ABOVE: Michal Rynkiewicz at the bivy above pitch 12 during his and Stamati Anagnostou's redpoint push on Bluebell. Tragically, Rynkiewicz died in a rappelling accident later in the year. *Stamati Anagnostou*

a similar rock type to Mt. Index. A couple of years later, my experience on Sonnie Trotter's Canadian Alpine Trilogy—three 5.14 multi-pitch routes in the Rockies—deepened my interest. I saw the potential for a similar style of alpine route: namely, bolted face climbing on rock deemed too loose or unprotectable for trad climbs.

Unbeknownst to me, the local Index phenom Michal Rynkiewicz had for years had a similar project in mind. I learned this in the spring of 2023 through our mutual friend Stamati Anagnostou, who put Michal and me in touch after we both sent Stamati photos of the NNB with nearly identical route lines drawn! Michal and I decided to team up, and after pushing the route above pitch 12, we convinced Stamati to join.

Mt. Index's North Norwegian Buttress, with the line of Bluebell (21 pitches, 5.13-). See *AAJ 2021* for lines of the prior routes on the buttress. *Nathan Hadley*

As an expectant father, my preference would have been to develop this new route from the top down so that any loose rock could be dealt with safely. Despite ethical considerations, it's hard to dispute this approach often leads to a more thoughtful route for future climbers. However, hiking all the way to the summit of Mt. Index, then traversing technical terrain to the top of Middle Index, and finally descending further technical terrain down to the top of the NNB—all with 2,000' of static rope in tow—was an impractical endeavor. Ground-up was the only option.

We planned our route using high-definition photos that I took from Lake Serene in early May. We aimed to take the most central line up the buttress, going directly up clean faces and confronting head-on the big roofs at midheight and the headwall near the top, which the earlier routes had avoided. Our route would be completely independent of those routes, joining them only for the short heather scramble to the summit.

The inaugural day on the climb ranked among the most terrifying—at least for me. At a precarious point on the first pitch, I reached far above a questionable cam to screw a hanger onto a rusting bolt stud, left from an unknown earlier attempt. Then I committed myself to some steep 5.11 climbing, with an alder as one handhold, praying that if I fell, neither the rusty bolt nor the cam would fail. The lead that later became pitch three was rife with unstable stacks of loose blocks. I tiptoed around them, strategically placing protection to avoid a catastrophic chain reaction.

From May to mid-August, we worked tirelessly on the climb, with at least one of us on the NNB for 25-plus days. Our approaches to advancing the route included free climbing, drilling on lead, and aid. Since the gabbro is both hard and brittle—providing numerous face holds but few cracks for gear—we made the decision to protect

Michal Rynkiewicz aiding pitch ten of Bluebell during the route's initial ascent. *Nathan Hadley*

the entire route with bolts, using a power drill. (The NNB is outside any wilderness area or park.) We consciously drilled only about half the bolts on lead, allowing for more intentional placements once the line was established.

While the rock on the NNB may not be as solid as on Dolomite Tower, we found the pitches to be far more diverse in flavor, from slabs to roofs. Each pitch offered pleasant surprises—the "3D Dike" on pitch six, for example, or a key pinch on pitch nine that provides passage through a roof. The rock overall is quite smooth, but on several pitches we found incut and textured, limestone-esque holds.

We believe our route to be one of the steepest long free climbs in North America, with approximately one-third of the 21 pitches overhanging. Imagine two of Yosemite's Leaning Towers, with sections of slab before, in between, and after. Most of the route is consistently rated 5.11–5.12, with pitches six and 14 just crossing into the 5.13 range.

Due to its length and sustained difficulty, many climbers may choose to tackle the route over multiple days. (A portaledge is recommended.) The entire route can be descended with a single, uncut 70m rope.

Michal, Stamati, and I finished working the pitches on August 8. I freed the route on August 11, with Luke Stefurak's support. Michal and Stamati then both freed the route over two days, August 21–22. Afterward, they derigged the rest of our fixed lines and gear on the way down.

Michal, who had a fondness for birds and flowers, proposed the name Harebell for the route, inspired by the resilient flowers that could be found in unexpected locations along the wall. Another name for this flower is the Scottish bluebell or simply bluebell, which led us to settle on the name Bluebell for the route.

Just two short months after freeing the NNB, on October 27, Michal died in a rappelling accident at the Index Town Walls. His death was a devastating loss to his new wife, Sara, his family, his friends, and the larger Washington climbing community.

Michal and I had plans for many more climbs in the Skykomish Valley. His passion for finding and creating new climbing experiences was unmatched. Despite this, he managed to maintain a balance between his time with Sara, his friends and family, his work, and personal training. Earlier in 2023, he and Sara had made the decision to move to Index, a decision that only served to amplify his accomplishments. In an impressive display of energy and dedication, over the course of a single summer he established numerous routes on Index's Upper Town Wall and a new bouldering area, and spent nearly every weekend between early June and late August on the NNB with me.

I am immensely grateful to have had the opportunity to meet and work alongside Michal, and I am certain that Bluebell will stand as a lasting testament to his genius and his impact on the climbing community. [*A photo-topo of this route is at the AAJ website; a pitch-by-pitch description is at Mountain Project.*] 📄 📷

Adrian Vanoni on the crux sixth pitch of Prayer for a Friend (600', 5.14a), on the southwest face of Prusik Peak. *Victoria Kohner-Flanagan*

PRUSIK PEAK, PRAYER FOR A FRIEND, FREE ASCENT

Prayer for a Friend, a striking line on the southwest face of Prusik Peak, had been waiting for a free ascent for 20 years, ever since Fitz Cahall opened the route at 5.12- C1 in 2003, along with Becca Cahall and Aaron Webb. The only pitch that didn't go free then was the striking headwall splitter, a feature that anyone who has climbed Prusik's West Ridge (4 pitches, 5.7) has goggled at: beautiful, black-and-white-checkered rock, speckled with bright green and orange lichen, slightly overhanging—and split by a singular finger crack. I first saw it in 2019 as I was downclimbing the West Ridge; I took a picture and kept it as my phone background for the next four years.

The lower pitches on the route are stellar in their own way—mostly technical 5.11 and one pitch of 5.12—but all ten days I spent on the route, spread over two seasons, were consumed by the final splitter. Lots of this was spent top-rope soloing, trying to figure out exactly how to hold each of the sloping locks. The pitch begins with some exciting 5.11+ up to a

bolt and a crimp, where you can shake out, followed by 19 hand movements and three gear placements. Some final easier stemming leads to the top.

Fitz established the route with minimal bolts, but it was made safer (with Cahall's permission) by Nik Berry, who worked on freeing the route and added a number of solid bolts in 2018. Even with these in place, the route still has a heads-up feel.

My free ascent was in imperfect style: I started from the ground, supported by Will Vidler, on October 5 and sent all the pitches to the base of the crux (onsighting except for a foot slip on a 5.11 pitch), and then gave the headwall a go in the sun. I two-hung it. We topped out and went back to camp.

The next day, we soloed up the West Ridge and rapped in to the crux pitch. I tried it two times, placing all the gear on lead, and sent on the second try. Obviously the best way to do the route would be a single-day push, but this was the best I could do at the time. I am excited for someone to improve upon my style. Prayer for a Friend (600', 7 pitches, 5.14a) is an experience not to be missed for those up to it.

—**Adrian Vanoni**

OREGON | Wallowa Mountains

The 1,200-foot west face of the Matterhorn in the Wallowa Mountains. (1) West Face Chimney (IV 5.9 A1, Coughlin-Jensen, 1973). (2) Cigarette Tree (13 pitches, 5.11 R, Gray-Shtilman, 2023). (3) West Face Wall (V 5.8 A3, Coughlin-Jensen, 1974). *Spencer Gray*

MATTERHORN, WEST FACE, CIGARETTE TREE

In mid-August, Mo Shtilman and I climbed a route up the prominent central buttress of the west face of the Matterhorn (9,826') in the Wallowa Mountains. In a state characterized mainly by basaltic crags and broad-shouldered volcanoes, the Matterhorn's west face is a singularly impressive alpine wall.

The mountain's current name, an unimaginative co-optation of the famous Swiss Alp, obscures its unique aesthetic, cultural, and geologic features. The valleys below the Matterhorn were home to the Wallowa band of Nimiipuu (Nez Perce), the band of Chief Joseph, before their flight in 1877 and subsequent exile following violent conflicts with settlers. Some versions of the Nimiipuu creation myth describe Coyote binding himself with a vine to the Matterhorn in a face-off with a great devouring monster. With such rich associations, perhaps there's a better moniker for this mountain than that of another continent's iconic summit, to which it bears no resemblance.

The west face of the Matterhorn is the outstanding metamorphosed (later glaciated) exposure of a thick layer of limestone, originally a reef that formed around a tropical island in the proto-Pacific, then accreted onto the ancient North American core. As the Wallowa terrane was colliding with the continent, a granitoid pluton formed underneath; the intense heat and pressure of the contact zone caused overriding limestone to transform into marble. This marble is cut by many basalt dikes, some of which appear as swirling flows in the white host rock.

The slopes below the Matterhorn are covered in disconcerting mounds of sugary calcite gravel, a preview of the rock above. The marble on the west face is not what you would find in a Tuscan quarry, ready for Michelangelo's chisel. Rather, it's as if the mountain was pulled out of the oven too soon—not quite ready for climbers.

The west face's soaring central buttress is a nose-type feature, the left flank of which ranges from overhanging to vertical, the right from vertical to steeply inclined. Farther left is another overhanging face; farther right is a distinct tower. The junctures of those features with the flanks of the central buttress are where Dave Coughlin and Dave Jensen established the West Face Chimney (1,200', IV 5.9 A1) in 1973—a free line except for 20' of aid to avoid loose rock—and the West Face Wall

(1,200', V 5.8 A3) in 1974—which aids through a traversing, overhanging crack for most of its length. Those are the only recorded routes, but I wouldn't be surprised if others have been completed.

The hike into the Matterhorn is seven miles from a popular U.S. Forest Service trailhead on Hurricane Creek, followed by a few hours of scrambling up loose slopes. Mo and I bivouacked at the base of the wall. To access our route, Cigarette Tree (1,200', 13 pitches, 5.11 R), we climbed one of the few free-able cracks below the 1973 West Face Chimney route and quickly traversed left across moderate terrain to reach the nose of the central buttress. We then followed the nose, more or less, to the summit, climbing two necky roofs (mid-5.11) to surmount sections of jumbled, suspended blocks. We bivouacked once midroute and relied frequently on assorted types of pins. Alex Marine and I had attempted a similar line several years earlier, before retreating due to an ankle sprain.

Mo Shtilman stretches across the opening moves of pitch six (5.10) of Cigarette Tree, having clipped the complex, extended belay anchor for his first piece. *Spencer Gray*

The closest climbing analogue to what we found might be a rock face with aggressively decomposing granite. In the case of the Matterhorn, large pillars and blocks are often split by hairline fractures only visible up close, and the surface of most of the mountain rubs off under your palms and feet, like grains on cheap sandpaper. Reasonably sound handholds and footholds can be found on the sloping edges after two or three swipes. Deep cracks exist, and they periodically offer acceptable protection, but it's best to double up the critical placements.

The actual movement was satisfyingly similar to that on a steep granite wall—short boulder cruxes, occasional mantels, and plenty of jamming. But the quality of the gymnastics was entirely colored by the uncertain protection. Climbing such a "Big Rock Candy Mountain," like terrain out of a fable ("Where the boxcars all are empty, and the sun shines every day / On the birds and the bees and the cigarette trees," as Harry McClintock sang in 1928), isn't particularly about discovering a retraceable line or a classic route to share. It's more like a game whose point is to stay on the safe side of deadly, conjuring a reasonable way through unreasonable features, seeking the nicotine without the tar.

There is ample room for new variations and independent lines on the Matterhorn, for those into this kind of thing. We can't recommend this wall—it's falling apart too much—but it is a gorgeous siren. 📷

—**Spencer Gray**

THE THING, WONDER WOMAN

In early October 2023, Brandon Adams and I put up a new route in Little Slide Canyon on a formation called the Thing, which is down-canyon from the Incredible Hulk. This was the first first ascent of which I've been a part, so I was stoked. The route starts about 100m to climber's left of Gambit (800', 6 pitches, III 5.10c)—another route that Brandon put up in 2023, with Miles Fullman—and 150m left of Causative Striations (900', III 5.11-, Fasoldt-Finkelstein, 2015). [*The 2016 AAJ report for Causative Striations incorrectly referred to the Thing as the "Incredulous Bulk."*]

On our first trip, we climbed two pitches of hand cracks and 50' of a third pitch before we pulled off a large block that narrowly missed Brandon. I pushed that pitch another 50' and placed a few bolts before we decided that we'd had enough excitement for one day. We stashed our gear and made a plan to return the following week.

Next time out, Brandon completed the unfinished third pitch by placing some

Wonder Woman (700', III 5.11c), on the Thing, down-canyon from the famed Incredible Hulk in Little Slide Canyon. Other routes on the formation are not shown. *Brandon Adams*

beaks and bolts. The result was a beautiful face pitch through a band of crystals. At the anchor, we got our first sun of a very cold day, and a beautiful finger crack invigorated us. After climbing this fourth pitch, we descended in the setting sun.

The next day, after patiently waiting for the wind to calm and the sun to warm our camp, we set off. Each pitch seemed to go down effortlessly as we swapped leads to reach our high point. Brandon took the last pitch—another phenomenal hand crack to finger crack. We reached the summit with daylight to spare, and reveled in the canyon's solitude. Several routes on the Thing, as well as the formation itself, are named after male superheroes; we decided to name ours Wonder Woman (700', 5 pitches, III 5.11c). 📄 📷

—**Trish Matheny**

REGGE POLE, FREE RADICAL

Of the hundreds of climbers who enter Little Slide Canyon every year, only a few venture onto the cluster of soaring, granitic spires positioned on its west slope—collectively known as Little Slide Spires—rising above the approach to the famed Incredible Hulk. The tallest and steepest of these spires is the Regge Pole (10,340'+), whose square-cut geometry is reminiscent of a 700' skyscraper. This pinnacle is rarely climbed because of its reputation for low rock quality and poor protection.

Several years ago, Brandon Adams and I separately noticed a thin fracture splitting the virtually featureless southeast face, which had been more or less—and confusingly—ascended by the South Face, Right Side route (5.7 A3, Gocking-Warburton, 1973).

In the fall of 2022, in preparation for a push on a challenging nailing route on El Capitan, Brandon and I decided to refresh our aid skills on the thin crack system

(which shares about 150' of terrain with the South Face, Right Side, split between pitches two and three). The minute we got to the base, the rock quality, the stunning position, and the unique nature of the line were evident. We abandoned our El Cap plans and decided to put in the work on a well-constructed free climb. We knew this would be a first ascent worthy of effort.

Over the next year, Brandon and I somehow found enough time away from work and family responsibilities to venture repeatedly to the project, either together, alone, or with other partners, in order to find the line with the most enjoyable climbing. Much of this was on crackless faces; nearly every pitch has stretches of bolt-protected climbing.

On September 16, 2023, the line was prepared, and the time had come to enjoy the fruits of our labor.

We swung leads up the route, laughing the whole way. The highlights just kept coming: the laser-cut crack on pitch two that we called "Critical Mass"; the crackless right-angle corner topped by a steep roof traverse on pitch three, "The Particle Accelerator"; a gently overhanging, thin crack capped by a V5 crack-switch boulder problem on pitch four, "Quantum Leap"; the wildly featured, sport-bolted arête on pitch five; and even the incredible, rarely trodden summit. The first ascent of Free Radical (7 pitches, IV 5.12) took us only a few hours.

As storm clouds gathered, we dropped to the south over the subsummit and descended the rappel line—which mostly follows the route and is equipped with bolted rap stations—back to our packs. Twenty minutes later, it began to rain. We watched a glorious rainbow arc over Mt. Walt from the shelter of a cave under a late-season snowbank, happy in the knowledge that we had created something beautiful, free, and radical. 📷 🔍

—**Roger Putnam**

ABOVE: Brandon Adams leading 5.10 knobs at the start of pitch four on the first ascent of Free Radical. *Roger Putnam*

ABOVE LEFT: Free Radical (7 pitches, IV 5.12) on the southeast face of the Regge Pole. *Mark Thomas*

THE HOURGLASS WALL, GOLDEN CORNERS

I have always been impressed with Kevin DeWeese's eye for new routes on obscure formations in Yosemite Valley. Perhaps no route exemplifies this better than Blue Collar (1,200', 9 pitches, V A3) on the Hourglass Wall, right of Ribbon Falls Amphitheater, which he put up in 2014 with Steve Bosque and Josh Mucci. Josh told me it had the best rock he had ever climbed in Yosemite. Travis Heidepriem and I first sampled Blue Collar in January 2023 and realized Josh's impression was spot on. This route was special—and freeing it would be even more so.

In February, we recruited our close friend Robert Kennedy and went all in. In total, we spent nearly 11 months on the project. By necessity, most of this time was on weekends, as we all live in San Francisco and have full-time jobs.

As we began exploring, equipping, and piecing together free variations, Robert focused on the first two pitches; he was able to forge 200' of independent and high-quality bolt-protected climbing on overhanging rock. I spent much of the spring trying to free the third pitch, which mostly follows the original line of Blue Collar. This became one of the two crux pitches on the route, with extremely thin and hyper-technical face climbing up to a redpoint-crux traverse. Travis focused on developing the free variations above pitch three, which deviated significantly from the aid route until the two rejoined at a massive bivy ledge 600' off the ground.

Our team worked as a unit to establish the pitches above the bivy ledge, most of which were independent from Blue Collar until the ninth pitch. About 200' above the ledge is one of the route's namesake golden corner pitches, with superb rock and exciting laybacking. The free variation's tenth pitch is the route's second crux,

Travis Heidepriem on the tenth pitch of Golden Corners. *Samuel Crossley*

a steep and sustained section of crack climbing to a boulder problem guarding the chains. The free route again breaks off Blue Collar for the 12th pitch, ascending a beautiful golden layback flake for 70' to a stance and then a V4 horizontal dyno. It was truly one of the most wild and unlikely pitches that any of us had ever climbed.

Our free variation ended up with six pitches of 5.12 (two of which are 5.12+). Throughout the development process—during which we installed a number of new bolts, all with approval from the FA team—we had plenty of help from close friends, notably Benj Wollant.

In November, Travis, Robert, and I went for a continuous push of Golden Corners (1,200', 12 pitches, V 5.12+) in a team-free style. At least one climber redpointed each pitch, while the others followed free. By sunset on the third day, we were taking group selfies at the top, stoked that we had accomplished something that each of us had, at one point, thought impossible. That moment was bittersweet: I was stoked to have completed our year-long obsession, but sad to see it come to an end. The time spent up there with close friends, arguing about bolt placements and bullshitting about life, will remain some of the best moments of my climbing career. 📷 🔍

—Mark Westerberg

Mark Westerberg leading the 12th and final pitch of Golden Corners. *Samuel Crossley*

HALF DOME, SOUTH FACE, FREE ASCENT OF HISTORIC KARMA ROUTE

In 2017, when I climbed Growing Up (VI 5.13a A0, Borchard-Jones-Jones-Montoya-Watson, 2007) on the south face of Half Dome, I had a look at the dike that makes up the infamous line called Karma. I was blown away by the beauty of that line, which zigzags up the right side of the big south face. I knew one day I'd try it, and not just because of the aesthetics, but also because of its rich history.

Karma is a testament to visionary climber Dave Schultz's boldness and skill. In July 1986, Schultz, along with Jim Campbell and Ken Yager, opened the 14-pitch route in Yosemite's traditional ground-up style, drilling on lead. The meat of Karma follows a huge dike that meanders left-to-right diagonally across the wall. According to a story Ken wrote to accompany the original topo, Dave, joker that he was, convinced his friends to go up with him by telling them "that tourists often walked down the upper portions of it from the summit of Half Dome to take pictures."

Dave led all the pitches and was climbing for his life—at times, quite literally. Falling was not an option—due to the traversing character of the line, Dave feared that a pendulum fall would result in the rope cutting on the sharp dike. Nine of the route's 14 pitches required some aid, and the line was graded 5.11+ A1. The numbers do not reflect the seriousness and character of the route.

The route might have been forgotten except for a few rusty bolts and the vision of another Yosemite legend, Brooke Sandahl. When Brooke saw Ken Yager's pictures of Karma around 2010, as he told me in an email, he was "absolutely blown away by this mind-blowing dike which stretched on across the face like the writhing backbone of a dragon. It was one of the most amazing features I had ever seen in climbing." He immediately called Dave and said, "We have to try and free it." Dave emphatically said no—he was still scared of the route after the first-ascent experience.

But Brooke prevailed, finally convincing Dave to go back to Karma and try to free it with him. From 2016 to 2021, they returned six times to Half Dome. They carried loads of supplies up to their camp and labored for weeks on rebolting the route to bring it into a state that repeaters could enjoy. They added a number of bolts at the cruxes and moved the placement of many others to make things considerably safer.

For five years, Brooke and Dave toiled away, in hot sun, in freezing shade, even in rain that turned the face slick. Not even a 2020 heart attack kept Dave away. By the end of their efforts in 2021, Brooke, now 62, and Dave, now 63, realized that, strong as they were, some of the pitches were beyond them. They estimated the final pitch might be 5.14. Having freed all but three of the route's 14 pitches—and having unlocked every move except for four meters at the beginning of pitch nine—they graciously opened the project up to others.

Brooke had been telling me about Karma since 2016. It sounded desperate. But after finally seeing the line in 2017, I was in.

In October 2023, Oliver Schmidt (Germany) and I packed food and supplies for a week and started up Karma. While climbing the route, I constantly thought what it would have been like to be up there with a handful of homemade 1/4" machine bolts crudely pounded into the holes. The original bolts were so sparsely placed that just thinking of the potential falls was terrifying. The new bolts made the climb safe and a pleasure.

Pitch after pitch went down. The first test came at pitch six, where there is an interruption in the dike. Brooke had told me they found a solution with a long sideways reach they called the "Iron Cross." He also said that, given my five-foot-six height and shorter wingspan, I might not like it. But it went.

The last obstacle was pitch nine. We spent several hours seeking a solution—and replacing some old bolts that Dave and Brooke hadn't gotten around to—and eventually put it down. When we topped out on the third day of climbing, even before we took a summit photo, I sent a text message to Brooke: "We did it!"

Free Karma is a spectacular route surrounded by the best scenery imaginable. We graded the crux pitch 5.13d, and there are four other 5.13 leads. We based the grades on our experience on other Yosemite lines, including several we climbed in the four weeks immediately prior to making Karma's first free ascent: Wet Lycra Nightmare (5.13d A0), Nexus (IV 5.13a/b), Misty Wall (5.13a), and the Free Heart Route with the Freeblast start (5.13b). Based on all of that, 5.13d feels like it fits. 📷 🔍

—**Tobias Wolf,** *Germany*

OPPOSITE PAGE: Oliver Schmidt on pitch five (5.13a) of Karma. The incredible dike continues traversing up and right for about 700 feet, with four more 5.13 cruxes along the way. *Tobias Wolf*

ABOVE: Approximate line of Karma on the south face of Half Dome. Other routes not shown. *Vitaliy Musiyenko*

Jack Cramer on the crux fourth pitch of Troll Toll on the northeast face of Mt. Morrison. *Tad McCrea*

MT. MORRISON, NORTHEAST FACE, TROLL TOLL

The Sierra Nevada is a range where pristine golden granite dominates the landscape. Mt. Morrison, however, doesn't care about fitting in with the masses. Known as the "Eiger of the Sierra," the 12,240' peak's notoriously chossy northeast face, made of ancient metamorphosed sandstones and muds, towers above Highway 395, sending chills down the spine of any climber who considers it.

Unlike the real Eiger, which gets climbed all the time, the northeast face of Morrison sees very little action. [*In 2014 and 2015, Preston Rhea and partners made several first ascents on the complex north and northeast faces, including Caught Inside (9 pitches, IV M4 steep snow), with Kia Ravanfar, in April 2014, and Psychopomp (8 pitches, IV M4+ moderate snow) in December 2015, on the far left side. The main northeast face had only one full-length route, the Northeast Wall and Buttress, climbed in summer in 1946 and in winter 1968.*] In mid-April, Jack Cramer and Tad McCrea invited me to join them on an attempt to climb a new route up this monster.

Jack and Tad had tried the same route, starting on the left side of the main northeast face, twice before, in 2021. Those attempts—hindered by sustained climbing, challenging route-finding, bad bivouacs, and lack of ice—ended in retreats after six and nine pitches.

But 2023 was different. With record snowfall blanketing the Sierra Nevada, the conditions were ripe. Our climb followed a good freeze, and we didn't experience any rockfall. All we found was pitch after pitch of engaging mixed climbing—some even had plastic ice. The rock was generally as solid as an alpinist could wish for. In fact, the rock might be described as *too* solid in places—pro at times was hard to come by, but thankfully the climbing dropped in difficulty at those spots.

On the crux fourth pitch, Jack followed blobs of ice and cracks straight up rather than staying in a dominant right-facing corner to the left—this variation was a total classic and surprisingly well-protected. By the evening of our first day on the wall, we had surpassed Tad and Jack's previous high point and settled in for a night of recovery in our two-man tent. On our second day on the route, venturing into uncharted territory, we found more ice and engaging mixed climbing on shockingly solid rock.

If I were to describe Troll Toll (600m, WI3 M5/6) in one line, it would be "not particularly hard, but tricky." It provided a sense of precarious security, with holds often plentiful but not always positive or reliable. The route was sustained, with most pitches having at least some M4/5 moves.

Just five days later, the route witnessed a swift second ascent by Dylan Johnson and Josh Wharton. With a description and photo overlay, they completed the climb in mere hours, simul-climbing and using Micro Traxions. They confirmed the route's moderate yet classic character. For someone with similar skill to Wharton and Johnson, Troll Toll will feel like a good warm-up for mixed routes in Alaska. For those with little experience on gear-protected mixed routes, don't underestimate the difficulty based on the moderate grade. 📄 📷

—**Vitaliy Musiyenko**

TORRE DE MIERDA, NORTHEAST FACE, TWO NEW ROUTES

Frozen lakes weren't part of my childhood in Rhode Island, so I was a little nervous when Jack Cramer and I skied out onto Convict Lake at dawn. The ice came alive with sound: booms, cracks, and all sorts of sci-fi noises. Panicking, I started poling and skating as hard as I could. Jack, a native of the Upper Midwest, found my fright quite humorous.

The north face of Mt. Morrison, along with its subpeak, the Torre de Mierda (10,040'), has been a focus of Jack's energies for several years, and he had spotted two potential lines on the northeast face of the Torre: a prominent red dike and a ramp system to its left.

The Torre De Mierda is not made up of the Sierra's exceptional granite, but of an ancient metamorphosed rock. Secure-feeling holds are rare, as is protection. Ledges, chimneys, and couloirs are covered with rubble; it's best to climb in winter, when the loose stuff is covered by snow and the holds are (hopefully) frozen in place.

In March 2021, Jack led up the first pitch on the red dike, using all of our 60m rope and almost all the rack. Thinking ahead, he found a belay to the right of the dike— which presented as a wide but shallow chimney—that kept him out of the fall line.

In the dike, I found the red rock was slightly better than the surrounding stone,

Mt. Morrison with (1) Troll Toll (600m, WI3 M5/6) partially visible on the northeast face. The original summer routes up the northeast and north faces are in the center. Torre de Mierda is to the right, showing (2) Artem's Ramp and (3) Jamaican Lager, first climbed in the winters of 2022 and 2021, respectively. *Jack Cramer*

though pro was still sparse. The third pitch was the crux, as Jack climbed the steep right wall of the dike on decent rock. As the dike became more of a low-angle gully, we simul-climbed, doing just one more belayed pitch on steeper rock right of the dike. We topped out with just enough light to navigate the third-class start of the descent, a gully on the west side. Given that we'd followed a big red stripe, there was an obvious name: Jamaican Lager (800', 5 pitches, III M4).

In February 2022, we were back, this time for the left-leaning ramp system to the left of Jamaican Lager. We followed two easy but run-out pitches to a ledge at the start of the ramp. Above, the route-finding was straightforward. The challenge was once again finding good protection and anchors. Though it didn't have a single move harder than anything on Jamaican Lager, this route felt more sustained. Somewhere around pitch eight of the nine-pitch route, we put on our headlamps.

We had talked a lot about Ukraine and Russia on the way in because the military buildup was all over the news. An interview on NPR with Ukrainian writer Artem Chapeye had moved me, so we named the route Artem's Ramp (1,200', IV M4+). A selection of pitons, including beaks, is useful on both routes. 📄 📷

—**Ian McEleney**

CALIFORNIA | Sequoia National Park

Josef Maier leads the tenth pitch (5.11) during the first ascent of Mother of Pearl on the east face of Moro Rock. *Brian Prince*

MORO ROCK, EAST FACE, MOTHER OF PEARL

On December 17, Christian Black, Chris Koppl, Josef Maier, and I completed a project that I had originally envisioned in 2016. After multiple trips over several years, including a three-pitch false start that dead-ended at unclimbable terrain, we established the first free route up the imposing left side of the east face of Moro Rock.

While the right side of Moro's east face has easily accessible and mostly moderate routes, the left is home to dramatic overhangs that, until now, had only allowed for impressive aid lines. Our climb, Mother of Pearl (1,200', 10 pitches, 5.12-), is predominantly on knobs, which are

ubiquitous on Moro Rock and part of what makes the formation so special.

Mother of Pearl starts left of Pièce de Renaissance (1,400', 8 pitches, IV 5.10 A1), first climbed by Jon Gatti, E.C. Joe, and John Vargas in 1989. The upper pitches climb through a spectacular headwall, which holds the crux. The line mostly follows new terrain, but we commandeered two pitches in the middle from an old, abandoned route simply labeled "incomplete" in the out-of-print *Southern Sierra Rock Climbing: Sequoia/Kings Canyon.* Christian, Chris, Josef, and I completed a team-free ascent. [*This report at the AAJ website includes a photo of all routes on the left side of the east face of Moro Rock.*]

—**Brian Prince**

BEARPAW DOME, WEST FACE, TWO ROUTES

Working as a fire and fuels assessment tech for the U.S. Geological Survey in Sequoia and Kings Canyon National Parks (SEKI), it seemed like every backcountry work trip revealed unclimbed granite. In the summer of 2022, I attempted to scramble the south ridge of a wall—which I later learned is called Bearpaw Dome, just north of Bearpaw Meadow Ranger Station—but was turned back by a 5.9 slab move. I recruited fellow UMass Outing Club alum Chris Hebert to join me for some more exploration that fall.

Bearpaw Dome is immense: a half-mile-long system of walls and buttresses facing due west, with a long north–south ridgeline on top. We believe the wall had only one prior route: In July 2017, Chad Namolik and Matt Zussman put up Brownies and Lemonade, a five-pitch 5.8 that winds up the far right shield of the dome.

Chris and I did the 12-mile approach from the Wolverton trailhead in mid-October and climbed two long routes: UMOC Connection (1,400' of climbing, 8 pitches, III 5.9), following the obvious left-leaning crack system that splits the center of the main face; and Long Distance Runner (2,800' of climbing, III 5.8+) on the far left buttress. We left no gear on either route. 🗎 📷 🔍

—**Peter Murphy**

Connor Herson and Fan Yang in high spirits after sending all three of the hardest pitches with no falls during their first free ascent of Hairline. *Fan Yang*

MT. WHITNEY, HAIRLINE FREE

Standing beneath Hairline (12 pitches, IV 5.10d C2+) for the first time in 2018, looking up at Mt. Whitney's imposing east face, I could hardly imagine the vision and audacity it had taken Bruce Bindner and Alex Schmauss to attempt this route back in 1987. An obvious line, yes, but mind-boggling to contemplate: The route's blank, overhanging headwall, situated above 13,000', was split by what seemed the thinnest of cracks, stretching upward for several hundred feet.

I returned for a reconnaissance mission, and it seemed clear that Hairline could go free—albeit with a lot of blue-collar cleaning. I applied for and received a Live Your Dream Grant from the AAC to help fund the project.

In 2018 and 2019, I made two more trips to clean the rock and try to climb pitch three, the obvious crux. A monster pitch of nearly 60m that overhangs by 15° to 20°, it starts with an insecure, pumpy layback and becomes progressively more bouldery. The hardest sequence guards the anchor. On my final trip in the summer of 2019, I surprised myself by redpointing this crux pitch, with Ronnie (my girlfriend at the time) on belay.

COVID-19, wildfires, and a lack of partners forced me to keep Hairline on the back burner. But in the summer of 2023, I met Connor Herson in Tuolumne Meadows. We got to chatting about Hairline, and it was clear he would be a perfect partner. A week later, we were both giddy as kids as we packed on my front porch in Bishop and drove up to the Portal that afternoon.

Connor—who, among other mind-blowing feats, freed The Nose of El Capitan at age 15, in 2018, and in 2023 repeated Beth Rodden's masterpiece Meltdown (5.14+) in Yosemite—is just as much of a hard worker as he is a phenomenal rock

The east face of Mt. Whitney (14,505') showing the approximate routes of Hairline (red line) and the East Face route (yellow line). Many other climbs are not shown. *John Scurlock*

climber. We hiked up to Iceberg Lake laden with 65-plus-pound packs on the afternoon of Tuesday, September 19. For the next two days, we scrubbed, hand-drilled, and jugged up and down the crux pitches to rehearse the moves. At night we endured 40–50 mph gusts and single-digit windchill in our pitiful two-person tent.

Most of the bolts on Hairline are old 1/4-inchers, but all of the bolts on pitch one and most anchor bolts were upgraded to 3/8" in an ASCA rebolting effort in 2004, led by Bindner himself. In our first two days together on the route, Connor and I hand-drilled six new bolts to make the route a sensible free climb, including one to protect a 5.12 slab section that climbs around three bolts of A0. Aside from that last bolt, the entire route is protected by cams, wires, and in situ gear (including old bolts, pitons, and copperheads). Bindner and Schmauss had placed their original anchors every 50m (the length of their ropes), but this resulted in heinous hanging belays and poor holds for clipping the anchors; we placed five bolts for anchors at better free climbing stances, making minimal changes to the nature of the aid climb.

On Friday, September 22, Connor and I were worn out from two days of hard work, but there was no time to rest—he had to be at a meeting at Stanford University on Sunday morning! Our planned tactics were simple: We would take turns leading each crux pitch until one of us freed it, then push on to the next pitch.

After two 5.10 pitches at the base, we sat on a big ledge to wait for shade to hit the three hardest pitches—three, four, and five—which wouldn't happen until 1 p.m. However, Connor got impatient and decided he'd take a run at the crux pitch in full sun. I could see he was nervous, but I wasn't worried for him, knowing he had enough fitness and grit for multiple good tries; rather, I was concerned for myself—if he fell, I'd be up next!

As I fed rope through the Grigri, Connor dispatched boulder problem after boulder problem. At the very end, he grunted through the technical V7ish sequence to the chains. I felt at once relieved that I wouldn't have to lead this pitch again, and also slightly vindicated that even the wunderkind Connor Herson had to try really hard on the pitch. To my surprise, I followed the crux cleanly. Later, we agreed to grade this pitch 5.13d.

We both sent the next two pitches, a 5.12 and 5.13-, making it a no-fall day. However, by the time we reached the top of the ninth pitch, it was already 5 p.m. There were only three moderate pitches and some 4th class to reach Whitney's summit, but the 3rd-class Mountaineer's Route—our way down—was particularly icy and snowy that summer; without crampons, it would have been dangerous to descend it at night.

We decided to save the summit for the next day and scrambled down the East Face route (5.7) to return to our bivy. The next morning, we reversed the previous night's descent and swung leads on Hairline's remaining pitches, topping out around 11 a.m. in glorious sunshine, along with dozens of hikers. After a brief celebration, we practically skipped down to Iceberg Lake in the highest of spirits, but once there the respite was brief: We still had to break camp, hike out, and get Connor to school.

The rock on Hairline Free (1,000', 13

pitches, V 5.13d) is generally very good for the Whitney zone, but there are sections that, while not quite R-rated, are certainly fragile. Those looking to repeat the route should tread lightly—but above all enjoy the spectacular climbing and setting. [*Herson and Yang spoke in depth about this climb in episode 62 of the AAJ's Cutting Edge podcast.*] 📷 🔍

—Fan Yang

AIGUILLE EXTRA, EAST BUTTRESS

To those who look upon it from the east, Aiguille Extra (14,048'), a peak in the Whitney Massif, cries out to be climbed. The steep formation was first ascended by Bill Sumner and Mike Heath by the East Face route in 1971; their route was freed by Pat Brennan and Kenn Kenaga in 1993. In 1978, Kenny Cook and Werner Landry climbed an obvious line to the right of the original route: the East Buttress (V 5.10 A2). The only sections they didn't free were a tension traverse on pitch three and the start of the final pitch. Kenny and Werner's route was a proud achievement, but it has largely faded into obscurity, perhaps because schlepping aid gear so high into the Sierra Nevada doesn't have universal appeal.

James Holland and I embarked on a ground-up free attempt of the East Buttress in August 2023. After a bivy at the base of the needle, we climbed to the summit via engaging face and cracks—from tips to wide—without adding any bolts or using any aid. We added a three-pitch direct start (5.9+, 5.10+, 5.10) instead of climbing the two blocky 5.8 pitches of the original route. Pitch two, the physical and mental crux, involved a sporty, gear-protected traverse to gain a steep hand crack. Our fourth pitch (originally A2, now 5.10) followed a sustained and steep right-leaning hand and fist crack. Pitch nine (originally A2, now 5.10+) had excellent bouldery movement through a steep dihedral.

TOP: Cam Smith leads pitch four (5.10) of Aiguille Extra's East Buttress. *James Holland*

BOTTOM: The East Buttress (10 pitches, IV 5.10+) of Aiguille Extra. *Cam Smith*

We were impressed by the free climbing that Kenny and Werner did back in 1978, but not surprised: They were both native to San Diego and frequented Mt. Woodson, a crack training mecca. Having spent much time at Woodson myself, I felt a kinship with them on Aiguille Extra, knowing our endeavors had overlapped in space, if not time. James and I hope the free version of the East Buttress (1,230', 10 pitches, IV 5.10+) will encourage others to check out this unsung gem of the Eastern Sierra. 📄 📷

—Cam Smith

The Allotrope (900', IV 5.10- R) on the south face of La Madre. One older route took a line to the right. *Joey Latina*

the wall, after one last short section of 5.10-, the climbing became scrambly. We hit the summit and hiked out to the car on a pleasant ridgeline. Though most of the climbing on The Allotrope (900', 7 pitches, IV 5.10- R) is run-out, chossy, or both, the position is fantastic and it's a great way to escape the Red Rock crowds. 📷 🔍

—Joey Latina

NEVADA | Red Rock Canyon

MT. WILSON, AEOLIAN WALL, SALAMI WAND KENOBI

Having climbed with Sam Boyce on several occasions, including a handful of first ascents, I'm well aware that he is into the kind of weird, ungroomed terrain that most strive to avoid. I also knew—despite never having climbed with him—that Kyle Willis has an appetite for wide cracks in obscure areas of Red Rock. So, when they invited me to attempt an intimidating unclimbed line on the Aeolian Wall, I knew it'd be a grand adventure.

On December 9, we shouldered heavy backpacks filled with a huge rack, from ball nuts to the gigantic number 7 Black Diamond cam. We also brought a big assortment of pitons and beaks, as a large roof 1,000' up—the unmissable feature that had attracted us to this line—looked like it would require some good ol' nailing. The plan was to bivy once and then climb to the summit the following day. We packed two gallons of water, a gallon of coffee, and enough salami to feed the Swiss army for a week.

Two long pitches got us to the top of a triangular tower. From there, we climbed three pitches of Woman of Mountain Dreams (17 pitches, V 5.11), after which we veered right into another chimney system. Woman of Mountain Dreams was first climbed in 1997 by my parents, Joanne and Jorge Urioste, along with Dave Krulesky and Mike Morea, and then freed by my mother and Aitor Uson in 1998.

NEVADA | La Madre Mountains

LA MADRE, SOUTH FACE, THE ALLOTROPE

High above the Las Vegas valley, between Red Rock and Mt. Charleston, is the south face of La Madre (8,154'), a 1,000' wall of limestone. Few people make the approach to climb here—it's more than two hours if you know the way, and upwards of four hours through thick brush and talus if you don't. The rock is typical Mojave limestone, which can be very chossy.

The only known prior route was done nearly 30 years ago, by Andrew Fulton and Dan Briley, leaving no fixed protection. While the idea of repeating their route was appealing, I figured a new route probably wouldn't feel much different. I wanted to explore a large corner system about 100' left of the original line (based on Andrew and Dan's description).

On a cold day in November, Mike Starr and I met at 4 a.m. to drive to the "trailhead"—an unmarked pullout on an unmarked dirt road on La Madre's north side. Our plan was to climb long pitches and hand-drill bolted anchors (mainly because the rock quality isn't good enough for confidence-inspiring trad anchors). Protection on the route wasn't great, but I found gear where needed. About 750' up

We stopped to bivy on a nice ledge at the end of our sixth pitch. The next morning, after jugging a pitch we'd climbed and fixed the night before, we continued up until we were under the 120' roof (yes, 120' *horizontal*), chilling at an epic stance that we dubbed the "Womb with a View Belay."

Like a bat emerging from the depths of hell, Sam aided through the enormous roof on micro-cams, back-cleaning to make his followers' lives more pleasant. Awkward C2 led to a squeeze chimney (protected by the number 7), which ended at a nice stance. Sam belayed us up, and we then quested up several pitches of fun, crispy crack.

It was getting dark, so we rigged a rappel into a gully that led to the top of the Wind God Tower; we bivouacked on top of this tower for an unplanned second night out. (Since no other climb ascends Wind God Tower, and dangerous scrambling would be required to reach it otherwise, we're fairly certain we were the first people on it.) Thankfully, we had enough cell service that I could call into work and request a substitute teacher to cover my class the next day. As I roasted salami for dinner using a "wand" that Kyle fabricated from a nearby bush, he looked over at me and said, "Salami Wand Kenobi." Our savage laughter filled the canyons to the brim.

The following morning, to put the finishing touches on Salami Wand Kenobi (2,000', 14 pitches, V 5.11- R C2), we climbed two 200' pitches up the Aeolian headwall. We high-fived on the majestic crown of Mt. Wilson and hiked down Oak Creek with smiles on our faces and leftover salami in our packs. 📄📷

—**Danny Urioste**

TOP: Sam Boyce transitioning into the squeeze chimney of the enormous pitch-nine roof on Salami Wand Kenobi. *Kyle Willis*

BOTTOM: Salami Wand Kenobi (2,000', 14 pitches, V 5.11- R C2) on the Aeolian Wall of Mt. Wilson. Other routes are not shown. *Sam Boyce*

THE RED ROCK TRAVERSE; MONUMENT PEAK, NORTHEAST RIDGE

Over six days in early October, Lani Chapko and I completed The Red Rock Traverse (RRT). A couple of iterations of Red Rock traverses had been done in the past—including The HURT, an impressive ultra-running crossover by Alex Honnold in 2022—but a complete *climbing* traverse (more on what that means in a bit) had yet to be done. Kyle Willis suggested the possible link-up that would become the RRT in 2016, though timing and life prevented us from giving it an attempt.

Basically, there are 11 canyons that open to the east in Red Rock, defined by 12 ridgelines or peaks. Traversing north to south, the idea would be to summit the high point of each ridgeline via a technical route on the north side, assuming that peak *had* a technical north face. It is certainly a bit contrived—you can hike and scramble the Keystone Thrust behind Red Rock, thereby eliminating much of the technicality, and this has been done a number of times—but the RRT is a more direct traverse, up and over each peak. The HURT is somewhere between the RRT and scrambling the Thrust, as Honnold climbed about two-thirds of the peaks via technical routes and ran along the backside to tag a few more.

The ground we covered consisted mostly of well-established scrambling, climbing, and canyoneering routes, but there were a couple of question marks going in. The biggest was the north face of Monument Peak. There is little published climbing history on the walls in Mustang Canyon; the only established route to the top of Monument's north face seemed to be Slim, a 19-pitch 5.10c.

During the RRT, we fell behind our planned pace, and we determined that another Grade V route would likely set us up for failure. At the base of Monument's north wall, we weighed our options and decided to take an obvious, low-angle ridge splitting the face. The Northeast Ridge (2,000, III 5.9) climbed like an alpine route, with isolated roped blocks interspersed with long sections of scrambling; we climbed around eight pitches up to 5.9 and soloed a fair amount of low-fifth-class terrain. We did not encounter any signs of prior travel but cannot be certain this was a first ascent.

We did the RRT in a "supported" alpine style, bivying in the canyons without returning to civilization, but relying on water and food caches that we or friends had stashed. We logged 90 hours of moving time during the six-day traverse, climbed over 120 guidebook pitches, and gained around 30,000' of elevation. [*This report at the AAJ website includes a list of the peaks and routes climbed during the traverse.*] 📄

—**Sam Boyce**

Woodland Nymph (1,100', III 5.10+ M5), on the north face of Mt. Heyburn's west summit, follows the broad couloir in the center of the picture and then a big left-facing corner on the highest rock formation. This photo was taken in summer, but the route was climbed in May, when the couloir was filled with snow. *Matt Ward*

IDAHO | Sawtooth Mountains

MT. HEYBURN, WEST SUMMIT, NORTH FACE, WOODLAND NYMPH

On May 4, Brad Ward and I climbed a new route on the north face of the west summit of Mt. Heyburn (10,229'). From the upper Bench Lake, our route ascended a large snowfield before entering the broad couloir directly below the summit. We soloed snow in the couloir for 500' before roping up for a pitch of steep snow and easy mixed to reach beautiful rock at the base of the upper face. An exciting M5 pitch through snow mushrooms and great stone got us to dry rock, where we switched to rock shoes and enjoyed four more pitches of excellent climbing up an obvious corner that splits the face.

Brad led the crux fifth pitch of the route in fine style and called it 5.10+. It seemed harder to me, but somehow, by the time I followed that pitch, both of our pairs of boots, crampons, and ice tools, along with the pin rack and water, had found their way into my pack—so who knows the actual grade? We experienced some loose rock on the sixth and final pitch, but nothing like the rotten rock on the west side of the mountain. We descended the Stur Chimney and were back in town before dark.

We climbed the route in May for a couple of reasons. First, I had previously looked at the route in the summer, and it seemed unlikely we could get up the very loose, steep rock in the couloir without snow cover. The spring snowpack made that part easy. Second, we were unsure what we would find above, as Heyburn has a reputation for heinous rock (apart from the classic Stur Chimney); we thought we might need tools and crampons even if the rock was dry.

Ultimately, we were pleasantly surprised by the rock quality. If someone took the initiative to clean the last pitch, perhaps on rappel, Woodland Nymph (1,100', 6 pitches, III 5.10+ M5) could be a classic early season Sawtooth route.

—Matt Ward

ROTTEN MONOLITH, NORTH RIDGE, TOO LATE TO SAY SORRY

The legendary duo of Fred Beckey and Louis Stur made the first ascent of Rotten Monolith in 1961 via its 150' west face. In a report for the *AAJ*, Stur described decomposing stone and wrote that the "conspicuous tower...presents a formidable impression from the east" and rises "at least 500 feet, smooth, perpendicular and holdless all the way." I read these words ten years ago, after the east face first caught my attention from Idaho Highway 75, and they were enough to make me forget about the mountain for a decade.

In May, when Brad Ward and I stood on the summit of nearby Mt. Heyburn (10,229'), I finally got an up-close glimpse of the east face of Rotten Monolith. What we saw was beautiful Sawtooth stone, more like 1,000' tall than 500', and split by multiple crack systems.

Returning in September, I made a solo trip to shuttle gear for an attempt. Four hours after stepping off the Redfish boat shuttle, and after a 4.3-mile and 3,300' vert approach, I stood at the base of a true Sawtooth gem with no established routes—possibly due to Stur's discouraging words, possibly because of the difficulty of reaching the base.

On September 28, Brad and I returned with more gear and bivvied at the base. The next morning, we started up a crack system that generally followed the north ridge; this seemed like it had a better chance of leading to the summit than options more on the face. We found pitch after pitch of excellent crack climbing, mostly in the 5.10 to 5.10+ range, on quite good rock. The fifth pitch was the crux; I aided a short section, but Brad followed it

Too Late to Say Sorry (10 pitches, IV 5.10+ C1) on the north ridge of Rotten Monolith. *Matt Ward*

Brad Ward climbing the first pitch of Too Late to Say Sorry on the north ridge of Rotten Monolith. *Matt Ward*

mechanism. I waited until we were committed to the approach trail before sharing the trials of Stur and Beckey—the insanely bad rock, the 3,300' slog, the lack of water where I planned to camp. And by then it was, well, Too Late to Say Sorry (800', 10 pitches, IV 5.10+ C1). 📷

—Matt Ward

THE ELEPHANT'S PERCH, SOUTHEAST FACE, TAKIN' 'ER BY THE TUSKS

From September 13 to 15, Greg Rickenbacker and I finished a new route up the southeast face of the Elephant's Perch. I grew up in the nearby town of Stanley, so establishing a route on the formation was a longtime dream come true.

I first attempted the line in early July, supported by my good friend Gracie Hornsby. The moderate first pitch began just left of the first pitch of Sunrise Book (5.12-). An exciting 5.11 second pitch ended at the anchor below Sunrise Book's second pitch. The third pitch of our line, the free climbing crux (5.12a R), went straight left—a thin traverse with beautiful, sculpted edges and a horizontal seam that accepted small cams and tied-off knifeblades. Unfortunately, I injured my shoulder when I fell off the crux sequence and swung hard into a corner below, forcing us to bail.

In September, I returned with Greg. Focused on pushing the route higher, we climbed the first pitch of Sunrise Book on September 13 to go straight to the crux traverse on the new line. We fixed ropes and returned the next day. I successfully climbed through the section where I had fallen to reach decent protection, then was faced with 25 more feet of insecure, unprotectable traversing. At the end of this, a tenuous stance allowed me to hammer in a beak at the base of an incipient crack, which widened to steep 5.11 fingers and hands, at the top of which I built a belay.

After this taxing two-hour lead, Greg took over for his own two-hour push up

free and suggested 5.11a. The sixth pitch traversed climber's right for 60' and was the only time the route left the ridge.

After nine quality pitches, we finally encountered the horrendous ball-bearing rock to which Stur had alluded. Our tenth pitch was intense and gearless, although not steep. I scooped away sand and gravel, and sometimes kicked steps. I wished I had ice tools. The pitch finished at a small gendarme on the ridge, around 200' below the summit. Although the sandy summit pitches appeared climbable (likely with aid), they did not look appealing in the late evening light. We chose to call it a route. We rappelled our line with some difficulty and reached camp in the dark.

Brad had failed to ask many questions before agreeing to try the route—which, based on other things I've gotten him into, might be some sort of mental defense

steep A3 on a thin seam. We again fixed ropes and returned to the ground. On the third day, Greg led another beautiful A3 across left-rising, parallel beak seams on orange rock. Two more pitches took us to the summit. Two days later, we added a higher-quality and more direct first pitch (5.11).

Takin' 'er by the Tusks (625', 7 pitches, 5.12a R A3) covers all new terrain. To our knowledge, this is the first route through the prominent, steep headwall between Elephant's Eye (5.8 A3) and Sunrise Book. A continuous ascent awaits. While the route might go free, the bolting ban in Sawtooth National Forest means it would involve a lot of scary climbing and almost certainly require headpointing tactics.

—**Benj Wollant**

IDAHO | Lost River Range

MT. BREITENBACH, NORTH FACE, FIRST SKI DESCENT

Benj Wollant finishes the crux sequence of pitch three (5.12a R) on Takin' 'er by the Tusks on the Elephant's Perch. *Greg Rickenbacker*

I became interested in the north face of Mt. Breitenbach (12,140') in the early 2000s as an alpine climbing objective. There had been several attempts over the years, but only one route, the Grand Chockstone Couloir (III 5.8 A2, Boyles-Olson-Weber; *AAJ 1983*), had been found through the complex, steep terrain.

After many years of climbing and skiing in the Lost River Range, I wondered if a skiable line existed on the cliff-riddled face of Breitenbach. In 2017, conditions looked favorable for an attempt, but when my partner bailed at the last minute, I settled for a climb and ski of the north face of Mt. Borah. In June of 2019, favorable conditions lined up again, and I climbed a new alpine route up the north face of Breitenbach with Paddy McIlvoy: Cowboy Poetry (2,800', IV 5.7 R AI2 50° snow; *AAJ 2020*). In the spring of 2023, conditions once again looked promising for a potential ski descent.

I reached out to fellow guide Jon "JP" Preuss to see if he was available for an adventure. With access to the east side of the Lost River Range still blocked by snow, I chose Jones Creek for our approach and exit. This meant we'd be approaching the north face top-down; I'd have to rely on photos and my prior experience on the mountain for reference. On April 26, we brought the whole kit—sharp points, rope, harnesses—but I had picked out a line I thought would go free of the rope.

And it did. Our descent line, The Last Cowboy, is a steep-skiing

TOP: Jon "JP" Preuss cowboying up in the Right Leg Couloir on Mt. Breitenbach. *Marc Hanselman*

BOTTOM: The line of The Last Cowboy, the first ski descent of Mt. Breitenbach's 2,500-foot north face. *Wes Collins*

adventure through one of the most complex alpine faces in Idaho. From the first turns to the last, it's a no-fall zone where stability and conditions are critical.

The route lulls you in with some casual turns off the summit and along the shoulder before dropping into the Central Couloir (40°). The Walk the Line traverse that followed looked scary and improbable, but with an axe in hand, skis on our feet, and the stable conditions we had, it felt quite secure. The traverse ended in a hanging bowl above the Long-Legged Couloirs, some of the steepest terrain on the route. A cornice had collapsed far to skier's left, wiping all the good snow clear of the lower bowl and the Left Leg Couloir; consequently, we aimed for the Right Leg. (We named these features according to a skier's perspective.) An exceptionally steep traverse above a 50' cliff got us to the Right Leg's entrance. Once in the couloir, we linked turns through a spectacular narrow hallway to reach the easier lower face.

The descent took us 1.5 hours. The Last Cowboy covers 2,500' of vertical, has slopes up to 55°, and winds through couloirs as narrow as eight feet wide.

—**Marc Hanselman**

MONTANA | Glacier National Park

BEARHAT MOUNTAIN, NORTHWEST FACE, THE ANDERSON-CAREY

In late November 2017, Brent Anderson and I made our first trip into Avalanche Basin in Glacier National Park to climb the ice routes formed by runoff below the Sperry Glacier. We left completely enamored by the beauty and abundance of ice in the back of the basin.

Inspired, I combed through old *AAJ* reports from Glacier and perused Google Earth, and I noticed a cascade of water flowing down the northwest face of Bearhat Mountain (8,689'), which rises just east of the Avalanche Lake Trail. I followed the cascade up and up and up until it terminated in a perennial snowfield that sits in a large bowl between the main and false summits of Bearhat. A quick measurement showed the cascade to be approximately 3,100' high. From the snowfield, it was another 800' to Bearhat's summit. Stunned by the potential route's length, and its close proximity to a well-traveled trail, I sent a message to Brent. We made plans to attempt the route early the following winter.

Several days prior to Thanksgiving in 2018, Brent and I headed into the park. Heavy packs, slow climbing, and a small weather window forced us to retreat just a third of the way up Bearhat. We returned in November 2019, thinking we had learned from our previous mistakes: We launched with minimal food and fuel, planning on climbing the route in a single push. Some poor navigation during the night put us off route in an unclimbable corner. After many time-consuming rappels to correct our mistake, we realized we didn't have sufficient food or fuel to complete the climb. Terrible weather and park construction

The northwest face of Bearhat Mountain and the Anderson-Carey Route (1,210m, V WI4 M5). This is possibly the second ascent of the face. The late Mason Robinson reportedly soloed a route up the northwest face in 2002, but the line is not known. *Google Earth*

Dallin Carey leads a step of good ice low on the northwest face of Bearhat Mountain. The full route took 26 hours to climb, with another 11 hours for the descent. *Brent Anderson*

projects kept us away for the next three winters.

November 2023 proved unusually warm and dry, but on the 29th, Brent and I found ourselves standing below the face yet again. Around 11 a.m., the clouds dissipated enough for us to see that our cascade was frozen. By noon we were climbing.

We soloed several hundred feet of low-angle ice steps to a dubious pitch of poorly formed ice that poured through a narrow cleft. We belayed each other up this pitch, then happily simul-climbed ice that increased in quality as we got higher.

After 600', we arrived at the crux, a steep WI4+ curtain that ended with a beautiful pillar. Overjoyed by the sticky, one-swing ice, we belayed this pitch and then raced up a steep snow slope to the base of a two-tiered curtain of ice. We climbed aerated but still enjoyable ice here, then stomped out a platform to boil water as the sun dipped below the horizon.

After rehydrating and enjoying some snacks, we simul-climbed approximately 1,000' of steep snow with the occasional step of ice up to the base of what Brent and I had previously dubbed the "Black Face." On Google Earth, this appeared as a vertical face of black rock, about 150' high, with water streaming down it. We had fantasized about it for years but were dismayed to find it completely dry. Instead, 50' to the left, we headed up a V-slot of engaging mixed climbing over two-inch-thick névé.

Past the slot, we simul-climbed 600' of steep snow up the bowl between Bearhat's northeast ridge and north rib. We climbed out of the bowl via a steep snow ramp to just a few hundred feet below the summit, where large, compact blocks halted our passage. Seeking a way past this obstacle, we traversed across the top of a hanging snowfield for two pitches to the north rib, where we found a slot through the blocks. Exciting mixed climbing for one and a half pitches—including an overhang that we each surmounted with a tenuous tool placement on the right and a hand jam on the left—deposited us on the west ridge, 50' from the top of Bearhat. We stood on the summit at around 1 p.m. on November 30, 26 hours after beginning.

With a storm incoming, we fired off a few messages to friends and family and began the descent. After 11 hours of downclimbing and rappelling, we were back at the base and soon hiking back to the car—just as the storm broke.

After we made the news of our ascent public, we were informed by Michael Robinson that his brother, Mason Robinson, had possibly soloed Bearhat's northwest face in 2002 and, in true Montana style, never told anyone except for his brother. Mason died on El Capitan in 2013. No more information about his ascent is known. So, while we believe our line, the Anderson-Carey (1,210m, V WI4 M5), to be a new route, it was probably not the first ascent of Bearhat's northwest face. 📷

—**Dallin Carey**

BEAR'S FACE, DANCING BEARS

While approaching the classic California Ice route in East Rosebud Canyon in late November, I noticed ice pouring down the upper left shoulder of the mythical Bear's Face. In an area known for either very compact or very loose rock, and a scarcity of routes on the most impressive formations, I knew that a winter ascent of this northwest-facing wall would likely take some work.

Charlie Faust and Paul Shaughnessy joined me on a scouting mission, which then led to not one, not two, but three failed attempts on the line. We tried forcing a line through the roofs halfway up the face, dreaming of Stanley Headwall–like multi-pitch dry-tooling. Twice, about 600' up, we were foiled by unprotectable slabs above the roofs—not ideal terrain for crampons. The slabs also would have required way more bolts than the ground-up onsight style we prefer.

Up to this point, we'd ignored the path of least resistance leading to the ice: a dark vertical dike system cutting a groove through the wall left of the roofs. On our third attempt, we took a stab at this, reaching it via an easy leftward traverse from our second-pitch anchor. However, an intensifying storm brought near-constant spindrift and, after I battled for two hours up this third pitch, we decided to return in better conditions.

Confident that we'd unlocked the route and tired of hiking overnight loads up the five-mile approach, on our fourth attempt, Charlie, Paul, and I opted to climb the route car-to-car. On December 31, 2023, we got an early start from the trailhead. The first two pitches went smoothly, thanks to our practice

Paul Shaughnessy navigating the thin and delaminated ice headwall on Dancing Bears. This feature, visible from the ground, was what enticed Adrien Costa, Charlie Faust, and Shaughnessy to try the first winter route up Bear's Face multiple times. *Adrien Costa*

runs. This time Charlie led pitch three's corner, which turned out to be the route's crux, a delicate and loose M6 R. Paul's and my doubts steadily crescendoed as Charlie inched upward for over two hours, but they instantly evaporated when he finally called, "Off belay!" He'd extended the pitch to a full 60m, belaying at the base of an iced-up corner interrupted by a roof. This quality corner pitch was yet another rope-stretcher, bringing us to a short traverse onto the treed ledge directly below the start of the glorious ice headwall.

Paul Shaughnessy starts up pitch two during the third attempt to climb Dancing Bears. An intensifying storm stopped this attempt on the next pitch, but the climbers succeeded on their fourth try. *Adrien Costa*

Paul took over here, navigating thin and delaminated ice, and skirting left on rock briefly to avoid a detached curtain. His 65m lead (pitch six) brought us to a tree and a surprise final pitch featuring a "V4" boulder problem on tools. (Going left looked like it could offer an easier alternative.) A lower-angle groove led us to the trees that mark the top of the route.

The unknown descent included a handful of rappels from trees. At one point, a small snow runnel avalanched on Paul; thankfully, we'd kept the rope on. When we hit the easy snow couloir between Bear's Face and Giant's Foot, we unroped and stumbled back to the car, reaching it 19 hours after setting off the previous year.

While there are a couple of summer lines farther right on Bear's Face—Alex Lowe and Andrew McLean's 1998 route Ursus Horribilis (9 pitches, VI 5.10 A4) and the new route Ménage Trout (13 pitches, 5.10 R A2+; *see story below*)—we believe this to be the wall's first winter ascent.

We named our route Dancing Bears (310m, WI5 M6 R) for the amount of time we spent dancing around the face's various features as we tried to piece together a line, and for our collective love of music and good times in the hills with close friends. 🗏 📷 🔍

—**Adrien Costa**

BEAR'S FACE, MÉNAGE TROUT

In early August, Matt Cornell, Jackson Marvell, Austin Schmitz, and I set off for a two-week base camp–style trip up East Rosebud Canyon to complete a line on Bear's Face that Jackson, Matt, and Justin Willis had started in 2020. The road to East Rosebud

Lake was still closed due to historic flooding the previous summer, so the approach was more than ten miles and arduous. Once near Bear's Face, we established camp in a protected cave—a clutch move, as it rained heavily for much of the following week.

We killed time pleasantly during these damp days by fishing, swimming, packrafting East Rosebud Creek, cooking steak over the fire, and drinking wine, but we were eager to be climbing. The only known route up the vertical to slightly overhanging, northwest-facing main wall of Bear's Face was a line climbed by the late Alex Lowe and Andrew McLean in August 1998, named Ursus Horribilis (9 pitches, VI 5.10 A4).

With just a few days left on our trip, the weather cleared. On day one, we repeated pitches that Jackson and Matt had climbed three years earlier—wandering, often dirty, blue-collar climbing up to 5.10+, located climber's right of Ursus Horribilis. This brought us to a big ledge, from which we fixed lines to the ground.

The following day we hauled loads to the comfortable bivy ledge and climbed an additional three pitches (also from the 2020 attempt) up beautiful left-facing dihedrals. We fixed lines and rappelled back to our ledge, where we were greeted by our friend Chris Kulish; he had jumared up to deliver essentials, such as LED party lights for the ledge hang. He then opened a new BASE jump exit off our ledge—an incredible thing to witness.

On day three we opened three more rope-stretching pitches

TOP: Jackson Marvell climbing the sixth pitch of Ménage Trout, high above East Rosebud Creek. *Austin Schmitz*

BOTTOM: Schlepping gear to the East Rosebud Canyon trailhead because the access road was closed to cars. From there, the seven-mile hike to base camp began. *Austin Schmitz*

at 5.10 A2+. The following day, we Micro Traxioned those pitches, freeing as much as possible. We added one more long new pitch, after which we joined the final two pitches of Ursus Horribilis. We made a quick trip to the summit in the early evening light, collected some dead wood, and started rappelling and cleaning our fixed lines in the dark. We celebrated with a small campfire on our five-star ledge and descended the next morning.

Though we ran out of time on this trip, we plan to return and free climb our new line. As it stands, Ménage Trout is 13 pitches and comes in at 5.10+ R A2+. The rock quality is generally pretty good, but not always. There is a mix of bolted and gear anchors. We did a phenomenal amount of cleaning on this route and got rid of the vast majority of loose, dangerous blocks. 📋 📷

—**Chantel Astorga**

Bear's Face, with Giant's Foot behind, in early August. (1) Partial view of Dancing Bears (310m, WI5 M6 R), the first winter route up the face. (2) Ménage Trout (13 pitches, 5.10+ R A2+). The original route up Bear's Face, Ursus Horribilis (1998), took a direct line up the face to the left of Ménage Trout; the two routes share the last two pitches. See the AAJ website for a topo of the 1998 route and a complete route photo for Dancing Bears. Austin Schmitz

SILVER RUN PEAK, QUANTUM DIRECT

In early November, Blake Berghoff, Aidan Whitelaw, and I attempted to repeat the route Quantum Entanglement (2,100', WI5 M4, Hoiness-Kisner-Willis, 2020) on Silver Run Peak's (12,542') northwest aspect. We found less ice than reported on the first ascent, and after getting off route and ending up in a terribly chossy chimney with a 20' chockstone roof, we bailed. However, earlier that day, I climbed a new pitch on the face's central cliffband. It seemed like a direct line through the steep rock guarding Quantum Entanglement's upper ice would be possible and exciting.

Blake and I returned with Paul Shaughnessy the following week. From the snow ledge where Quantum Entanglement cuts right onto easier terrain, we headed left up the pitch I had established the previous week: a full rope length of three-dimensional M6 climbing on good rock. A short section of dry-tooling then brought us to a snow ramp heading up and right. Two more pitches of easier but slabby mixed climbing, interspersed with snow hiking, brought us directly to the ice headwall of Quantum Entaglement, which we did in two long pitches.

Our variation, Quantum Direct (WI5 M6), adds about 300m of new ground, and we highly recommend it for those seeking a relatively easy approach to varied, engaging climbing, with just enough protection and moss sticks to keep the difficult climbing fun.

—**Adrien Costa**

Adrien Costa leading the second mixed pitch on Quantum Direct, a long new variation to Quantum Entanglement on Silver Run Peak. *Paul Shaughnessy*

WYOMING | Teton Range

MT. OWEN, NORTH RIDGE, DIRECTISSIMA

Perhaps the most striking long line in the Tetons is the 1,000m north ridge of Mt. Owen (12,928'), leading into the north ridge of the Grand Teton. The only routes that compare would be climbs on the south buttress of Mt. Moran continuing to its summit.

This Owen–Grand line is most prominent when viewed from the mouth of Cascade Canyon near the Callis Slabs (named after Exum guide Pat Callis). I enjoyed teaching climbers to move over stone at this spot in part because it is surrounded by the achievements of so many legendary climbers. When teaching someone how to tie a bowline around their waist, I could point out Symmetry Spire, where Jack Durrance put up his eponymous route in 1936 before the modern harness was invented. When coaching a 5.8 move, I could point up to the Direct North Face of the Grand Teton, where Richard Emerson made similar moves in mountain boots in 1953.

I commonly told my guests, "The biggest and best climbs were done in mountain boots, with just a handful of pitons and a rope tied around the waist." The statement wasn't entirely true, however—some climbs could be improved. The most obvious example was right behind me: the north ridge of Mt. Owen.

The original North Ridge Route was climbed in 1951, by William Clayton and Richard Emerson, at IV 5.7 A1 (free at 5.9). This route angles in from the left, then follows a huge corner left of the ridgeline; it doesn't hit the actual crest until near the Great

(A) The Grand Teton. (B) Mt. Owen. (1) The original North Ridge Route (1951). (2) Directissima (2023). Both routes continue up the long ridge to the summit of Mt. Owen. *Acroterion | Wikimedia*

Yellow Tower at around 12,400'.

Unable to beat the style of climbing the ridge for the first time, I was determined to climb a line staying as true to the crest as possible. In July 2020, Matt Meinzer and I made it roughly halfway up, where a headwall, split by an offwidth crack that stretched farther than we could protect with the gear we had, stopped us in our tracks. Chuck Pratt would have put the rope up, but I would not.

We escaped the ridge by wandering onto the north face and continuing up to the summit by what we called Escape Route, detailed in *A Climber's Guide to the Teton Range* (4th edition, 2023). We climbed pitches up to 5.10, watched the Neowise comet from our bivy, and slaked our thirst at the upper snowfields. Matt once again got us through a climb where I had bitten off more than I could chew. The next day we walked out through Valhalla

with a deeper friendship.

In August 2023, I returned with three "friends": Karen Kovaka and numbers 4 and 5 Camalots. We quickly reclimbed the lower north ridge and continued up through the offwidth crack, a full pitch of 5.10. Confident that I had unlocked the key to the route, we wandered up easy ledges for a few hundred feet to the next headwall—this one completely devoid of cracks. We bivvied below it, uncertain once again, but next morning found passage via a 60m 5.10 traverse to the left. Another rope length put us on the edge of the ridge, just to the right of the original route's corner system, and we continued to the top of what is now the Directissima (V 5.10).

Later that day, on the top of Mt. Owen, we decided that we would not be the first to climb the most striking route in the range by continuing up the north ridge of the Grand Teton. We would go home.

Climbing a direct line up the north ridge of Owen had also been the goal of my friend Nate Brown, who, along with partners Tobey Carmen and Eric Draper, climbed a route in 2001 that they named the North Ridge Direct. Although it's documented in the 2023 guidebook, the description relied on a somewhat vague *AAJ* report. I remember Nate telling me that his line joined the big dihedral of the original North Ridge Route, and that the rock out on the arête (where we climbed) looked "pretty good." It's quite possible our routes share terrain—maybe a lot—in the lower part. 📷

—**Michael Abbey**

DEVILS LEAP, THE FALL OF SATAN

In early May, Zach Lentsch and I set our sights on a massive and unclimbed sandstone cliff near the town of Shell, just west of the Bighorn Mountains. Standing roughly 700' tall, Devils Leap is certainly the largest sandstone cliff in Wyoming, and the top 200' of the feature is separated from the hillside behind it by a cavernous chimney. However, with rock reminiscent of Utah's Fisher Towers, we were ill-prepared on our first try. After one grueling pitch, we realized we needed more gear, more ropes, and more time.

We returned a week later and started up one of the largest weaknesses on the south face of the buttress. Zach dispatched two excellent leads up to 5.10+ C3 on very soft rock. I took the lead for the next two pitches through extremely steep terrain, with wild open-book climbing and lots of sand. At dark, we left our ropes fixed and slept at the car, just a half mile away. The next morning we jugged back up, eager for what looked to be enjoyable cracks. Though the rock improved for a short while, the quality quickly declined and we found ourselves, again, climbing daintily over extremely loose ground.

Before too long, we arrived at the base of the final chimney separating the "tower" from the hillside behind it. As I began up, I saw something white sticking out of the back of the chimney. Lo and behold, it was an American bison horn. We realized the Leap may have been an ancient bison jump—a location where Native American tribes of the region would, on horseback, funnel bison herds to the top of a cliff and run them off as a means of efficient food gathering. A bison must have fallen into the chimney, where it has remained for well over 100 years. I continued on, making sure to not touch or disturb the horn.

The rock again became atrocious. Both sides of the chimney's final 15' consisted of overhanging stacks of sharp limestone blocks the size of footballs. Feet dangling in space, I jammed my body through the rubble and squeezed to the top of the tower, where I could find not even the remotest possibility for an anchor. I climbed back into the chimney and gave Zach an uncomfortable body belay, yelling to him to please not fall. Zach, being the choss-wrangling expert that he is, did not fall.

Luckily, the descent was casual: We were able to simply step over the chimney that separates the tower from the hillside and walk back to the car.

We would like to go back and free the route someday. Each anchor is bolted, and we placed a few protection bolts where absolutely necessary. Meanwhile, The Fall of Satan (700', 7 pitches, 5.10+ C3) is an excellent adventure in a wild setting. 📄 📷

—**Justin Willis**

TOP: The Fall of Satan (7 pitches, 5.10+ C3) on Devils Leap. At the top, it's possible to step over the chimney separating the formation from the hill behind it and walk down. *Justin Willis*

BOTTOM: The ancient bison horn discovered about 100 feet down the final chimney pitch on Devils Leap. *Zach Lentsch*

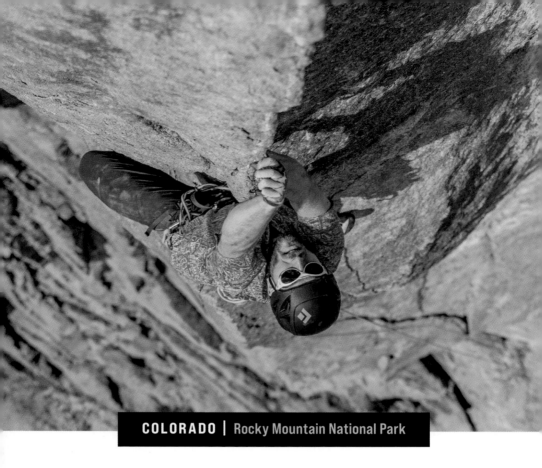

COLORADO | Rocky Mountain National Park

MT. ALICE, EAST FACE, THE MAD HATTER

"It'll be, like, 5.10 for you guys! You'll be able to pull it off in a weekend trip, and, man, it'll be great climbing!"

These were the encouraging words from Estes Park guide Harry Kent when I approached him about free climbing his 1976 route Good Vibrations (V 5.9 A3) on the east face of Mt. Alice (13,310'), deep in the Wild Basin backcountry. In late August 2021, I wrangled two friends for the nine-mile slog into the Mt. Alice cirque.

We shouldered heavy loads, and by the time Alice came into view, our spirits were broken. We bivouacked nearly two miles from the wall, and in the morning, with low morale, we shifted gears and spent the weekend bouldering and doing possible single-pitch FAs around Trio Falls.

One week later, with a better understanding of the approach, I recruited Josh "Sender" Bender, my most reliable partner and a great crack climber, to head back. We found a bivy closer to Alice's east face, and the next day, Josh cast off early on what we believed to be the first pitch of Good Vibrations. He soon found himself in a dirty corner about 100' off the ground, with only one piece of gear, 50' below him. I'll never forget the sight of his body falling toward me when he pulled off a chunk of granite, before miraculously stopping himself with an improbable spread-eagle stem after a ten-foot fall! We eventually bailed from pitch two. Good Vibrations, we realized, was not the quick and easy one-weekend route Harry Kent had promised.

Still intrigued by Alice, we kicked off the next summer season, 2022, with a recon mission. It became obvious that

Rob Scrivner halfway through the sixth pitch of The Mad Hatter, below the crux roof. Julia Cassou

Keith Lober and Joe Hladick's 1979 route Jabberwocky (V 5.10 A3), which climbed obvious features some 300' left of Good Vibrations, would make for a much higher-quality free climb. From miles away, a viewer could appreciate the enormous orange dihedral in the wall's center or the immaculate shield of granite with an arching crack one pitch below.

Josh and I spent nearly every weekend of July on the wall, averaging less than one pitch per day and bailing in terrifying electrical storms nearly every time. As weekend warriors, we'd hike into the cirque late on Fridays, spend the weekend climbing, and stumble out Sunday night to start the workweek. We pieced together an independent four-pitch start, above which we followed the steep crux pitches of Jabberwocky. By the end of 2022, we had established our line to within 100' of the summit. With the goal of producing a high-quality free climb that would be fun to repeat, after much deliberation, we decided to install two-bolt anchors at each belay and to place three necessary protection bolts.

As the season came to a close, we made one ground-up free attempt—and both walked away with bloody hands and bruised egos from the hard ring locks of the pitch six crux. We knew we needed to level up, and we went to work honing our skills with trips to Indian Creek and a winter of strength training.

A few more rainy trips during July 2023 allowed us to finish work on the route, and on August 23 everything aligned for a free attempt. The possibility of one of us sending and the other failing haunted us—we had both invested so much.

We made quick work of the lower route, dispatching progressively harder crack and slab pitches, up to 5.12-, before arriving at the crux, pitch six, at 10 a.m. This pitch starts with a boulder problem through a hanging dagger we'd named the Wild Fang, then tests every skill in the toolbox, including burly ring locks, offwidth, tricky aspect changes, roofs, hard laybacking, and technical face climbing. It was my lead, and I still had never sent two sections of the pitch. Josh had Tupac's "Ambitionz az a Ridah" bumping from his phone as I left the belay. Before I knew what was happening, I had sent the crux of our multi-year project and was lowering off to support my friend. When Josh, too, clipped the chains, our cheering echoed through the cirque.

One hour later, we had a rushed celebration on the summit before the typical noon storm had us sprint-rappelling toward the ground. We called our route The Mad Hatter (8 pitches, 5.12). [*A detailed description and topo for this route are at the AAJ website.*] 📄 📷

—**Rob Scrivner**

TOP: The Mad Hatter (8 pitches, 5.12) on the east face of Mt. Alice (13,310') in the Wild Basin area of Rocky Mountain National Park. The new route is a free version of Jabberwocky (Hladick-Lober, 1979). Other routes on the face not shown. *Rob Scrivner*

BOTTOM: Josh Bender on the burly laybacking of pitch four's arching crack. *Julia Cassou*

CHIEFS HEAD, NORTHEAST FACE, SPIRIT ANIMAL

Given that I'd never stepped foot into Glacier Gorge, you might say my plan to rope-solo a new line up the 1,500' northeast face of Chiefs Head (13,577') was ambitious. Maybe, but my buddy Greg Davis, who'd established some classics on that alpine wall—including Ten Little Indians (IV 5.11a) and Cowboys and Indians (IV 5.11c)—about 30 years earlier, assured me there were still plums to be picked, and spoke of an amazing, untapped upper headwall. My only question was, *Why hadn't these climbs been done before?*

The line of Spirit Animal (10 pitches, 5.11) on the northeast face of Chiefs Head (13,577'), with the summit in back. Other routes on the face are not shown. *Bill Duncan*

When I made it out there, in mid-August 2022, some of the answers became clear. Just getting to the base of Chiefs Head's northeast face requires an hour's hike past Spearhead, which is already deep into Glacier Gorge, six miles from the road. The final approach involves either snow travel (early season) or horribly loose scree (late season)—apparently refreshed with razor-sharp rocks daily. After considerable effort, I managed to assemble a small mountain of gear at the base of the cliff. I was exhausted, but also psyched to tackle some of the most pristine granite I'd ever seen, stretching to the skyline.

I'd spent decades rope-soloing new routes, both big and small, in the mountains of North Carolina, with only my dogs as witnesses. Since I'd moved to Colorado, six years earlier, most of my work had been on smaller crags, so I was ready for some "real climbing" again. Unfortunately, Chiefs Head's sheer size, plus the requisite hand-drilled bolting inside the national park, would make things more "real" than I'd become accustomed to in recent years.

Greg had given me a photo with possible lines drawn in, but his topo didn't do this wall justice. There were amazing cracks and corners everywhere. To me, the most obvious line started up a left-arching series of corners with a small ledge at 90'. After some shenanigans sorting out a ground anchor, the pitch went off without a hitch. Unfortunately, the second pitch was soaked from the previous day's rain, so I used the extra time to work out an excellent 5.11 variation to pitch one that I would bolt during inclement weather on a subsequent trip—this would become a common theme up along the Continental Divide.

It's hard to remember exactly how many trips I made that season. Suffice it to say, the pitches that followed required days of effort. It had been a while since I'd hand-drilled on lead, but the time came on pitch four, and after a few minutes I was tapping away. Most of the pitches above have some bolts (up to five or six per pitch), but each also requires a rack. Pitch six finishes up what some have dubbed "Lost at Sea"—a steep, bushy crack that's an unintended variation to Cowboys and Indians, where many get lost. My version makes a beeline to a spacious, grassy ledge that provided a nice bivy the following summer.

In 2023, the weather and conditions weren't good enough for me to return until late August. After a long day regaining my high point, I was exhausted. There was still a lot of new ground to cover, including the still-unclimbed headwall above Long Ledge, where all previous routes had veered right around a roof. I considered just gunning for the summit the following day on Cowboys and Indians. Torn, I slept on it.

That night, my only companion on the grassy ledge was an unusually large rat, who seemed a little too interested in my anchor; it gave up trying to chew through my tether only after I doused him with a few squirts of precious water. I awoke tired but seeing the route in a whole new light. The fabulous, knob-riddled "Golden Arête," my seventh pitch, glowed in the morning sun, shooting straight up to Long Ledge. By afternoon, the bolting was done. I was out of time, though, so down I went, again.

The last push was in early September. So far, I'd been approaching from the bottom, but the climbing season up there would end very soon, so I decided to come in from the top for the final pitches. To my surprise, the exposed headwall, while having a few scary flakes, wasn't bad—it went at 5.11 on bolts and gear.

Greg had flippantly pointed to an "easy crack" in a photo to finish the route—a feature that ended up being a pinched-off, dead-end seam. However, Greg's "crack" did lead me to discover a double finger and hand crack slashing diagonally across the face to the last few feet of knobby rock. A couple more bolts and the route was complete.

Was all that work worth it? Several times I felt I'd reached the end—a figurative one, as the literal end still loomed far overhead. But I just kept going, cajoled by Greg every time we'd meet at a crag, until finally Spirit Animal (10 pitches,

5.11) was done. After the memories of hellish, gear-laden approaches had faded, only the vital essence of the ascent remained: getting after it high on that massive wall with only my spirit animal there to watch. It was just like old times. [*The online version of this report includes a detailed pitch-by-pitch description and photos of the route.*] 📄 📷

—**Nathan Brown**

DARK SIDE WALL, PRIDE IS THE DEVIL

Across Canyon Creek from Camp Bird Road, above Ouray, is a forbidding wall, up to 425m high, that locals affectionately call the Dark Side. It never sees the light. Legends such as Steve House, Hayden Kennedy, Jeff Lowe, and Charlie Fowler all left their marks on this wall. Since 2021, I'd climbed three new routes on the Dark Side, but all toward the margins, where it's shorter. For a while I had been eyeing a long, faint system of corners just left of the classic Bird Brain Boulevard (IV

Pride Is the Devil on the Dark Side Wall. The arrow marks the start of Bird Brain Boulevard. *Charlie Faust*

Charlie Faust leading pitch five of Pride Is the Devil, which involved dangerously run-out climbing and a collapsing snow mushroom. *Jonathan Zaugg*

WI5 M5, Fowler-Lowe-Wilford, 1985). On February 20, 2023, with an okay window in the avalanche forecast, I convinced Jonathan Zaugg to attempt the line. His only condition was that I lead every pitch.

After two fun pitches, I quested up a snow-filled groove for around 30m before finding a decent piton placement. I pulled rightward through a bulge, slung a dead bush, tooled farther right, slung another dead bush, and scanned the face above: no gear in sight. Deep breaths and some tenuous sticks in thin, semi-frozen blobs of turf took me to the end of our 70m rope.

The remaining four pitches followed the same theme—very little solid protection and mostly difficult anchors. By the time I finished pitch five, the crux, it was dark. Jonathan jugged the pitch, stoked to be moving again after over two hours, but as I climbed the next pitch—once again horribly run-out—he endured a miserable and scary hanging belay with spindrift funneling down on him. As he followed the final pitch, a 20m chimney choked with a car-sized snow mushroom, Jonathan made three light kicks and sent the entire mushroom down. We rappelled the treed buttress left of the route and got back to the car at 2 a.m.

Assigning a grade to this climb seems futile: While it might be able to capture the physical difficulty, it could never speak to the insecurity or seriousness. Let's call it 5.9 M6 X. It probably shouldn't be repeated without a bolt kit. I called the route Pride Is the Devil, a reference to the J. Cole song whose name and lyrics I reflected upon after the experience. [*In February 2023, Faust and Jay Karst also put up a 220m line on the same buttress, called 3 Nil. The route is poorly protected and not recommended.*] 📄 📷

—**Charlie Faust**

TEXAS | Hueco Tanks State Park

NORTH MOUNTAIN, THE FRONT SIDE, THE TEXAS LONGROUTE

"**What about traversing** the front side of North Mountain?" Nate Vince asked me on the porch of the Hueco Mountain Hut. With a history of world-class bouldering, Hueco Tanks does not attract many roped climbers, let alone multi-pitch trad climbers. As John Sherman is quoted in the Matt Wilder guidebook, "Rope climbing at Hueco is like drinking wine at Oktoberfest."

The Texas Longroute (1,640', IV 5.10+ R), a left-to-right girdle traverse across the Front Side of North Mountain at Hueco Tanks. *Ross Andrea Collection*

But after tweaking a muscle in my shoulder while bouldering, I turned to Nate and asked, "Do you want to go for the traverse today?" His eyes lit up. It was late in the day, but we drove over to the Front Side—the west-facing aspect of North Mountain. We started near the left end of the mountain on Cakewalk (5.6) and climbed up and down to enter chimneys or bypass seriously overhanging sections like the Cowboyography (5.13b/c) wall. This included a lot of new-routing on loose terrain, including a serious runout with tedious rock-craft gear placements after crossing Purple Microdot (5.10).

Another serious section traversed from Uriah's Heap to the first anchors on Sea of Holes (5.10-). This pitch is dead horizontal, about 80' above the ground, and a fall by either climber would result in serious injury. Since the park closes at 6 p.m., we rappelled down Sea of Holes.

On our second outing, a week later, we quickly simuled all the terrain we'd covered on the first try. We then followed Indecent Exposure (5.9+) before making a final upward traverse to the Pink Adrenaline anchors near the top of the mountain. We had climbed 900' in a few hours and added a great adventure climb to the Front Side. However, back on the porch, I realized that although our route was gigantic for Texas, it was not *the* longest route in the state. That distinction belonged to the obscure Grand Canonical Finale, a 1,200' traverse at Enchanted Rock.

A week later, Nate came up to me with a big smile on his face. "I found the *true*

start of the traverse," he said. The next day we were at the entrance to the Cueva de Leon sector, several hundred feet farther left than where we'd started before. We climbed through a massive hole that led into a horizontal tunnel, with the pitch ending after a wild step to a magnificent perch about 50' up in the cave. The next two pitches had more of the same. We dubbed this three-pitch start The 4-Dimensional Time Tunnel (5.8).

We traversed above Flake Roof and around the corner to the Hourglass. Now simuling, I led the way, placing our smallest cams in good horizontal seams. As I neared the bolted anchors of Cakewalk, where we'd started earlier, I heard Nate yell, "Falling!" A handhold had broken. Thankfully, one of the small cams prevented what could have been a much more serious fall.

We continued and I eventually reached the top of the mountain, unware that, below me, Nate was being attacked by Hueco's notoriously aggressive bees. But he was fine and soon reached the top. After 1,640' of climbing up, down, sideways, and through caves, we had completed the longest route in Texas. Back at camp, Nate's dad suggested an inspired name: The Texas Longroute (1,640', 16 pitches, IV 5.10+ R).

Unhappy about his fall, Nate dragged me back a final time in April. We simuled the entire thing in just over two hours, completing the first no-fall, no-bee ascent. 📄 🔍

—**Ross Andrea**

Canada

BRITISH COLUMBIA | Coast Mountains

Nakula Spire, showing the line of Quartz Arête (600m on the rock buttress, 5.9), and Mt. Arjuna on the right. Arjuna's northwest ridge (the probable line of the 1952 first ascent) finishes along the right skyline. *Andrew Councell*

ARJUNA SPIRES, NAKULA SPIRE AND OTHER CLIMBS

The town of Bella Coola rests in a deep, shadowed fjord along the central coast of British Columbia, amid the Great Bear Rainforest. Similar to Squamish, Bella Coola is surrounded by huge granite cliffs, many of which have rock climbing routes. However, the incredible nearby peaks are largely hidden by steep-sided valleys too arduous to climb.

Guiding heli-skiers throughout the area for many years, I've marveled at the climbing potential visible from a bird's-eye view. Finally, in a culmination of years of desire to climb these mountains, mixed with a fatalistic shrug toward my bank account, I planned an exploratory trip with my brother Daniel.

In early August, we took a ten-minute flight southeast from the Bella Coola Airport and landed on a mellow glacier below Mt. Arjuna (2,787m), one of the few

named peaks in the area. (Arjuna was first climbed in 1952, most likely by the obvious line of the northwest ridge.) During our trip, we did a number of first ascents up to 5.11, including a five-pitch route, Friends in High Places (5.11a), up an overhanging formation we called Sahadeva Spire, at the east end of the Arjuna group. We did a number of single-pitch routes on the Bhima Buttress, alongside the Arjuna Glacier. We also climbed Mt. Arjuna by its northwest ridge. (Details of these climbs can be found by searching "Arjuna Spires" at Mountain Project.) However, our new route up the north side of a big spire just east of Arjuna was the highlight.

From camp, we hiked about an hour across the Arjuna Glacier, passing a few devious crevasses, to the toe of the north-facing arête. Armed with one battery for our drill, a dozen bolts, and one rope, we had the tools to instill extra confidence while not overequipping ourselves. We climbed in boots, smedging up clean, solid, whitish rock and then into furry, lichen-covered steps for the first 300m, with difficulties mostly in the 4th- to low-5th-class range. This lower ridge terminates at a headwall through which a quartz band diagonals up and left. We encountered a couple of steeper pitches (around 5.8) on very good quartzite, with decent protection. Moving onto the final arête, the angle eased off for a bit before rearing into the crux, climbing through a small notch. The top was then a few short, easy pitches away.

We quickly downclimbed to the top of the crux and from this point began rappelling, using bolts and fixed nuts. Rather than diagonal back along the line of ascent, we rapped a bit more directly. We downclimbed much of the last 300m of low-5th-class terrain, rapping off single bolts through steeper steps in the waning light. After 14 hours on the go, we reached camp, thrilled to have climbed such an amazing line at moderate difficulties.

We called the route Quartz Arête (600m on the rock buttress, 5.9), due to the large quantities of quartz crystals we passed. I called the tower Nakula Spire after one of Arjuna's four brothers. My hope is that continued development of climbing in the Bella Coola backcountry will encourage fellow adventure seekers to discover this untapped arena of alpine climbing potential. 📄 📷

—**Andrew Councell,** *Canada*

WADDINGTON RANGE, SERRA PEAKS, EAST–WEST TRAVERSE

As the moon rose from behind a jagged ridgeline, the world exploded beyond the fading beam of my headlamp. I struggled to comprehend the scale of the mountains in front of me. From down on the Tiedemann Glacier, the monolith of Mt. Waddington rose 2,000m above us. The moon reflected brightly off glacial seracs cascading down shattered black rock. On the other side of the valley, innumerous sharp granite spires protruded from broken icefalls, like

Ethan Berman starting up the Duck 'n' Cover Couloir (climber's right) after rappelling down the Serra 4–5 Couloir on the left. The previous year's accident occurred halfway down the 4–5 Couloir. The steep granite on the lower half of Serra 5's north face (directly above) is unclimbed. *Matteo Agnoloni*

nails hammered through wood. The days we'd spent swirling in the clouds above felt like a dream.

As dawn cracked like a yolk on the horizon, we made our way back up 800m of talus and bare ice to the Plummer Hut. We had left our previous camp at 6 p.m., perched on a high col between Serra 5 (3,579m) and Mt. Asperity (3,716m). We reached the hut at 6 a.m., and by early afternoon, after a long helicopter flight, we were at a beach bar in Campbell River. "Looks like you guys have been out hiking," the waitress said. I suppose you could say that.

A couple of weeks earlier, in mid-July, bad weather had taken hold after an exceptionally dry spring. Although Matteo Agnoloni, Sebastian Pelletti, and I were poised to launch into the Waddington Range, we had to wait patiently in Squamish to see if our opportunity would come. Finally, on July 31, we committed to what looked to be a good window of clear weather, which unfortunately (and not all that surprisingly) didn't quite pan out. We took the ferry to Vancouver Island, boarded a helicopter in Campbell River, and flew 150km north to the Plummer Hut, perched above the Tiedemann and Tellot glaciers.

Our goal was a "reverse traverse" of the Serra Peaks, from east to west (Serra

The five Serra Peaks from the north in winter. The east-to-west traverse (left to right) took three days, followed by an all-day rest at the Serra 5–Asperity Mountain col (far right) and an all-night descent to the south to reach the Tiedemann Glacier. *John Scurlock*

1 to 5), plus whatever peaks we could reach beyond. These spires have been traversed twice in the opposite direction (Croft-Foweraker-Serl, 1985, and Bunker-Haley, 2004) during traverses of the full Waddington Range. The conditions we found were far from ideal. Amid low visibility and light flurries, the Serra spires were in full mixed conditions, which made for really fun climbing, but much slower than anticipated.

From the Plummer Hut, we headed up the Tellot Glacier and camped in a white-out. On August 1, we started up the north face of Serra 1 (5.7 55°), simul-climbing from the 'schrund all the way to the summit. On Serra 2, we climbed a new route on the northeast aspect, which we called Nor'easter (230m, M5); it had a five-star iced-up chimney pitch leading directly to the summit. We descended from Serra 2 and camped. It was storming in the morning, so we stayed put and then climbed for just a few hours in the afternoon, summiting Serra 3 and camping just below the top.

Farther along the traverse, we faced the emotional stress of revisiting the scene of a rappelling accident during our attempt on

the same traverse in 2022. While rappelling from Serra 4 and down the north side of Serra 5, Matteo and I triggered some rockfall and Matteo was hit in the thigh, suffering a deep laceration and partially severed quad muscle and tendon, leading to an extrication by Bella Coola SAR (*see Accidents in North American Climbing 2023*).

Thankfully, this year the rappels went smoothly: two raps off Serra 4, then some downclimbing on snow, and four more rappels down the Serra 4–5 Couloir. We then opened a new route up Serra 5 by a hidden couloir full of blue ice and a stellar mixed pitch that connected us to the existing routes on the upper north face, which were caked in wet snow. We called it Duck 'n' Cover Couloir (400m, AI3 M6, with 200m of new terrain at AI3 M5). Given the snowy, insecure nature of the climbing, we likely chose a harder line than necessary, opting for steep terrain with better protection rather than low-angle slab.

It was cool to make the first ascent of Serra 5 coming from the east, a puzzle that had confounded climbers since the 1950s and '60s. The east face is unappealing, consisting of vertical and

loose basalt. I surmise that the idea of rappelling down the north side and climbing ice back up was not a feasible option given the equipment and techniques of earlier eras. It is a simple solution with V-threads and modern ice equipment.

After a 20-hour day to climb Serra 4 and 5 in tough conditions, we found ourselves at the Serra 5–Asperity col around midnight on the third day of the traverse. The forecast was for two more days of seemingly good weather before another big storm. We tried to rationalize continuing to Asperity, Tiedemann, Combatant, and ultimately Waddington, but given our pace, it seemed all too likely we might end up descending from Waddington on the heavily crevassed Bravo Glacier in a vicious coastal storm. We decided to escape while we could.

The most accessible escape route was Carl's Couloir, which in good conditions would consist of downclimbing snow slopes for 1,400m. I was nervous to commit to an unfamiliar south-facing descent given the late-season conditions on the lower mountain, but the alternative was to reverse the traverse, which was certainly not appealing. After a full day of lounging in the sun, we started down in the evening to mitigate the threat of overhead hazards. My skepticism about the descent was well-founded, as we spent 12 hours rappelling chossy cliffs recently exposed from snowmelt, huge broken bergschrunds, and a 40° glacial tongue littered in debris that severely damaged our carabiners and belay devices in only two rappels. Finally we reached the relative safety of the Tiedemann Glacier and then trudged back up to the Plummer Hut.

As with other ranges around the world, it may be time to rethink the climbing season in this part of the Coast Mountains. High-pressure systems in the traditional season of late July and August now bring warmer temperatures that exacerbate hazards. Many of the snow, ice, and glacier routes in the guidebook, as well as approaches to the rock spires, are becoming inaccessible, and descent options are deteriorating. Steve Swenson wasn't far off when he told me that the Waddington Range is "as hazardous as the Canadian Rockies." Yet with the right partners, motivation, and mentality, the experience and solitude of climbing in the range are hard to beat. 📷

—Ethan Berman, *Canada*

TOP: Sebastian Pelletti climbing steep granite on the south side of the Serra 3–4 ridge. The climbers rappelled twice in this section to avoid a large gendarme and regain the ridge farther along. *Ethan Berman*

BOTTOM: Matteo Agnoloni and Pelletti traversing the ridge between Serra 1 and Serra 2 on the first day. *Ethan Berman*

Mt. Klattasine (2,561m), left of center, is the high point of the Klattasine Ridge and was first climbed, solo, by John Clarke in 1974, following the prominent southeast gully (1). The next formation to the right now has two routes: (2) Warbird (Beckey-Diedrich-Nelson, 1987) and (3) The Lonesome Crowded West (Pelletti-Stanhope, 2023). *Kieran Brownie*

KLATTASINE RIDGE, THE LONESOME CROWDED WEST

Inspired by a 1988 *Canadian Alpine Journal* that I'd found lying around during a piss-wet Squamish spring day, Kieran Brownie, Seb Pelletti, and I ventured onto the Klattasine Ridge in August. Given all of my trips to other parts of British Columbia (mostly the Bugaboos), I had spent an embarrassingly small amount of time in the Coast Mountains in my own backyard.

Located at the northwestern corner of the Homathko Icefield, the Klattasine Ridge is named after a chief of the Chilcotin (Tsilhqot'in) people. Klattasine was a major figure in the 1864 Chilcotin War, a gruesome conflict in B.C.'s history. The highest point of the ridge, Mt. Klattasine (2,561m), was climbed solo by John Clarke in 1974, following a gully up the southeast face. A trip in August 1987 by Carl Diedrich, Jim Nelson, and Fred Beckey yielded two fine new routes in the big south cirque of the Klattasine Ridge

on what they deemed excellent granite. In 1998, Bill Durtler, Bruce Fairley, and Kirt Sellers climbed a 12-pitch 5.8 up the southwest buttress of the southernmost tower in the cirque, which they called Tootsie Roll Tower. To our knowledge, no climbers have ventured back there since.

Flying out of Bluff Lake on August 14 in Mike King's helicopter, we set up camp south of the towers in a little snow basin about ten minutes' walk from the peaks. We immediately set our sights on repeating Golden Klattasine, the Diedrich-Nelson route up a west-facing formation on the right side of the cirque; they reported about 450m of climbing at 5.10 A2. We encountered a very loose flake feature on the lower half of the climb that I climbed gingerly; it flexed every time I exerted hand-jam force on it. Other than this, the stone was excellent. Our ascent cleaned up the lichen on the route considerably; we freed it on top-rope, and it is ripe for a future redpoint.

After topping out, we descended the north side of the formation and then back through a notch to the south. This was in many ways the crux of the day: dusty, steep tiptoeing down a long slab rife with loose blocks. In the future I would recommend a careful rappel descent of the Golden Klattasine route, as there are many bolted belays from the first ascent.

Next, we set our sights on the southeast face of another formation climbed by the 1987 team; their route Warbird climbed the prow of the first prominent formation east of Mt. Klattasine. A perfect, left-facing open book at around half height, to the right of the 1987 route, struck us as the king line of the wall. We spent an afternoon questing around to see if it was feasible. The dots looked like they connected, so we fixed around 100m of static line to the ground, fired up for a bid the next day.

After an early start with some coffee and maté, Seb and I Micro Traxioned our fixed line

Will Stanhope and Seb Pelletti on a 5.11 pitch on The Lonesome Crowded West, a 400-meter route up the Warbird formation. *Kieran Brownie*

while Kieran flew his drone to gather footage. A crisp finger and hand crack gained the corner. It felt similar to the Split Pillar on the Stawamus Chief, and we were overjoyed at our good fortune. By midafternoon we were on top, where we found an enormous cairn standing vigil. With epic views of Mt. Bute (2,810m) to the south and the Waddington Range to the north, we felt elated to be in such a remote, special place. We rappelled the route, adding bolted anchors with a power drill. [*The 1987 party rappelled and downclimbed to climber's left of the formation to reach the Clarke route on Klattasine and continued down from there.*]

Our pickup was delayed for a day while Mr. King was busy fighting forest fires. We spent the day reading and relaxing, spitballing names for our new route, and enjoying this beautiful little cirque deep in the Coast Range. I'd been listening to my favorite Modest Mouse album on repeat throughout the summer, and eventually suggested the name The Lonesome Crowded West (400m, 5.11). The Klattasine, while lonely, is certainly not crowded, and it's a far cry from the sad, monochromatic mallscapes of the Pacific Northwest, as described in the lyrics by the guys from Issaquah, Washington. Not so far as the eagle flies, but a different Cascadia entirely. 📷

—Will Stanhope, *Canada*

ABOVE: Mt. Habrich from the north, showing (1) the upper pitches of Life in Space (27 pitches, 5.10, completed in 2022) and (2) Blood Moon (2023). *Colin Moorhead*

LEFT: Jacob Cook on the crux pitch (5.13a) of Blood Moon on Mt. Habrich. *Pim Shaitosa*

SQUAMISH AREA, MT. HABRICH, NEW ROUTES

Mt. Habrich (1,792m) is located high above Squamish and is accessible either via the Sea to Sky Gondola, followed by a hike of about two hours on the Sky Pilot Valley Trail, or by hiking the Sea to Sky Trail to the upper gondola station, adding 900m of elevation gain to your day.

Recently there has been a renaissance in development on Habrich, including a 300m 5.13a trad climb called Blood Moon on the peak's north face. This route was completed during the summer of 2023 by Jacob Cook and Drew Marshall, and is characterized by steep, challenging crack climbing for five pitches (5.12b, 5.13a, 5.12a, 5.9 R, and 5.12d). Another 180m of 5.7 leads to the top. Cook described the crux as a thin tips crack protected by small offset cams. Both Cook and Marshall sent all the pitches.

In September 2022, Colin Moorhead and Nick McNutt completed Life in Space, a 27-pitch 5.10b route that finishes on Mt. Habrich. Life in Space starts by climbing The Goldilocks Zone, an earlier route established by Moorhead, McNutt, Nick Bejcar, and Jamie Selda in 2021, located on the Stawamus River Headwall. (This cliff is below the northeast side of Mt. Habrich and is accessed by a separate approach involving a 4WD road and a hike of 45 to 60 minutes.) The Goldilocks Zone on its own features 15 pitches of climbing up to 5.10-. From the top, a brief hike accesses the northeast ridge of Habrich, with another 12 pitches up to 5.10. Culminating on the summit, the link-up totals 750m of technical terrain, the longest climb in the Sea to Sky region.

Additionally, in May 2023, Jim and Jola Sandford added Earthshine, a 200m 5.10 route, to the south face of Mt. Habrich.

—**Whitney Clark,** *AAJ*

LILLOOET RANGE, TRAVERSE OF THE SEASONS

Our hopes of taking my 4WD up Kwoiek Creek Forest Service Road were squashed by an impassable slide only a couple of hundred meters up the road. Seb Gulka and I were heading to the long alpine ridgeline that leads westward over four peaks (informally named Winter, Autumn, Summer, and Spring) to the summit of Skihist Mountain (2,968m). I didn't quite realize what I was getting into, as

The Traverse of the Seasons from the southeast. The traverse went from right to left over Winter, Autumn, Summer, and Spring peaks to reach Skihist Mountain (2,968m), the highest summit left of center. *Alessandro Lanius-Pascuzzi*

Seb had fueled this idea and done much more research. Notably, the traverse was attempted by Robert Nugent, Margaret Saul, and Don Serl in July 1995; they bivouacked between Summer and Spring and bailed in a storm the next day (*see Canadian Alpine Journal 1997*).

We walked ten kilometers up the Kwoiek Creek Road, then turned onto the poorly maintained North Kwoiek Road (where we'd hoped to park) and then into alder thickets. When we finally broke free of the steep bushwhacking, we found ourselves in a beautiful alpine bowl. Gaining the ridge, we rambled along the crest to a sheltered nook with a patch of snow for water about three kilometers east of Winter Peak (2,446m). We stopped there for a starlit bivy.

In the morning, we continued to the straightforward 3rd-class scramble up Winter's east ridge, then down the southwest ridge. Autumn's northeast buttress was much steeper and more formidable. We found a stunningly white quartz ramp that led to some low-5th-class steps, then followed the northeast buttress up solid and sustained 4th class. Beyond Autumn Peak (2,784m), the rock quickly deteriorated as we downclimbed the south ridge. We continued over loose 3rd class to the summit of Summer Peak (2,713m), then descended once again, eyeing up the northeast ridge of Spring Peak (2,822m), which was steep straight out of the col.

After we traversed the right side of the ridge along loose 4th-class blocks, Seb belayed me up to the crest by a short 5.7 chimney that protected nicely with our small rack of cams. After a bit more 4th class, we reached the top of Spring. Continuing toward Skihist, we romped along and around large orange blocks that jutted above the ridgeline—mostly low 5th class save for one memorable gaston move. From the summit, we hopped down orange talus and bivvied in the bowl between Skihist and Antimony Mountain (2,668m).

In the morning, we headed up the north ridge of Antimony, then down green slopes on the south face, dropping back toward the overgrown Kwoiek Creek Road. What followed was a creek crossing, more alder thrashing, a nest of angry yellowjackets, and a much more difficult crossing of the hip-deep, fast-moving creek. Climbing out of the water, we finally gained a section of the forest road that was in good shape, leaving us with nothing but 20km of road hiking to go. I plugged into my iPod to distract myself from tired legs and battered feet.

All in all, it was an amazing adventure, following about ten kilometers of alpine ridgeline to the tallest peak in southwest British Columbia. Despite being only a few hours from Vancouver, this spectacular area is rarely traveled. 📖 📷

—**Alessandro Lanius-Pascuzzi,**
Canada

SLESSE MASSIF, MT. PARKES, RUSSIAN ROULETTE

In early June, Will Kovacic and Jeremy Roulette climbed a route up the east side of Mt. Parkes (ca 2,100m), a summit on the long Crossover Ridge that runs north from Slesse Mountain. The two had been aiming to climb the North Rib of Slesse, but snow on that route prompted them to change plans. Instead, they climbed a broken buttress in about nine pitches to reach the summit of Parkes, near the Crossover Pass descent route from Slesse, then continued along the ridge and upper North Rib to Slesse's top. They called the new route Russian Roulette (5.9). 📷

—Information from Will Kovacic

B.C. | Selkirk Mountains

VALHALLA PROVINCIAL PARK, GLADSHEIM PEAK, SOUTH FACE

Sara Lilley and Isobel Phoebus had been to the Valhallas the prior summer, making an ascent of the complete north ridge of Little Dag (Lussier-Senecal, 2015). The south face of Gladsheim Peak (2,830m), the highest summit of the Valhallas, caught their eyes, and later they learned that the last route on this face had been put up 15 years earlier. They reached out to me about some potential new-routing, and, since I was on sabbatical from my job as a wildfire crew leader, I was able to say yes to summer adventures for the first time in eight seasons.

In mid-August, we made the approach to Mulvey Basin, and during the first week there we climbed the classic West Ridge (Deane-Oswald-Stewart-Stovel-Williams, 1963) and the South Dihedral (Koedt-Rowat, 1974) on Gladsheim and Etoile Filante (Lussier-Shute, 2011) on Asgard Peak (2,825m). The idea was to immerse ourselves in the history of adventurous climbing in this area, much of which took place in the 1960s and 1970s.

After studying the south face of Gladsheim for over a week, a line was obvious. The anticipated crux, a hanging, serrated left-facing corner in the center of the face, lit up in the morning sun. We packed a drill, a small bolt kit, pins, offset nuts, and a triple rack of cams.

On the first day, Sara launched up the 55m opening pitch, and Isobel and I followed, enjoying the flowy movement along granitic cracks. We swapped leads

The line of Crystal Pocket (435m, 5.10d), which leads to the West Ridge of Gladsheim Peak (2,830m). *Sasha Yasinski*

to reach the top of pitch three, feeling surprised and elated at how good this line was proving to be.

Returning the next day, we continued to the summit ridge of Gladsheim, completing Crystal Pocket (435m, 5.10d) clean and free. I was lucky to lead the crux pitch, discovering a magical pocket full of crystals on my way into the overhanging terrain. Good finger locks, wild stemming, and solid protection brought me to the top of the intimidating roof section. I smiled, lichen in my teeth, as I hauled the bags.

Our line bisects the south face of Gladsheim, climbing six pitches of cracks before joining a 5.6 corner system for 100m and then some low-5th-class scrambling. The upper West Ridge leads on to the

summit. [*The new route is left of the Beckey-Martinson Route (1976)
and may briefly follow an earlier line that is not well-documented.*]
We had the West Ridge descent dialed from our previous mission,
efficiently rappelling several short rock steps to reach the descent
gully in about three hours.

Sasha Yasinski below
the crux of Crystal
Pocket (435m, 5.10d)
on the south face
of Gladsheim Peak
(2,830m). *Isobel
Phoebus*

As we hiked back to camp, we began to doubt this route had
never been climbed—it was too good to be true. We held off from
celebrating until we could meet guidebook author David Lussier
over coffee at Nelson's famous Oso Negro and realized we had
achieved our trip's purpose: an all-female first ascent in the
Valhallas. [*This trip was supported by a Jen Higgins Grant for Young
Women from the Alpine Club of Canada.*] 📄 📷 ▶️

—**Sasha Yasinski,** *Canada*

ALBERTA | Jasper National Park

OLDHORN MOUNTAIN, LUNCHLORD BUTTRESS

In 2021, during a traverse of the Trident Range (*AAJ 2022*),
Maarten van Haeren noticed the big, steep northeast face of
Oldhorn Mountain (ca 3,000m) to the south. It had about 600m of
quartzite (the good stuff in the Rockies). Although it was hard to
imagine the face hadn't been climbed, I remembered that this is
the Rockies, and these days the majority of climbers focus on sport
projects or flock to Squamish for splitter cracks.

So there we were, on July 8, at 3:30 a.m., looking down at the
peanut butter and banana bagels in my Tacoma. "Coffee first," I
declared, and then off we went to the Tonquin Valley trailhead. A
kilometer down the trail, I realized that I had left my lunch bagel
in the truck. "Guide's lunch, good for two," we laughed, repacking

Lunchlord Buttress (600m, 5.10+) on the northeast face of Oldhorn Mountain. The summit is out of frame to the left. *Ethan Berman*

our shared bag below Oldhorn.

Maarten's first block led through steep and exposed corners, which were surprisingly moderate thanks to the plethora of crisp, square edges. Progress slowed on pitch three, as the singing of Maarten's hammer indicated his tenuous position. I followed his great lead up the "Beak Pitch," struggling to remove the Peckers he had placed to protect delicate face climbing.

Our route continued up a deep corner to a roof, then four pitches over moderate terrain. I skirted two massive gendarmes, then followed an exposed fin to a headwall. A steep black corner veered upward, with loose blocks and grainy features; the climbing on the "Zion Pitch" was technical and serious. More steep, burly climbing waited above. I haven't done enough Rockies summer choss wrangling to say for sure, but I thought this climbing was pretty good. "Way better than your average Rockies alpine route!" Maarten exclaimed, reaching the end of the rope-stretching pitch we called "The Corner."

We were now in the middle of the

headwall. The turquoise Astoria River ran far below in the valley; to the east, the summit of Mt. Edith Cavell seemed close to level with our position. Maarten climbed two pitches of easy, loose ground—not what we'd expected halfway up the headwall, but mountain features are often more three-dimensional than they appear from below. The final pitch was marked by white and pink quartzite, in horizontal stacks, full of discontinuous roofs. I nibbled half a bar and started up the wild "Bloc Party Pitch," climbing slowly and meticulously, placing big cams, and pulling on juggy holds into and around corners and roofs. Cresting the ridge, I brought Maarten up to where we could finally sit down, coil the ropes, and take the climbing shoes off our throbbing feet.

We scrambled the final hundred meters, blocks leaning this way and that, somehow suspended above the abyss. It was 7:30 p.m., 10.5 hours since we had started. The 600m route had gone at 5.10+.

With three hours of daylight left and a long, convoluted descent ahead of us, we shared the last candy bar and began the downclimb, heading more or less southwest on loose ledges and through scree hell. The next evening, we were back in Canmore. "Hah!" Maarten's wife, Lin, remarked to him. "You were like Ethan's lunch lady...the Lunchlord!" 📄 📷

—**Ethan Berman**, *Canada*

NUNAVUT | Baffin Island

AUYUITTUQ NATIONAL PARK, MT. ASGARD, LOKI'S MISCHIEF

On June 23, as Waldo Etherington, Leo Houlding, and I flew into Pangnirtung (Pangniqtuuq), pure excitement surged as we gazed upon the magnificent valley we would be exploring for the next month and a half, contrasted by trepidation as we observed the first of many hurdles. The fjord was still frozen, but large leads crossed the ice, preventing travel by boat or snow machine. This meant an additional 20-mile hike just to reach the trailhead. The initial miles proved to be the most challenging, with deep, boggy tundra, difficult river crossings, and heavy packs.

During the arduous approach to Mt. Asgard (2,015m), we crossed the Arctic Circle and retrieved a gear cache dropped by outfitter Peter Kilabuk earlier that winter on a snow machine. After seven challenging days, we reached Summit Lake, which would serve as our base camp.

We spent about a dozen days shuttling gear and waiting out storms, hoping to climb the north side of Asgard. But continuous rainy weather made that impossible. Remaining optimistic, we established a new camp at the northeast toe of Asgard's North Tower.

Right of the classic 1972 route (Braithwaite-Hennek-Nunn-Scott), we eyed a line of striking discontinuous splitters up the center of the east buttress. The line appeared challenging for the first 200m and dried out faster than anything else around. We picked away at it whenever the weather allowed. On pitch two, I quested left through mantels and flakes, hand-drilling our only bolt of the route from a stance and placing beaks for protection. Pitch four proved to be a challenging beak seam that Waldo aided through the rain at A3.

Nearing the bottom of our food supply, we seized a weather window to attempt our route to the top. I top-roped the fourth-pitch seam at 5.13-, then Leo and I alternated leads in blocks, climbing long pitches of mostly 5.11 in a fix-and-follow style, while Waldo, in hero style, jugged with a large backpack of bivy gear. We slept on ledges at the top of pitch nine, as the sun traveled slightly under the northern horizon before rising again.

After 12 new pitches, we connected with the Scott Route and followed it to the summit, free climbing the wet crux offwidth and completing a total of 29 pitches. We called our 500m alternate start to the 1972 route Loki's Mischief

The first 11 pitches of Loki's Mischief (500m of new climbing, 5.11+ R A3). Prior routes up this buttress are not shown. *Wilson Cutbirth*

(total of 1,300m, 5.11+ R A3). [*Several other lines have been completed on the lower east buttress of the North Tower, including Line of Credit (Condon-Easton-Prohaska, 1998) and Whiskey Gonzales (Favresse-Favresse, 2009), both to the right of Loki's Mischief, and the Brazeau-Walsh Route (2009) to the left.*]

Experiencing the greatness of Baffin when the weather cooperates, we were hungry for more but out of food and time. The expedition concluded with Loki teasing us one last time, with splitter weather for our walk out. 📷

—**Wilson Cutbirth,** *USA*

CORONATION GLACIER AREA, FOUR NEW ROUTES

The ice around me gleamed as I slid into my dry suit. I fashioned an improvised harness out of skinny Dyneema and tied in—it hardly seemed like real life as James slowly lowered me down steep ice into cobalt-blue water. I stretched across the moat and grabbed beautiful golden granite. Soon, the three others were sliding across a taut rope and racking up at the base of our fourth new route—likely

Noah Besen on The Salami Exchange Commission (800m, V 5.10), above the Coronation Glacier. *James Klemmensen*

the fourth climb ever established near the outlet of the Coronation Glacier in southern Auyuittuq National Park.

Shira Biner, Amanda Bischke, James Klemmensen, and I had arrived in the village of Qikiqtarjuaq on July 7. Our plan was to paddle 70km south and west to Coronation Fjord using inflatable sea kayaks. However, the sea ice surrounding southern Baffin Island had not yet broken up. We had hoped to do this expedition as humanly powered as possible, but some things were out of our control. We compromised by asking outfitter Billy Arnaquq to deliver a large load of equipment and food to an island near the southern extent of the sea ice while we walked over the ice. After 20km, we arrived at our gear cache.

The next phase of our trip consisted of waiting and growing increasingly antsy. We dubbed the tiny spot where we were marooned Faffin Island—it accurately described how we felt by day five. Finally, we were able to shuttle massive loads of gear across the thinning ice, pack our boats, and carefully scoot them into the open water. We were off!

The rest of our journey to Coronation Fjord was relatively uneventful. After 50km of paddling, we arrived at the end of the fjord and began another gear shuttle ten kilometers up the valley to our base camp.

Finally it was time to climb. Alpine new-routing in such a wild environment is not easy, and successes and failures came in equal measure. On their first attempt, Amanda and Shira learned several critical things about the Coronation Glacier. One was that traveling up the glacier was easy, but traveling laterally involved stream crossing after stream crossing. Second, they discovered that the cleanest-looking walls lacked continuous crack systems.

In time, we managed to complete four routes between rainstorms and rest days. James and I climbed two long routes: The Salami Exchange Commission (800m, V 5.10) on a prominent buttress on the north side of the Coronation Glacier, and Escape from Azkaban (650m, IV 5.10+), above the north side of the glacier's north arm. Amanda and Shira teamed up for The Big G (350m, III 5.8), a pretty ridge on the south side of the glacier. All four of us joined forces for our final climb, back up the north arm. A glacial lake guarded a beautiful ridge of golden rock—so that's when I got to don the dry suit to set up a Tyrolean traverse. Bathed in pale Arctic sunlight, we completed Raise the Drawbridge (300m, III 5.10-), with breathtaking views over the Penny Ice Cap, a perfect ending for our 20 days by the Coronation Glacier.

After hiking out and paddling 70km back to Qikiqtarjuaq, we departed the village on August 19. Our expedition was supported by a Cutting Edge Grant from the AAC and a Jen Higgins Grant for Young Women from the Alpine Club of Canada. [*More details and coordinates of climbs are at the AAJ website.*] 📄 📷 🔍

—Noah Besen, *USA*

GRINNELL GLACIER AREA, NEW ROUTES

One hundred and fifty kilometers southeast of Iqaluit is the broad ice cap of the Grinnell Glacier and the Everett Mountains, rising more than 600m from the ocean. The tallest peak, at 2,230', is

Angijuqqaaq, meaning "where the leader sits."

In July, after many days of canceled flights ended our hopes of heading north to Auyuittuq National Park, Erik Boomer, Sarah McNair-Landry, and I quickly shifted plans to a new area. Sarah and Erik had scouted the mountains around the Grinnell Glacier previously by boat, and after seeing a couple of photos, I was excited to explore.

Sarah and Erik convinced a friend to carry us to a cove near the north end of the glacier in his small boat. After two days, he waved goodbye, leaving us and our gear on shore. We set up camp by a creek with a view of the ice cap, only a couple kilometers from a polar bear we'd spotted on our way in.

It was early afternoon, but after establishing camp, we were so excited by the cirque of rocks surrounding us that we started questing up the southwest face of the closest formation. We were happy to find the rock was more than acceptable. Our first route involved perfect hand cracks and roofs, with a memorable pillar perch. We reached the summit in time to watch the sun set over Frobisher Bay, a beluga whale swim by, and a bear stroll along the coastline. Due to our late start, we had a short shiver bivy on top, so we called the route Power Nap (440m, 5.10).

TOP: Ky Hart soaking up the ambience from Faffin in Baffin. The team's base camp was near the mouth of the valley at right. *Erik Boomer*

BOTTOM: The line of Faffin in Baffin (14 pitches, 5.10), near the Grinnell Glacier. *Erik Boomer*

We next climbed the northeast face of a formation about 40 minutes' hike from camp. Faffin in Baffin (335m, 5.10) had 14 pitches of fun climbing, gradually getting harder as we made our way up and away from a massive rock scar.

Finally, Erik and I sought out a route on the gorgeous north-northeast face of Angijuqqaaq, our steepest line. We climbed 12 pitches of 5.10 to 5.11 cracks and decided to name it Polar Frenzy (300m, 5.11 C2), after a scary incident involving a polar bear the day before. [*Coordinates of the climbs and more information are at the AAJ website.*] 📷

—Ky Hart, *USA*

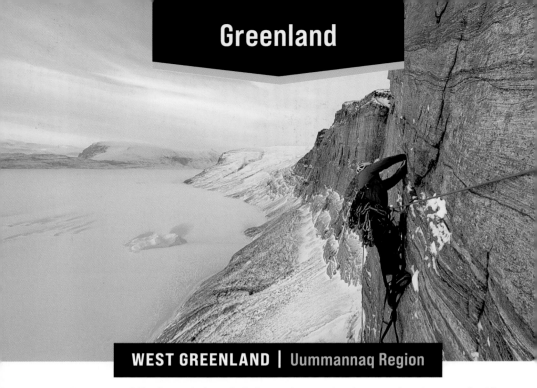

WEST GREENLAND | Uummannaq Region

Marcin Tomaszewski leading on the lower half of Fram. The ascent in February took 14 days. *Pawel Haldas*

OQATSSUT WALL, FRAM, WINTER FIRST ASCENT

Pawel Haldas and I quickly learned that the temperature in West Greenland varies enormously in winter, and speed is often key to success when one's access is dependent on sea ice. Our original goals lay on the walls of Storen, Uummannaq, and Agpat islands, but our local guide advised against them, warning that we could be stranded by melting ice. Instead, we set off on snowmobiles into the depths of the fjords, toward longer-lasting ice and walls that had been seen by local hunters.

We settled on a 6km-long cliff, locally known as Oqatssut Wall (70°42'13.82"N, 51°13'48.07"W), on the south coast of Qaqugdlugssuit peninsula, northeast of Storen. The right edge of the face, dropping directly into the fjord, was named Goliath Buttress by an American-Belgian team that climbed two routes there in 2014 (*AAJ 2015*).

On February 9, we pitched tents on the surface of the fjord, attaching them to the ice with screws. For cooking, we used ice from a nearby floe, as both the snow and fjord surface were salty. The following day, we packed our gear and headed for the southwest face, roughly 750m to the left of the 2014 routes. It took 14 days to climb to the top.

During the initial days the weather was sunny, but we experienced temperatures down to -40°C. On the lower wall, the climbing was not technically difficult yet proved very demanding due to loose rock. Sedimentary and metamorphic rocks prevail in this area, but the black bands of rock cutting completely across the face at two distinct points proved to be poor granite, with a high risk of spontaneous rockfall. Because of the brittle rock, we placed 12mm bolts at each belay for rappelling and hauling.

Seven hours of daylight meant we were unable to complete more than one or two pitches each day, either using aid or free climbing up to M5. Climbing at night was out of the question due to the cold. Every day we were on the verge of frostbite to toes and hands. A moment's carelessness would have ended our expedition.

Despite the cold and wind, the weather was fine and we made the most of each day. One of us would lead the whole day, wearing light clothes, while the other belayed in a down jacket and trousers. We fixed ropes progressively up about half of the route and slept at our fjord camp.

On the 18th, we hauled all our gear and the portaledge to the top of pitch nine, where there was a good snow shelf. We deliberately had not bivouacked lower for fear of damaging the ledge with falling debris.

After passing the second black rock band, Pawel took the lead on a demanding A3 pitch, while I stood beneath booming flakes, feeling like a condemned man at the guillotine. Bat-hook moves led to safer formations, and after a couple of hours, Pawel finished the pitch. I was proud of him: We now had the chance of reaching the top the next day—the last chance before a predicted spell of warming and 110 kph winds.

Oqatssut Wall from the approach above Uummannaq Fjord. The arrow marks the start of the 17-pitch route Fram. *Marcin Tomaszewski*

February 19 was windless and warmer than usual. I quickly led two long pitches of easy aid to the top of the wall, where we untied and walked up to the summit. One of the ice floes trapped in the frozen fjord reminded us of the ship *Fram* (the three-masted vessel that was used by Norwegian polar explorers Amundsen and Nansen), which may once have sailed below this wall. We named our new line Fram (700m of climbing, 17 pitches, M5 A3 C1).

We descended to the last bivouac and prepared for the next day's rappels—time was not on our side. Fortunately, we were able to reach our tents on the fjord by mid-day, finding them already sitting on melting pulp. We were collected by snowmobile and driven to Uummannaq. An hour after our arrival, the ice cracked and the route we had traveled from the wall closed. Two days later, much of the fjord had melted out.

This is likely the first big wall climbed in winter in Greenland. 📷

—Marcin Tomaszewski, *Poland*

MIRROR WALL, DIRECT WEST FACE, ATTEMPT

The spectacular 1,200m west face of Mirror Wall (2,030m) appeared on most climbers' radar during the first decade of the new millennium, when it was named and photographed by a British expedition. It was climbed in 2012, when a four-member Swiss team completed routes up both the left and right edges of the face (*AAJ 2013*). Three years later, a primarily British

Mirror Wall, showing (1) Midnight Solarium (2012), (2) Reflections (2015), (3) the 2023 attempt, and (4) Ledgeway to Heaven (2012). *Matt Pycroft | Coldhouse Collective | Berghaus*

team climbed the left side of the smooth central wall at 5.12c A3+ (*AAJ 2016*). In the summer of 2023, Ben Ditto (USA), Franco Cookson (U.K.), Nico Favresse and Seán Villanueva O'Driscoll (Belgium) went to try a new line right of center. The team sailed from Scotland, via Iceland, to Renland, then ferried loads up the 30km approach. During the initial carry, Favresse tripped and put a large gash in his leg, keeping him largely out of action.

The quartet established a camp atop a pillar toward the right edge of the wall and then broke left onto the central section. Here, Villanueva O'Driscoll took the lead. Highly run-out free climbing was interspersed with tenuous aid. He climbed with minimal bolting, often spending eight hours a day for around 40m of progress.

About halfway up the wall, having drilled a total of 18 holes, Villanueva O'Driscoll reached a corner leading to a crack system that might take them all the way to the summit. However, the corner proved to have blank, flaky rock with no protection. Twenty meters up, Villanueva O'Driscoll managed to place a bolt from a hook. He could see a cam placement four meters higher. For two days, he tried unsuccessfully to free or aid the upper corner, taking many falls. A team with strong personal ethics, the climbers had agreed that they could place bolts and then free climb or aid above them, but they would never place a bolt from another bolt, thus avoiding even a two-bolt ladder.

In the end, Villanueva O'Driscoll had to accept defeat. "In some ways,

the impossible is what makes climbing worthwhile…" he wrote later. "It cannot be the summit above all…. You have to give failure a chance, too."

—**Lindsay Griffin**, *AAJ*

HISTORICAL EXPEDITIONS IN RENLAND

An *AAJ 2018* **report** about an ascent of Grundtvigskirken in Renland mistakenly reported that an earlier name for this 1,977m formation—Penguin Tower—was proposed by a 1985 expedition. In fact, it was given this name by the 1987 team that visited this area in the yacht *Penguin*. The members were Daniel Caise, Philippe Cowez, Michèle Héralie, and me, all from Belgium.

On August 13 and 14, Daniel and Michèle climbed the south ridge to where it becomes very steep, then retreated due to inadequate equipment. [*The south ridge eventually was climbed in 1999.*] We then decided on another objective: triple-summited Peak 1,882m, about four kilometers to the southwest. On the 15th, Daniel and I climbed the northeast face, which presented no great difficulties. [*Reports in the AAJ and elsewhere credited the first ascent to a Swedish team in 1999.*] Given that Grundtvigskirken is the accepted name for the 1,977m summit we named Penguin, perhaps Peak 1,882m now could be called Penguin Tower.

I also went alone up a glacier immediately west of Skillbugt Fjord, naming this glacier Belgica. Where it bends west, I continued north into a side glacier that I named Glacier du Solitaire, and at the head of this, I climbed a summit at 71°12'07"N, 25°47'16"W and named it after my father—Pierre Baguet—who had helped purchase the yacht. [*Seemingly unnamed on today's maps, the Belgica Glacier system has since been explored by several parties. See the online version of this report, which also documents first ascents in 1991 by the author and partners near Mt. Shackleton in Goodenoughs Land.*] 📄 📷

—**Paul Baguet**, *Belgium*

EAST GREENLAND | Kangertitivatsiaq Fjord

CIRCUS MAXIMUS

A COMPLETE TRAVERSE OF THE MYTHICS CIRQUE AND OTHER ASCENTS

By Martin Feistl, *Germany*

In every part of Felix Bub's and my expedition to the Mythics Cirque, we placed the "how" above the "what." Our journey to East Greenland from Innsbruck was made by train and yacht. This resulted in a direct carbon cost of only 280kg per person, roughly the equivalent of a single-person car journey from Munich to Chamonix and back. All of our completed objectives were climbed free and emphatically without bolts. We climbed more than 3,000m of new ground in alpine style up to 7b+.

Arriving in the Mythics Cirque at the end of July, Felix and I spent August 1 to 3 making the first complete traverse of the Mythics. As seen from the shore, we climbed from left to right, creating a route we called Circus Maximus (39 hours of climbing, 6c). The route was comparable to the Peuterey Integrale on Mont Blanc, but looser. We belayed 22 pitches (2,130m of climbing), rappelled 14 times, and climbed 16 peaks and gendarmes, half of which were probably first ascents.

We began with the strangely named No Tower 1 East, then followed the rim of the cirque west, north, and then northeast to the last summit, Damocles, from which we descended southeast back to the valley. The new routes included a 270m 6a climb up Ganja Tower (a.k.a. the Squid), a long 6a/b route up Gendarme de Papi and Ataatap Tower, and Sirens of Change (6c) on Siren Tower. [*A full list of the summits and a description of the routes climbed on the Circus Maximus traverse is included with the online report.*]

From August 6–9, Felix and I made the second ascent of Forum (840m, 7c, 2021; see *AAJ 2022*) on Siren Tower. We took a portaledge and two haulbags. Every pitch was redpointed by the leader and climbed

The Mythics Cirque from the east. The 2023 traverse went from left to right, took three days, and crossed 16 peaks, many of them first ascents. (A) No Tower 1 East. (B) Ataatap Tower. (C) Siren Tower. (D) Aurora Tower. (E) Prometheus. (F) Tantalus. (G) Sysyphus. (H) Damocles. *Martin Feistl*

Felix Bub on the ninth pitch (7b) of Forum on Siren Tower. *Martin Feistl*

without falls by the second; both of us led the crux pitch free.

Low on the route, we climbed a four-pitch variant, taking a path of least resistance somewhere between Forum and The Wall of Planck (also established in 2021). On pitch nine I avoided the second bolt on Forum by a hard traverse right and a devious line back left via hollow flakes. [*This variation was climbed by the first ascensionists on their way down after climbing the route.*] It took four attempts to lead this. Near the top, we also diverged from the original line, probably following parts of The Wall of Planck before moving farther left. From the summit, we descended the wall following an almost fully equipped rappel piste.

Back in base camp, Michelle Dvorak and Fay Manners, whom we knew from before, turned up unexpectedly at the tent door. Over the 13th and 14th, the four of us attempted a new route on Siren Tower, right of The Wall of Planck. We turned around after completing seven pitches (245m of climbing), up to 7b onsight and with two pitches that were not redpointed, probably in the French 8th grade. We retreated having reached an unprotected section. I was simply too weak mentally after a demanding first day on the wall, immediately after climbing Forum, to decipher the remaining five meters of free climbing above a micro-cam.

It would have been easy to place a bolt that would have allowed us to continue and probably complete the whole line. However, we strongly criticize the current development in the Mythics Cirque, and elsewhere in Greenland, regarding the use of bolts. Justifying bolts purely for safety or convenience reasons is not sustainable.

Later, while climbing a new route on Ataatap Tower, we were disturbed by the awful roar of a power drill used by a Spanish women's team that had arrived in the area. They placed bolted anchors on their route to aid a rappel descent of the face. In my opinion, given that the rock here is so easily protectable, this shouldn't be an argument made by an elite national alpine team. It will relegate Ataatap Tower, which is strategically very difficult to access and descend, to a one-day undertaking.

To keep the adventurous character of climbing in Greenland and leave space for future parties, there must be a rethink toward less egoism when putting up new routes and toward a much greater acceptance of failure among the climbing community. [*The author's new route on the northeast face of Ataatap Tower, climbed with Dvorak and Manners (Bub had injured his shoulder and was unable to climb) is described on the next page.*] 🗎 📷

(A) Ganja Tower. (B) Ataatap Tower. (C) Siren Tower and approximate lines of (1) Coronis (2012), starting on the back, (2) Rostoll Verbenero (2023), (3) The Mental Breakdown (2023), (4) Daddy's Sweet Tooth (2021), (5) Built Fjord Tough (2012), (6) La Jubi (2023), and (7) Northeast Face (2018). *Martin Feistl*

MYTHICS CIRQUE, ATAATAP TOWER, THE MENTAL BREAKDOWN; CHASTITY TOWER, THE PRINCESS BRIDES

Fay Manners (U.K.) and I arrived in Tasiilaq on August 7, after a delay of several weeks due to reports of impassable sea ice in the east coast fjords. A boatman then took us on a journey north of about 350km, and on the 10th we arrived in the alpine valley of the Mythics Cirque.

There, we ran into Felix Bub and Martin Feistl, who had arrived two weeks previously by yacht. The two had recently repeated Forum (840m, 7c, 2021) on the north face of Siren Tower and had scoped a new line on the face that looked inspiring. The four of us spent two days attempting this line, but retreated after encountering a blank section that we were unable to free climb without placing a bolt (*see previous story*).

A few days later, on the morning of the 17th, Fay, Martin, and I found ourselves at the base of a steep column on Ataatap (a.k.a. Father) Tower. We hoped to make a two-day, alpine-style ascent of a new line dividing the steepest part of the northeast face from a pinnacle on the left side.

What had appeared to be a long, splitter hand crack turned out to be three pitches of vertical offwidth or chimney—Fay carefully and boldly dispatched these without a number 6 cam. Above this, Martin continued to a thin finger crack and then climbed through sparsely protected 7b/b+ terrain for two long pitches, never falling or hanging, and providing us with the best free climbing of the trip.

From there, two more rather loose pitches, which required extreme delicacy and a nut tool to clean out cracks for protection, deposited us on top of the pillar, a comfortable spot for our one-Pod-

Michelle Dvorak on the eighth pitch of The Mental Breakdown on Ataatap Tower. *Martin Feistl*

voyage to nearby Chastity Tower (*AAJ 2022*). Fay and I found what appeared to be an easy and quick line on the west face, but it proved to be deceptively long: 370m and nine pitches up to 6c+, with involved route-finding, offwidths, loose blocks, and a smattering of nice cracks. We stood on the summit after nine hours of climbing, calling our route The Princess Brides. Amaia and Miriam were not able to complete their route.

Back in Seattle, after enjoying—with gratitude—a week of stormbound hospitality with new friends in Kulusuk and then in Iceland, I reflected on how happy I was that this remote expedition had turned out to feel not so remote after all. 📷🔍

—**Michelle Dvorak,** *USA*

MYTHICS CIRQUE, MANY NEW ROUTES

The Equipo Femenino de Alpinismo (Women's Alpine Team) from the Spanish Mountaineering Federation arrived in Kulusuk on August 4 and stayed in Greenland for one month. The group comprised Ángela Altaba, Julia Casanovas, Ruth Fornós, Uxue Loizu, Miriam Marco, Maialen Rojo, and Amaia Segurola, and was accompanied by two males, mountain guide Rubén Sanmartín and cameraman Juan Miguel Ponce.

The team established base camp below the Mythics Cirque, where two fjords intersect: Kangertitivatsiaq and Sangmilik. The first few days were spent exploring the area and scoping possible new routes. Approaches were either on foot or using inflatable packrafts, which allowed gear and supplies to be moved faster through the fjords.

The first new route was climbed on the August 7, when Altaba, Casanovas, Fornós, and Sanmartín put up El Espolón de las Zorras (1,000m of climbing, 5+) on the southeast buttress and northeast ridge of Aurora Tower. [*The upper part of this route is similar to a 2018 ascent by a French team; see AAJ 2019.*] They descended via the very

for-the-three-of-us seated bivouac.

The following day, 120m of nice face and crack climbing brought us to the ridgeline, where we joined Coronis (*AAJ 2013*) and followed this to the summit, proud of our accomplishment but slightly bewildered as to the best way down. Downclimbing the 2012 Libecki route on the south ridge turned out to be progressively more exhausting, with loose and involved terrain, followed by a tricky circumvention of a black-ice glacier that forced us to slide down its moraine—a first-hand experience of the effects of climate change in Greenland.

We called our route The Mental Breakdown (765m of climbing, of which 580m were new, 7b/b+ R, natural gear throughout). Between tears and German expletives, it was apparent that each of us had been close to this feeling over the course of the two long days.

We returned to a base camp that had become even more sociable due to the presence of a team of Spanish women. We quickly made plans to accompany Miriam Marco and Amaia Segurola on a packraft

loose Tortures Traverse (5.4), a crossing of four small summits to the northeast, first completed by Matthew Bunn and Mike Royer (*AAJ 2013*).

Ruth Fornós during the first ascent of Lady Garsa (9 pitches, 7a) on Punta Juanillo. *EFAExpedition | Juan Miguel Ponce*

The climbers then used packrafts to reach the glacier south of the Mythics Cirque. From there, on the 10th, Altaba, Marco, and Segurola repeated the 2012 Bunn-Royer route Assembling the Tupilak (450m, 5.10), on the southeast buttress of Hidden Tower. At the same time, Loizu, Rojo, and Sanmartín climbed a new route a little to the left, which they named Fumantxus (400m, 8 pitches followed by easy ridge, 7a).

The next day, Casanovas, Fornós, and Sanmartin moved farther up this glacier and opened one of the hardest and most sustained routes of the expedition: Lady Garsa (325m, 9 pitches, 7a). It takes a steep pillar they named Punta Juanillo.

After returning to base camp, Altaba, Fornós, and Rojo spent three days establishing La Jubi (600m of new climbing, 7a) on the northeast face of Ataatap Tower. After starting up the initial pitches of Built Fjord Tough (Libecki-Pringle, 2012), the route moves right and climbs a parallel line until rejoining the Libecki-Pringle route high on the face. Later, Casanovas, Loizu, and Sanmartín would start up the first part of the 2018 French route on this face, join La Jubi, and finish up the final section of Built Fjord Tough, giving "1,000m of amazing climbing in a breathtaking environment."

Prior to this ascent, Casanovas, Loizu, Sanmartín, and

Lady Garsa (350m, 7a) on the previously unclimbed Punta Juanillo. *EFAExpedition | Juan Miguel Ponce*

Segurola had used packrafts to reach Borsch Soup Tower, first climbed in 2021 by Nico Favresse, Aleksej Jaruta, and Jean-Louis Wertz (*AAJ 2022*). It took two hours on the rafts and three hours of walking up the glacier to reach the foot of the tower, where they split into two parties to climb a pair of new lines just left of the original route, Borsch Soup.

Casanovas and Loizu put up Izar Askea (600m, 11 pitches, 6c), while a little to the left Sanmartín and Segurola climbed Gure Gidari (600m, 6c). The teams began a rappel descent upon reaching the summit ridge.

After a few days of bad weather, there was just time to climb two more routes. Altaba, Fornós, and Sanmartín headed to the far left side of the northeast face of Ataatap, where they climbed Rostoll Verbenero (750m, 6c+). This route ascends an east-facing wall for eight or nine pitches before joining Coronis (*AAJ 2013*), which it follows to the summit. Meanwhile, Loizu and Segurola explored the south

face of Damocles (ca 1,250m, the most northeasterly summit in the cirque), where they climbed the 200m Azken Aukera (6b) to a point they called Pico Osobucas.

With a forecasted storm now on its way, the expedition beat a hasty retreat to Kulusuk, where they sat out a hurricane in the town's community center, kindly offered by the residents, before starting their journey home. 🄰

—Information provided by Miriam Marco, Spain

Schweizerland

ATTEMPTS AND ASCENTS NORTH OF KULUSUK

Over ten days in August, Ben Kincaid, Kennon Kincaid, Scott Lockhart, and I explored the coastal mountains extending north from Kulusuk to the east of the lower Knud Rasmussen Glacier. We were supported by IFMGA guide Matt Spenceley, head of Pirhuk Guides. I was provided with limited financial support from the AAC's Live Your Dream Grant.

Our expedition greatly benefited from the use of a rigid inflatable boat (RIB) and ample fuel to access various islands and points of interest on the mainland coast, otherwise inaccessible to larger vessels. We attempted four ascents, two of which failed due to potential hazards and issues with route selection; poor weather also reduced our available climbing time.

After an ascent of the previously climbed Inntugai (a.k.a. Tatsukajik) on the south side of Apusiajik Island, our next target was an unnamed peak at 65.66299°N, 37.00288°W (marked as 830m on the Danish Map but seemingly well over 900m), accessed from the north side of the same island. Although this mountain was previously climbed, we traversed the northeast ridge (Oscar's Ridge), which we believe to be new. We generally moved together as two rope teams on the ridge, which was of

The upper part of Oscar's Ridge (the northeast ridge) on Peak 830m on Apusiajik Island. The traverse went from left to right, then descended snow and a glacier on the far side of the mountain. *Josh Alcorn*

mixed quality and low 5th class, then descended snow and a glacier system to the west and back north, resulting in a near circumnavigation of the peak.

We later tried an unnamed peak (918m, 65.76611°N, 36.82814°W) on an island with no name on the map, southeast of Ikâsak Fjord. Route-finding was complex, due to dense fog on the maritime approach to the island and during the initial ascent from the southeast, resulting in poor route selection. An approach from the north or northeast would have likely provided much easier access and a potential non-technical walk-up. We climbed extensive unstable rock and moraine, eventually stopping on the east ridge at around 800m. The continuation looked loose with very limited protection. (*See note below about an ascent of this peak.*)

We then used the RIB to access the snout of the Knud Rasmussen Glacier. We followed the east side of the main glacier to the base of a side glacier flowing from the southeast, then followed a broken ridge to the south toward a summit at approximately 66.07584°N, 36.18338°W, which we were unable to reach in daylight. Although we had brought bivouac equipment, we decided to descend to the RIB. [*Editor's Note: Islands and peaks north of Kulusuk received much attention in the 1960s and '70s, and it is very difficult to ascertain what has been climbed here before.*]

—Josh Alcorn, *USA*

PEAK 918M ASCENT: *In early summer, I was guiding in the Kulusuk region area, and it was suggested we try a possibly unclimbed peak on the island southeast of Ikâsak Fjord. On the Danish map of Tasiilaq, the island is unnamed, but other maps call it Fugleholmene. The summit is also unnamed but has a spot height of 918m. The island can be identified by two other named mountains: Blokken (a.k.a. Ittikasaat Qaqqaat, 840m) and Hjelmen (735m). My clients and I reached the summit (65.76611°N, 36.82814°W), where my inReach recorded an altitude of 920m.* **—Juliana Garcia, *Ecuador***

TASIILAQ FJORD, PEANUT WALL; QIANARTEQ ISLAND, PEAK 620M

Our "fair means" expedition lasted from July 6 to August 10 and began in Tasiilaq, where Anne Flechsig, Timon Kaufman, Ramona Volken, and I (all Swiss) loaded 250kg of gear and food into four kayaks and spent the next two and a half days paddling to our first objective: the Fox Jaw Cirque.

Peanut Wall, south of the Fox Jaw Cirque, showing (1) Was Für ein Peanuts and (2) Double Peanuts (both 12 pitches). *Lydiane Vikol*

We had hoped to visit the Mythics Cirque, but large quantities of sea ice made this impossible in kayaks.

Once at Fox Jaw, we climbed three established routes on Baby Molar, Left Rabbit Ear, and Incisor before paddling back south half a day to access an impressive gray wall near the fjord entrance. From a camp near the shore, we followed traces of a path to reach the glacier, then walked up this easily for four hours to reach the north-facing rock wall at 65°59'09.8"N, 36°55'17.4"W.

We decided to try two lines on the left side, which appeared to have the most stable rock. Anne and I headed for a dihedral, and Ramona and Timon took the most logical line farther right. Both lines had sections of loose rock—including huge blocks on our route—where we needed to climb carefully. In the middle of the wall, we joined Ramona and Timon's line. It was already midnight, so we moved right onto easier terrain and climbed a final three or four pitches to a point where we discovered a bolted anchor, astonished to learn we weren't the only fools to climb this wall. By 1 a.m. we were on top.

We made ten rappels down the face, the first two from previously established anchors. Our name for the formation was Peanut Wall. We called the left-hand route Was Für ein Peanuts (500m, 12 pitches, 6c, with an A1 pendulum). Ramona and Timon's line was Double Peanuts (500m, 12 pitches, 6b+), with a wonderful crack on pitch four.

Following two delightful days of kayaking, we reached Ikateq Fjord and camped on Qianarteq Island, beneath the northwest face of Peak 620m. An hour's hike and 30 minutes of scrambling brought us to the face.

Again, we began climbing in two pairs. Ramona and I started left of Timon and Anne, who reached and then climbed the big left-facing corner on this part of the wall. When we encountered a badly protected section, Ramona and I moved across to join the other team. Above this point, Anna led the crux pitch (7a) over a big roof. We followed a series of beautiful cracks through the twilight hours and arrived on the summit at 3:30 a.m. We descended the west ridge and arrived back at camp after a 20-hour day. The 600m route (15 pitches) was mainly 5c–6b, with a few pitches up to 7a.

During our stay in Greenland, we climbed everything clean and left only slings and two nuts where we rappelled. [*The team's route on Peak 620m, Eternal Sunshine, appears to share significant ground with a line climbed solo in 2019, with a self-belay in places, by David Gladwin. He also followed the large left-facing corner low on the face, then finished about 50m right of the summit. He estimated his route to be British E2 5c (AAJ 2020).*] 📷

—Lydiane Vikol, *Switzerland*

Lydiane Vikol climbing through a band of distinctive red rock on the northwest face of Peak 620m, with Ikateq Fjord behind. *Ramona Volken*

Mexico

Nuevo León

LA POPA, EL CACOMIXTLE DE LA NOCHE

I needed a change of scenery. For once, I wanted no glaciers, no heavy backpacks, no wind and cold. I wanted to climb in shorts. Where there was plenty of limestone and, above all, where you could still explore. So, I and three friends, Gio Ongaro, Simone Pedeferri, and Max Piazza, went to Mexico in February.

When we first traveled to Mexico, in 2015, we felt that energy that only climbing in a place in its infancy can give you. Simone, Marco Maggioni, and I went to El Salto, where we opened a multi-pitch route on the El Chamán face (*AAJ 2017*). There were only a few climbers, and almost all of us were there to bolt routes.

Now the community of El Salto lives on climbing tourism, there are cafes for climbers, and during the day you meet a lot of people at the crags. It is beautiful, but there is also something missing: that energy in the air given by new places, where you experience more than just the climbing. That's why our main objective in Mexico was again off the beaten path: a new route climbed ground-up on La Popa, where the closest village has only a few inhabitants and no cafes or shops. The east face of La Popa is up to 300m high, almost 3km long, and largely overhanging.

I could tell you about the romance and the ethics of trying to open a route from below. But, unfortunately, it all went wrong. The wall's steepness made it difficult to find a good line, I got injured low on the face, and Simone and Max ended up in a large area of rotten rock. Our attempt stopped after about 50m.

We were back to square one, but still with food and water for ten days. We had

Paolo Marazzi climbing one of the final pitches on El Cacomixtle de la Noche (11 pitches, 5.13b). *Gio Ongaro*

to compromise, and we decided to bolt a sport route from above. We wanted to find the most logical and aesthetic line, to give something to the climbing community.

We didn't do anything crazy or extraordinary in the end. We just climbed a route on magnificent limestone, first on technical walls, then on gray overhangs with perfect pockets. A route that, from our point of view, could become a great classic. The route begins about 350m to the right of El Gavilán (Gallagher-Jackson, 1997). We named it El Cacomixtle de la Noche (11 pitches, 5.13b) after an encounter I had one night when I woke suddenly and saw a beautiful and rare cacomixtle (a mammal in the same family as raccoons and coatis) next to our food bag. 🗎 🔍

—**Paolo Marazzi,** *Italy*

LA POPA, EL VISITANTE

In February 2023, Jacob Cook and Drew Marshall opened another route on the east face of La Popa. El Visitante (7 pitches, 5.13c) is now the hardest route on the wall. The duo dedicated six weeks to exploring the remote desert and establishing the fully bolted route, which climbs an overhanging corner system to the right of El Gavilán and Los Naguales, the latter of which Cook and

Marshall established in 2022 (*see AAJ 2023*).

Cook faced setbacks due to injuries and was unable to send the crux sixth pitch, but Marshall climbed it free. The extremely overhanging crux demands pure resistance, navigating crimps and pockets. Neither climber achieved a continuous ascent (opting to redpoint each pitch individually), but they reported being delighted to open the line. It is possible to rappel the route with a single 70m rope, using directionals on the overhangs.

—**Whitney Clark,** *AAJ,* **with online**
information from the climbers

EL POTRERO CHICO, EL TORO, LA SOMBRA DE MUERTE

In January 2023, Sam Boyce and I bolted and freed a new route on the north side of El Toro over three weeks. La Sombra de Muerte (1,500', 16 pitches, V 5.12) climbs the clean face about 100' to climber's right of El Sendero Luminoso (15 pitches, V 5.12d, Jackson-Smith, 1994) and summits the same feature, known as the Central Pillar.

The new route boasts sustained 5.11 pitches, a few 5.12-leads, and one solid 5.12 pitch. It climbs similarly to El Sendero Luminoso, with lots of fun and delicate limestone dancing. It also has some crack climbing, including a wildly overhanging 5.11d hand crack near the top. Pitch 13 is a wildly exposed 5.11d arête.

As we started bolting the route, ground-up, we spent a few

TOP: Lani Chapko sending the fifth-pitch crux (5.12d) of La Sombra de Muerte. *Max Barlerin*

BOTTOM: The north face of El Toro at El Potrero Chico, showing (1) El Sendero Luminoso (15 pitches, V 5.12d, Jackson-Smith, 1994) and (2) La Sombra de Muerte (16 pitches, V 5.12d, Boyce-Chapko, 2023). *Sam Boyce*

nights on the wall so we could trundle rocks in the dark when no one would be climbing. We also rappelled a few times with rocks in haulbags, in an effort to be as safe as possible.

Sam and I both tried the crux fifth pitch on top-rope during a few days while sussing out the route. When we got there on our free push, the finger pods seemed to be a little smaller than we remembered, the crimps a little farther apart. But it was incredible, sustained, balancey climbing. On my first redpoint attempt, I surprised myself by hanging on all the way to the last bolt before the juggy finish.

We bivvied that night on the massive ledge at the top of pitch six—the same one used for El Sendero Luminoso. The next day, I whipped at the last crux of the fifth pitch once again. At that point, I was wrecked; I probably had only one more go in me. But at the final crux, I executed the tenuous move that never feels like it's going to work. I climbed the last few moves to the anchors slowly, wanting to savor the way my body was moving and the intense focus.

Sam sent this pitch, too, and the rest of the climb went much smoother. At the summit, we moved our ropes over to El Sendero Luminoso so that we could rebolt its top ten pitches, with gear courtesy of the American Safe Climbing Association.

La Sombra de Muerte is a slightly less sustained alternative to El Sendero Luminoso, and the 5.12 climbing is better protected, too. Later that season, a few other parties climbed La Sombra de Muerte, and the reviews were everything we could have hoped for. 📷 🔍

—**Lani Chapko,** *USA*

LA HUASTECA, PICO NEGRO, ETERNO OPTIMISTA

In the fall of 2019, I headed out to the limestone area of La Huasteca in search of a new-routing adventure. My dream team consisted of Kai Jacobson (Canadian photographer extraordinaire), Will McEvoy (English rope ninja), and me, the one who

Eterno Optimista on Pico Negro. An earlier route (Medina-Vera, 2003) climbed this face, but the location is unknown. *Kai Jacobson*

came up with the daft idea. We spent a few days getting accustomed to the limestone and learning the local ethics before settling on an objective: the southwest face of Pico Negro. Only one other full-length route is known to exist on the steep, blank face—it was put up in 2003, but there is little information available and it's believed to be out of commission.

The peak was satisfyingly intimidating, towering over the valley. It also had access to the top, making it possible to bolt on rappel. We hoped this would help us to pick the best line and create a masterpiece—it was the first route we'd ever bolted.

Each day for the next two weeks we hiked 3,000' up through a cactus forest, a boulderfield, a relentless scree slope, and a ridge leading to the summit. From here we rappelled down the face, armed with all manner of hardware, to dislodge monster blocks, loose flakes, and cacti. The days were both brutal and utterly incredible. Every day was a riddle of how to make progress and endure the weather—

Will McEvoy leading exposed face moves on pitch seven of Eterno Optimista (350m, 5.11 A0). *Kai Jacobson*

unrelenting heat one day, icy rain the next, with thunderstorms sending us fleeing from the face. We cut it right down to the wire, with only one day left and absolutely no time to rest between preparing the route and attempting to climb it.

So, on November 20, after a solid night of three hours of sleep, we got to the base by sunrise. I started up the crux first pitch, a techy 5.12b corner. (Our route begins from a broad ledge that can be approached by four pitches of bolted 5.10.) The climbing was just beyond my limit—I tried as hard as I ever have, but still fell on the final move.

We continued up the pocketed wall with more straightforward climbing that still required focus due to the variable rock quality. A second crux came on the fifth pitch, which required a bit of aid, and pitch eight delivered a final bold slab that Kai heroically led in the dark. We made it down to the car 21 hours after leaving—and with only six hours to get to the airport.

We named the line Eterno Optimista (350m, 5.11 A0) due to our team's consistent ability to drastically underestimate timing. And, yes, we did make it to the airport in the nick of time. 📷 🔍

—**Sally Lisle**, *England*

PERU | Cordillera Blanca

The Line Under the Sky on Tuctubamba West (5,140m). This peak rises along the ridge extending southeast and then east from Taulliraju, whose summit can be seen at left, rising behind the ridgeline. *Marek Radovsky*

TUCTUBAMBA WEST, SOUTHWEST FACE, THE LINE UNDER THE SKY

Ďuri Švingál and I flew to Lima on July 18, then traveled to Huaraz. Aguja Nevada I (5,840m), above Laguna Parón, was our choice for acclimatization. Then, after consultation with the mountain guides' office in Huaraz, we chose a new destination. Several days later, we arrived at Laguna Tuctubamba (4,200m), below the east side of the Taulliraju massif, and set up base camp.

On August 3, after a bivouac at the base, we started up the unclimbed southwest face of Tuctubamba West (5,140m), a peak on the long ridge extending southeast and then east from Taulliraju. [*The climbers initially called this peak Marva, believing it was unclimbed. They later discovered it was called Tuctubamba West (8°54'12"S, 77°33'30"W) and was first climbed in 1960 by an Italian team, who ascended a glacier on the southeast side, then traversed around to the north side to finish.*]

Our route began with several hundred meters of chimneys and corners, around 6a. After reaching a big ledge and ramp system, we traversed up and left. Above this, we simul-climbed for several hundred meters, then more chimneys and corners led to the first snowfield. After two snow pitches, we put aside the tools and climbed a beautiful 6b rock pitch, followed by steep snow and run-out M6+ mixed. Some loose rock led to a final pitch of 6b and the summit.

Our descent involved 14 rappels and took six hours, and we returned to the bivouac below the face after a total of 19 hours. We called our new route The Line Under the Sky (1,100m climbing distance, 6b M6+). 📷

—**Marek Radovsky,** *Slovakia*

AGUJA NEVADA I, SOUTHWEST FACE, UN HILO DE STILO

On July 8, Jedrzej Jablonski (Poland) and Christian Junkar (USA) climbed a route up the southwest face of Aguja Nevada I (5,840m), reaching the plateau below the summit. The climbing began at 5,100m and consisted of 12 pitches of ice, mixed, and steep snow, exiting the face by a weakness in the middle of the

ice cliff that spans the top. After 13 hours of climbing, they ended the climb at about 5,700m and descended to the east with some rappels. They estimated they were several pitches below the summit. The route was called Un Hilo de Stilo ("A Thread of Style," TD+ AI4 M4 80°). 📷

—*Information from Christian Junkar, USA*

RANRAPALCA, NORTHWEST FACE, YA PE' CHOLO

In 2022, we made an attempt on the unclimbed northwest face of Ranrapalca (6,162m), but we'd barely reached its base before we retreated, exhausted. We had been active in the Cordillera Blanca for two months and found the ascent too difficult in our current state.

We decided to return at the end of the 2023 season with Micher Quito, a friend and guide in Peru. The uncertainty of what we were going to encounter on Ranrapalca was enormous. Above all, we were worried about the quality of the rock and how many days the climb would take us.

We arrived in the Cordillera Blanca just a week before attempting Ranrapalca and acclimatized quickly on two beautiful, snowcapped mountains: Yanapaccha (5,460m) and Cashan (5,716m). As a local guide, Micher was very acclimatized. It was late August, very late in the season. Ranrapalca was quite bare of snow, and the weather forecasts were not very encouraging, but we still wanted to give it a try.

TOP LEFT: Battling *nieves penitentes* en route to the rock face on Ranrapalca.

TOP RIGHT: Blocky granite and limited ice on the northwest face of Ranrapalca.

BOTTOM: Ya Pe' Cholo (900m, 6b 80°) and the bivouac site on Ranrapalca. *All photos: Eneko and Iker Pou*

The northwest face is comprised of a big rock wall to the right of the snow and ice routes on the north and northeast faces. On August 29, Eneko led the initial nine pitches while we (Iker and Micher) hauled the packs. The climb began with some slabs that were difficult to protect and not easy with the weight we were carrying. Little by little, we gained height. After 13 hours of climbing, we reached a bivy site at 5,700m. It was small and uncomfortable, and we couldn't sleep a wink due to the continual rockfall. The next morning, we decided to change our planned route and move left onto a spur that seemed more protected.

We began very early on the second day. By midmorning, we were up on the spur, and we saw the top getting closer, but the climb seemed endless. Iker led all the pitches until the finishing slabs, where Micher took over.

Once atop the wall, we encountered several large crevasses on the summit slopes. Micher was essential to help us avoid falling into them, as he is well accustomed to this type of terrain. We reached the summit around 4 p.m., with a storm on our heels.

On the way down the normal route, our biggest problems began. It started to snow, with poor visibility. Thank goodness Micher knew the descent well.

Halfway down, Eneko was hit by a stone that could have killed him, but luckily only grazed his helmet. He was unconscious for several seconds, and he finished the descent with severe dizziness and pain in his neck and head.

At 2 a.m., after countless rappels, we arrived safely at the Longoni refuge (5,000m), where our friend Alex was waiting for us with very hot soup.

We named the route Ya Pe' Cholo, which is a Peruvian slang term for an affirmative, roughly translating as "Yes, Amigo" (900m vertical, 1,200m of climbing, 6b 80°). 📷

—**Eneko and Iker Pou,** *Spain*

The line of Zamba de los Adioses on Rasac Oeste, with the main summit of Rasac (6,017m) to the right. *Adam Matthews*

Cordillera Huayhuash

RASAC OESTE, ZAMBA DE LOS ADIOSES

On September 2, I soloed a significant variation on Rasac Oeste (ca 5,700m), starting on the southwest face. This peak is a major spur of Rasac (6,017m).

I approached from Huayllapa, via the Segya Valley, and camped 300m above Laguna Caramarca (4,600m). The initial couloir on my route had two 30m sections of 70° and 80° ice, followed by a short, vertical mixed passage. After the couloir ended, I traversed to the west ridge with some steep snow and mixed sections. Once on the west side, my line likely intersected the Jaeger Route. [*In 1979, Nicolas Jaeger (France) soloed the west face of Rasac Oeste (500m, TD), descended the far side, and continued up the west face of Rasac to the main summit; see AAJ 1980.*] A continuous 60° couloir led up the west face to the top. The summit had a small serac in bad condition, so I did not climb the final ten meters.

I downclimbed the safest way, which again was probably along the Jaeger Route. The descent to Rasac Pass took several hours; my complete climb and descent took seven hours. I named my line Zamba de los Adioses (400m, D 80°).

—**Juan Cruz Rodríguez,** *Argentina*

NEVADO MINAFIERRO OESTE, PASEO CON SOLEDAD

The Cordillera Venturosa is a small range of about 20 summits, with a few small glaciers, west of the Cordillera de la Viuda and east of Lima, about a four-hour drive from the city. Many of the summits are unnamed; one of the highest is Nevado Minafierro Oeste (ca 5,260m).

Steve Meder, a Frenchman living in Peru, soloed a partial new line on Nevado Minafierro on November 16. His route started at 5,000m on the left side of the southwest face, near a 2015 route called Escudito Camycam. That route climbs left of a rock buttress splitting a couloir, then up an icy headwall. Meder ascended to the right of the rock buttress on mixed terrain (M3), then up the right side of the ice wall, where he found 70m of WI3 (max. 75°–80°).

From the summit, he descended the normal route down the glacier, well to the right of the ascent route. Meder christened his route Paseo con Soledad (250m, D- WI3 M3). 📷

—**Marcelo Scanu,** *Argentina*

Cordillera Urubamba

NEVADO VERONICA, DIRECT EAST FACE

In September 2021, I climbed a route on the east side of Nevado Veronica (5,911m) that joined up with the normal route at the shoulder on the northeast ridge around 5,500m. I had considered climbing the ice directly on the east face, but my client wanted to finish on the northeast ridge (*AAJ 2022*).

Nevado Veronica (5,911m). The east face is on the right, with the new route leading directly from the upper glacier to the summit. The northeast ridge is along the right skyline. *Nate Heald*

In April 2023, Humberto Rada, a young Bolivian living in Lima, and my local friend Leo Rosalio joined me to climb the direct line on Veronica. We used the same camp as in 2021. On April 29, we left at midnight. Instead of going through the broken lower glacier, we accessed a ramp and chute that got us onto the upper glacier, right below the east face headwall. Now we were in the sun and had great snow conditions.

From below, the top-out had looked straightforward, but a hidden bergschrund cut off the summit slopes. I explored out north but was blocked by huge seracs. We followed the bergschrund south and rounded a corner that brought us to the final slopes. At noon we reached the summit.

We descended the upper northeast ridge to the glacier, rejoining our ascent tracks at dusk. The rest of the descent in the dark was slow and tiring, but we made it back to camp at 11:30 p.m. 📷

—**Nate Heald,** *Peru*

PERU | Cordillera Vilcanota

JAPONÉS DIRECTO

THE NORTH FACE OF NEVADO AUSANGATE

By Yudai Suzuki, *Japan*

Kei Narita and I saw a truly beautiful photo of the north face of Nevado Ausangate (6,384m), and we thought, "This is the perfect objective to climb alpine style." I didn't know why this magnificent wall was still unclimbed. Maybe the rock was too loose and the serac at the base was too huge, or maybe there was a lot of avalanche risk? I didn't know of any previous attempts. We decided to go on a trip into the unknown. It felt like there was only a 30 to 40 percent chance that we would even be able to start the climb.

Because this would be an ice and mixed route, we thought July or August (the usual season for this range) would be too late. By that time, we expected the ice would have melted. So we planned to climb in May, and that was a key decision. We acclimatized on the normal route, climbing the east and south faces to the summit. Several teams usually do this route every year, but this season, apparently, no one climbed it.

On May 17, we headed for the north face. We left our bivouac at Laguna Azul Cocha (4,500m) at night and passed the broken glacier as quickly as we could. The glacier was threatened by the huge serac, but we passed the most dangerous part in about an hour. At the 5,300m level, we made an excellent bivy in a little cave that was completely protected. After we had reached the cave, the sun hit the face and we heard countless avalanches.

We started climbing again at midnight so we could minimize the rockfall and avalanche risk. Kei led an initial pitch of WI4+ that was like a waterfall, so it was difficult to use ice screws. The second pitch was also WI4+, including some vertical mixed climbing. While passing this vertical section, I was struck by a huge spindrift avalanche that included some falling rock. I stabbed in my axes as hard as I could and held on. It felt like I was pounded for more than three minutes.

Fortunately, the intense shower eventually slowed and then ended. I climbed quickly to the left for the protection of a rock wall and made a solid anchor. It was hard to find the route in the dark, so I had to trust my feeling.

The third pitch was the crux of the lower half of the route. It was still completely dark, yet somehow Kei found a crack in the rock and climbed through the hard section at about 5.10a. Climbing this with crampons and gloves took some hard effort. It was an absolute miracle that a crack existed here—we could not have passed the vertical section without it.

After this first crux, we merged into an obvious snow and ice couloir. Here we mostly simul-climbed to move rapidly, hoping to avoid potential avalanches and rockfall. After reaching 5,700m, we were super lucky to find a small, flat bivy spot covered by a huge rock roof. Our tent was slightly too big to fit on the flat space, but we both managed to lie down and recover body and mind.

We left the bivy around 3 a.m. and simul-climbed the rest of the couloir in one super-long pitch that would have been about eight or nine rope lengths had we belayed. I only placed one or two pieces of protection every 60m to save on gear.

This brought us to the base of the vertical ice section on the upper wall. When the sun had only just hit the ice, we started up the first pitch. The ice was really hard, like metal, so it was quite tough both to lead and to follow while wearing the heavy pack. The 50m first pitch was WI5. The second pitch was 40m and WI6. On the latter, I was about to give up on free climbing the slightly overhanging ice, but I wanted to push as hard as Kei did on the hard rock crux of the previous day. I was really relieved after topping out without hanging on the rope. The ice crux at 6,000m felt much harder than the last pitch of Polar Circus in the Canadian Rockies or any ice I had climbed in Japan.

I quickly realized that the real crux of our climb was probably still to come. We had to simul-climb, breaking through soft snow that was melting in the intense sun. It felt like it went on forever, and we also were threatened by seracs in some sections. We had hoped to camp at a flat area on the foresummit, but we couldn't reach it that day because we climbed so slowly in the knee-deep snow. I was feeling somewhat sick from the altitude, and I took a minute to climb every meter. We decided to bivy on a snow slope at 6,250m. We had carried an 80-liter plastic bag, and I filled it with snow and hung it from the wall to make additional space for the tent. After two hours, we had created a ledge that was nicer than the previous bivy, giving us a safe spot to recover and stay motivated.

The next day, I led the final snow slope at sunrise, when the

ABOVE: Japonés Directo (1,100m, 5.10a WI6), the first route up the north face of Nevado Ausangate (6,384m). The climbers bivouacked once at the foot of the wall, twice on the route, and once on the summit ridge. They descended the far side. *Yudai Suzuki*

OPPOSITE PAGE: Moving across the complex summit ridge of Ausangate. The climbers had to rappel and traverse across the south face to bypass the pinnacle of snow and ice behind them. *Yudai Suzuki*

Yudai Suzuki leading the 40-meter WI6 ice pitch at around 6,000 meters on the north face of Ausangate. *Kei Narita*

snow was still firm, and we reached the summit ridge relatively smoothly. Yet Andean ridges are rarely simple and easy. A complicated rock barrier stood in front of the foresummit, and it was obvious we would not be able to climb over it. Instead, we rappelled for 40m and made a big traverse on the south side. It was a difficult decision, because losing altitude at this elevation is mentally and physically tough. However, after the rappel, we could see an obvious traverse to a 60° slope leading to the base of the true summit.

Again, the strong sun hit us and we had to break a trail through deep snow at 6,300m. When we finally reached the foot of the summit cone, about 20m below the top, the weather turned bad. We were completely blind in the whiteout. After an hour of drinking hot tea, we decided to spend another night there (6,360m), because descending from the top with no visibility would have been unrealistic. That night was so cold. Our small sleeping bags were wet at this point, but we survived with big hope for the next day.

On the fifth day of our climb, we started before daylight, hoping to avoid the melting seracs and crevasses on the upcoming descent. The visibility was good, but the wind was the strongest we'd felt during our month in Peru. Our hands and feet were freezing. We reached the summit about 15 minutes after leaving our final bivy. The suffering of the past five days turned to pleasure. The 360° view at sunrise was stunning, and I was glad we hadn't climbed to the summit in the whiteout.

We started down the normal route, rappelling three pitches down the steepest section and downclimbing. We had a near miss when the wire on a snow picket snapped as I tested it before rappelling on a 60° snow slope. At the bottom of the face, we carefully managed the dangerously crevassed glacier.

We descended from the summit all the way to the tiny settlement at 4,300m at the base of the mountain, and there we caught a ride on a small motorbike that was passing by—two climbers with big packs struggling to hold on to the bike as we left Ausangate. After a bus ride, we returned to the village of Pacchanta and woke the owner of our hostel, who was surprised to see us and offered hearty congratulations.

The north face of Ausangate was still faintly visible under the starlit sky as I soaked in a wonderful hot spring and felt the warmth of the steaming water all over my body. Looking up at the line we had climbed, it was hard to process the intense five days of climbing. I felt sad, happy, and an emotion that is inexpressible in words. I wanted to bask in that afterglow for a while.

We called our route Japonés Directo (1,100m, 5.10a WI6), after a Peruvian friend suggested the name. 📷

NOTES ON AUSANGATE'S NORTH SIDE:
The only prior route on this side of Ausangate was on the northwest face, a shallow buttress well to the right of the 2023 route. A line on this face was climbed in 1982 by an Italian team, who descended the far side without going to the summit. In 1983, a Swiss trio climbed the face and continued to the summit, where they were forced to bivouac for two nights before the weather cleared enough for them to navigate down the south side.

NEVADO TINKI, RÍOS ATMOSFÉRICOS

In early June, Peruvians Bruno López and Rodrigo Mendoza made the second ascent of the west face of Nevado Tinki (a.k.a. Tinke, 5,450m), southeast of Cusco, with significant variations to the line opened by Luke Bird and Pete Takeda in 2022.

The pair set up base camp at 4,700m and began their climb on June 2. Low on the rock face, a cut rope (reduced to 40m) slowed progress, as did 40cm of new snow on the upper ridge. They climbed left of the 2022 route low on the face, then to the right in some of the middle section. They bivouacked three times, summited on June 5, and returned to base camp that evening. The pair called their line Ríos Atmosféricos (800m, TD/TD+ 5.10 M3/4 80°). 📷

—**Rodrigo Mendoza,** *Peru*

PERU | Cordillera Apolobamba

CHAUPI ORCO NORTE, WEST RIDGE

In November, Canadians Samuel Gagnon and Valery Bilodeau, Samuel Crispin (Peru), and I drove past the mining town of La Rinconada to a valley on the eastern slope of the Andes, to access the west side of Chaupi Orco (6,044m). We followed a dirt road to a large mining area at the head of the valley. A miner named Avad allowed us through the gate and offered us his sheet-metal hut to stay in.

On November 9, we woke to 20cm of snow and an icy wind from the north. For two days, we could not see Chaupi Orco. The Maps.me app said that Chaupi Orco Norte (ca 6,000m) was higher than the main peak, so we went for that.

Chaupi Orco Norte (ca 6,000m), with the west ridge along the right skyline. The climb began with a steep ascent of the icefall at far right. *Nate Heald*

The morning of the 11th cleared long enough to get some photos of the face and a route leading onto the west ridge. By afternoon it was raining again, but the forecast said it would be clearer the next day.

We left a bivy cave just before midnight and made our way onto the glacier, then up a large cascade of ice. This was fun AI3, with great views of Ananea (5,853m) and Callijon (5,829m). From the top of the cascade, the route was mostly walking, with two sections of steeper AI3 that we pitched out. As we hiked the summit slopes, the clouds came in and we did not get extended views of the other peaks; it wasn't obvious to me if the main or north peak of Chaupi Orco was higher. We descended the route, with some rappels, and made it to our bivy just before dusk.

Our route on Chaupi Orco Norte gained about 800m above the glacier and was around AD in difficulty. 📷

—**Nate Heald,** *Peru*

Bolivia

Cordillera Real

HUAYNA ILLAMPU, VIA DEI NEMBRESI

In 1973, an Italian expedition led by Carlo Nembrini climbed Illampu (6,368m) and then moved to Illimani. After climbing that peak, they joined a search for the bodies of Pierre Dedieu (France) and Ernesto "Coco" Sanchez (Bolivia), who had been killed on the mountain. Sanchez had been considered the best alpinist in Bolivia at the time, climbing new routes with French resident Alain Mesili. The Italians located the body of Sanchez, but tragically, during the evacuation, Nembrini fell to his death.

In 2022, Rosa Morotti, a niece of Nembrini's, wrote to me about her dream of opening a new route on Illampu, 50 years after the death of her uncle. I had visited Laguna Glaciar, a beautiful lake between Illampu and Ancohuma, four years earlier, and during that trip I saw a possible new line on the south side of Huayna Illampu, a 5,940m summit on the southwest ridge of Illampu. When Rosa wrote, I immediately thought of this potential line. [*Information on Huayna Illampu's climbing history is scant. The only prior reported line is the Mesili-Sanchez Route on the southwest face, climbed in 1973 and graded TD.*]

On June 27, Rosa, Maria Teresa Llampa Vasquez (the first female IFMGA aspirant guide from Bolivia), and I made a five-hour trek from Sorata to reach the bottom of the face, where we camped. Carrying all of our equipment, we left at 4 a.m. for the face. The first part of the route followed a fine couloir for 300m, with two hard pitches of AI4 and M5. The route then became easier, but the snow was bad, forcing us to climb ice close to a big serac barrier. Above, a ridge led to the flat summit of Huayna Illampu, which we reached at 2 p.m.

We opted to make a second camp at this point and then left at five the next morning to continue up to Illampu's main summit. Following the southwest ridge (normal route), we reached the top at 8:15 a.m. Rosa dedicated the route to her husband and all the people of Nembro (immediately northeast of Bergamo), where her father and Carlo were born: Via dei Nembresi (700m, ED AI4 M5).

Editor's Note: The author is a guide based in the village of Peñas in the central Cordillera Real, and his company, La Cordillera Experience, is training and employing local people in adventure sports and tourism, as well as adding routes to the local cliffs. The red sandstone crags in Peñas now have more than 100 bolted routes, from 4 to 8b. 🖼

—**Daniele Assolari**, *Italy/Bolivia*

Huayna Illampu (5,940m) from the south, showing (1) the approximate line of the 1973 Mesili-Sanchez Route and (2) Via dei Nembresi (700m, ED AI4 M5, 2023). The climbers in 2023 continued up Illampu (6,368m), which is hidden behind Huayna Illampu. *Daniele Assolari*

HUALLOMEN, SOUTHWEST FACE, VIA DEL TRIANGOLO AND RUTA IMANTATA

At the start of June 2022, Maria Teresa Llampa Vasquez and I decided to try one of the mixed routes on the southwest face of Huallomen (5,463m). Looking at the face from Condoriri Base Camp, we immediately saw the potential for a new line.

We left the refugio at 3 a.m. and by 5 a.m. were slanting up the lower wall to access the first goulotte and the left-slanting ramp above. [*This ramp lies below and left of the route Canaleta del Angel.*] The first part of this ramp was in excellent condition, with perfect ice and short, easy mixed sections. The ramp took us to the top of a large triangle of rock that forms the lower southwest face. Above, two hard rock pitches got us to the final icefall, after which we reached the ridge. At 2 p.m. we were on the summit, having belayed nine pitches. It's one of the hardest routes I've climbed, mainly due to bad rock with little protection. We named the route Via del Triangolo (500m, ED+ AI4 M6 A2).

In June 2023, at the start of Bolivia's dry season, Ronaldo Choque Camargo, Maria Teresa, and I decided to attempt another route on the southwest face. Ronaldo and I had seen a possible line during a guides' course and had been waiting for the right conditions. We checked it out from the base of the wall on the 14th and it looked perfect, with the face very well iced. We left the next morning at 6 a.m.

Our route began down and left of the 2022 line, slanting left up an obvious snow and ice ramp. Two mixed pitches then led toward a snowfield in the middle of the face. The final passage of this section was one of the best pitches we had ever done—a very delicate ice/mixed traverse, full of exposure.

Above the snowfield we climbed two pitches in a fine couloir, with a 30m icefall to finish. We were then able to sit in the sun and eat. It wasn't easy to see how best to finish the route, but we opted to follow a ramp on the left with a final hard pitch. The summit ridge was difficult due to very bad rock, but at 5 p.m. we were standing on top. We named our new line Ruta Imantata (500m, ED AI4 M5). In Aymara, *imantata* means "hidden." 📷 🔍

—**Daniele Assolari,** *Italy/Bolivia*

TOP: Ronaldo Choque Camargo on Ruta Imantata, southwest face of Huallomen. *Daniele Assolari*

BOTTOM: The southwest face of Huallomen (5,463m). (1) Ruta Imantata (2023). (2) Via del Triangolo (2022). (3) Canaleta del Angel (climbed in 2017 and possibly earlier). (4) Via Mesili (possibly 1976, definitely in 1996). (5) Via del Querubin (2017). Other routes have been climbed, but their whereabouts are unknown. *Alexander von Ungern*

The south face of Mururata (which actually faces more southwest). (1) Normal route (1915). (2) Matti ma Felici (2022). (3) Guias AGMTB (2013). (4) Goulotte Marie (1987). (5) South-southeast ridge (1970). Another route on the south face, Power to the Process (2018), is off picture to the left. *Daniele Assolari*

MURURATA, SOUTH FACE, MATTI MA FELICI

On July 4, 2022, Maria Teresa Llampa Vasquez and I climbed a new route on the south face of Mururata (5,871m). [*Although always traditionally called the south face, this broad snow/ice wall faces more southwest.*] We started near Guias AGMTB, the April 2013 route climbed by Sergio Condori and a group of UIAGM guides and aspirants (*see AAJ 2014*). We made a short leftward traverse to a prominent narrow couloir, then climbed this couloir throughout, finishing via the last section of Guias AGMTB, just to the right of the huge capping serac. It is a logical ice line with a few short mixed sections, and we made the ascent in just four hours. Anything falling from the large serac would sweep the route, and for this reason it is important to be fast. This is also why we called our new line Matti ma Felici ("Crazy but Happy," ca 600m, TD AI3 M3).

—Daniele Assolari, *Italy/Bolivia*

PICO MILLUNI, NORTH SUMMIT, NORTHEAST FACE; CHAUPI ORCO ASCENT

On August 24, Gregg Beisly and I climbed a short new route up the northeast face of the northern summit of Pico Milluni (ca 5,450m), following a prominent corner system (4 pitches, New Zealand 21). However, the main goal of my visit to Bolivia was to climb Chaupi Orco (6,044m), on the border with Peru, which I achieved with Gregg, Andy Baker (USA), and Ronaldo Choque Camargo (Bolivia), thus completing an almost 30-year project to summit the dozen 6,000m peaks in Bolivia. Climate change, resulting in collapsing glaciers, is nowhere more apparent than in the Andes, and this has turned the traditionally straightforward ascent of Chaupi Orco into a demanding climb. [*This report at the AAJ website also describes route variations on Huayna Potosí resulting from glacier loss.*] 📷📄

—Erik Monasterio, *New Zealand*

CORDILLERA QUIMSA CRUZ SKI ASCENTS AND DESCENTS

On April 23, Mikiko Fischel, our camp cook Lucrecia Chambi, and I camped by the shores of Laguna Huallatani in the central part of the southern Quimsa Cruz. The following day, Mikiko and I skied the glacier northeast of the lake to reach Coricampana (5,550m, 16.98662°S, 67.33743°W) at the northernmost point of the glacier. We skied to a point around 100 vertical meters below the summit, then put on crampons for the short headwall and knife-edge summit ridge. In descent, we skied the headwall (35°–40°) from the ridge on good snow.

Getting onto this glacier was fairly easy and required about one hour of walking from the end of the mining road on the northwest shore of the lake. Several other peaks, such as Huayna Cuno Collo (5,640m), are accessible from the glacier, but skiing to and from the summits would be difficult due to the rocky and narrow summit ridges.

We then moved base camp northwest to the roadside Laguna Octa Khota (Octacota), with its disused Malla Chuma mine, and skied an unnamed peak at the top of the glacier north-northeast of the lake. [*This snow peak is around 5,590m and is situated at 16.92111°S, 67.38904°W, immediately east of Cerro Nikko (5,630m), first climbed in 1968. The mountain lies northwest of Cerro San Enrique in what is sometimes referred to as the Choquetanga Group, between Atorama and Gigante Grande.*] The glacier here has receded significantly, and one must navigate a newly formed lake and several sections of glacier-polished rock interspersed with glacial debris. However, it is a relatively big glacier by Quimsa Cruz standards, and the skiing was good aside from some ice in the lower part.

We skied to within 30 vertical meters of the summit, using ice axes at the top, although in hindsight we could have skied all the way. Many other peaks of equal or lesser elevation appear to be skiable from the same glacier.

The scale of ski mountaineering in the Quimsa Cruz is smaller than in the more heavily traveled Cordillera Real, but mining roads allow relatively easy access to the glaciers, and there's a very good chance that you'll have the place entirely to yourself.

—Josh Fischel, *Bolivia*

TOP: Mikiko Fischel on the Huallatani Glacier with the lake of the same name below. *Josh Fischel*

BOTTOM: An idyllic base camp by Laguna Huallatani. (A) Jacha Cuna Collo (5,800m), the highest peak of the Quimsa Cruz. (B) Huayna Cuno Collo (5,640m). (C) Huallatani (ca 5,600m). (D) Coricampana (5,550m). (E) Anco Collo (5,460m). *Josh Fischel*

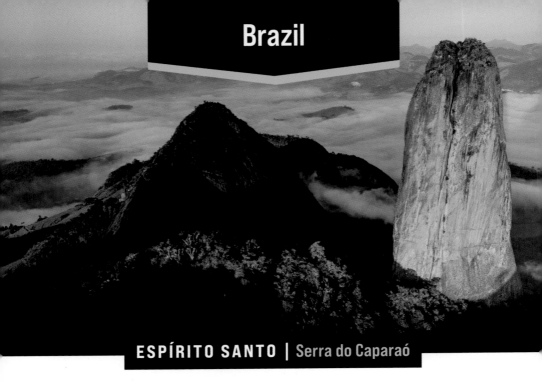

Brazil

ESPÍRITO SANTO | Serra do Caparaó

Pico do Itabira from the north. The new route Ao Ao (9 pitches, 5.13c A2) ascends the steep face just to the right of the left skyline. An earlier route, the Northeast Face, climbed the face to the right of Ao Ao. The original route (1947) is mostly around the corner to the right. *100 Limite Filmes | Murilo Vargas*

PICO DO ITABIRA, AO AO

Conceiving of and realizing big climbing projects, at least for me, requires an obsessive mindset. I've spent many late nights in the last decade diving down internet rabbit holes in search of the world's most unusual rock formations. When I came across the slender tower of Brazil's Pico do Itabira in 2016, with only a handful of established routes, I knew I'd found a gem.

Climbing out of that rabbit hole and to the top of Pico do Itabira was a long journey. It took seven years to piece together the logistics, a team, and the free time to climb the peak. In June 2023, I finally met up with Brazilian climber Neni Gabbardo and Brazilian filmmaker Murilo Vargas in Rio de Janeiro, and we traveled about 400km northeast to Cachoeiro do Itapemirim, the town below Pico do Itabira, in the state of Espírito Santo.

Pico do Itabira is on private land, so we needed to arrange permission to climb. After several calls to a number in the climbing guidebook, and after hanging outside of a bicycle shop for most of a day, we managed to connect with one of the local landowners, Ezequiel Vieira. He was wary of our intentions, but after I tried some "Port-añol"—my attempt at Portuguese despite only knowing Spanish— Ezequiel welcomed us to his home and shared in-depth knowledge of Pico do Itabira. He explained how to access the base, where the existing lines went, and which face stayed shady. Access to the peak is guarded by thick jungle and stretches of nearly featureless slab, but Ezequiel had installed a via ferrata in 2020, saving us days of effort shuttling loads. [*This via ferrata to the summit of Pico do Itabira was controversial among many climbers, leading to a formal statement of opposition from the Espírito Santo climbing association.*]

We climbed another via ferrata to the top of a peak opposite Pico do Itabira to

Neni Gabbardo
establishing pitch two of
Ao Ao on the northeast
face of Pico do Itabira.
Eventually this 30-meter
pitch was equipped
with bolts and freed at
5.12a. *100 Limite Filmes
| Murilo Vargas*

select a potential line. Heeding Ezequiel's advice about shade, we identified what appeared to be the only possible line on the northeast face, a thin, direct crack system to the left of the Northeast Face route, climbed in 1999 by Luciano Bender, Marcel Leoni, Magno dos Santos, and Leandro Siqueira.

The tower itself was first climbed from June 7–22, 1947, by Reinaldo Behnken, Júlio Maria de Freitas, Índio do Brasil Luz, Sílvio Joaquim Mendes, and Reinaldo Santos. Their ascent was part engineering project, part rock climb. They used fixed ropes, drills, and sledgehammers; installed iron rungs and homemade bolts called "crow's feet" (they did not have pitons); and made ample use of a portable, three-meter iron ladder. Their route began on the north face and midway up the tower crossed onto the northwest aspect.

Our plan for working on the new route was to fix ropes to our high point each day before finally committing to the wall, using a portaledge, once we were several pitches up.

I took the first lead, following an obvious crack system past a death block (since removed) and through the treeline to a small ledge. Though the climbing was only 5.10d, the protection was dubious, made up mostly of cams positioned between the rock and a tree that had melded into the crack. Neni took the next pitch, a perfect hand crack that ended in a corner and forced him onto 5.12 face climbing, for which he added some protection bolts before stopping at a hanging belay.

Over the next few days, we alternated leads, adding bolts when necessary. By pitch six, the crack system that we had observed from the neighboring peak had disappeared, and we opted to go directly up the face to avoid crossing onto the Northeast Face route. The face climbing was technical and thin, offering pitch after pitch of sustained 5.12. Pitch seven was the hardest we freed, at 5.13a. We did not completely free the 50m eighth pitch; at present, it comes in at 5.13c A2, with 20 bolts. The final 15–20m of the route joined the Northeast Face to the summit. So as not to modify that route, I kept with the first ascensionists' style and hooked my way up, which led to very long runouts. We topped out Pico do Itabira on June 16.

We named our route Ao Ao (305m, 9 pitches, 5.13c A2), after the indigenous Tupi-Guarani god of hills and mountains, in a gesture of thanks to the wonderful locals who made this dream possible. [*A pitch-by-pitch description and additional photos are at the AAJ website.*] 📄 📷

—**Gareth "Gaz" Leah,** *U.K.*

Pedra Riscada, showing Rabiosa (900m, 8a). Two earlier routes climbed the face and prow to the right (see the AAJ website). *Jonathan Crison*

Minas Gerais

PEDRA RISCADA, NORTHEAST FACE, RABIOSA

I first encountered Pedra Riscada in 2021 during a trip with friends to repeat some lines there. What blew me away as much as the soaring granite walls was that there was no established route up the heart of the steep and beautiful northeast face.

When we rapped down the superb line of Viaje de Cristal (900m, 8a)—first climbed in 2015 by Ignacio Elorza, Horacio Gratton, María José Moisés, and Cintia Percivati, and located on a light-colored pillar on the right side of the northeast face—I tried to scope the middle of the face to the left. On some similar formations in Brazil, the rock can be very slick and virtually blank—which would make a climb up the vertical center of this face all but impossible—so I scanned for distinct features, and I thought I saw enough to make an ascent possible.

I kept the line in mind and proposed it as a project for the Roc Aventure Programme (RAP), a French rock climbing team under the auspices of the Fédération Française de la Montagne et de l'Escalade (FFME). Gérôme Pouvreau and I direct RAP, and some of France's leading competition climbers are members, including Esteban Daligault, Léa Delacquis, Margaux Deschamps, Thomas Joannes, Kenza Slamti, and Tanguy Topin.

All of us traveled to Pedra Riscada in mid-May 2023. We chose an obvious line in the middle of the northeast face, up a whitish gully, and tried to stay as direct as possible. The start is about 100m climber's left of the start of Place of Happiness (850m, 7c, Gerais-Gratton-Glowacz-Heuber-Fengler, 2009). It took us nine hard and long days to reach the summit, bolting as we went, rotating in teams of three to four people every one or two days. We established a single camp with two portaledges in the middle of the face, about 500m up.

After getting to the top, we then spent four more days cleaning and freeing the route. As there are no cracks, the route is fully equipped with stainless-steel bolts. Compared with most climbs in the area, it is very well-protected, without long runouts; we wanted to offer future climbers an enjoyable and accessible line. Nonetheless, Rabiosa (900m, 21 pitches, 8a) is a big undertaking for those seeking a sustained challenge. Twelve pitches, all in the upper half, are between 7a and 8a.

Big ups to Mother Nature: Our entire team agreed that Pedra Riscada was one of the most spectacular places any of us had visited. And thanks again to Edmilson Duarte for his warm welcome at Recanto Pedra Riscada, a perfect base camp.

—**Jonathan Crison,** *France*

Argentina & Chile

CORDILLERA FRONTAL, CERRO SANTA CLARA, NORTHWEST SLOPES

In late March 2023, Lisandro Arelovich, Federico Barberis, and Glauco Muratti (all from Argentina) climbed Cerro Santa Clara (ca 5,400m, 33°10'21"S, 69°41'35"W) via its northwest slopes. The mountain is approximately eight kilometers west-southwest of Cerro del Salto (ca 5,350m), which Muratti climbed in 2021 (*AAJ 2022*), and 30km south of the town of Punta de Vacas. Even though the mountain has appeared on maps for some time, the approach is long and difficult, and the peak was unlikely to have been climbed before.

Their approach from Punta de Vacas took four days and included crossings of the Río Tupungato (plus a 100m rock traverse above the river at UIAA IV+), Río Taguas, and Arroyo Chorrillo. The climbers made a high camp at 4,600m. From there, on March 31, they climbed a rocky couloir on the northwest side of the mountain, with 35°–40° scree and some easy but exposed rock steps. This led to a 5,300m plateau where they traversed across hard snow patches toward the summit. The summit comprised an exposed and rotten perch that admitted only one person at a time. They had a three-day journey back to Punta de Vacas, reaching it on April 3. 📷

—**Marcelo Scanu,** *Argentina*

Crossing the Río Taguas en route to Cerro Santa Clara. The approach to the previously unclimbed 5,400-meter peak took four days. Glauco Muratti

CERRO CAPICUA, PICAFLOR, FIRST FREE ASCENT

Cerro Capicua is a 1,000m wall whose name derives from a Catalan phrase meaning "head and tail." In early 2017, during my first trip to Cochamó, a new aid route on Capicua called Picaflor (Spanish for "hummingbird") caught hold of my imagination and wouldn't let go for seven years.

The route was put up by Tom Ireson, Martin Håskjold Larsen, Clare Mains, Barry Smith, and Fernando Virot (*AAJ 2017*). Although they had hoped to create a free route, they found the relentless sealed cracks and blank slabs too difficult. After abandoning those ambitions, they continued to equip the route so it might be freed by another party in the future. (The 24-pitch route initially went at around 5.10+ A1.) During stints of rain, when the Picaflor team would

Will Sharp on the long, immaculate 5.13b stemming corner two pitches above the Plaza Catalunya bivy ledge on Cerro Capicua. *Ian Dzilenski*

return to the valley floor, Tom would talk about what a gem the route was and that it would "certainly go free."

Fast-forward to January 1, 2022. Bronwyn Hodgins, Danford Jooste, Tyler Karow, and I were heading to Chile to give our best effort at freeing this spectacular wall. We spent approximately 21 days living on the wall, with Plaza Catalunya (a huge ledge ten pitches up) acting as our wall camp. With Tyler as our big-wall ace, we first aided the pitches, added supplementary bolts where it felt necessary, cleaned the pitches, top-roped them, and eventually led them in a team-free style. By the end of our 2022 trip, our team had freed all of the 1,050m route—with difficulties up to 5.13+—except for one desperate slab move on pitch 20.

I had invested around ten days of work into pitch 20 and deemed it possible, but just barely. The line of incipient features would surely be the most difficult piece of granite slab climbing I had touched. I knew that I'd need to improve my climbing level if I wanted to stand a chance at freeing Picaflor, so for the next two years I trained

with that specific intention.

I returned to Cochamó in early 2024 with a new team: Bronwyn's husband, Jacob Cook, and budding Yosemite master Will Sharp. For five weeks, we dedicated ourselves to Picaflor. We spent many nights sleeping on the midway ledge and used fixed ropes to ease access to the most difficult pitches, which are around 800m up the face.

While swinging around on our ropes, Will spotted an unlikely variation I had failed to explore on the previous expedition. It climbs more directly into the original line out a featured roof, using knee bars and granite wizardry. This allowed us to skip the slab traverse that had shut me down before. Despite being "easier," this pitch still clocked in at around 5.13+, and we gave it the tongue-in-cheek name "The Strenuous V4." Above was a second 5.13+ pitch, featuring the sort of wild slab climbing one might find in a bouldering competition—we dubbed it "The World Cup Pitch."

After about a month of work on the route, we started a continuous push as a team on February 23. Over seven days,

Will, Jacob, and I free climbed every pitch from Plaza Catalunya up, with each of us leading the two 5.13+ crux pitches; we split the rest of the leads evenly. We topped out on February 29.

Over my two trips, I spent around 45 nights camped on Plaza Catalunya, working on Picaflor. For me, that time shared on the wall represents the duality of the climbing experience. The heavy workloads and exhausting days, when paired with the endless laughter and joy of discovery, came together to create an experience that only climbing can provide. Capicua, true to its name, helped us to see and appreciate both sides of the coin: head and tail, dark and light.

—**Hayden Jamieson,** *USA*

Cerra Capicua and Picaflor (24 pitches, 5.13+). Other routes on the face not shown. Jaron Pham

FREE ASCENT OF ENTRE CRISTALES Y CÓNDORES IN COCHAMÓ: *Shortly after completing a team-free ascent of Riders on the Storm (1,300m, 5.13a) on the Central Tower of Paine (see p.218), Siebe Vanhee (Belgium) headed to Cochamó Valley and made a free ascent of Entre Cristales y Cóndores. Located up the Anfiteatro Valley on Atardecer, the 11-pitch route was established at 5.12- C1 in 2022 by Thomas Gilmore and Kevin Heinrich (AAJ 2023). Only the 30m tenth pitch had yet to go free. Vanhee freed the 5.13b overhanging hand and finger crack on his third try, placing gear.*

—**Whitney Clark,** *AAJ*

CHILE | Aysén Region

CORDILLERA EMPERADOR GUILLERMO: CERRO MESA, CERRO MIRADOR, AND PUNTA RINCÓN, NEW ROUTES

The Cordillera Emperador Guillermo is located north of Coyhaique and a few kilometers west of the town of Villa Ortega. Despite the proximity to town, the range emanates a great deal of mystery and solitude. Spanning about five kilometers from southwest to northeast, the most prominent summits include Punta Rincón (ca 1,915m), Cerro Azul (ca 1,900m), Cerro Mesa (ca 1,941m), and Cerro Emperador Guillermo Norte (ca 2,100m), the tallest in the range. Climbing began here only recently, in the early 2000s, and has concentrated on the south and east flanks. For me, the range is an old acquaintance, which I first began to know in 2010.

In mid-September 2023, I visited the range with Gustavo Durán, intent on climbing a new route on the south face of Cerro Mesa (45°19'06"S, 72°11'44"W). Cerro Mesa was first climbed by Francisco Croxatto and Samuel Esmiol in April 2005 (route unknown). Daniel Zapata and I made the second ascent, climbing the southeast face in December 2010.

Approaching the Cordillera Emperador Guillermo from the east, with Punta Rincón in the center, Cerro Mirador to its left, and the blocky summit of Cerro Azul on the right. *Marco Poblete*

With Gustavo's 21 years to my 41, we achieved a good synergy based on vitality and experience. To approach, we followed the Río Azul, hiking south-southwest for three hours to a campsite at the moraine. The mountains were very heavy with snow.

The next day, we set off at 5 a.m., moving through the dark with snowshoes and headlamps. At 7:30 a.m. we reached a steep south-southeast-facing glacial ramp. I led two pitches of snow and ice up to 70°, then we simul-climbed for about 120m until reaching the upper ramp, where the slope and the exposure lessened. Nonetheless, the upper ramp demanded a lot from us. We felt tired and the cold was intense (I never took off my down jacket).

From the top of the ramp, we continued up the rocky south ridge to the summit, progressing around gendarmes covered in ice. At 12:15 p.m., we stood on the summit of Cerro Mesa, our wintertime effort resulting in a well-deserved reward: Diagonal Sur (500m, AD 70°). It took us three hours to descend, using one rappel to avoid the initial, steeper pitches.

In mid-October, Gustavo and I

returned with the goal of climbing the east face of Punta Rincón (45°20'11"S, 72°12'32"W). I first saw this face with Eduardo Jara in December 2012, when we made the first known ascent of Punta Rincón. On that climb, we chose an east-facing gully north of the summit (climber's right of the central east face); this led to an obvious col from where we rounded onto the west face, overcoming some rock steps in the final section. It had been a long time since a goal generated so much anxiety and uncertainty in me.

We followed the same three-hour approach and rested the evening before our climb. The next morning, we were on the move by 3:30 a.m. The snow was hard, progress was rapid, and we gained altitude easily up a left-trending couloir that leads toward the col on Punta Rincón's southeast shoulder. As this gully steepened, it appeared that a diagonal, rightward-trending snow slope would lead us onto the east face. However, the slope turned out to be quite vertical and exposed for hundreds of meters, with snow of dubious quality. We opted for plan B: continuing up to the col, from where we could ascend the south face.

The col separates Punta Rincón from a likely unclimbed summit to the south that we propose to call Cerro Mirador (ca 1,700m). We decided to climb Cerro Mirador first, and we ascended snow slopes on its east-northeast shoulder to arrive at the summit by dawn. The summit is crowned by a prominent ten-meter rock step that we overcame to the east. On the summit, we enjoyed an incredible sunrise and analyzed the route we would attempt on the south face of Punta Rincón.

We first descended back to the col and then began zigzagging up the face between rock steps and ledges, keeping the rope mostly in our backpacks. Eventually, we anchored in the ice below the first real pitch, and Gustavo led a narrow, exposed gully to the upper snowfield. From there, it was my turn. After placing a couple of short ice screws, I used snow stakes to

CLOCKWISE FROM TOP LEFT: Dos Generaciones (400m, AD+ 65°) on the south side of Punta Rincón; Gustavo Durán and Marco Poblete on top of Punta Rincón; on the summit of Cerro Mirador at dawn, looking toward the south side of Punta Rincón, which the climbers ascended next. *All photos by Marco Poblete*

protect the steep slope. It was a perfect morning—cold, always in the shade, but windless—as we made our way up a forgotten staircase of the Patagonian Andes. We climbed one final steep section, using cams to protect the rocky exit.

On the summit ridge, the sun was shining brightly, offering some warmth to our extremities. The summit was close, about 60m away, but first we had to solve about eight meters of mixed climbing (M3). I did this without much style: After breaking through rime crust to place a couple of cams, I *crawled* the final meters. At 12:30 p.m., we both stood on the tiny summit of Punta Rincón. The descent by the 2012 route did not bring any major surprises, allowing us to reach our vehicle again at 7 p.m., exhausted, broken, but infinitely satisfied. We called our route Dos Generaciones (400m, AD+ 65°).

—**Marco Poblete**, *Chile*

NOTES ON THE CORDILLERA EMPERADOR GUILLERMO:

The first reported ascent of Cerro Emperador Guillermo Norte (45°18'38"S, 72°10'57"W) was by Richard Mansilla and Ignacio Vergara in December 2013; their route was repeated in October 2016, by Pablo Cid, Sebastian Jans, and Marco Poblete. The route climbs the east face to the col between Cerro Emperador Guillermo Sur and Norte, then up the latter's south side.

In April 2017, Hugo Castañeda and Martin Hatmann climbed a new route on the northeast ridge of Cerro Emperador Guillermo Norte over three days, using two bivouacs; they reported six pitches with maximum difficulties to 5.11. Cerro Emperador Guillermo Sur (ca 1,960m) may be unclimbed.

The other prominent summit of the range, Cerro Azul, located between Punta Rincón and Cerro Mesa, had its first recorded ascent in September 2012 by Hugo Espinoza and Marco Poblete, who ascended a northeast-facing gully to its summit; they called that route Canalón de los Coyhaiquinos (240m, 60°).

PUNTA MILLER, SOUTHWEST FACE

In early November, Andres Bosch, Lucia Guichot, Nico Tapia, and I climbed the obvious gully in the middle of the southwest face of Punta Miller (1,930m, 46°25'46.3"S, 72°34'05.4"W), at the head of the Miller Valley. We drove from Puerto Sánchez and then walked seven hours up the valley to camp below the south face. Our route gained 400m and had one crux pitch of WI4+ and another of M4. [*The first known ascent of Punta Miller, west of the better-known Avellano Towers, was in October 2017, by César Ibáñez and Marco Poblete, who climbed the northwest couloir and proposed the name Punta Miller.*]

—**Oriol Baró,** *Catalunya*

CERRO NORA OESTE, WEST RIDGE

In November, Luca Schiera and I made our fourth trip to the Campo de Hielo Norte (Northern Patagonian Icefield), this time with Andrea Carretta and Giovanni Ongaro, who came along to document the trip. Our goal was Cerro Nora Oeste, a peak we had glimpsed in 2019 from the summit of Cerro Mangiafuoco (*AAJ 2019*) but only saw with binoculars in 2020 when we entered the icefield via the Steffen Glacier. [*Cerro Nora*

The south face of Cerro Nora Oeste. The ascent was by the west ridge (near left skyline). *Paolo Marazzi*

Oeste (-47.106269, -73.434797) is about 1.5km from Cerro Nora (2,460m), first climbed in 2021 by Nadine Lehner and Isidora Llarena; see AAJ 2021.]

We started our approach on November 17. We walked up the Nef Valley for three days with the help of gaucho Don Aguilino, until thick vegetation made it impossible for him to continue with the horses. Since a good weather window was coming, we decided to take climbing gear and a week of food and continue on foot. We walked for two more days, crossing a pass to enter the Cachet Valley, at Lago Cachet Dos, and then continued to the edge of the icefield.

At this point, Giovanni and Andrea decided to rest, while Luca and I continued toward Cerro Nora Oeste. Early in the afternoon of November 23, we reached the base. The peak is huge and impressive, but it was in winter conditions on both the south and north faces after recent storms. We were about to turn back when we caught a glimpse of a possible safe line along the west ridge.

On November 24, Luca and I climbed to the western summit of Cerro Nora Oeste following this ridge. The ascent entailed about 900m of elevation gain, with 300m in a snow gully and 600m of mixed climbing (up to M6+) and rock. The upper ridge was covered with a thick layer of rime. On top, we measured the elevation at 2,420m. [*The mountain has three tops of similar elevation;*

the central summit may be the highest by a few meters.]

That same day, we descended to the glacier and returned to its edge, where we found Giovanni and Andrea waiting. On the ninth and tenth days of our expedition, we returned to the gear cache, then rested and sat out some bad weather for three days. We then started shuttling loads to Lago Colonia. On December 3, with four packrafts loaded with all the gear, we crossed Lago Colonia and rafted part of the Río Colonia. The following day, we finished descending the river to the road at La Rinconada.

We called our route Zenin (900m, 6a+ M6+) and dedicated our ascent to Mario Conti, one of the climbers who made the first ascent of the Ragni Route on Cerro Torre. Mario disappeared on a hike close to his home around the same time we climbed Nora Oeste.

—**Paolo Marazzi,** *Italy*

SOUTHERN PATAGONIA | Chaltén Massif

AGUJA POINCENOT, SOUTH FACE, POT

When Luka Lindič and I stood on top of Aguja St. Exupery after climbing our new route Mir on its south face (*AAJ 2020*), the view to the north was of the imposing south face of Aguja Poincenot (3,002m). We knew about some unclimbed terrain on that section of the wall, but the lack of crack systems and obvious blank rock made it clearer why there were no routes. During our descent from Exupery, we took a couple of photos, having no idea we would look at them so many times in the years to come.

In January 2022, we found ourselves under the wall. On that first visit, we scoped options for a new line and climbed some entering pitches that start from the SUSAT col and traverse onto an obvious buttress shared with Historia Interminable (Cobo-Murcia, 1987); after a few pitches on the buttress, Historia Interminable traverses left, and our line stays 50m to 100m to the right. We later made a second, two-day attempt and climbed 11 pitches, turning around after spending half of the second day climbing 20m of a smooth traverse between two crack systems, one of the major puzzles of the route. It took us two and a half hours to place a single bolt, and we had to lasso a horn high overhead to overcome one blank section.

Before the biggest weather window of that season, I suddenly had to leave for home, so Luka and a friend went back to retrieve the gear we had left under the wall. Fortunately, they hadn't planned to go climbing. Before dawn, one of the biggest rockfalls

Luka Krajnc climbing the amazing corner and "great roof" pitch on Pot (750m, 6c A3) on the south face of Poincenot. *Luka Lindič*

ABOVE: The line of Pot (750m, 6c A3) on the south face of Aguja Poincenot, with Cerro Chaltén in back. *Luka Lindič*

LEFT: The lasso move during the key traverse on the south face of Poincenot. *Luka Krajnc*

in recent times occurred in the approach couloir. Our equipment therefore remained below the wall.

In 2023, we returned to the "scene of the crime," but bad weather and uncertainty about the rockfall situation diverted us to easier goals. In early February 2024, we decided to go for a recon, and a 24-hour round trip from Polacos camp equipped us with the knowledge that our gear under the wall was in great condition. We also managed to climb an additional ten meters of the traverse, add two bolts, and peer into the next crack system, which promised a way forward.

The end of February finally brought good weather for a proper try. On the 23rd, we climbed the familiar first eight pitches and bivouacked. On the second day, we climbed the remaining known meters in the morning, then headed into unknown terrain, using Peckers and all the aid tricks we had. Then, every climber's dream came true in the form of incredible pitches and amazing rock. Splitter cracks that rival any Yosemite classic brought smiles to our faces. Plus, we were rewarded with a perfect bivouac ledge in the middle of a steep wall.

On the third day, an overhanging "changing corners" crack awaited for breakfast, followed by a huge roof visible even from Chaltén. In the afternoon, we found ourselves in less steep terrain. We followed the last 200m of the Whillans-Cochrane Route (1962), where the climbing was easier but the fatigue and weight of the equipment we carried became more evident. At the top, we were rewarded with almost no wind and a vividly glowing sunset, which, together with the inner peace we felt, needed no words. Twenty meters below the summit, we set up a third bivouac on a wedged boulder under a roof. We were woken that night by snowfall but didn't care much. In the morning, we rappelled Whiskey Time (Eggler-Pitelka, 1994) on the east face and stumbled back to town.

In harmony with the changes that happened to us during the life cycle of this project and the history of a climbing partnership that began 20 years ago, we named the route Pot, which is a Slovenian word for "The Path." The route gained 750m (6c A3), with 500m of new climbing. We used nine bolts, three of which are on belays, and climbed the route without fixed ropes. Peckers were used on the crux sections. Low wind or strong fingers are recommended for the lasso move. The rock is very good to amazing in quality. 📷

—Luka Krajnc, *Slovenia*

CERRO TORRE, SOUTHEAST RIDGE, ALL-FEMALE ASCENT

Fanny Schmutz, Maud Vanpoulle, and I all came to El Chaltén for the first time around ten years ago. When I first saw Cerro Torre (3,128m), I knew that one day I'd stand on top of that mountain. Cerro Torre is quite intimidating, but our previous trips to Patagonia had helped a lot in getting us used to the range, the style of climbing, and the long waiting game in town. This year, we felt more than ready to climb it—we just needed a chance.

We arrived in mid-January and made a gear cache at Niponino, focusing our attention on the Southeast Ridge (*AAJ 2012*). [*The Southeast Ridge, or Filo Sureste, is the line established to avoid the bolts on the southeast face placed by Cesare Maestri in 1970. After several attempts, the route was finished in 2012 by Hayden Kennedy and Jason Kruk, who then removed more than 100 of Maestri's bolts. The 800m route has a few variations and goes at around 7a+ C2 WI5 or free at 7c.*] After a month of mostly bad weather, we thought we would go home without even having the chance to give it a try. But finally, ten days before our flight, a good window arrived.

With all the new snow that had fallen in the previous weeks, and after seeing conditions in the mountains, we left our camp at Niponino with the idea of taking it one pitch at a time. On February 23, it took us 11 hours to get to the Col de la Paciencia, our first bivy site, at the foot of the ridge. Breaking trail with fresh snow on the glacier and cleaning the pitches while climbing was time-consuming. Fortunately, we shared the task with two other parties.

After arriving at the col, we could see snowy cracks and a very frozen headwall high above. We planned a leisurely morning, starting around 8 a.m., so the temperature could rise a bit and the rock could dry. One of the teams decided to bail, as they were not optimistic about the conditions.

Fanny Schmutz following the wild ice chimney just below the headwall on Cerro Torre's Southeast Ridge. *Lise Billon*

Fanny Schmutz leading the first 7a+ and third pitch of the headwall, with Cesare Maestri's rime-covered compressor and the summit visible above. *Maud Vanpoulle*

The first pitches in the morning were cold and took us quite a while to get through. However, after three pitches, the terrain eased and the temperature rose, so we managed to get back in the flow. We could hear the other team ahead of us, and it was a very nice feeling to be with another party on such a big route. It was still daylight when we reached our bivy spot on pitch 15. It took us an hour and a half to create an adequate ledge on the ice, where our shoulders could fit while lying down.

On the 25th, we opted for the same strategy as the day before—not starting too early. We were ready to climb by 7:30 a.m. The ice chimney above was absolutely unique: 50m in a steep, narrow corridor that barely allowed you to swing your axes and crampons into the ice. This pitch brought us to the base of the headwall. The hardest was still to come.

We changed boots for climbing shoes and nervously started up. The first pitch, a 5c, was a good warm-up for the 6c pitch: wet, flaky, and intimidating. So, when we arrived at the 6c pitch, although it was still wet and flaky, it was a little less intimidating.

And then came the last two hard pitches. We opted for the right variation, climbing to a belay to the right of and level with the famous compressor that Maestri used to drill all those bolts. Leading up to this moment, there had been a lot of fear and worry about these pitches. Yet somehow they didn't even feel that hard. You still have to have focus and climb, but when you reach that point, it feels like you're flying to the top.

It was 7 p.m. on the 25th of February when we stood on top of Cerro Torre and realized our common dream. Some tears were shed, some laughs were shared, and a selfie was made. We started rappelling soon after, as our goal was to make it down to our previous bivy. Going down the headwall, we could see the meltwater begin to freeze. The path we had taken up to the summit was now closed.

When we reached our bivy ledge atop pitch 15, the platform we'd chopped had shrunk in the heat of the sun. But we still decided to set up the tent, which was a good call because it snowed that night much more than predicted. We felt lucky to be on our way down and thought of all the lights we could see in the Fitz Roy massif and our friends up there.

Fortunately, we had good weather on the 26th, so we took it easy on the descent. When we reached Niponino at 6 p.m., the call of our comfy beds was too strong, so we decided to hike all the way back to El Chaltén. As always, the way back from the Torre Valley felt quite long, but this time, it had a slightly different taste. 📷

—**Lise Billon,** *France*

CHALTÉN SEASON SUMMARY

The 2023–2024 season in the Chaltén Massif was statistically "average" for weather, meaning there were few windows and conditions were challenging. For a change, and thankfully, there were no fatalities in the massif. There were only two serious accidents, both in the Cerro Torre valley. Because of how much the glacier has receded, the trail into this valley is exposed and difficult, so the rescue team avoids making retrievals on foot. For both rescues, helicopters were used, and they flew from Río Gallegos, three hours away, at a cost of $30,000 in each case. Before coming to climb in this area, be sure to obtain rescue insurance that covers at least that much.

On the far right side of the north face of Cerro Grande, Giovanni Zaccaria and Claudio Migliorini (Italy) benefited from a cold spell during poor weather and climbed a 300m new line (65°). The crux was descending in the storm, with low visibility, following the line of ascent.

Two variations were climbed on El Mocho. Yannick Glatthard and Jonas Schild (Switzerland) started up Moribito and, halfway up, traversed to a splitter immediately right, climbing four pitches (Plan YX, A2 6c) to join Bizcochuelo. In the stunning shield to the right of Frader Pisafe, Nicolas Lewin and Leon Riveros from Chile and Ignacio Mulero from Spain climbed a six-pitch splitter—a jewel. They returned a few days later to free it (Arigato Chaltén; one 5.13 pitch, mostly 5.10 and 5.11). On Aguja de la Medialuna, Nicolás Gutierrez, Alexis Rojas, and Hernan Salas (Chile) climbed Con la Calma (300m, 5.11), a line to the left of Harvest Moon, which it joins for its last two pitches.

The Southeast Ridge of Cerro Torre was climbed four times, its eighth to 12th ascents, including the first all-female ascent—one of the hardest done yet in the area (*see report above*). On Cerro Chaltén, Laura Tiefenthaler (Austria) and Thomas Bukowski (USA) summited via El Corazón in difficult conditions; Tiefenthaler's was the first female ascent of the route. On the opposite side of the peak, Lucia Guichot and Nieves Gil, two members of the Spanish young female alpinist team, climbed Supercanaleta, doing its second all-female ascent.

On the east face of Aguja Guillaumet, Matías Korten and Pedro Navarro (Argentina) climbed a beautiful rock pillar, finding six pitches with difficulties to 5.11. On the west face of Aguja Val Biois, Korten and Pierrick Saint-Martin (France) climbed a massive right-leaning corner that was gritty in the lower half but had good Patagonia granite after that. The nine pitches of Gracias a Vos have difficulties to 6c C1. Yet another crack system was climbed on the north face of Aguja Poincenot: a five-pitch variation, said

Laura Tiefenthaler en route to the east face of Cerro Chaltén, where she and Thomas Bukowski made the sixth ascent (and first female ascent) of El Corazón over two days. The route climbs the pillar in the center of the face. *Thomas Bukowski*

to be of very good quality, to the left of the middle section of 40° Gruppo Ragni, done by Michał Czech and Jakub Kokowski (Poland).

There were a number of thefts at Niponino camp. Although some of the gear was recovered when the thief was apprehended, this must be kept in mind when leaving caches and choosing a storage method and hiding place.

With a donation from Edelrid, the local rescue team was able to replace the 300m of rope across the approach slabs to the base of Mermoz and Guillaumet's west faces. The previous ones had been placed over ten years ago and were in very bad shape. ▤

—**Rolando Garibotti**

CHILE | Torres del Paine

CUERNO PRINCIPAL, SERENVIDA

In early 2023, Diego Arredondo and Camila Monsalve (Chile) started working on the first route up the north face of Cuerno Principal in Torres del Paine National Park, approaching via the Bader Valley. That season they made two attempts, the second with Shutaro Fujiwara (Japan).

In February 2024, the three of them, along with Angela Cardenas (Chile), were able to finish the route, though they did not make the summit. Their line starts on a pedestal 100m right of the col with Cuerno Este, and at two-thirds height traverses left to follow an obvious corner. This leads to the slate band on the upper mountain. There were two aid sections that required pitons, including Peckers, and a handful of copperheads.

Once on the slate, they traversed right to the original 1968 line, climbing two pitches up it before retreating, five pitches below the summit. In all they covered 500m with difficulties up to 5.11 and A2+. It took them three days, spending two cold nights on the wall. They christened their route Serenvida.

—**Rolando Garibotti**

The north face of Cuerno Principal, showing the new route Serenvida on the left and the original 1968 route coming in from the right. Arriba Quemando el Sol, climbed in 2023 on the west face (hidden), finished on the 1968 route. *Rolando Garibotti*

CUERNO PRINCIPAL, ARRIBA QUEMANDO EL SOL

On December 6, 2023, Javier Reyes and I ventured into the French Valley in search of adventure on the west face of Cuerno Principal. A big winter snowpack meant that the first warm weather window of the season had left most features dripping wet and out of condition. A long pillar that leads to the upper metamorphic rock on Cuerno Principal had caught my eye while guiding other mountains in the French Valley, and its exposure to the strong westerly winds and prow-like nature meant it would probably be dry enough. There are two routes farther south on this wall: The first to the right is Junto a Vasquez (Labarca-Retamal, 1998), which is around three pillars farther over, then the normal (1968) route up the southwest ridge.

After spending a night under a large boulder on the moraine below the west face, Javi and I were on route at 7 a.m., simuling some 5th-class dihedrals before belaying ten rope lengths to the "headwall"

Sebastian Pelletti leading pitch six of Arma de Doble Filo (800m, 5.11+ A1). The climbers would bivouac on the big ledge just above, then continue up the headwall in the morning. *Hernán Rodriguez*

of the pillar. Here, the golden-red rock proved to have amazing climbing; we transitioned from one side of the prow to the other before pulling onto the shoulder of the west face and then scrambling some 200m. After previous experience on Los Cuernos (*AAJ 2022*), new-routing on this loose metamorphic rock seemed frivolous, and it made sense to continue up the 1968 Chilean line to the summit. Another team was on the route, so we waited until they had summited and descended, to avoid any rockfall, before climbing the seven loose and run-out pitches to the top.

After rapping the metamorphic rock back to the shoulder, we decided to bivy and descend the original route at sunrise. We watched the shadowed silhouettes of Cuerno Norte, Mascara, Hoja, and Espada stretch and project themselves against the glowing red west face of Paine Chico before dozing off, then returned to the beech forest and the bustling tourist trails the next day.

We named our route Arriba Quemando el Sol ("Up High the Sun Is Burning," 650m, 5.11-) after a classic Chilean folklore tune, by Violeta Parra, that rang true at our boulder bivy below the route. 📷

—Sebastian Pelletti, *Chile*

LA ESPADA, ARMA DE DOBLE FILO

At the end of February 2024, after a season of bad conditions and weather, a spell of high pressure appeared in the forecast for Southern Patagonia. I prepared to make my third foray into the Bader Valley of the season, hoping to finish a line I had spotted in the spring. When powder snow coats the enormous east faces that line this cirque, it reveals features and textures that otherwise camouflage into the immensity of steep granite. After reading about Jimmy Haden, Sean Leary, and Russel Mitrovich's first ascent of the east face of La Espada (Under the Knife, *AAJ 2001*), and having stood below the face during other trips into the valley, a direct line on the left side of the face had piqued my curiosity.

Hernán Rodriguez and I had already ventured to this far end of the valley during a windy 30-hour window in early February, and we'd managed to climb to just below the steep, golden headwall before the impending front of bad weather—and the considerable difficulties ahead—convinced us to descend.

As we trudged up to the Welsh Camp

The line of Arma de Doble Filo (800m, 5.11+ A1) on the east face of La Espada. The original route (Haden-Leary-Mitrovich, 2000) was to the right. The peak to the left is La Hoja. *Ankar Patagonico*

once again, we contemplated the stunning east faces of Los Cuernos, La Mascara, La Hoja, and La Espada, all plastered in snow that had fallen in the last 48 hours. Our line started about 100m to the left of the 2000 route, on lower-angle slabs. A system of flakes and rooflets would funnel snow and water onto us, and we doubted whether we'd even be able to reach our high point. Fortunately, the following day we were able to resolve these first six pitches before the sun turned our line into a torrent of snowmelt. We dug out a bivy site on ledges halfway up the face, just big enough for two.

The east faces in Torres del Paine receive sunshine as soon as the sun crests the horizon. Bathed in amber light, we began the upper pitches of our route, with amazing 5.10 and 5.11 free climbing for five pitches up a corner system to reach the top of a pillar that provides access to the golden-red headwall. From the valley floor, through binoculars, I had barely made out a fissure that snaked through this dead-vertical panel. The climbing here proved truly spectacular, as the 100m crack went straight up and then horizontally, with one beak move to switch systems at half height. After two more rope lengths, we had

escaped the east face. We connected with the scrambly south ridge to the summit and basked in sunshine on top. A small can of muscle relaxants glistened among the rubble at our feet. Inside, we found a roll of paper and a perfectly sharpened pencil, along with the signatures of the South African team that had made the first ascent of La Espada in 1972.

We traveled back to 1972 in our minds, envisioning their six-man team fixing lines and questing up the west face from the French Valley, and then to the year 2000, when Russel, Sean, and Jimmy had embarked on their voyage. We added our names to this small roll of history, buried it back where it belongs, and descended our line to high camp on the slabs below.

We named our route Arma de Doble Filo (800m, 5.11+ A1), which translates to "double-edged sword," a metaphor for anything that possesses a certain duality, such as alpine climbing, thin taglines, slung rappel blocks, and many other elements of our adventure. ◙

—**Sebastian Pelletti,** *Chile*

CENTRAL TOWER OF PAINE, RIDERS ON THE STORM, FIRST FREE ASCENT

In 1991, Germans Kurt Albert, Bernd Arnold, Norbert Bätz, Peter Dittrich, and Wolfgang Güllich made the first ascent of Riders on the Storm (1,300m, 7c A3). The 38-pitch rock line, which tracks up the center of the east face of Torre Central, was primarily climbed free, with only five aid pitches, including a long pendulum traverse (*AAJ 1992*).

In the three decades since, a completely free ascent of the line has been attempted by a number of teams, including Nicolas and Olivier Favresse, Mike Lecomte, and Seán Villanueva O'Driscoll (Belgium), who freed all but four pitches in 2006 and noted a possible free variation to avoid the pendulum. In 2016, Ines Papert (Germany), Mayan Smith-Gobat (New Zealand), and Thomas Senf (Switzerland) freed two of the original aid pitches and unlocked the potential five-pitch free variation after pitch 13; they summited, but rockfall and poor conditions prevented them from completing the free ascent (*AAJ 2020*). Smith-Gobat returned the following year with Brette Harrington (USA), documented by photographer Drew Smith (USA), but did not make any progress. Harrington, Jacopo Larcher (Italy), and Siebe Vanhee (Belgium) were similarly stymied in 2023.

Over three weeks in January-February 2024, the team of Vanhee, Nicolas Favresse, and Villanueva O'Driscoll, along with photographer Smith, finally made the route's complete free ascent, encountering difficulties up to 7c+ on the free variation, as well as no shortage of snow, ice, and wind upwards of 80 mph.

The 2024 team reached the summit in 18 days, swapping leads, with each team member (except Smith) following all pitches free. The free variation entails a downclimb followed by two pitches at 7b+ leading into

Siebe Vanhee leading pitch 17 during the first free ascent of Riders on the Storm (1,300m, 7c+) on the east face of the Central Tower of Paine. This pitch was the crux of a five-pitch variation to the original route. *Drew Smith*

the 7c+ crux—two side-by-side cracks running up to a roof—which was led by Vanhee. Another 7c crux is found before rejoining the original route. They reached pitch 26, the enormous Rosendach roof, by their sixth day, but cold and ice then paralyzed them below the roof for a week. When the weather cleared, they pushed ahead and—after another pause for two days due to heavy spindrift—summited on February 9.

The team said conditions, not technical difficulty, were the primary hurdle on this route, both in this effort and in previous ones. Their success, they said, came as a result of patience, luck, and the drive to take advantage of every possible weather window, no matter how small.

In 2017, the same trio freed the 1,200m El Regalo de Mwono, at 8a, on the east face of the Central Tower. Favresse, Villanueva O'Driscoll, and Ben Ditto freed the South African Route on the same formation in 2009. 📷 🔍

— **Owen Clarke, *AAJ*, with information**
from the climbing team

The complete traverse of the Torres del Paine went from southwest to northeast over (A) Torre Sur, (B) Torre Central, (C) Torre Norte, and (D) Peineta. The line and bivouacs are marked. *Francisco Bedeschi*

LA TRAVESÍA DOBLE M

A SOLO TRAVERSE OF THE FOUR TORRES DEL PAINE

By Rolando Garibotti, *with information from Seán Villanueva O'Driscoll, Belgium*

On February 22, Seán Villanueva O'Driscoll walked to Campo Británico in the French Valley. It rained all night. In the morning, his sleeping bag, rope, and other gear were wet. He spent a slow morning drying things out, then, around mid-day, started hiking into the De Agostini Valley.

The forecast predicted four days of stable weather, but it was cold and there was ice and new snow from the previous night's deluge. It was not quite the kind of weather window that suggests the amount of climbing that Seán had in mind, but he has never been short of poetic faith, the ability to suspend disbelief and to allow oneself to, against all preconceptions, walk forward, one step, move, or pitch at a time. The dream of traversing the four Paine towers spurred him on.

While a number of traverses of the towers have been done, only on one

occasion had the skyline been followed continuously: Pedro Cifuentes did it in 2013, going from north to south. No traverse had included the fourth tower, La Peineta. Discussing options with a friend, Seán concluded a southwest-to-northeast traverse made the most geographic sense, starting via the west ridge of Torre Sur and then tackling the south faces of the Central and North towers and Peineta.

As his first climb, Seán had set his sights on Il Lungo Sogno (900m, 5.10 A2 60°), a beautiful climb that initially tackles a prominent corner on the north side of the west ridge of Torre Sur. He climbed two pitches to a recess and another up the corner, then rappelled back down to spend the night. The freezing line was quite low, and the ice and snow from the previous night had not melted out. Conditions did not improve in the morning. A steep, iced-up section, which normally would be free climbable, required aid using a Pecker and a few micro-nuts.

After a few more pitches, he reached the crest of the ridge, where conditions improved, allowing him to make faster progress. He belayed every pitch and followed with a heavy pack, carrying a light tent, food for five days, two gas canisters, two light ice tools, crampons, a light sleeping bag, and a good bit of clothing. He reached the summit of Torre Sur in the evening and quickly started rappelling the Aste Route along the north ridge. Two-thirds of the way down, he turned on his headlamp and continued to Col Condor, at the base of Torre Central, where he set up the tent and slept for a few hours.

On the morning of the 24th, the Kearney-Knight Route (850m, 5.10 A2) on the south face of Torre Central beckoned—a climb that has seen only a few ascents. The original topo was unclear, so he took some time to identify the start, and more time to find the splitter through the steep middle headwall. On two pitches here, he resorted to aid. In the upper third, he made faster progress, scrambling up to reach the summit. Without delay, he tackled the descent to the north, via the Bonington-Whillans Route. Three parties bivied partway up that route were surprised to see their favorite bearded bard descend upon them from the heights.

Night had already fallen when he reached Col Bich, but he was aware that the new day would bring some marginal weather, so he continued, climbing the Monzino Route (200m, 5.10b) on the southwest side of Torre Norte to bivouac one pitch below the summit. He slept only two hours, and with the first light of February 25, he tagged the summit, then began downclimbing to the north, crossed over the north summit of Torre Norte, and descended Spirito Libero to the base of Peineta, the fourth tower.

The best bit of climbing on this traverse turned out to be the last. Puro Filete (300m, 5.11 A1) follows a striking

On the summit of Torre Central during the second full day of the traverse. *Seán Villanueva O'Driscoll*

splitter on the south face of Peineta, a queen line. Seán did the seven-pitch route in four long pitches. The climbing is challenging, with two cruxes: a thin crack in the lower part and an offwidth near the top. He aided the lower crux and French-freed two moves elsewhere. At the top of Peineta, with clouds already covering most of the summits, he could finally take a short break. After a chat with two climbers there, he traversed north along the ridge, then descended northwest, partially down the Via dell'Agordino, making several steep rappels to reach a ramp that led back to the base.

In a weather window that was far from promising, with challenging climbing conditions, and in spite of fatigue from having just spent 18 days on the east face of Torre Central free climbing Riders on the Storm (*see previous pages*)—and while still recovering from a broken elbow suffered in November—Seán navigated a seemingly endless roller coaster of golden granite, entering the park via one valley and exiting at the opposite end via another. He named his line the Travesía Doble M, a nod to other Paine traverses and treks named after their appearance, including the popular W hike and the W Traverse of the Torres del Paine (pioneered by Steve Schneider in 2002). It had taken 90 minutes short of 72 hours to ride the longest and most complete traverse of the Torres yet. [*See Pataclimb.com for more history of Paine traverses and details on the individual routes.*]

Antarctica

Skiing the east face of Mt. Bridgman (1,410m GPS) on Liard Island, with Glen Peak in back on the right. The skiers made the first known ascent of Bridgman by the same route. *Phil Wickens*

Antarctic Peninsula

LIARD ISLAND, MT. BRIDGMAN

In January 2024, I led a team of six aboard the yacht *Icebird* to make a number of ski ascents in the Grandidier Channel and Crystal Sound areas. After an ascent of frequently climbed Mt. Scott (880m), the team summited a 530m peak on Lahille Island (first climbed by a group led by me in February 2019), followed by two minor unclimbed summits on Larrouy Island.

We then headed south of the Antarctic Circle and on January 14 landed on a small cape on the east coast of Liard Island. We traversed to the unnamed glacier that flows northeast from Mt. Bridgman, the highest point of the island (approx. 66.825442°S, 67.368824°W), and established a camp.

The following day, in perfect weather, we made the first known ascent of Mt. Bridgman, via an improbable-looking line up its east face, following a minor glacier to reach the south ridge and southwest summit slopes. We measured the elevation on top as 1,410m. We then made a very enjoyable ski descent via the line of ascent. 📷

—**Phil Wickens**, *U.K.*

Ellsworth Mountains

HERITAGE RANGE, FIRST ASCENTS

Alex Brough, Ryan Burke, and Will Reno (USA), with ALE guide Eli Potter, made a number of ascents on the ridge between the Splettstoesser and Gowan glaciers in the northern Heritage Range, east of the Founders Peaks. After an initial attempt to reach the area by Twin Otter on January 2, 2024, the team traveled 85km north in 3.5 hours the next day aboard an ALE Sno-Cat, then established an intermediate camp on the southern side of the Anderson Massif. On January 4, they continued west on skis and established a camp at 79°14'S, 85°30'W on a plateau of the upper Splettstoesser Glacier. The next day they climbed the north-northwest ridge of Mt. Herrin (1,756m, 79°26'S, 85°76'W), starting with a 40° snow slope followed by 4th-class scrambling along a mixed ridge, for a total gain of around 360m.

On January 6, the team climbed two small peaks nearby, mostly on skis. The first they named Wolverine Peak (1,497m, 79°13.36'S, 85°40.39'W), climbed via Red Dawn Ridge, rising 120m on 40° snow. The second was the Kraken (1,480m, 79°14.49'S, 85°37.27'W), climbed up its northern side for 210m, also at 40°. The next day they skied to the eastern side of a peak they had been calling the Shark's Fin and climbed the north ridge on firm 45° snow to its 1,512m summit (79°14.71'S, 85°40.67'W). At the top, the team decided to continue along an attractive rock ridge for more than a kilometer to a prominent humped snow summit they named Moby Dick (1,558m, 79°15.17'S, 85°42.75'W), with the summit reached by a slope of 50° alpine ice.

On January 8 the team returned to the ALE camp at Union Glacier, and the following day Brough, Reno, and Potter climbed a new couloir route on Mt. Rossman, the popular 1,450m peak close to camp. Their ascent involved six pitches of 45°–50° snow and ice, plus some simul-climbing. The gully ended in a short, steep rock wall that the trio avoided by moving right over easier mixed ground to the summit. They named their route The Warriors' Way. 🅾

—**Damien Gildea,** *with information from Ryan Burke and Eli Potter*

Climbing the northern side of Moby Dick, having traversed the long ridge from the Shark's Fin (center), climbed earlier in the day. The truncated rock summit left of center is Landmark Peak (1,840m), first climbed in 1992. In the far distance is the Sentinel Range. *Eli Potter*

Queen Maud Land

RITSCHERGIPFEL, SECOND ASCENT AND NEW ROUTE

On my seventh expedition to Queen Maud Land, I and the experienced New Zealand mountain guide Mike Roberts climbed a new, short, and relatively safe route up the eastern flank of Ritschergipfel (2,791m, 71°24'21"S, 13°20'52"E). From Novo Airbase, we flew to a plateau east of the peak and reached the summit on November 6 after four hours of ascent and 800m of vertical gain using skis and crampons. On the summit it was bitterly cold, with a temperature of -32°C and strong wind.

Ritschergipfel is the highest peak of the Gruber Mountains in the northeastern part of the Wohlthat Massif. It was discovered on February 3, 1939, on a reconnaissance flight during the third German Antarctic Expedition, using a Dornier Wal flying boat catapulted from the MS *Schwabenland*. The peak was named after the expedition leader, Captain Alfred Ritscher.

The first ascent was made on December 17, 1991, by German scientists Wieland Adler and Gerold Noack, based at the former GDR Georg Forster station in the Schirmacher Oasis. They reached Lake Unter-See with tracked vehicles and from there climbed the mountain in 10.5 hours. On February 9, 1996, the German geologist Joachim Jacob and Austrian mountain guide Joe Rainer reached the summit after a helicopter landing and ten-minute walk—a practice that has been quite common in the mountains of Antarctica. 🅾

—**Christoph Höbenreich,** *Austria*

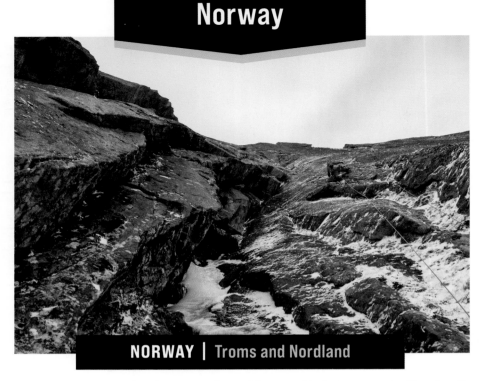

Norway

NORWAY | Troms and Nordland

Greg Boswell heading into the unknown on pitch two of The Horns of Segla. "To my surprise," he writes, "I found just enough tiny hooks for my picks to keep moving up." *Hamish Frost*

SENJA ISLAND, SEGLA, THE HORNS OF SEGLA

My wife and I visited Senja during a van tour around Norway in the summer of 2022, and I took a photo of the northeast face of Segla. I've had it set as my laptop background ever since. I've spent a lot of time daydreaming over this beautiful mountain, and there's one line that always had my attention.

I returned to the Arctic island in February 2023 with Guy Robertson and Hamish Frost. We stayed at Senja Lodge, whose owner, Bent Eilertsen, knows the area extensively. After a few days, a window arrived and we found ourselves trudging up through deep snow to the beautiful but imposing granite face. Even in the winter, the mountain has a moderate approach from the village east of the mountain, Fjordgård.

We were aiming for a groove system that splits the wall, but there were some obvious blank sections higher up. I opted to take the first two pitches, knowing the climbing would calm my nerves. Or so I thought—the first pitch was much trickier than expected. I had to wrestle up an icy offwidth, with poor feet and minimal protection. As this pitch had looked straightforward from below, doubts about the harder-looking upper sections started to gain momentum, but I hid my worried thoughts.

The protection was a little suspect as I moved up slowly on the second pitch, looking for a way through the blankness. To my surprise, I found just enough tiny hooks for my picks to keep moving up and away from my last runner, which was now well below me. I committed to a strenuous rock-over onto the blank slab and past the point of no return. Thankfully, I've been in this situation many times in Scotland, and I knew to compose myself and focus on getting to the safety of the belay. I followed a line of weaknesses and gained a

ledge at the foot of the main corner line that cuts straight up the face.

The route didn't let up, and every time we finished a pitch and looked at the next, we were sure our adventure would end. We kept pushing on upward into the night and found ourselves at a horizontal weakness we had seen from below. Guy pulled off a scary leftward traverse with the full length of the face dropping away below him, and then we had only one hard pitch left before easy ground. I took the sharp end, and, to my delight, the steep, intimidating corner succumbed with little fight. After six challenging pitches, we moved over easy terrain to the summit.

As I sat on top of Segla looking down on the lights and beautiful fjords below, I was in a small state of shock. The route had been truly amazing to climb, but also one of the more mentally engaging battles I'd had in the mountains in quite a while.

We called the route The Horns of Segla (Scottish IX,10). [*The Scottish team opened the second winter route on the northeast face (with one established summer route). The first was Jim Bird and Richard Cross' Aegir (400m, WI5 M6, 2014) up the gully left of the 2023 route. During the 2023 trip, the Scots also established a direct start to Aegir, at a similar grade to the original line, and climbed it to the top.*] 📷

—**Greg Boswell**, *Scotland*

TOP: Starting the fourth pitch, a sustained lead of more than 60 meters. *Hamish Frost*

BOTTOM: The remarkable spire of Segla from the north. The Horns of Segla route ascends the dark face in center, facing the camera. The 2014 route Aegir climbs the obvious steep gully just to the left. Both routes gain about 400 meters. *Hamish Frost*

Aerial view of Stetind (1,392m) and the line of the Southwest Face route. The classic west ridge and south pillar define the edges of the triangular face. *Lars Westvig*

STETIND, SOUTHWEST FACE

With its vertical, anvil-like shape, Stetind (1,392m) rises straight out of the ocean, about 80km southwest of Narvik, and for sailors it's a well-known landmark. In 2002, Stetind was selected as Norway's national mountain. Stetind has a climbing history that dates all the way back to 1910, and there are a few really high-quality routes that are very popular. Most parts of the mountain have been explored, but if you look close, this vast ocean of rock has plenty of potential between existing lines.

By chance, Andreas Widlund and I bumped into each other while waiting for the ferry to Lofoten. Full of excitement, Andreas told me that he had just been to Stetind, scouting and rope-soloing a few pitches on the southwest face. Eighty meters up, the corner he had been following suddenly disappeared and blank slabs forced him back down. "I'm sure it goes in some way! Plus, I've never seen it this dry," he said with a grin. Without

any fixed plans for the coming few days, we quickly decided the only sensible thing was to drive back to Stetind and give it a proper try together. This face had been on my mind for a few years and a lot longer for Andreas.

After sleeping under a large boulder at the base of the wall for a few hours, we racked up and started the first pitch on June 30 around 5:30 p.m. We planned to climb through the night and the next day, and longer if needed. After arriving at Andreas' high point, we climbed a tricky and somewhat bold slab traverse to reach another corner system. This would turn out to be the crux of the entire route at N7 (6c+).

For hours we searched our way higher and higher up the face, freeing every pitch onsight. At times we took wrong turns, resulting in some scary downclimbing or run-out traverses. There was one A0 section on the very last pitch. After 33 hours (with two long breaks), we topped out, happy and very tired.

Our route, the Southwest Face (790m,

N7 A0), climbs straight up the highest part of the face. In the middle we seem to have crossed an existing route (Guldfisken, 11 pitches, N6, Nilsson-Lindberg, 1981). Our route offers everything from tricky slabs and runouts to well-protected corners and steep cracks. The rock quality was mostly good, with occasional wet sections and loose blocks.

—Joda Dolmans, *Norway*

LAPPVIKSTINDEN, LAPPBLAD: *Juho Knuuttila (Finland) rope-soloed a new route up a shallow buttress on the northeast side of Lappvikstinden (1,338m), at the south end of Skjomenfjord, south of Narvik. The route is called Lappblad (600m, Norwegian 6). More details and a photo are at the AAJ website.*

LOFOTEN, KLOKKTINDEN AND RULTEN, NEW ROUTES

For about the last decade, I've made a yearly pilgrimage to the Arctic north, where each winter I hope to squeeze some climbing into rare days off from ski guiding. The Nordland, more than anywhere else I've climbed, is a hard place for weather, conditions, free time, and the right partner to align, but sometimes they do.

When I met Stian Bruvoll, a strong, young guide and native of Narvik, in 2019, our first day out yielded an excellent new route. Due to the pandemic and other issues, we didn't reconnect until 2023. As my departure date for Norway neared, Lofoten's mercurial weather took a turn for the worse and I moved my ticket to the first day in the forecast when temperatures looked to drop below freezing. By the time I arrived, all of that rain and snowmelt had turned to ice, and Stian and I eventually were able to establish three genuinely high-quality and difficult new lines in Lofoten.

We began by pulling on a thread I had seen years ago during a scouting mission to Lofoten's west islands. A few hours' drive through the morning of March 8 landed us at a dark pullout by the side of the E10 below Fjøsdalen, some 12km north

Approaching the north face of Klokktinden. Part of Beyond Cod and Eagle (400m, WI5 M8) is shown. The arrow marks Nowhere's Finest (WI4 M6), hidden to the left. *Stian Bruvoll*

of Reine. We decided to make our approach on foot instead of skis, a decision we'd regret for the entire three hours it took us to reach the face, and again on our return. The tortured post-holing brought us to the northeastern shoulder of Klokktinden (860m) and its east summit—the spire I had seen previously.

A host of icy veins split the dark facade of the 400m north face, with the two most continuous emanating from a shared approach gully. We decided upon the one going right from the top of the gully to the main summit of Klokktinden.

A few hundred feet of snowy wallowing brought us to a belay below an enormous chockstone, and as I racked up, I realized with a shock that one of the nuts attaching the pick of an ice tool was missing. Not having any spares, I reasoned that the bolt, which was still present, was essentially functional, and all I needed to do was keep it in place. I exhausted half a roll of athletic tape in that effort and, with considerable embarrassment, set off.

The route's first crux was surmounting a blank section of overhanging rock. After hanging my pack, I was able to stand as tall as I could and tap a pick into a glaze of ice. Pulling over the lip involved some of the more desperate campused swinging I've

done, followed by pumpier than expected climbing through the drips above.

Luckily, this granted us entry to the runnel we'd seen from below, which in turn brought us to the summit slopes via a succession of ludicrously good ice pitches, most of which Stian led. Unluckily (though perhaps unsurprisingly), my tape did not hold, and the pick of my tool began shifting disconcertingly. I executed another round of repairs, this time with bailing wire in place of the bolt, and set off on the steep sheet of ice at the apex of the ice hose. What looked like a straightforward lead turned out to be more vertical than expected and at times no more than 10cm thick, the difficulties compounded by my frightfully wonky tool and Stian's frightfully dull screws. Copious swearing, both internal and shouted, found us on top of the pitch after almost a full 70m. We topped out as sunset lit the islands in a stunning palette of red, black, and white.

We descended by traversing until we were able to rappel down the peak's steep but short northeast wall, then downclimbed snow slopes to the shoulder from which we had started. We reached the car after 17 hours on the go, and named our route Beyond Cod and Eagle (400m, WI5 M8).

The morning of March 11 again found us driving through the dark toward Klokktinden, aiming for the left of the two lines we'd scoped on the north face. This time we used skis and found the approach considerably less painful.

Upon reaching the face, we set off up the approach gully and were greeted by a firehose of graupel powerful enough to hasten a belay. Stian led out to the left and into a classy mixed corner system, which again offered pitch after pitch of remarkable climbing on mostly moderate ice. That brought us to a shoulder below the east summit, which presented a compact and formidable horn about 150m high. I led into a series of iced corners, and with some considerable hardship, we managed to stitch

into a hidden couloir between it and the headwall, and continued directly.

A few pitches of challenging mixed climbing brought us to an uncomfortable, semi-hanging belay and the route's crux: a terribly overhanging, exposed, and rimed slot, which gave way eventually to ice. Stian dispatched it in great style, and with both of our packs and howling biceps, I barely managed to follow.

From the top, we descended the western ridge and rappelled Syklotronen, benefiting greatly from Stian's knowing the way. After we skied back to shore, the boatman met us with tea and a banana, and we reached Vestpollen about 20 hours after leaving. We named our route No Sleep till Rulten (600m, WI4+ M7), though I had to explain the Beastie Boys before Stian agreed.

On April 1, I flew home. A few days later, Stian messaged me to say that spring had come and the climbing season was over. 📄📷

— **Chris Wright,** *USA*

KJERAG, SILVERBACK

On the north face of Kjerag, the 1,100m wall rising above the south shore of the Lysefjord, Jon Egil Auestad and Jan Eivind Danielsen (Norway) completed a new route on September 9 and 10. The two had explored the upper route earlier in the summer, approaching by the climb Hoka Hey, because the bottom of their intended line was wet; they returned in September to add the start and free the full climb.

The new route shares a start with Nordøstpassasjen ("Northeast Passage," Båsen-Bjørgen-Jensen, 1995) and then climbs between that route and La Vida Es Bella (Marin-Vales, 2005), crossing the latter about two-thirds of the way up. The route is called Silverback (1,000m, 20 pitches, 7b+).

— **Dougald MacDonald,** *with information from Brattelinjer.no*

together a fairly direct line to the summit through continued wind and snow.

We reached the top half plastered in rime and as the light was fading, but were heartened by already knowing the way down. From the shoulder where we'd left our skis, we enjoyed an excellent powder run down. We called this one Nowhere's Finest (400m, WI4 M6).

Some days later, we boarded a fisherman's boat to cross the Austnesfjorden from Vestpollen to Rulten. Known as the "Eiger of Lofoten," the northwest face of Rulten is one of the area's most imposing walls. Finding a way across the fjord had always stopped me from trying it, but Stian got the beta on a boat after repeating the classic Syklotronen on the face while I was busy working.

We began in the same series of runnels that Marko Prezelj and Bjørn-Eivind Årtun took on their 2009 ascent of The Bullocks (600m, M6+), then continued direct where they branched left. Outlandishly good pitches led up to a gendarme at three-quarters height on the face. Where previous routes had veered right here, we made a rappel from the gendarme

ANAFI, MT. KALAMOS, SOUTHEAST FACE, THE RITUAL OF HARDSHIP

Ten years ago, during a flight over the Aegean Sea, I spotted a remarkable rocky mountain rising from the water. The flight attendant could name the neighboring isle of Santorini, but it was only after returning to an internet connection that I discovered the mysterious island's name: Anafi.

The fascination with Anafi resurfaced during conversations with two friends, Nikos Hadjis and the late Yiannis Torelli, who mentioned their route Halcyon on the island's Mt. Kalamos, which rises nearly 500m from the sea at the eastern tip—it is the second-biggest monolith in the Mediterranean, behind Gibraltar. They also mentioned the mountain's potential for new routes. In May 2023, Constantinos Andreou, Andreas Rossidis, and I (all from Cyprus), along with Daniela Banc (Romania) and Jenny Schauroth (Germany), embarked on a journey to unlock Anafi's climbing potential.

Before our visit, the island only had two documented routes: Argonaftiki Ekstratia and Halcyon. In 1999, Thomas Michaelides and Aris Theodoropoulos established the former at 5b, climbing a distinctive pillar on Mt. Kalamos's south-southwest face using trad protection. In 2008, Nikos Hadjis, Yiannis Torelli, and Theodoropoulos established the aesthetic and fully bolted Halcyon (435m, 7a+/7b, 6b+ obl.) on the south face, right underneath the currently unoccupied Kalamiotissa Monastery; the route was freed in 2012 by Nicolas Morell, Iliana Peikova, and Sylvain Perrin.

Navigating logistics on this remote island, as well as figuring out how to put up a route rising directly from the sea, created a unique set of challenges. Daniela and I began by hiking up Mt. Kalamos to look at its virgin southeast face, which we'd picked as our objective for its steep, aesthetic headwall. The hike was a wild and remote ascent, offering the first taste of the exposure that would define our expedition. The wall itself was breathtaking, the high quality of its orange and tan limestone and amazing marble features visible from a distance, its vast scale hard to fathom against the Aegean. Choosing the exact line would not be easy.

As the rest of the team arrived, we

formulated our strategy: For the headwall, we'd employ a top-down/ground-up approach in which we'd abseil to the start of each pitch and then bolt it on lead to get back to the bottom of our fixed lines. This would help us choose the most logical line and also let us install the route in suboptimal weather, when a boat couldn't access the base.

Using this strategy, we equipped ten pitches on the headwall in four days. Meanwhile, on a rest day, a boat ride let us see the wall for the first time from the water and locate our access point, a perfect belay ledge right above the waves. On our fifth and final working day, we divided the labor among all members of the team, stripping our fixed lines and then rapping down the easier lower section, installing anchors as we went.

On May 28, late in the afternoon, we embarked on a bumpy boat ride to the wall. Over the next two and a half days, we cleaned and free climbed the route. The initial climbing was a combination of slabs, steep pitches, and ledges with loose debris. On the first day, we reached Mouse Ledge at around 200m above the water. The second day, we tackled the challenging headwall, working hard as a team to clean holds, free pitches, and navigate the technical terrain. We split into two separate rope parties, and the leader of each team freed every pitch first go except for the crux 15th pitch (7b). For this one, we had to abseil back down from Party Ledge, where we spent our second night on the wall, and free the pitch first thing on our final climbing day.

Our route, The Ritual of Hardship (19 pitches, 7b/6c+ obl.), was bolted where necessary; a rack of cams up to number 3 and wired nuts also are necessary. The climb was a testament to the spirit of adventure and the satisfaction that comes from overcoming challenges as a team. Anafi, a relatively unknown gem in the Aegean, had captured our hearts. We'll certainly be back for more. [Editor's Note: The online report includes a pitch-by-pitch description of the route.] 📷

—**Kyriakos Rossidis,** *Cyprus*

ABOVE: Kyriakos Rossidis on pitch 15 (7b) of The Ritual of Hardship, the first route up the southeast face of Anafi's Mt. Kalamos. *Jenny Schauroth*

OPPOSITE PAGE: The Ritual of Hardship (19 pitches, 7b/6c+ obl.). The photo was shot with a drone during sunrise on day two of the free ascent. Two earlier routes finished near the monastery, circled on the left. *Kyriakos Rossidis*

Middle East

JORDAN | Wadi Rum

JEBEL RUM, ZION AND OTHER ROUTES

During a 28-day frenzy on the sandstone walls of Wadi Rum, in January and February 2023, Alberto Luque and Albert Segura (both from Spain) established seven new multi-pitch climbs from 6b to 8a. It was a particularly meaningful trip for Segura, who was on the rebound from chemotherapy for a tumor and who'd had to curtail his guiding work for six months during treatment.

Their standout climb was Zion, a 12-pitch 8a up an eye-catching buttress on the west side of the Jebel Rum massif, with its crux on pitch ten. Segura had learned of the potential on the west face from French climber Arnaud Petit, and when they showed a photo of it to their local guide, Atayek Hamad, he took them there the next day.

Alberto Luque and Albert Segura established seven long routes in 28 days on the otherworldly formations of Jordan. *Albert Segura Collection*

This objective took four days to complete, leaving the climbers with time and bolts to spare. (The climbers used bolts sparingly on their routes—there are only 20 protection bolts on Zion's 12 pitches, for example, plus bolted anchors.) Taking only 1.5 rest days on their trip, the duo put up six more climbs ranging from 6b to 7b, and from 130m to 450m. Four of these were in the remote area of Jebel Suwebit, south of Rum, near the border with Saudi Arabia. [*A list of all the new climbs and many photo-topos are at the AAJ website.*] 📄 📷 🔍

—**Matt Samet,** *AAJ, with information from Desnivel and Albert Segura*

OMAN | Musandam

KHOR ASH-SHAM, JEBEL SHAM AND QARN SHAM

From our campsite at the edge of the Khor Ash-Sham (Ash-Sham Fjord), on yet another deserted white-sand beach, we watched the sun sink low over the Strait of Hormuz. A single thought occupied our minds, and Aniek was the first to put it into words: "I don't want to leave tomorrow." Aniek Lith (Netherlands), Marius Rølland (Norway), and I had just spent eight glorious days kayaking with dolphins, wading shin-deep through bioluminescent algae, and climbing multi-pitch routes on virgin limestone. After the magic of the previous week, I wondered how anyone could ever leave.

The Musandam Peninsula is an Omani exclave that extends into the Strait of Hormuz from the United Arab Emirates (UAE), making up the northernmost point of the Arabian Peninsula. This mountainous region is called the Norway of Arabia, thanks to the numerous fjords that gouge deeply into the landmass. It was the largest of these fjords, the ten-mile-long

Khor Ash-Sham, that we explored in late January 2023. Climbers most often access the Musandam Peninsula via motorboat charter, but Aniek's desire to rely solely on kayaks made leaving from the port town of Khasab and exploring nearby Khor Ash-Sham the logical choice for us.

We were tipped off to the peninsula's climbing potential by Mark Synnott's 2013 *AAJ* report. Although climbers have been visiting the Musandam for deep-water soloing (DWS) for upwards of 20 years, and some longer routes have been established, the potential for new multi-pitch lines remains substantial. In the Khor Ash-Sham alone, there were 15 miles of steep rock walls with no recorded ascents—until our visit.

Our first route, Good from Far, Far from Good (400m, IV 6b), begins to the right of a prominent pillar on the southeast face of Jebel Sham and climbs around 12 pitches to a large cleft in the center of the face. Aniek and I climbed the route onsight, leaving no fixed protection. Marius scrambled up the south ridge and then graciously guided us down a

walk-off route that would have been impossible to find in the dark.

A few coves farther west, Taste the Paste (360m, III 6a+) climbs the centerline of the obvious prow feature on the southeast face of Qarn Sham. We managed to find a lengthy and complex walk-off descent. Major kudos go to Marius, as this was his first multi-pitch climb!

Both routes proved to be longer, steeper, and more difficult than estimated from the ground. While the rock generally provided ample cracks for gear placements, the limestone was often poor, requiring a light touch to climb safely. In the Khor Ash-Sham, the potential for DWS is quite low. For the adventurous, roped climbing opportunities abound, most notably on the long walls that make up the southeast faces of Qarn Sham and Jebel Sham, and the walls near the village of Sibi. (Please note, though, that official policy forbids travelers from entering the villages along the fjord.)

On our last morning, we paddled away from our peaceful oasis and back toward civilization. A handful of hours later, we were in the bustling world of downtown Dubai, where a very different type of adventure awaited us. 📄 📷

—**Alan Goldbetter,** *Finland*

TOP: Alan Goldbetter following the final pitch of Good from Far, Far from Good (400m, IV 6b) on the southeast face of Jebel Sham. *Marius Rølland*

BOTTOM: Aniek Lith and Alan Goldbetter paddle into the Khor Ash-Sham, towing their packraft trailer filled with water and gear for a week's adventures. *Marius Rølland*

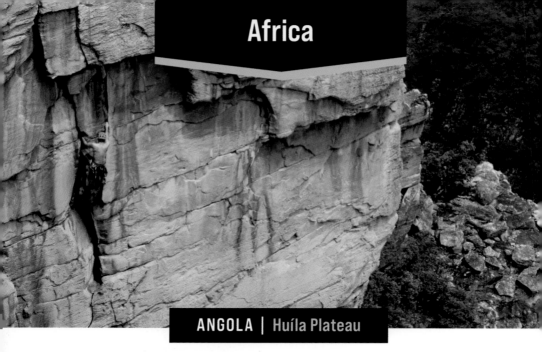

ANGOLA | Huíla Plateau

Nathan Cahill working on the route Dez Mangas (5.11c) at Serra da Leba, Angola. *Diogo Rebelo*

FENDA DA TUNDAVALA AND SERRA DA LEBA, NEW ROUTES

In the sunbaked land of Angola, the Huíla Plateau rises majestically above the Namib, a coastal desert in southwest Africa. The plateau provides a welcome escape from the pervasive heat in the country. Lubango, Angola's second-largest city, sits atop this elevated landscape at 1,760m. At the edge of the plateau is a remarkable sandstone cliffband that stretches for hundreds of miles in a semicircle around the city.

In February 2024, I traveled 900km south from the capital, Luanda, to open new routes on these cliffs. Driving down the Atlantic coast, the trip takes almost 14 hours on a highway cratered with potholes. (My wife and son chose a 90-minute flight on the local TAAG airline.) During the drive, I met up with two backpackers from Portugal, Tiago Cruz and Diogo "Reebz" Rebelo, who were relatively new climbers but brought tons of energy to the trip.

Lubango, a significant settlement for colonial Portuguese since 1885, only welcomed its first climbers in the early 1990s. Jim and Claire Harvey were stationed in Lubango with the nonprofit CARE Canada in 1992, only a year after peace accords paused Angola's long civil war. While there, Jim and a Belgian friend top-roped on the cliffs. When the war resumed that year, they were forced to relocate to Zimbabwe. Since then, there have been sporadic visits by climbers from Namibia and South Africa, but no concentrated effort to open new routes.

About 26km northwest of Lubango, the Fenda da Tundavala (Tundavala Gap) is a breathtaking rift in the cliff line, with sheer walls dropping hundreds of feet to the valley. A beautiful place with a sad history, the rift was used to kill prisoners during the civil war. After discussion with the locals, we limited our exploration to the top pitch of the gap out of respect. In any case, the rock face is only accessible via rappel, as there are no paths leading to the base on this northwest aspect of the plateau. I opened two airy trad lines on the headwall, which had bulletproof sandstone with edges, splitter cracks, and chicken heads. The grade of both 35m routes was around 5.10.

Serra da Leba, our main objective, is a deep canyon renowned for a picturesque switchback road that descends steeply off the plateau, 42km west of Lubango. A river swollen from the rainy season and dense jungle prevented us from trying a ground-up route from the bottom of the canyon. Instead, I rappelled over a majestic headwall towering over the valley. The sandstone is etched with a maze of cracks—a trad climber's paradise. It is also remarkably clean, apart from the occasional loose block or pile of hyrax droppings.

We bolted anchors at the top and bottom of the headwall, and Tiago and I both tried a route on top-rope. Later, I sent the headwall pitch on trad gear, giving us Dez Mangas (32m, 5.11c). Completing the full route from the bottom would add five or six pitches.

A hundred meters away, a long rib of stepped walls drops into the canyon. I rappelled down to check out the rock and then rope-soloed from the bottom in three long pitches (lead climbers typically would do this in six pitches). This 200m effort became N'Gola (5.10c).

There is potential in Serra da Leba for many lines, particularly in the alcove above the waterfall at the head of the canyon. I cleaned and bolted a couple of rap stations there for an eventual six-pitch sport route on impeccable vertical rock.

I am developing climbing across Angola, particularly in Conda and Sumbe, along with local climber Pedro Cunha, through the new collective Climb Angola. As of this writing, we have several more trips planned in 2024, culminating in Angola's first international climbing festival, in Serra da Leba, August 16–25.

—**Nathan Cahill,** *USA*

TOP: A sandstone headwall floating above the mist at Fenda da Tundavala. *Nathan Cahill*

BOTTOM: The cliffs above the waterfall at Serra da Leba are 150 to 225 meters high. A nearby canyon has walls estimated to top 600 meters. *Nathan Cahill*

MOROCCO | Anti-Atlas

ADAD MEDNI, SOUTH PILLAR

On December 4, Dominique Lalot and Raphael Thomé (France) completed the upper South Pillar of Adad Medni in the western Anti-Atlas. This line, which begins partway up the 1,000m south face and is accessed by a traverse from the east, had been attempted in 2019 to within about 100m of the summit (*see AAJ 2023*). The completed route was nine pitches (300m) and 5+/6a.

—**Information from Bernard Amy,** *France*

The view from Chambe's midway terrace of the 800-meter upper northwest face, showing (1) Kuche Kuche (2023) and (2) West Face Direct (1977). *Mark Richey*

CHAMBE, NORTHWEST FACE, KUCHE KUCHE

Across the African plateau, rising smoke from slash-and-burn agriculture gave an orange haze to the setting Malawian sun. One by one, electric lights illuminated the towns far below us, and the rhythmic drumbeat of pop music from small bars gathered in volume. A troop of blue monkeys, rare in these parts, traversed the wall above our camp, foraging and chattering. A four-inch-long African millipede slithered along the cliff, then disappeared under our tent.

"That's why I'm up *here*," piped Will Carey, cocooned in a hammock he had suspended between boulders. He and Ray Rice—two of my three partners on this trip, along with Taki Miyamoto—had been very concerned about snakes and other critters when I convinced them to come halfway across the world to Malawi.

We'd been at the Mulanje Massif, in southern Malawi, for two weeks, equipping a new route on the dramatic, 800m upper northwest face of Chambe. One of 62

named peaks in the massif, Chambe and its two-tiered face is a sight to behold, and we were a hair's breadth from finishing the first modern route on the upper wall. But we only had two days left before we'd fly out—and, of course, for the first time on our visit, it had just rained. Mist clung to the wall, delaying—and possibly foiling altogether—our final chance to free the route.

On my first trip to Mulanje, in 2022, James Garrett, Mark Jenkins, Geoff Tabin, and I focused on repeating routes. After climbing James' 2018 line Passion and Pain (630m, 11 pitches, IV 5.9), a slab climb on Chambe's lower wall, we added (but didn't free) a 60m 12th pitch to the terrace at 5.11 A0. From there, we gaped at the bigger and much steeper wall looming above. Except for one chimney system, the West Face Direct (VI 5.10 A1), climbed by Frank Eastwood and Ian Howell in 1977, the huge wall was untouched.

With that brief up-close glimpse of Chambe's upper face, I hatched a plan to return and establish a direct new route. The upper wall has the same highly featured, solid rock as the lower face and

similarly few cracks. I imagined it would require a serious ground-up bolting effort, so I invited a crack team of close friends—Will and Ray, both from New Hampshire, and Taki from Maine—all with deep experience in exploratory rock climbing and bolting.

On June 19, we arrived in Blantyre, Malawi. We spent the first morning gathering supplies before our friend, hotelier, and local fixer, Ruth Kalonda ("Auntie Ru"), picked us up in her van for the two-hour trip to Mulanje and the Hiker's Nest, the cozy guesthouse that would be our base. The following day, we repeated Passion and Pain to regain the terrace and inspect the upper wall. Pulling onto the roughly 3km by 0.5km terrace, where a tangle of ancient trees and massive boulders guards the upper cliff, we were met by local hiking guides George Pakha and Witness Stima, whom we had hired to help us out. They had reached the terrace by hiking up steep slabs at the north end of the lower face.

After a few hours and some drone inspection, we settled on a direct line up the tallest section of the face, about 500m left of the start of the Eastwood-Howell route. A small, flat area at the base would make a perfect camp for three-to four-day missions away from the Hiker's Nest to clean, bolt, and work the route.

Following Witness and George, we descended to the valley along 2,000 vertical feet of polished slabs and steep trails. Local woodcutters—many just young boys and girls—use these daily to access the terrace. It was humbling to see these tough people at work, gracefully descending fourth- and even fifth-class slabs with incredibly heavy loads, barefoot, often laughing and singing. Along the trails were little streams and myriad red, blue, and orange flowers, from begonias to balsams. Tiny malachite and double-collared sunbirds flitted hummingbird-like between the flowers, flashing their brilliant gorgets. Back at the trailhead, Auntie Ru was waiting to shuttle us back to the Hiker's Nest for hot showers, home-cooked food, and plenty of Kuche Kuche—the local light beer, which translates to "all night long" in Chichewa.

Though we had already obtained a permit from the Mulanje Mountain Forest Reserve and had been in touch with Ed Nhlane, a board member of Climb Malawi, to ask advice and share our plans, we also set up a meeting with the local village chief as a sign of respect and to ask his permission to climb on the upper wall. Chief

TOP: Mark Richey on pitch two of Kuche Kuche. Although the face has significant vegetation, the climbers found it easy to clean the rock on their line. *Ray Rice*

BOTTOM: A woodcutter starts down the 2,000-foot lower slabs with a heavy load. *Mark Richey*

Camp on the terrace below the upper wall of Chambe. *Taki Miyamoto*

M'Pwanye, his wife, and several elders welcomed us warmly, expressed interest in our adventure, and said they would alert the woodcutters so they would not be alarmed by our activities.

Over the next few days, George and Witness began ferrying supplies up to the terrace as we set up camp and started the methodical job of establishing our climb. We quickly realized we could leave behind all of our trad gear—there simply wasn't any opportunity to use it. We also found that the climbing was going to be fantastic. The rock was steep but not overhanging, and there was far less gardening than anticipated. Although the rock is syenite, similar to granite, it climbs more like limestone, with delicate crimps, tufa-like rails, and huge solution pockets. The climbing only got better as we pushed higher.

We worked in teams of two: one pair would lead, drilling from stances or hooks; the other team would follow up fixed ropes, cleaning, working the hard sections, and adding bolts as necessary. Rope-stretching pitches of 70m led to perfect belay ledges, including a killer bivy site on pitch eight. It was cool in the morning and at night, but warm enough to climb with just a long-sleeve shirt during the day.

After four missions on the wall, with rests in between at the Hiker's Nest, we had reached the summit slabs. On the afternoon of July 3, we all scrambled to the top of Chambe. The view was magnificent: The steep mountains and cliffs of Mulanje gave way to ancient erosional plains stretching as far as we could see. After making 15 rappels and removing all of our fixed ropes and gear, we were back at our tents—tired, dirty, but ecstatic. All that remained was a bit of rest and a one-day free ascent.

Then something unusual happened—it started raining. The wet approach slabs were too dangerous to ascend; we had to wait for the weather to clear. Finally, with only a day to spare before flying out, we made it back to our terrace camp. That night, as the sun set and we listened to the now familiar bar music, it rained again.

Fortunately, July 19 dawned clear with a chilly wind. We struggled to heat coffee over a tiny fire of sticks, since our petrol stove had died. I worried whether we could keep our fingers warm for the sustained crimping of the 5.12a second pitch. But as we got moving, our bodies warmed and the familiar pitches flowed by. As Taki sent the powerful 5.12b crux on the sixth pitch, I could hear Will and Ray whooping and hollering as they cruised the sunbaked pitches above.

By late afternoon, we had passed the Caves, a series of massive solution holes big enough for all of us to lie down—this section held some of the best climbing of the route. My fingers were sore and my hands had started to cramp, but two pitches later we all stood on top. At least one person had led every pitch free, and all four of us had freed each pitch either while leading or seconding. Later that night, after a four-hour headlamp descent, we settled into our tents and hammocks on the terrace and cracked a round of delicious Kuche Kuches.

In establishing our new route Kuche Kuche (800m, 15 pitches, 5.12b), our goal was not just to get up the wall but also to create a fun climb that other people, including the growing local climbing community, could repeat and enjoy safely. And, for the record, there is no concern of venomous snakes in Mulanje. 🗎 📷 🔍

—**Mark Richey,** *USA*

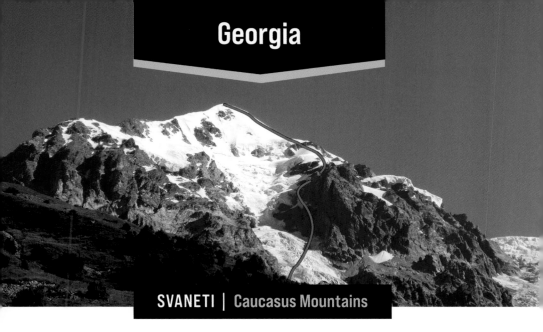

SVANETI | Caucasus Mountains

The south face of Tetnuldi (4,858m) and the 2023 route, which gained about 1,700 meters. The normal route up the southwest ridge finishes near the left skyline. *Archil Badriashvili*

TETNULDI, SOUTH FACE

On August 29, Temo Qurdiani and I drove in a 4WD vehicle from Mestia to the remote village of Adishi. (This road still does not appear on Google Maps.) Our idea was to climb the iconic Tetnuldi (4,858m) by an impressive and "forgotten" face.

The Adishi valley provides access to Tetnuldi's regular route, the southwest ridge, but also to the unclimbed south face, which rises about 2,000m above the lower Adishi Glacier. This face is split by a prominent rocky buttress, with the glacier's jumbled icefall on its right and a smaller glacier on the left. From the lower main glacier, we found passage through the left (west) moraine by a stream gully and then followed bear tracks up the steep grass above. By early afternoon, we were at 3,100m, right under the face, where we set up camp.

As we studied the face, a few potential lines were revealed, but clouds hid essential details. Our arsenal was vast, as we were prepared for mixed and rock climbing and had brought supplies for up to three days.

We set off the next morning at 6:30 a.m. First we checked out steeper climbing options on the south pillar but found only loose granite. Instead, we climbed left of the pillar, quickly simul-climbing a couple of rope lengths of easy to moderate mixed and ice. Above, snow and ice on the west side of the pillar brought us to its top at 4,000m. A snow and ice crest led directly to the summit, passing some short but loose bands of rock. It was only noon, but we still had 800m remaining, so we wasted no time, simul-climbing most of the way. We found traces of mountain goats, indicating that the most curious among them may have reached the summit by this line. Thus, our goal became to make a first human ascent.

A beautiful sunset and a breeze welcomed us to the summit at 6:15 p.m. We descended the southwest ridge to that route's base camp on the edge of a plateau. We slept there and took a direct descent to our car the following morning.

Our 1,700m ascent, graded 4A/4B with 55° ice and snow, is the first known route on the south face of Tetnuldi. It is an exciting line, with ever-changing character and with a few exposed sections that are safer to climb early and fast. 📖📷

—**Archil Badriashvili,** *Georgia*

Gulba (3,725m) from the southwest: (1) West-to-east traverse (2023 and possibly earlier); (2) Ivasuxari Roza (2014); (3) Khachapuri (2021); (4) Amaia eta Iker (2023). *2021 Spanish Mountaineering Team*

GULBA, SOUTHWEST FACE, AMAIA ETA IKER

Our initial plan was to open a new route on the south face of the main (south) summit of Ushba (4,710m). However, the forecast was not very good, with a risk of storms in the afternoons. Therefore, our trio—Basque climbers Julen Berrueko, Jon Inoriza, and I—changed plans to attempt an objective that wouldn't require bivouacs on the wall.

We opted for Ushba's smaller neighbor Gulba (3,725m) and its 700m southwest face. Our planned line would go up a buttress to the right of Khachapuri (7b) and Ivasuxari Roza (6b+), established in 2021 and 2014, respectively.

We started early in the morning on July 6, following weaknesses we had seen from our tents the previous day. The first four to five pitches were very nice, around 6a+, and we were able to climb quite quickly. Then our doubts about the path ahead began. We opted to take a dihedral that ended up requiring aid for a couple of meters, protecting with

small nuts, though the seconds climbed it free at 7a+. The next pitch was the most beautiful on the route: a small, sustained, and technical 7b dihedral. We were able to open this pitch onsight, an experience that made us feel like kids again. We climbed two more pitches of 6a before reaching easier terrain, simul-climbing the remaining 200m to the summit.

For the descent, we used the same route as the team that climbed Khachapuri in 2021, following the south ridge. After plenty of downclimbing and one rappel, we reached a couloir. From here we rappelled to the glacier.

Our new route, Amaia eta Iker, was protected entirely with cams and nuts. The name is in memory of our two friends, Amaia Agirre and Iker Bilbao, who died in Patagonia in January 2023. *Beti bihotzean*—always in our hearts.

During our climb, other members of our team—Adria Fidalgo, Rafa Gomez, and Mikel Larraya—completed a west-to-east traverse of Gulba, pushing through difficulties up to 6a on the lower southwest face before taking easier terrain and the ridgeline to the summit, then following the same descent we did. A similar line likely has been climbed before. 🖼

—Tasio Martin Elorrieta,
Basque Country

GULBA, SOUTHWEST FACE, IVASUXARI ROZA: *Previously unreported in the AAJ, the Basque team of Kepa Eskribano, Raul Gonzalez, and Mikel Saez de Urabain put up a 550m climb on Gulba's southwest face in 2014. Their one-day effort, christened Ivasuxari Roza, followed seven technical pitches up to 6b+ before a steep ridge scramble to the summit. The team reported that the initial two pitches seemed previously trafficked; beyond that, the terrain appeared untouched. They descended via four short rappels and much downclimbing, including an extremely loose chimney. The trio named their line in honor of the hostess at their guesthouse in the nearby village of Mestia.*

USHBA NORTH PEAK, SKI DESCENT FROM FORESUMMIT

In May, Tiphaine Dupérier and Nouria Newman (both from France) made a nearly complete ski descent of the North Peak of Ushba via the north ridge and northwest face. Ushba's North Peak (4,690m) was first skied in 2017 by Miroslav Pet'o (Slovakia), following the peak's original route to the south and east.

Dupérier and Newman climbed Ushba's north ridge on May 18, leaving their skis at around 4,500m and continuing along the narrow ridge for another 30 minutes before poor snow turned them around, close to the top. They returned to the skis and then to the North Peak's foresummit at around 4,450m, then began their 800m ski descent to the Ushba Glacier, mostly on the steep northwest face. Two 30m rappels were made to pass seracs low on the face.

—Dougald MacDonald, with information from Tiphaine Dupérier and Rodolphe Popier (Chronique Alpine)

Ushba's north (left) and south summits, with the line skied down the north ridge and northwest face in 2023. (R) The area of the two 30-meter rappels. *Archil Badriashvili*

SHKHARA, TRAVERSE VIA BEKNU KHERGIANI AND ROLLESTON-LONGSTAFF ROUTES

At 5,203m, Shkhara is the highest peak in Georgia. This broad-shouldered mountain boasts a long, narrow ridgeline running east to west, and various traverses of the peak and its neighbors have long been among the most significant mountaineering feats in the Caucasus.

On the Georgian (south) face of Shkhara, two routes outshine any others: the Beknu Khergiani, or south pillar, leading directly to the main summit, and the Rolleston-Longstaff Route to the lower west summit (5,068m). The Beknu Khergiani (2,200m, 5B or ED, 1950) is Himalayan in scale, usually requiring four bivouacs up and down. The Rolleston-Longstaff (2,000m, 5A or TD+, 1903) follows a curving line up the south-southwest ridge, crossing over the south peak (4,320m) along the way. By the numbers, it is one of the easiest ways up the south face; nevertheless, the route is wild and tricky.

In August 2023, Temo Qurdiani and I aimed to traverse Shkhara's main, central, west, and south summits in a grand way: combining three hard routes in a fast and light style. We'd link the Beknu pillar, an east-to-west traverse of the ridge, and a downclimb of the Rolleston-Longstaff. This link-up had never been done—it would be a serious feat for a small team.

Temo and I started the climb on August 4, maintaining fast and flexible dynamics on constantly changing terrain that felt

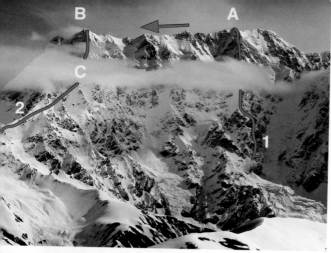

like it lasted forever. The climb was mainly on ice and rock—snow was lacking. We climbed mostly during the first part of each day, as clouds, snow, and wind picked up every day around 1 p.m., transforming the climbing experience into pure punishment.

We completed the Beknu Khergiani at 4 p.m. on August 6, celebrating the first phase of our three-part traverse at 5,203m. We bivouacked near the summit, throwing aside all of our steel tools as thunderstorms neared.

In the tent, Temo revealed to me that he was experiencing severe pain in both of his knees, aggravated by a high season's work in the mountains. I gave him an analgesic and later an injection of diclofenac. Unfortunately, it did not help. He had to bear the pain during the remaining climb, but he held strong.

TOP: (A) Shkhara's main summit (5,203m) from the south. The six-day traverse began with the Beknu-Khergiani Route (1), continued along the ridge to the west summit (B), and descended the Rolleston-Longstaff Route (2), passing over the south summit (C; hidden in clouds). Guillaume Vallot

The traverse of the ridge proved to be very tenuous. We moved on frontpoints for hours and finally progressed to the central summit, just above 5,000m. Beyond that, we bivvied on a small plateau near a huge serac, in a total whiteout. The fifth day started cold and with a stunning panorama. Just before 10 a.m., Temo and I were rewarded with the west summit at 5,068m.

We then downclimbed icy and loose terrain on the Rolleston-Longstaff pillar to approximately 4,500m in rain and lightning. We rappelled as little as possible to avoid leaving gear and to keep the rope safe, in order to ensure it would be intact when rappelling was absolutely necessary—such as a three-pitch stretch of M5, one of the route's cruxes. Despite our caution, a stone cut one rope in the middle of our descent.

BOTTOM: Traversing from Shkhara's main peak (in back) toward the west summit. Archil Badriashvili

At 4,500m we renovated the very same bivouac site built by a young alpinists' team led by Marko Prezelj and me in 2018 (the last time this route was known to have been climbed), ate the last of our food, and on the next day reached the refreshing Enguri River near Ushguli, after a descent that was quite painful due to big boots and rapidly rising temperatures. We returned to the village of Mestia that night, then drove to the Black Sea to heal our wounds.

The Express Traverse combined routes of 5B, 5B, and 5A (ED+); the traverse spanned August 4–9. [*The online version of this report includes substantial notes on the history of these routes and various other Shkhara traverses.*] 📄 📷

—Archil Badriashvili, *Georgia*

The line followed up the east side of Alpomish for the probable first ascent of the peak. The steep granite walls are about 400 meters high. *Eric Gilbertson*

ALPOMISH, FIRST ASCENT AND NEW COUNTRY HIGH POINT

Until recently, it was widely accepted that the broad, rocky 4,643m mountain at 38.948396N, 68.172312E in the Gissar (Hissar) Range, on the Uzbekistan-Tajikistan border, was the highest peak in Uzbekistan. This was based on the 1981 Soviet topographic map, the most accurate and recent map of the area. (In recent times, Peak 4,643m acquired the name Khazret Sultan, mostly in online sources, but another, better-known peak in Uzbekistan already had this name. Consequently, the name is not accepted by Uzbekistan's mountaineering community.)

While researching Peak 4,643m, possibly first climbed by Soviets in the 1960s, I realized that a border peak about 6km to the south, known as Alpomish in the local climbing community, was potentially taller than Peak 4,643m. Google Earth showed the highest points on each peak at exactly the same elevation (though this is often inaccurate). The

Soviet map showed no spot elevation for Alpomish. Andreas Frydensberg (Denmark) and I laid plans to carry a differential GPS unit and sight levels to both summits and determine which was higher.

We planned to go in late August when snow levels would be lowest. Acclimatized from ascents of Pik Korzhenevsky (7,105m) and Pik Ismoil Somoni (Pik Communism, 7,495m), Andreas and I headed to the Uzbekistan border region, and on August 21 started our approach from Sarytag village in Tajikistan. We hiked southwest alongside the Dikondara River, cached a few days of food to pick up after we returned from Alpomish, and continued south over several glaciated 4,000m passes and many talus fields, around 23km in total. Our base camp was near an unnamed glacier below the steep east face of Alpomish.

The four-spired peak loomed above camp with 400m granite faces on each spire. The southernmost spire looked to be the tallest, which I verified with sight levels. Using the known location and altitude of the tarn and angular inclination

View to the north from Alpomish to Peak 4,643m.
Eric Gilbertson

measurements with the sight levels, I measured Alpomish at 4,660m to 4,670m—significantly higher than Peak 4,643m.

On August 23, we hiked to the east face and found a big gully leading up to the notch between the summit and the next spire to the right. We scrambled up the gully on scree until it was blocked by a huge chockstone. I led the face to the right to an overhang, then traversed left delicately to reach the top of the chockstone.

We continued up the gully to a constriction with a small waterfall in the middle, where we decided to belay again. Above the waterfall, ice filled the gully all the way up to the notch, and since we hadn't brought technical ice tools, I started up the rock wall to the left and eventually moved left to a ridge crest with a good belay ledge.

The next pitch would be the crux. I climbed a steeper finger crack directly up the ridge crest, then made a delicate traverse left into a cleft. I continued up the cleft, then crossed back right to nice ledges and eventually the gendarmed summit ridge. A final knife-edge led to the top.

I first verified with the sight levels that all the nearby spires of the peak were shorter—we were definitely on the highest point of Alpomish. I set up the differential GPS, but it had trouble acquiring satellites. So I pointed my sight levels toward Peak 4,643m, and with each level measured 10min–20min angular declination looking down at the distant summit. Clearly it

was lower. There were no anchors, cairns, or any sign of human passage anywhere on Alpomish, so it seemed very likely we had made the first ascent. My handheld GPS recorded the summit at 38.89307N, 68.179583E. The sight level measurements showed that Alpomish is 25m (+/-8m) higher than Peak 4,643m, giving an elevation for Alpomish of ca 4,668m.

We made five diagonal rappels to reach the gully just below the ice as darkness set in, then downclimbed and made two more rappels to get into the lower gully. We staggered back into camp shortly before midnight. Our route was the Upper East Face (300m, 5.8).

To be absolutely certain about the relative elevations, I wanted to take measurements from the top of Peak 4,643m, looking back to Alpomish, so the next day we retraced our route over the glaciated passes, picked up our food cache, and hiked to the base of Peak 4,643m.

On August 25, we climbed the standard northeast ridge route, with long stretches of 4th-class scrambling on a knife-edge and two pitches of 5.7. On the summit, I used sight levels to measure 10min–20min angular inclination up to Alpomish. All six measurements showed that Alpomish is higher than Peak 4,643m, making it the highest point in Uzbekistan. We rapped off Peak 4,643m in a snow squall and hiked out to Sarytag the next morning. 🗒

—**Eric Gilbertson**, *USA*

THE SEVEN 'STANS: *Alpomish was one of the final summits of a five-year quest to reach the highest point of all seven nations whose names end with "stan." In 2019, Gilbertson and Frydensberg climbed Noshaq (7,492m, Afghanistan). In 2021, they summited Khan Tengri (7,010m, Kazakhstan) and Pobeda (7,439m, Kyrgyzstan). In 2022, it was K2 (8,611m, Pakistan), without bottled oxygen. In 2023, they finished with Ismoil Somoni (7,495m, Tajikistan), Ayrybaba (3,139m, Turkmenistan), and Alpomish (ca 4,668m, Uzbekistan). Gilbertson's ultimate goal is the high point of every country in the world.*

Tajikistan

PATKHOR, NORTHEAST SPUR, ATTEMPT AND ORDEAL

British alpinists Mick Fowler and Simon Yates attempted the northeast spur of Patkhor (6,083m), the highest peak in the Rushan Range, in mid-July. This unclimbed line had been the aim of Pete Dronkers and Spencer Gray (USA) in August 2017; they retreated from about halfway up because of rockfall concerns.

On July 13, Fowler and Yates gained the eastern side of the northeast spur via a couloir leading to a col at around 5,200m. At this col (the American high point), they poisoned themselves on freeze-dried meals that had gone bad and concluded that six of their remaining ten meals also were contaminated. This resulted in significant gastrointestinal issues and a much-reduced food supply for the climb.

The following day they moved very slowly up 50° ice slopes and easy mixed, bivying not far below a couloir leading through the upper face. The couloir provided Scottish IV/V climbing, which deposited them at their third bivy, below the final ridge. On July 16, the pair continued up despite poor weather. They found the ridge crest corniced and icy, so they traversed below it. Eventually, in a whiteout, they were forced to retrace their steps to the previous bivy. They estimated their high point was about 6,000m.

The next day, in continuing poor weather, they ate their final food and agreed to descend. After rappelling to the bivy site on the col, they set an alarm for midnight to ensure cold conditions for descending the lower couloir, but the alarm did not go off, forcing them to stay at the col another day. In the early hours of July 20, on their final rappel down the couloir, a V-thread anchor failed and Yates fell

Patkhor and the 2023 attempt, with a high point of about 6,000 meters. The lowest bivouac shown is at the 5,200-meter col. *Mick Fowler*

around 100m, sustaining broken ribs and back injuries. Fowler downclimbed to Yates, and they continued down to the glacier at 4,200m. Here, they called for a helicopter rescue, but after waiting two nights with no tent and one missing sleeping bag (lost after Yates' fall), and after five days with no food, they concluded Fowler would have to walk out for help. Four hours down the valley, he met a rescue team, which eventually reached Yates. With no helicopter likely to arrive, Yates and his rescuers spent three days walking the remaining 25km to the road. 📷

—**Damien Gildea,** *with information from Mick Fowler, U.K.*

RUSHAN CASTLE, FIRST ASCENT

On August 19, starting from a camp at 4,350m in the eastern branch of the Shteklozar Valley, Antonin Borovka, Lukas Kroker, Jaroslav Musil, Josef Smrtka, and I ascended the west side of the Shteklozar Glacier, along an icefall, into the cirque between Patkhor (6,083m) and Klunnikova (5,422m). A glacier then led southwest to an unclimbed peak (37.8713911N, 72.1754588E) that we called Rushan Castle, estimated to be 5,375m. [*Rushan Castle is a subpeak on the northeast ridge of Klunnikova, which was first climbed in 1946.*] 📄 📷

—**Michal Kleslo,** *Czech Republic*

Kyrgyzstan

KYRGYZSTAN | Pamir Alai

Peaks of the Jiptik Valley from the north. (A) Schurovsky (5,490m). (B) Muz Tok (5,066m); two attempts have been made on the aspect facing the camera. (C) Yuzhny. (D) Zemleprohodtsev (5,050m); arrow marks the 2023 attempt. (E) Khergiani. (F) Turkestan (ca 5,200m). *Christopher Elliott*

JIPTIK VALLEY, CHOKKO ZEMLEPROHODTSEV, ATTEMPT

On June 18, Russell Bate and I headed into the Jiptik Valley with the aim of attempting the north face of Muz Tok (5,066m). Knowing that a previous expedition had attempted it in early July (*AAJ 2017*), we factored in changing conditions due to climate change and arrived two weeks earlier. Despite this, we still observed a thin snowpack and conditions too warm for the north face of Muz Tok to hold ice.

To salvage our trip, we turned our attention to a possibly colder route on the northeast face of Chokko Zemleprohodtsev (Peak Zemleprohodtsev, 5,050m, 39.591803°N, 70.565173°E), whose summit ridge straddles the frontier. (The peak itself is south of the border in Tajikistan.) Based on information available to us, the peak did not appear to have been climbed since the Soviet era, when it was climbed along its east ridge, starting from the south. Studying the northern aspect, we observed a prominent 400m ice line on the right side of the face. We established an advanced base camp at 3,800m and prepared for an alpine-style attempt on the line after a few days of rest.

On the morning of June 24, we woke to rain after an unusually warm night, but set out across the glacier anyway. Crossing the bergschrund at dawn, we progressed up the face, encountering difficulties up to M4 and 70° ice. By afternoon, however, as we approached a near-vertical ice pillar at 4,700m, persistent warm temperatures forced a retreat under intense rock and ice fall. On the final rappel to the glacier, our V-thread—thankfully doubled up—was completely melting out.

In the following days, rain up to 5,000m stripped the remaining ice from most aspects in the range, forcing a relocation to the Karavshin for alpine rock climbing. The Jiptik area may be more suitable earlier in the season, although the April-May period would likely present its own challenges, because this has traditionally been a period of significant rainfall. 📷

—**Christopher Elliott,** *Canada*

AK-SU VALLEY, PEAK 4,431, WEST FACE

In July, Marina Popova and Denis Prokofiev (both from Russia) climbed the west face of an unnamed peak of 4,431m (GPS) on the east side of the Ak-su Valley. The peak (39°37'10"N, 70°18'57"E) rises along the ridge between the Ak-su and Jaupaya valleys and was accessed by a huge gully and scree slope to the north of Ortutyubek (3,895m). This approach took a day and a half.

Over two days, July 24–25, the pair climbed the west face in about 16 pitches, following a huge corner system in the center of the face (720m, Russian 6A/B), with a mix of free and aid climbing. (They placed no bolts). After a bivouac high on the face, they reached the summit around 4 p.m., finding no trace of prior visits.

Because of all the loose rock they had encountered during the approach and the climb, they opted to traverse the mountain and descend into the Jaupaya Valley. Fortunately, they found a reasonable descent along a stream that cut through the cliffbands and reached a bivy site in the valley after four hours. The next day, they hiked around 17km, trekking out of the Jaupaya Valley and back into the Ak-su, to return to camp. They later named the mountain Pik Breeze. 📷 ▶

View from below of the first ascent of Pik Breeze (Pik 4,431m GPS) by the west face. The climbers bivouacked on a ledge near the top of this photo; the summit is hidden beyond. *Popova/Prokofiev Collection*

—**Dougald MacDonald,** *with information from Mountain.ru and climber posts*

AK-SU VALLEY, PEAK 4,300, ESPOLÓN ÁLEX VILLAR

Alex Gonzalez and I took advantage of a good weather window in mid-July to open a new route on Peak 4,300m, a sharply pointed summit nestled between Odessa and Kyrkchilta peaks in the Ak-su Valley.

The new route runs up the northeastern spur of this peak. We simul-climbed most of the route, with difficulties up to 5. About 300m from the summit, we led several pitches up to 6b+. The descent was slow, and we had to place four or five bolts for rappels. We slept on some ledges about 800m above the ground and in the morning continued down toward the gully on the right side of the face. In total, we spent about eight hours on the descent.

Our route gained about 1,300m, with 1,700m of climbing distance. We named it in memory of our friend Álex Villar, who had died while wingsuit proximity-flying.

We later learned there was previous route on the northeast spur of Peak 4,300m, led by A. Kotelnikov in 1992. That party approached up our descent gully before starting their climb on the

Peak 4,300m, showing (1) Espolón Álex Villar (2023) and (2) approximate line of the Kotelnikov Route (1992). *Manuel Ponce*

face, making for a shorter route. Our line climbed the full height of the spur; it was mostly to the left of the 1992 route, crossing it near the top before finishing on the right.

—**Manuel Ponce**, *Spain*

The north side of Peak 5,914m as seen from Peak 5,860m. Both were reached from a camp in the col between the two peaks. *Oleg Silin*

PAMIR | Trans Alai

MINDZHAR VALLEY: PEAK 5,914, FIRST ASCENT; PEAK 5,860, NEW ROUTE

In the summer of 2023, our team from Latvia climbed two summits in the Mindzhar Valley near the Kyrgyzstan-Tajikistan border, which I had previously visited twice (see *AAJ* 2017 and 2018).

Nauris Hofmanis, Raivis Hofmanis, Edgars Madzulis, Inese Pučeka, Valdis Purinsh, Maksim Svoboda, and I arrived at the regular base camp for Peak Lenin on July 4 to acclimatize for a few days. We then traveled west by truck to a nomad camp in the Mindzhar Valley.

We ascended east to Mindzhar Pass

(5,050m, 39.379996°N, 72.604869°E), where we spent one night. We then traversed south over Peak 5,400m before turning west, dropping into the glacial valley, then climbing to the broad col between Peak 5,914m and Peak 5,860m, where we camped.

On July 15, Nauris Hofmanis, Madzulis, Pučeka, Purinsh, and I went to the summit of the previously unclimbed Peak 5,914m (39.33911°N, 72.57667E°). Our route was up the north ridge and involved snowy, glaciated terrain up to 50°. We reached the top in bad weather.

The next day, all except Pučeka climbed Peak 5,860m (39.35169°N, 72.56663°E) by a new line up the center of the south face. In 2017, our team had made the first ascent of this mountain from the northeast.

—**Oleg Silin**, *Latvia*

TIEN SHAN | Fergana Range

MANY ASCENTS ABOVE THE KARAKOMAN GLACIER

In late August and early September 2022, a team from the International School of Mountaineering, with a total of four guides and nine climbers, ascended numerous peaks in the northwest end of the Fergana Range. The team arrived at base camp (3,250m) on August 27 and spent the next eight days exploring two glaciated arms of the Karakoman (Kara-Karmin) Glacier. They climbed about a dozen peaks from 4,400m to 4,900m, most of which were likely first ascents. More details are at the *AAJ* website. [*This general area has been visited by climbers at least twice. A trio in 2007 climbed Uch-Seit (Uch Zeid, ca 4,900m), the highest peak in the area (also climbed by the 2022 team); see AAJ 2008. In 2013, a team from the U.K. made probable first ascents of four peaks above these glaciers (AAJ 2014).*]

—**Dougald MacDonald**, *with information from alpin-ism.com*

PIK ULUN, FIRST ASCENT, SOUTH FACE AND SOUTHWEST RIDGE

Turning the great roof on pitch 16 of Crack of Doom, the right-hand route on the south face of Pik Ulun. *Evgeny Murin*

Embarking on a mountain expedition is akin to taking a plunge into cold water: No matter how well you prepare, it still takes your breath away.

Our team from St. Petersburg chose to spend summer vacation along the Kyrgyzstan-China border. The approach to base camp took a total of seven days, at first with jeeps and an off-road vehicle, then by a strenuous trek with 50kg loads, including food for 18 days, using sleds on the glaciers.

We followed the same approach as a team in 2021: up the Dzhirnagaktu Glacier and then across the Uygrskyi Pass (Uighur, ca 4,630m, 1B), followed by a traverse southeast to Kechiksu Pass (ca 4,780m, 2B), and finally a descent to the east onto the Synarjar Glacier in China. [*This name for the glacier was used by the 2019 Russian trekking team, led by Ilya Mikhalev, that first completed this approach from Kyrgyzstan, but the origin is not clear.*]

This area has many beautiful peaks and so many unclimbed routes, but the weather here is a gamble. The night before crossing the second pass, we were struck by an electrical storm so vivid that it illuminated everything around, and the thunder was so powerful that it seemed the lightning would reach us

The south face of Pik Ulun (5,588m), showing (1) the Kochubey-Panov-Seryanov-Zhdanov route and (2) Crack of Doom (Lukashenko-Murin-Penyaev). Both routes were climbed in 2023, reaching the summit on successive days. The descent followed the right skyline of the peak before descending to the glacier. *Oksana Kochubey*

any moment. While we occasionally glimpsed the sun, we weren't prepared for the wintry conditions we experienced in August. We chose to start with Pik Ulun (Oolong, 5,588m, 41°0'44.96"N, 77°18'44.27"E) because its south face was the driest around. At the time we considered it a warm-up, expecting to climb other peaks. How wrong we were.

There were seven of us, split into two teams. Evgeny Murin would climb with Olga Lukashenko and Ilya Penyaev, while the second team comprised Andrey Panov, Sergey Seryanov, Ilya Zhdanov, and me. In our group, Andrey was the leader, having done several significant first ascents, Sergey was the strongest and calmest of us, while Ilya was the most positive and cheerful. Evgeny had tried this face on Ulun in 2021 (*AAJ 2022*) and wanted to complete his route. We opted for a line farther left. We expected the ascent to take two to three days. It took six.

Both teams started on August 23. From the base of the wall at 4,793m, we climbed the steep lower rock with two camps.

This section involved thin ice climbing, followed by a three-pitch chimney. Its walls were vertical, the left covered with a thin layer of ice that we climbed very carefully. (On one pitch, the leader had to ascend more than 30m before getting ice screws to engage halfway—this was the psychological crux of the route.) Then it began to snow and didn't stop until after the climb. We reached the southwest ridge on August 25 and then were stuck for two nights because of bad weather. We had taken one lightweight tent that could accommodate four people.

On the 27th we moved up the ridge and made our top camp only 15m below the summit, although at the time we didn't realize we were so close. The wind howled and we awoke to find the tent mostly buried in snow. Someone mentioned it was difficult to breathe. The tent zipper was under the snow, and we couldn't dig it out, so we were forced to use a knife. Crawling outside, we dug out the tent with our helmets, and after a couple of hours, exhausted, we were able to sleep until morning.

The unclimbed southwest face of Kyzyl Asker (right center) seen from the summit of Pik Ulun. To the left is Pik 5,632m. *Oksana Kochubey*

Next day, the sun was shining and we went to the summit. On the way back, we received a message that a strong storm would hit shortly and last for three hours. In fact, it lasted eight hours. We tried to shelter in the damaged tent, holding the fabric together to minimize the amount of snow coming inside.

On the following day, with no more food or gas, we would have to descend, and we opted to head east and then down to the glacier, rather than reverse our ascent route. We quickly crossed over the summit and then drilled our first Abalakov anchor. We made 20 to 25 rappels, which went relatively smoothly, and finally reached the glacier around 9 p.m.

It was only 2.5km to base camp (fortunately placed much closer to the wall than it had been in 2021), but the considerable amount of new snow made it impossible to progress unless we moved on all fours. We crawled for four hours, with our packs and duffels strung out behind our harnesses like tails. Each of us went through stages of denial and acceptance. I thought only about one thing: Keep moving my limbs and eventually it will end.

It did end, but base camp was nowhere to be seen. Everything was buried, and we had to dig again. We finally found the food barrel and ate all the dehydrated meals inside.

The 800m face had given us 1,200m of climbing with technical difficulties of F6a A2+ WI4 M6 and an overall grade of 5B.

Evgeny's team reached the summit a day after us, having climbed the south face with the same start he used in 2021. Once on the southwest ridge, they followed our line to the top to complete Crack of Doom. This 760m route (climbing length 960m) was graded Russian 6A (6b A3 WI3 M6). Like us, they descended to the east.

Without my climbing companions, those weeks of summer-winter would not have been so awesome. Thank you, guys! 📷 ▶

—**Oksana Kochubey,** *Russia*

NOCHNOI MOTYL, SKI DESCENT BY NORTH FACE

On May 19, 2022, the mostly French team of Thomas Delfino, Jean-Yves Fredricksen, Léa Klaue (Switzerland), Aurélien Lardy, and Hélias Millerioux skied and snowboarded the north face of Nochnoi Motyl ("Night Butterfly," 5,056m), the central peak at the head of the Dzhirnagaktu Glacier basin, just west of Kyzyl Asker. Access to the range was very difficult this early in the season, and they could get no closer than 45km from their planned base camp in a vehicle. They arranged to complete the journey on horseback, which cost time and limited their options.

After warming up with ski descents of Kucyk ("Pony," 4,705m) and Pyramide (4,812m), the riders climbed the south face of Nochnoi Motyl, the route of the peak's first ascent in 2010. They then started down the east ridge, climbed in 2013 by a British women's team. The quintet entered the north face (all belayed on the first steep pitch except for Lardy) then diagonaled down very exposed slopes. The ski descent was independent of the only route climbed up this face, North Face Corridor (Morrell-Zholobenko), ascended in late August 2012. 📷

—**Dougald MacDonald,** *with information from Chronique Alpine et des Montagnes du Monde and Montagnes magazine*

The line of the 2023 attempt on the southwest face of Pik Gronky. Arrow marks the start of the 2015 route. *Expedition Photo*

PIK GRONKY, ATTEMPT

In late August and September, a team of four from the U.K. (Clement Attwood, Thomas Walker, Calum Wesencraft, and Nick Whimster) aimed to establish new routes above the Kyzyl Asker Glacier. After acclimatization and several days of effort, an advanced base camp (ABC) was established on the glacier, a few kilometers from the steep faces of Pik Vernyi and "Pik Zabor." Initial reconnaissance of Zabor and a previously unconsidered face on Pik Gronky revealed lots of potential. [*The name Zabor or Sabor has been applied to two formations in this valley, leading to some confusion. See note below.*] With almost daily snowstorms, it was clear that big-wall rock climbs would be unlikely.

After a resupply, some rest, and poor weather at base camp, the team returned to ABC for a week of mostly good weather. On September 10, they attempted an obvious chimney system on the northernmost part of the east face of Zabor, to the right of Dry Ice Queen, climbed by a Slovak pair in 2022 (*AAJ 2023*). The climbers ran out of time and retreated after encountering thin ice and limited protection, then deep snow on an alternative line.

After a rest day, the team tried a route on the southwest side of Pik Gronky (ca 5,080m), starting with a snow gully, guarded by a pitch of ice, that leads to a notch in the west ridge. (This gully is to the left of Take a Walk on the Wild Side, climbed by a Slovenian party in 2015.) Above the notch, a burly mixed pitch and a pure rock pitch led to easier terrain, then a last steep rock band gained the summit ridge. The climbers moved up the ridge together until darkness forced a retreat about 100m beneath the top, followed by an open bivouac farther down. The incomplete route was called If You Like Piña Coladas (700m, TD+ VII). [*A comprehensive expedition report is at the AAJ website.*] 📄 📷

—*Information from Nick Whimster, U.K., and expedition report*

PIK ZABOR (SABOR) NOMENCLATURE:

In a report in AAJ 2023 on the route Dry Ice Queen, climbers from Slovakia identified the face as being on Pik Zabor (Sabor, 4,850m), "just opposite Pik Vernyi." This face, also attempted by the U.K. team in 2023, indeed rises opposite the northwest face of Vernyi, but the identity is confusing because Sabor was a name previously used for Vernyi. It was called that by the British expedition that climbed the north ridge in 2003. A report in AAJ 2005 as well as a map published by the AAJ also used the name Sabor. However, this mountain was named Vernyi in the Soviet era, when the peak was first climbed, and it has been called Vernyi in the AAJ since 2005. It's not clear if the formation climbed by Dry Ice Queen, on the northeast side of Kyzyl Asker, had any earlier name, but Zabor is coming into common usage.

NALIVKIN AND RUDNEV GLACIER AREAS, ATTEMPTS AND EXPLORATION

In July and August, Sam Spector and I attempted several unclimbed summits from a base camp at 3,943m below the Kotur Glacier in the Western Kokshaal-too. This we reached in a day from Naryn, thanks

to travel firm ITMC, our driver Anton, and his off-road-enhanced Mitsubishi SUV, which seemed much more reliable and comfortable than the Soviet-era trucks used on my previous trips to the area.

Unfortunately, our climbing attempts were stymied by conditions or weather. We planned to make the first ascent of Pik 5,611m, north of Pik Byeliy (Grand Poohbah, 5,697m), by traversing over the summit of Pik Korsun (ca 5,320m) at the northern end of this ridge. The latter was climbed by a Moscow party in 2000 and is sometimes incorrectly marked at the location of Pik 5,611m. Pik 5,611m itself was previously targeted by Pat Littlejohn and party in 2006, but they aborted the attempt at their glacier camp due to heavy snow (*AAJ 2007*).

From base camp, Sam and I cut across to the Nalivkin Glacier via vestigial icefields east of Pik Lvitsa (4,631m) and made a camp at 4,923m between Piks 5,055m and Korsun. We set off early on the morning of August 4 for the northeast ridge of Korsun in perfect weather but retreated at around 5,058m due to the hollow, unstable snowpack that seemed widespread across the northern aspect.

After returning to base camp, we later crossed Kotur Pass to reach a cirque on the southern (Xinjiang) side, overlooking the Rudnev Glacier. Since only its border peaks have been climbed, this cirque presents notable climbing objectives for future parties, especially if one were able to approach from within Xinjiang. The main summits appear well-guarded by rock walls and complex ridges, rising up to 600m to 700m above the snow *(more photos can be seen in the online report)*.

Below the pass, we found ourselves navigating complex glacial topography with several icefalls and only thin coverage of old snow. We camped at 4,574m at the base of straightforward-looking Pik 5,082m, immediately south of Pik Babouchka (5,282m), but withdrew due to exceptionally high overnight winds within a prevailing stormy pattern. 🖻 🔍

—Paul Knott, *New Zealand*

TOP: The eastern side of Pik 5,217m (located south of Piks 5,082m and Babouchka), with faces estimated at 600m to 700m high. *Paul Knott*

BOTTOM: The North face of Pik Korsun (ca 5,320m) with the summits of Pik 5,611m and Pik Byeliy (Grand Poohbah, 5,697m) rising along the ridge behind. *Paul Knott*

TROPHY HUNTING

A NEW ROUTE UP PIK ALPINIST IN
THE WESTERN KOKSHAAL-TOO

By Seth Timpano, *USA*

Dane Steadman (25), Jared Vilhauer (42), and I (41) traveled to the Western Kokshaal-too mountains of Kyrgyzstan for the month of September. We choose this time frame based on two factors: 1) the temperatures are significantly cooler than in midsummer and therefore better for ice climbing objectives, and 2) the weather seems to be more stable, with less afternoon convective buildup and precipitation. Generally, we found good weather and cold enough temperatures for most objectives, with the exception of those facing due south. We also had an uneventful exit from the mountains, although we snuck out just before a winter storm covered the roads in snow on September 30.

After ten days of acclimatizing and window shopping for different objectives,

Pik Alpinist (5,482m) from the northeast. (1) Trophy Hunt (Steadman-Timpano-Vilhauer, 2023). The route wrapped left under the summit cornice to finish on the south ridge. (2) Lebedev Route (1993), the first ascent of the peak, finishing up the north ridge. *Dane Steadman*

we set our sights on an elegant and sustained ice line on the northeast face of Pik Alpinist (5,482m). [*Pik Alpinist (41°03'04"N, 77°43'59"E) divides the Chon-turasu and Essledovatley glaciers. The peak's first known ascent was in August 1993, when a team led by Mikhail Lebedev climbed the east face—well to the right of the 2023 line—over four days, finishing up the north ridge to the summit. Two additional routes ascent the complete north ridge (1996) and northwest face (2001); see AAJ 2022.*]

Given the amount of steep ice climbing on our line, we determined our best strategy was to attempt the route without carrying bivy gear. We left our camp at the base of the wall at 3 a.m. on September 24 and crossed the 'schrund shortly thereafter. Using 70m ropes, we made 16 pitches, many of which required 10m or more of simul-climbing (difficulties up to AI4) on the steeper pitches and 60m or more of simul-climbing on the lower-angle sections.

High on the face, we climbed a mixed pitch with thin ice (M5) up and left of the direct fall line to avoid a pitch of steep WI6 ice. The mixed pitch deposited us on the upper southeast face about 200 vertical meters below the summit. We climbed snow and some ice up this aspect for roughly four rope lengths, which brought us to a point below a long cornice guarding the summit ridge. This pushed us on a slightly rising traverse to the southern snow and ice fields. Jared chopped through the cornice and gained the south ridge, exactly 60m from the true summit, at 8:15 p.m. We walked up the easy ridge for a few minutes to the top, high-fived, took a selfie in the dark, and left.

We walked back down the south ridge for a few minutes and then downclimbed through the cornice. From there, we simul-downclimbed the traverse of the south snowfields, placing ice screws in the same locations as on the way up, until we regained the top of the southeast snowfields. We then rappelled our line of ascent, except for a few deviations in hopes of finding thicker or better ice. We made 18 rappels using our 70m ropes, mostly from V-thread anchors. The limestone was very compact and made rock anchors challenging, both on the way up and down. However, we did leave a few stopper and piton anchors when necessary. We were back at camp 27 hours after departing.

Alpine climbing is inherently difficult to grade, due to the number of factors that can affect the perceived difficulties. Nonetheless, we felt our new route, Trophy Hunt, was AI5+ M5; it gained 1,100m from 'schrund to summit. We would like to thank the American Alpine Club for their support of this expedition through a Cutting Edge Grant. 📷

TOP: Seth Timpano leading the second of five steep pitches up the headwall in the middle of the northeast face of Pik Alpinist. Dane Steadman and Jared Vilhauer climbed this section while simul-climbing, as Timpano was forced to climb for 80 meters to find a suitable anchor. *Dane Steadman*

BOTTOM: Dane Steadman following one of the twin runnels on the headwall of Pik Alpinist. The steep ice visible in upper left was the WI5+ crux pitch of the route. *Jared Vilhauer*

The first-ascent route on Pik Trener (4,891m), up the east face and south ridge. *Christian Suys*

PIK BERNELINE, PIK TRENER, AND OTHER ASCENTS

In August, a team of six climbers—Niels Brack, Miel Cox, Annelore Orije, Loïc Puylaert, Cedric De Smet, and me, Christian Suys—spent four weeks in the beautiful Djangart Range. After three days of driving from Bishkek, we made it to some barracks used by hunters during winter at the southern end of the Kaichi Valley.

Our initial plan was to reach the Djangart Valley by driving up to Djangart Pass (4,158m) then descending into the valley, with our gear carried on horses, as a Dutch team did in 2018. Unfortunately, our GAZ-66 military truck was unable to get up the road to the pass. Instead, we decided to establish base camp at the hunters' barracks. Although this meant we had to hike an extra day over the pass on each outing to the Djangart Valley, we had a lot of luxury, including an oven and a sauna.

We left base camp on August 7 with backpacks up to 33kg and camped a few kilometers after the pass at 3,900m. From there, we noticed an easy-looking mountain to the south that was 4,870m, according to the map. Over the next two days, we attempted and then climbed it. We thought this might be a first ascent, but later we learned a Slovenian team had climbed it in September 2022, calling the peak Ak Ayuu, or "polar bear" in Kyrgyz. (*See report below.*)

Back at base camp, we split into two teams. Miel and Niels did some rock climbing and bouldering near the Djangartynbashi Glacier. Annelore, Cedric, Loïc, and I went to explore the highest summit north of the Djangart Valley. We had only one picture of this mountain, made by a 2008 Russian team, showing its spectacular north face. We wanted to explore the mountain from the south, as that looked easier on Google Earth.

After a reconnaissance below the mountain, we planned a rest day, but I didn't fancy staying in camp. Another easy-looking mountain was nearby, and so Annelore and I headed up. After traversing the glacier and a moraine, approaching from the west, we climbed a 30° icefield to the summit via the north-northwest face (PD). We named this mountain Pik Berneline (4,512m GPS, 41.726667°N, 78.864444°E), in honor of Annelore's mother (Bernadette) and my sister (Eline).

The next day, August 15, we went for our main objective, which we had been calling Pik Trener (4,891m, 41.745278°N, 78.828611°E) since we left Belgium. Pik Trener is the Russian translation of "Mount Coach," the two-year training program we had all followed.

We left camp at 4 a.m. and headed north toward the peak, then made a long western turn following the glacier toward the saddle between Trener and a lower top to its south. We crossed some massive crevasses before heading up steeper terrain (40°) to the col. From there, we got into the loosest terrain I had ever seen. After two 50m pitches, we made it to the top of Pik Trener (4,891m GPS; the route was AD). Looking down onto the north face, we saw a challenge for another time—or perhaps another team. We did two rappels down the ridge, then downclimbed the east face to the glacier.

During the third rotation, we all went to the Djangartynbashi Glacier, where Lore, Loïc, and Niels unsuccessfully attempted

Pik Howard-Bury (4,766m), while Cedric, Miel, and I went for Pik Illumination. On our first attempt, we descended due to avalanche danger. We went back the next day, August 24, and climbed a line farther to the right, on the northwest face, which almost entirely avoided loaded slopes. After crossing the bergschrund, we climbed a 60° ice face that eased to 50°–55° until we reached the north ridge. From there, we followed the first-ascent route on the northeast face to the peak (5,048m map, 5,104m GPS) on the frontier. Just like the first ascensionists, we decided to stop here. A higher summit is about 350m away and fully in China, but the traverse looked too long and difficult, given the time we had. In descent, we followed the same line, doing around 12 rappels off V-threads.

We also did some multi-pitch rock climbs on "Kaichi Mountain," the name we'd given the 4,100m prominence that splits the Kaichi Valley where the route to the Djangart Pass turns east. [*A trip report with more information and photos, including the rock routes this team climbed, can be downloaded at the AAJ website.*] 📄 📷 🔍

—**Christian Suys,** *Belgium*

PIK PETRA, AK AYUU, PIK BARSIK, AND OTHER ASCENTS

Luka Kramarič, Florjan Lajmiš, Špela Ozimek, Krištof Rener, Nejc Štebe, and Mojca Zajc, all Slovenians, arrived in Bishkek on September 3, 2022. We chose the Djangart region because it seemed like a good location to dip our toes into expedition climbing.

We arranged transportation, base camp equipment, food, and our cook (Davran) with the agency Kyrgyzland. On our third day of driving, we reached a point just below Djangart Pass (4,158m), then headed across the pass on foot and into the valley, where we set up our base camp (41.710150N, 78.887058E). Horses from Uch-Koshkon carried our gear over the pass.

We found the glaciers in very good condition, and the north faces seemed solid

and iced up. During the 15 days we were in the valley or climbing above it, the weather remained relatively stable and predictable. There were two days when it snowed down to base camp level, and otherwise only short afternoon showers. We split into three teams of two, making a number of two- or three-day excursions, with the first day usually involving a lengthy approach and a river crossing from base camp.

First, Nejc and Luka journeyed south to the head of the eastern branch of the Djangartynbashi Glacier. On September 10,

Distant view of Pik Petra (4,997m) near the head of the Djangartynbashi Glacier. The first ascent route is hidden by the big rock buttress. *Nejc Štebe*

they climbed the icy west face of Pik Petra (4,997m, 41.623100N, 78.922860E), making the first ascent. Their route (500m, D 70°) finished with a short ridge. At the same time, the other two teams climbed an easy glaciated peak south of Djangart Pass that they named Ak Ayuu (4,878m).

After some rest in base camp and a day of rain and snow, Florjan and Mojca attempted an unclimbed peak 5km south of base camp, but bailed because of bad snow conditions. Meanwhile, Nejc, Luka, Krištof, and Špela spent a day making the approach to the Djangartynbashi Glacier and setting up camp. Nejc and Luka then attempted to climb the northeast face of Pik Illumination but retreated because of deep snow and a storm. The next day, Krištof and Luka climbed an easy glaciated peak they named Pik Barsik (4,874m, 41.600533N, 78.856200E) and attempted an unclimbed peak (41.60070N, 78.85630E), stopping just below the top because they couldn't climb an overhanging cornice.

In the next window of good weather, team members climbed most of Horseman's Horror (700m, D+ 80°) on the 4,766m Pik Howard-Bury (*AAJ 2011*). However, they turned around below the summit because of a thunderstorm.

Unfortunately, our agency made a scheduling mistake that led to us being forced to leave the valley almost a week earlier than we'd planned. 📷

—Nejc Štebe, *Slovenia*

Dragon Peak from the northwest, showing the line of the first ascent. *Expedition Photo*

TIEN SHAN | Kuilu Range

OROY VALLEY: DRAGON PEAK, FIRST ASCENT; WOLF PEAK AND PERSEVERANCE PEAK, NEW ROUTES

Felix Hatzold, Annick Pietzonka, and I entered the Kuilu Valley on July 27 in a truck with the driver blasting Russian rap music. After a bumpy all-day drive from Karakol, we had an exciting crossing of the Kuilu River, which placed us very close to the start of the Oroy Valley. This point became our base camp (42.1675730N, 78.858877E). We then made two gear carries up the valley to a site at around 3,800m where we made advanced base camp.

South of here, Perseverance Peak (4,788m, 42.095989N, 78.836069E) caught our eye. It was first climbed in 2021 from the Bordlu Glacier on its west side, by a team from the U.K. On July 31, we set off up the Oroy Glacier and attempted to reach the east ridge. However, we turned around just short of a sub-peak because of loose rock.

During the next week, we turned our attention to a peak west of ABC and north of Perseverance: Wolf Peak (4,631m), which had been climbed in 2018 by the northwest ridge. On August 8, we climbed the northeast ridge, turning many rock towers on the left side and finding lots of loose scree. We grade the route PD+.

We returned to Perseverance Peak the next day, August 9, finding the climbing easier and much faster by going farther west on the slope up to the east ridge. We then followed the beautiful ridge either on rock (left side) or snow (right side). The crux was around 80m of 50° ice/snow, where two tools came in handy. Upon finishing this section, I assured Felix and Annick, waiting below, that the last 300m looked doable. They were scandalized that there was such a long way to go, but I'd been joking—we were on top in about 30m. We graded our new route up the east ridge AD 50°.

Our main objective was a higher peak, farther south up the Oroy Glacier. After one prior attempt, we departed ABC at 3 a.m. on August 10 under a sky full of shooting stars. After an hour on the bare glacier, we reached the first crux, a labyrinth of crevasses, some requiring belayed jumps across. Beyond this, we climbed the right side of a snow slope that rises to a col in the north ridge at 4,510m, reaching it as the sun rose. We followed the ridge to the top, belaying the steepest sections.

We graded the route AD with 50° ice and snow, and named the mountain Dragon Peak (4,820m, 42.090203N, 78.877262E), due to the scaly look of the glacier and some outrageously spicy soup we had eaten the day before. [*A full expedition report is at the AAJ website.*] 📄 📷

—**Sebastian Kegreiss,** *Switzerland*

Kazakhstan

TIEN SHAN | Ile-Alatau

Molodaya Gvardiya (center, 4,398m) from the northwest. The 2023 route went directly up the snow and ice face in the center. *Kirill Belotserkovskiy*

MOLODAYA GVARDIYA AND MURYN-TAU, NEW ROUTES

In August, I guided Austrian friends Geri Mairhofer and Traudl We on a 50km journey through the central Ile-Alatau range, south of Almaty. After traveling up Ozyornoye Gorge, we walked to the Kyzylsay hut and stayed the night. The next day, August 3, Traudl and I climbed a new route around 400m high, at AI1, up the center of the northwest face of Molodaya Gvardiya (4,398m, 43.00699°N, 77.08508°E), the highest peak at the head of this valley.

In the following days we crossed Turistov Pass (3,980m) from west to east and descended to the Left Talgar River, and then trekked upriver and then southeast to the Toguzak Glacier. On August 9, all three of us climbed a central line up the northwest face of Muryn-Tau (4,510m, 43.01068°N, 77.23766°E), about 300m at AI1, reaching the summit in poor weather. Descent was via the original 2B route down the north ridge.

Our return journey took us back down along the Left Talgar River and then west to Talgarskiy Pass (3,160m). We camped nearby and finished at Shymbulak ski resort on August 11. 📷

—**Kirill Belotserkovskiy,** *Kazakhstan*

TURGEN, NORTH FACE

In mid-June, Maxim Popov and I climbed a new route in the center of the north face of Turgen (4,410m, 43.108036°N, 77.595769°E) at the far eastern end of the Ile-Alatau, around 20km east of the range's highest peak, Talgar (4,973m). We spent two days approaching the mountain. Our 900m-high route followed an obvious gully slanting up from right to left. The 14 pitches of climbing on the main part of the route included eight pitches of ice up to 70° and some mixed ground near the top; the difficulties were up to AI3 M4. We reached the summit on June 22 and descended via the 2011 Scherbina-Vassiliev Route to the west. We believe ours was the third ascent of the mountain. 📷

—**Kirill Belotserkovskiy,** *Kazakhstan*

The north face of Turgen (4,410m) after fresh snowfall, showing the 2023 route, with 14 pitches up the main face. *Kirill Belotserkovski*

BURYATIA | South Muya Range

The line of the first ascent of Muisky Giant's south peak (3,040m), completed over two days with 1,300 meters of climbing. En route, the team climbed a spire along the ridge they named Pinnacle of the Pioneers of Transbaikalia. *Evgeny Glazunov*

MUISKY GIANT, SOUTH PEAK, AND KATYA REPINA PEAK

In late July and August, Ivan Shilnikov, Pavel Tkachenko, and I spent two weeks exploring the area west of Muisky Giant (also spelled Muiski or Muysky, 3,067m), the second-highest peak of Transbaikalia. This area of the South Muya Range (South Muiski Range) is far from populated areas and extremely difficult to reach. We hiked about 30km to reach our camp by Lake Geologov, with cumulative vertical gain of 1,500m. (We walked about 100km total during the expedition.) During two weeks in the mountains, we did not meet a single person. We carried all of our own loads, starting with about 40kg per person.

On August 7, we climbed an unnamed summit marked on the map as Peak 2,745m. We climbed this by the west ridge, starting from Mataika Pass, with about five pitches of easy climbing, descending by the same route. We named the peak in honor of Katya Repina, a girl who hiked and climbed with us, and who had died that summer in the Sayan Mountains.

Our main objective was the first ascent of Muisky Giant's unclimbed south peak (3,040m). Leaving our camp by Lake Geologov at 5 a.m. on August 8, we approached the southwest face in about 2.5 hours and started up the steep face. I led all day, and we climbed 16 pitches, using no bolts. We spent the night on the south-southwest ridge. This was an open bivouac, with just one sleeping bag for the three of us, but we found snow and ice to melt for water and we slept well.

The next day we continued up the long ridge to the summit tower. Five difficult pitches brought us to the top, where we left a cairn and a note. We descended the summit tower by rappel and downclimbed easy terrain on the northwest side of the ridge into a valley, then crossed through a pass to return to our camp by the lake by evening.

In all, our route was 1,300m (climbing distance) and had 24 pitches; we called it Team of Our Youth (Russian 6A).

To leave the mountains, we hiked to the

Muya River and assembled an inflatable catamaran, on which we rafted about 70km downstream, a journey complicated by rapids.

There are many objectives for new lines in this area; many peaks have not even been climbed. [*Several years earlier, Glazunov and Tkachenko, with various other partners, climbed many new routes in an area of dramatic granite peaks about 125km southwest of Muisky Giant; see AAJs 2020 and 2021. Tragically, in February 2024, Glazunov died while descending from Ak-Su in Kyrgyzstan after completing a solo winter ascent of the Chaplinksy Route (Russian 6B, 1988) on the north face.*]

— **Evgeny Glazunov,** *Russia*

MAGADAN | Kolyma Mountains

GREAT RAPIDS RIDGE, MANY ASCENTS

In late summer, the first known climbs were completed on the Great Rapids Ridge, a 70km-long system of granite domes and walls in the Kolyma Mountains of far eastern Siberia, an area better known for former Soviet gulags than for rock climbing. A team of 19 climbers from various parts of Russia traveled to Magadan Oblast in late August, led by Ivan Kergin and Alexander Yakovenko. From the village of Ust-Omchug, the team traveled 127km by truck and then hiked 15km of trailless terrain over two days to a base camp by the Tok River.

Over the next week, the climbers established an assault camp and climbed seven moderate routes (Russian 1B to 3A) up nearby peaks. Meanwhile, the trio of Ivan Kergin, Konstantin Bobrinsky, and Artyom Chikin selected a more difficult climb: the steep southern face of a mountain they called Peak 100th Anniversary of Russian Alpinism (2,112m GPS, 61°47.599'N, 150°24.362'E). After fixing ropes on about 100m of the route, they returned on August 31 and completed the ascent in one long day, with a total of 800m of climbing (16 pitches), graded Russian 6A.

The climbers observed many unclimbed walls in the area, including north and northeast faces estimated to rise 600m to 700m.

Climbers partway up the main wall of the 16-pitch route climbed on Peak 100th Anniversary of Russian Alpinism on the Great Rapids Ridge. Expedition Photo

— **Dougald MacDonald,** *with information from Mountain.ru and the Russian Mountaineering Federation*

Hindu Raj

CRUXING BOTH WAYS

THE FIRST ASCENT AND DIFFICULT DESCENT OF GHAMUBAR ZOM V

By Yudai Suzuki, *Japan*

Returning to base camp after eight days on Ghamubar Zom V, it felt like months since we had left. It was such a long adventure.

Three years earlier, I'd learned about this huge massif in the Hindu Raj through various publications, including the *AAJ*.

Ghamubar Zom (a.k.a. Dhuli Chhish, 6,518m) has five summits, and the entire north face had not been climbed. Only the middle and highest points had been summited, in 1973, by an Italian team climbing from the south.

Approaching from the north, Kei

Narita, Yuu Nishida, and I reached base camp (3,380m) in late August, one week after leaving Japan. We didn't require a liaison officer or cook, and so, after depositing our bags at the campsite, our porters and sirdar returned home, leaving the three of us to spend a month there by ourselves. We like this simple style.

It soon became obvious why the north side of the massif remained unclimbed. Climate change and the resulting glacial melt have left huge seracs hanging menacingly from the ridges and walls. The only safe and feasible line was the northwest ridge of Ghamubar Zom V (6,400m). It is a massive ridge: almost 4km long and gaining 2,000m vertically from the col at its foot, with a steep mixed headwall and a complex, 1.5km snow ridge above the technical crux. It appeared both challenging and adventurous, a perfect alpine-style objective for us.

As there were no easy mountains nearby for acclimatization and poor weather was predicted to arrive soon, we quickly began our attempt. At that point we had only climbed to 4,700m, the day after our arrival at base camp.

We placed our advanced base camp on the ridge, 200m above the col. Beyond this, a long, nasty, jagged ridge gave many pitches of 5.5 to 5.8 and M3 to M5. We tried to progress simultaneously, but the rope often got snagged. The ridge steepened into a mixed headwall above 5,400m, and we managed to climb through this and continue to 5,700m, but Nishida developed altitude sickness and we bailed. After descending to base camp, we continued down to the village of Darkot to rest for about a week. Unfortunately, the food

TOP: Ghamubar Zom V (6,400m); the northwest ridge, climbed in 2023, is along the right skyline. The camps along the ridge are shown; advanced base camp and the 4,400-meter col at the base of the ridge are off picture at far right. Ghamubar Zom's main summit is farther to the left. *Yudai Suzuki*

OPPOSITE PAGE: Moving toward the end of the rocky section on the northwest ridge of Ghamubar Zom V. *Yudai Suzuki*

there was bad, and we all had diarrhea.

Our agent, who until then had been very quiet, suddenly informed us that he needed to end our expedition within a week, because there had been a terrorist attack at the border with Afghanistan. Although far from being fully recovered, we rushed back to base camp for another attempt. When you're at the mercy of an agency, you don't always get to climb at your own pace.

On September 16, we returned to advanced base at 4,600m. The rock on the lower ridge was very unstable but bonded with snow and ice; the first crux on this day was a super-tough 60m of M5. Above this, we simul-climbed again for around 15 rope lengths with minimal protection, having to trust each other completely. We stopped for the night at 5,400m, below the crux mixed wall.

This 100m headwall looked like the rock section of Andromeda Strain in the Canadian Rockies. Two scary mixed pitches on fragile rock, followed by a dry-tooling pitch up 5.9 terrain, led to a final wall of better rock that proved to be one of the highlights of the route. Although this headwall was the technical crux of the climb, the long ridge above would be the mental and overall crux, both on the way up and coming back down.

Complicated ridge work brought us to a campsite at 5,750m, just above our previous high point. It took us more than two hours to excavate a platform, as the "snow" ridge turned out to be tough blue ice.

We left at 6 a.m. the next morning, and at 12:30 p.m., after climbing extensive 50°–70° blue ice, we reached a flat spot at 6,090m. We decided to leave our bivouac equipment there and head for the summit.

Passing under a serac, we continued up the ridge toward what appeared to be the top. We were dismayed to discover a false summit—the highest point was much farther away. We kept going, traversing more blue ice and climbing steep snow, to reach the true summit of Ghamubar V, at 6,400m, at 5:30 p.m., just as the sun was setting. With maximum focus, we downclimbed toward our bivouac gear and

ABOVE: Close to the end of the technical crux section of the northwest ridge of Ghamubar Zom V. *Yudai Suzuki*

OPPOSITE PAGE: Kei Narita negotiates a chossy pitch on the 100-meter mixed headwall. *Yudai Suzuki*

reached it, exhausted, at 9 p.m.

The next day, more traverses across blue ice awaited. Finally, near the top of the mixed wall, we could start rappelling. Nishida had a lapse in concentration that caused him to lose balance and pendulum against the side wall of the ridge; fortunately, no bones were broken, but his sunglasses were cracked and his eyes bloodied. During one rappel, rockfall chopped one of our ropes, and fortunately I noticed it before it was too late. We camped that night at 5,560m.

On the 21st we reached advanced base, having found the descent of the lower ridge as difficult as the ascent. On the 22nd, lightheaded due to fatigue, we hiked down the 1,200m of rough ground to base camp.

We had left only 20m of rope slings, one nut, and one piton on the mountain. From the col at the start of the ridge, our route was 2,000m and 5.9 M5 70°. We found it more taxing and more fulfilling than the Moonflower Buttress on Mt. Hunter in Alaska or the north face of Ausangate in Peru (*see report on p.194*). 📷

EARLIER EXPEDITIONS TO GHAMUBAR ZOM: *In 1973, Italians Carlo Platter, Silvo Riz, and Ludovico Vaia climbed to the 6,518m main summit of Ghamubar Zom via the southeast ridge. This summit also was attempted in 1990 and 1992 by Japanese expeditions, via the south ridge, starting from the Chhelish Glacier. The first year they reached around 6,200m, but in 1992 they discovered that a big serac, which they had previously circumvented, had collapsed, and they were unable to get above 4,500m.*

The Saraghrar massif with the northwest summit marked. The main summit is to the right. The Catalan Route, leading to Saraghrar Northwest II, is shown. The arrow marks the start of the 2021 first ascent of the northwest face, leading to Saraghrar Northwest (ca 7,300m). *Fatmap Image*

Hindu Kush

SARAGHRAR NORTHWEST II, SOUTHWEST PILLAR, ALPINE-STYLE ASCENT

In August 1982, after attempts by Spanish climbers in 1975 and 1977, a third Spanish team, comprising seven members led by Joan López, made the first ascent of the southwest pillar of Saraghrar Northwest, reaching an indistinct top on the northwest ridge that the Spanish named Saraghrar Northwest II (ca 7,150m).

Starting a little above 4,900m, this was one of the longest rock routes in the world and was graded VI 75°. The team fixed ropes to near the top of the major rock difficulties at over 6,000m, after which the leader, along with highly accomplished alpinists Nil Bohigas and Enric Lucas [*who just two years later would achieve the groundbreaking first ascent of the south face of Annapurna Central*], made a push for the summit. After four bivouacs, they reached Northwest II and elected to descend from that point. The higher summit of Saraghrar Northwest (ca 7,300m) would have to wait until 2021 for a first ascent, via the northwest face (*AAJ 2022*).

In the summer of 2023, Catalans Oriol Baró, Bru Busom, Guillem Sancho, and Marc Toralles first attempted the complicated rock pillar left of the 2021 route on the northwest face. They reached 6,000m, fixing a little rope, but two days of heavy snowfall forced them down. They decided instead to attempt an alpine-style ascent of the 1982 Catalan Route, aiming to complete it to the main summit.

Beginning on July 20, it took them two days to climb to 6,000m, whereupon it snowed all night. The rock next day was either covered in verglas or wet. They only gained another 300m. On day four they had reached 6,750m when they received a forecast that the weather would be bad on the following day. Baró and Sancho decided to retreat and equip rappel anchors, so the other pair could make an efficient and speedier descent. (They also removed some ancient fixed rope.)

Busom and Toralles continued that day to 7,000m and hunkered down for the expected storm. Fortunately, it never materialized. The next day the two reached the top of Saraghrar Northwest II, where they found the snow on the ridge leading toward the main summit in awful condition. Progressing too slowly, they turned around and descended, reaching the bottom of the face on July 25.

The 2023 team found over 2,000m of technical climbing, which changed from pure rock to more mixed terrain above 6,400m. They rated the ascent 6c M6 70°.

—**Lindsay Griffin,** *AAJ*

KARAKORAM | Ghujerab

SHAR IZAT PEAK, ATTEMPT ON SOUTH RIDGE REACHING THREE SUBSIDIARY SUMMITS

In September, Tim Oates and I hoped to make the first ascent of Dih Sar (6,200m) by the east ridge. Our plan involved crossing Joshi Pass (5,423m, 36°32'25.44"N, 75°18'26.63"E) to reach a base camp on the Dih Glacier. Unfortunately, Tim got altitude sickness approaching the pass. Ultimately, he had to return to Shimshal in hopes of recovering there.

Meanwhile, porters carried some climbing gear, a tent, and supplies up to Joshi Pass so that Tim and I could continue from there if he returned, either by descending to Dih Sar base camp or by climbing peaks above the pass. I went to Joshi Pass alone, and the next day I climbed along a ridge heading north from the pass; this is the long south ridge of Shar Izat Peak (5,930m), which had been climbed previously from Boisum Pass (*AAJ 2006*).

I crossed two tops on the ridge (Peaks 25 and 26 on the Wala map, the latter at 5,547m), which was easy but corniced. After 1.5km, I reached a third top, the highest, at 5,696m GPS, just before Wala Peak 29 (5,720m, 36°33'25.96"N, 75°18'43.23"E). Beyond this, the ridge dropped a short distance to a col before rising toward the summit of Shar Izat.

The ground beyond looked trickier for solo climbing, so I returned to my tent at the pass. The next morning, I learned by inReach that Tim was not coming back up, so we ended the expedition.

—Compiled from a report by Peter Thompson (U.K.)
to the Mount Everest Foundation

SOUTHEAST BOISUM GLACIER, VARIOUS ASCENTS

The lead-up to our planned trip to India had been a test of bureaucratic nerves, ultimately ending with it falling through at late notice. With little time, we managed to throw together a new itinerary in Pakistan, and on August 27, Arran Turton-Phillips and I landed in Islamabad.

The reformulated plan was to visit the Virjerab Glacier, several days' trek southeast from Shimshal. On our arrival in the village, however, the general feedback was that the glacier would be very difficult for porters. By our second morning in Shimshal, we had found only two willing porters out of the required 15. It was evident we would need to change plans to somewhere accessible with donkeys.

The eastern branch of the Southeast Boisum Glacier, showing the route to the col and up Peak 5,625m (left) and Boe Sar Southeast (5,880m). *Lee Harrison*

We opted for the north side of the Boisum (a.k.a. Boisam or Boesam) Pass, where I knew there remained several unclimbed peaks. In a matter of hours, the donkeys were loaded and we were on our way. The trek over the pass to our base camp at Perchudwashk (4,580m) took two days.

On the evening of September 3, we bivouacked in a strip of moraine on the Southeast Boisum Glacier, close to where it divides into southwest and east branches. The following morning, we used a one-day weather window to attempt Peak 5,810m (36°32'23"N, 75°23'20"E), first ascending the glacier's southwest branch, with a plan to gain the col west-southwest of the summit via its northwest slopes. However, a short way up

TOP: This spectacular rock finger is south of Shpodeen at approximately 36°29'46"N, 75°20'11"E. It is estimated to offer a couple of hundred meters of climbing, with a top at around 4,800m. This area appears to have largely good rock. Lee Harrison

BOTTOM: The southwest face of Koh-e-Brobar (5,985m GPS). The original ascent of this peak, in 2011, followed the right skyline (south-southeast ridge). Lee Harrison

these slopes, we decided there was too much avalanche risk.

We promptly switched to the east ridge of Pir Sar (5,683m, 36°32'03.1"N, 75°21'56.5"E), but insufficient acclimatization, together with the payback for our detour up the slopes of Peak 5,810m, caught up with us at 5,625m, and we retreated to base camp.

On the evening of the 7th, we were back at the same bivouac. Early next morning, we ascended the eastern branch of the Southeast Boisum Glacier and climbed to the col at its head, from which we made an impromptu ascent of the short south ridge of Peak 5,625m (36°33'01.2"N, 75°24'01.6"E) at PD. While erecting our tent on the col, we lost a pole down the mountainside, but after

some experimentation, we concluded the remaining pole would suffice, given the fine weather.

On the 9th, we started up the north buttress of Peak 5,880m (36°32'28.6"N, 75°23'59.6"E) from the col. Low on the route, we were startled by a thunderous boom that coincided with me striking an axe into the mountainside. Some excited discussion followed, and it became apparent that a section of serac had fallen off near Arran. Cracks were also visible in the surrounding névé, suggesting this was no place to linger. As we continued, we negotiated several serac barriers interlinked with snow slopes; the seracs' arrangement limited the objective danger, since any potential debris would be funneled down the faces on either side of us.

From the top of the buttress, we continued up the northeast ridge for a final rope length to the corniced summit. We downclimbed the same route. We suggest the name Boe Sar Southeast, since Peak 5,880m lies at the head of the Southeast Boisum Glacier. [*Boe Sar was the name given to the first peak northeast of Boisum Pass, climbed in 2005 by Abdullah Bai and Francois Carrel.*] We graded the route D-, partly for the less than straightforward descent.

On the 14th, we bivouacked on the Boisum right ice flow. Next day, we climbed a new route on Koh-e-Brobar (a.k.a. Barabar Sar, 5,907m map height, 36°34'09.9"N, 75°24'11.5"E), via the prominent central couloir on the southwest face. The couloir involved easy snow slopes in the lower half, increasing higher to a maximum of 50°. A short distance below the summit, we joined the south-southeast ridge and traversed beneath its corniced crest to the top (5,958m GPS, 850m of ascent, AD). Descent was via the same route.

Fine weather had prevailed for most of the trip, and then, on the 18th, we made a timely departure from base camp amid new snow and an unsettled outlook. 📷

—Lee Harrison, *Norway*

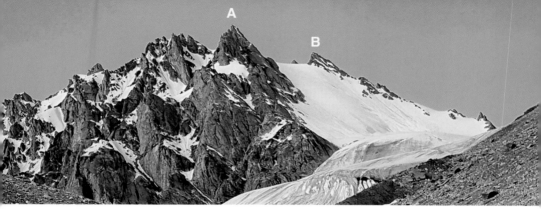

(A) Peak 282 and (B) Peak 283 (Tuki Sar, 5,850m). The ascent of Tuki Sar was near the right skyline. The climbers then traversed to Peak 281 (AK Sar), hidden behind Peak 282. *Jacob Dyer*

GUNJ-E-DUR VALLEY, TUKI SAR AND AK SAR

In August, after over a year of planning, Will Dixon, Job Klusener, James Rigby, and I arrived in Pakistan. While we had a lot of experience in the Alps and Scotland, this was our first time on an expedition aiming to make first ascents, so we wanted objectives that would allow flexibility, depending on conditions. After reading the 2017 British Shimshal Expedition report (*AAJ 2018*), we settled on the Gunj-e-Dur Valley, where the First and Second East Gunj-e-Dur Glaciers contained almost a dozen unclimbed peaks of varying style and difficulty just below 6,000m.

After three days of flights and driving, we reached Shimshal, from where a three-day trek took us to base camp. We then explored the Second East Gunj-e-Dur Glacier. We quickly saw the effects of what is now being described as the hottest year on record. Temperatures on the summits of 6,000m peaks were barely going below freezing, even at night. We could see debris from a couple of small avalanches, and most of the rock we came across was extremely loose.

Our first objective was Peak 289 (5,775m; peak numbers taken from Jerzy Wala's maps to the Ghujerab Mountains). Job and I attempted the south ridge, reaching the col between Peaks 289 and 290 via a 30°–35° snow slope. We continued up the ridge over loose, rocky terrain until reaching a four-meter blank wall. A mixed option to the left was too warm in the sun, so we headed down. [*This ridge was also the goal of a 2022 expedition, which turned back from the col; see AAJ 2023.*]

On the 20th, James, Job, and I climbed Peak 281 (5,907m, 36°34'26.38"N, 75°36'20.40"E) via the south-southeast ridge of Peak 283 (5,850m, 36°34'12.14"N, 75°36'30.57"E). After an initial snow slope to gain the ridge, we were able to pass most of the short rock sections on the right, using steep patches of snow. Below the rocky summit of Peak 283, we roped up and I led a couple of winding pitches until moderate terrain brought us to the summit, which we named Tuki Sar. After a short rappel and a slog across snow, bypassing Peak 282, we reached the top of Peak 281, which we named AK Sar after our two cooks, Ali and Khadim, who had been outstanding.

In the afternoon of August 21, as Will left to bivouac before an attempt on Peak 275 (ca 5,850m) from the Third East Gunj-e-Dur Glacier, Khadim commented that we were cutting it close to the porters arriving. This surprised us, as we didn't expect to leave base camp until day 25 of the expedition. It was only day 16. It turned out there had been some language confusion between "day" and "date"; we had planned a 24-day expedition, ending on August 29, but the porters were to arrive on August 24. As a result, we ended up losing five climbing days. We made the most of it by exploring Shimshal and Hunza as tourists. 📷

—**Jacob Dyer,** *U.K.*

The line of Thomas Franchini's attempt on the north face of Trivor (7,728m). Deep snow and warm weather halted the attempt at around 6,100 meters. *Thomas Franchini*

Batura and Hispar Muztaghs

MUCHU CHHISH AND TRIVOR ATTEMPTS

Two high peaks in the western Karakoram were the scene of attempted new routes in 2023.

In July, two teams attempted unclimbed Muchu Chhish (7,453m) in the Batura Muztagh, north of the Hunza Valley. As with previous expeditions, they followed a prominent ridge that extends to the south from the Batura Ridge. This was the route followed in 1983 by a Polish-German team that made the first ascents of Batura V (7,531m) and Batura VI (7,462m). The Muchu Chhish suitors have aimed to repeat the 1983 route to the Batura Ridge and then make a committing traverse eastward along the crest for almost two kilometers, all above 7,200m, to reach the unclimbed peak.

Two Norwegians attempting this line in 2023 gave up low on the mountain, but a Czech expedition, which had previously acclimatized on Spantik, managed to establish three camps, the highest by Radoslav Groh and Tomáš Petreček at 6,900m, just below the Batura Ridge. They then struggled in very poor snow to a reported altitude of 7,200m before descending.

Previously, in June, Thomas Franchini made a solo attempt on the north face of Trivor (7,728m) in the Hispar Muztagh. He approached up the Momhil Valley, where he had climbed the previous year (*AAJ 2023*). Unfortunately, the conditions were much worse in 2023, with large quantities of spring snow and very high temperatures. Although he planned a direct ascent of the face, he was forced to try a safer route toward the right side. At 6,100m, he decided it was too dangerous and retreated.

This shapely mountain was first climbed from the Trivor Glacier to the south and west to gain the high col at the foot of the northwest ridge. The summit was reached via this ridge in August 1960 by Wilfrid Noyce (U.K.) and Jack Sadler (USA). The only other known ascent was made by a Japanese expedition that approached up the Momhil Glacier and climbed a northeast-facing spur to access Trivor's northwest ridge; Atsushi Endo and Toshifumi Onuki reached the top. 📄 📷

—**Lindsay Griffin**, *AAJ*

Rakaposhi Mountains

DIRAN, NORMAL ROUTE WITH PARAGLIDER APPROACH

Antoine Girard, a pioneer in using paragliders to approach and descend from alpine climbs, climbed Diran (7,266m) in early July after flying to the mountain from the hills above Karimabad, about 23km to the north.

Girard launched his paraglider a little after noon on July 3, climbed to about 5,500m, then flew cross-country to Diran's west ridge (the upper part of the peak's normal route) at about 5,500m. Finding lift on the southwest side of the ridge, he continued upward to about 6,750m before landing, 2 hours 20 minutes after starting. He then used skis to climb the crevassed west ridge, sometimes in deep snow, to about 150m below the summit. From there he continued in crampons, reaching the top just before darkness fell, between 7:30 and 8 p.m.

Girard skied down the ridge to his

gear cache, then continued down on foot to around 6,500m, where he put up his tent at 11:30 p.m. In the morning, he descended to 6,240m and launched his paraglider at 11:20 a.m., just before a storm engulfed the mountain. The return to Karimabad was direct: He landed at 2,273m after about 40 minutes in the air, utterly exhausted.

In June 2021, Girard flew 40km from Karimabad to land at 6,400m on the southwest ridge of Spantik, climbed to the 7,027m summit, and flew back the same day, in a round trip of only eight hours. [*See "Fly and Climb" in AAJ 2023 for more about this technique. A self-filmed video of the Diran climb is at the AAJ website.*]

—**Dougald MacDonald,** *AAJ,*
with information from Antoine Girard, France

Antoine Girard flying back to Karimabad after climbing Diran's upper west ridge, visible in back. The summit, enveloped in storm clouds, is in upper left. *Antoine Girard*

KARAKORAM | Panmah Muztagh

BAINTHA KABATA, SOUTHWEST FACE TO SOUTH RIDGE, THE ALIEN FACE

Our goal, like many teams before us, was the unclimbed southeast pillar of Baintha Brakk (The Ogre) leading to the east summit. François Cazzanelli and Matteo Della Bordella (both from Italy), Symon Welfringer (France), and I arrived in Skardu in late June. The weather was hot and sunny during our trek to the Choktoi Glacier.

Deep snow on the glacier forced us to establish base camp several kilometers away from where we had planned, and the wonderful weather we had enjoyed came to an end. Nonetheless, starting on July 1, we made a four-day acclimatization trip to the Sim La and a high campsite at about 6,000m on the ridge northwest of Baintha Ahrta (ca 6,300m). We used skis during this outing, which meant we were able to travel long distances efficiently, and the ski descent from the shoulder was one of the highlights of the expedition.

The weather was then mostly bad until July 11. On the 13th, we left for advanced base, and on the 14th made the dangerous ascent to the col between Baintha Brakk I and II, at the base of the southeast pillar. This approach is threatened by seracs to the north and enormous snow mushrooms to the south. Considerable avalanche debris showed we shouldn't linger, and by mid-day we were back in base camp.

We set off with the next good weather forecast, but it began to snow heavily before we could climb to the col, forcing us back. A strong monsoon influence was making weather reports unreliable,

The Alien Face on the southwest face and south ridge of Baintha Kabata. The route started from the Sim La, just off picture to the right. The 2008 Haley-Turgeon route, making the first ascent of the mountain, was more on the right side of the ridgeline but shared some ground on the third tier of the rock buttress. *Silvan Schüpbach*

and we determined there would not be a sufficiently long window to climb the pillar. On the 23rd, we carried out the thankless task of retrieving our gear from the col, and the next day François left for Skardu.

On the 26th and 27th, there was enough good weather for Matteo, Symon, and me to climb the southwest face and south ridge of Baintha Kabata (ca 6,290m). Our route started above the Sim La, where we climbed 400m (M3 60°) to outflank the initial towers of the south ridge on the left (west) and reach a steep rock step. This gave 200m of 6a to 6c. The 200m second step was climbed at M5 6b to a snowfield below the upper wall, where we camped. Next day we climbed a further 250m to the summit (difficulties to 7a) and descended the same route in worsening weather.

Our new line, The Alien Face (800m, 7a M5), climbs largely on the left (southwest) side of the crest but shares some of the middle section with the route climbed in 2008 by Colin Haley and Maxime Turgeon to make the first ascent of the mountain. [*In the lower and upper section of the ridge, these two climbed on the right (southeast) flank of the crest at 5.9 M5; AAJ 2009.*]

—**Silvan Schüpbach,** *Switzerland*

UPDATED AAJ REPORT ON FIRST ASCENT OF BAINTHA BRAKK II: *The original AAJ report on the 1983 Korean expedition that made the first ascent of Baintha Brakk II (Ogre II, 6,960m) has been updated at the AAJ website with some corrections, additional information, and historical photographs.*

LATOK THUMB, FIRST ASCENT, VIA SOUTHWEST FACE

Latok Thumb is a 6,380m rock tower with a precipitous southwest face. Its northeast flank drops to a high col on the south-southwest ridge of Latok II; the upper section of this ridge, approached via the southeast spur, was climbed by an Italian team in 1977 to make the first ascent of Latok II (*AAJ 1978*). Mixed ground on the southwest face of Latok II, left of Latok Thumb, was ascended in 2012 by French climbers to reach the upper south-southwest ridge (*AAJ 2013*). But the rock formation that we named Latok Thumb was still unclimbed.

Miquel Mas and I spent 12 days on the southwest face in 2022. The face drops more than 1,000m from the summit: a very steep granite wall with significant mixed sections at the beginning and end. We established base camp on the Latok Glacier at 4,470m and advanced base at 4,950m, and then spent many days studying potential routes and their objective dangers. To reach the foot of the wall at 5,300m, we first had to climb a snow/ice couloir of about 350m (70° max). This had to be completed by 9 a.m.—later, it was raked by rockfall and avalanches.

The first six pitches of the wall provided difficult mixed climbing up to M5. This took us to 5,650m, where we established our first portaledge camp. Above, we continued to the top of pitch 14, with several run-out sections of 7a and A2+ at around 5,900m. We moved slowly, as the sun only reaches the wall at 11 a.m. and leaves at 4 p.m., giving a five-hour window for rock climbing in reasonable temperatures. At other times, it was very cold.

Above our high point that year was a steep section with obviously difficult roofs. Bad weather forced us down, and as we had no time for a second attempt, we fixed ropes down the route and left most of the equipment at Camp 1 for a return match the following year.

In July and August 2023, Miquel and I spent 18 days on the face. After negotiating the section of roofs, we moved the portaledge up to Camp 2, at 6,030m, 19 pitches up the wall, where there was snow to melt for water. We then climbed the top of the face in three intense days, arriving at the summit of Latok Thumb on August 18. Two more days were needed to rappel the route and remove all our gear from the face.

We named our route Atraccio Instintiva ("Instinctive Attraction," 1,100m, 7a R A2+ M5). On pitches 17–19, some 8mm bolts were used for aid moves. 📷 🔍

—**Marc Subirana,** *Spain*

TOP: Starting pitch 20 on Latok Thumb, above the portaledge at Camp 2 (6,030m). Marc Subirana

BOTTOM: The 2023 route Atraccio Instintiva on the southwest face of Latok Thumb (6,380m), showing the two portaledge camps. The route had 31 pitches above the steep snow gully at the base. Marc Subirana

KARAKORAM | Baltoro Muztagh

VARIOUS ASCENTS AND SKI DESCENTS

In the latter half of May, Sam Favret and Julien Herry (France) made a number of probable first ascents and ski descents of couloirs above the Baltoro and Biarchedi glaciers.

These included: an 800m northeast-facing couloir immediately to the southeast of Lobsang Spire South (5,594m); the 600m

The left of these two couloirs at the end of the long northeast ridge of Biarchedi was skied. Part of Peak 5,597m is visible on the left. *Julien Herry*

southwest-facing couloir that leads from the Biarchedi Glacier to the gap between Nuating I (5,868m) and II (5,860m; neither of these peaks has a recorded ascent); 800m of the northeast-facing couloir that reaches the col immediately north of a rock spire, Peak 5,597m (Polish map), toward the end of the long northeast ridge of Biarchedi, starting from the south col of the Baltoro Glacier; and, with two young Pakistani snowboarders, Hasnein Ali and Jibran Aziz, part of the 700m southwest-facing couloir that lies between Nuating III (variously reported 5,620m to 5,700m) and the first shoulder to the north.

Details of these climbs and descents, along with photos, are at the AAJ website. 📄 📷

—Lindsay Griffin, *with information from Julien Herry, France, and Rodolphe Popier, Chronique Alpine*

KHARUT II, FIRST ASCENT, VIA WEST-NORTHWEST RIDGE

Vicente Bárcena and I reached K2 base camp in early July and acclimatized on Pastora Peak (a.k.a. Khalkhal East, 6,206m), reaching a height of 5,800m.

We then established an advanced base camp at 5,500m, below the west flank of Kharut II (6,824m). There were many crevasses, which we fell into on several occasions, fortunately without

major consequences. Indeed, our biggest difficulty was finding a route along the ten kilometers of glacier.

Having deposited gear, food, tents, and gas, we returned to base camp, where we rested for two days during bad weather. Despite no improvement on the third day, we went back up to advanced base and spent the night.

The next day, July 18, we started up the west face. Not long after leaving camp, at around 5,600m, Vincent realized he had no strength and decided to go down. It was a difficult moment, but at no time did we discuss the possibility of me going down with him. I continued up with a small tent and sleeping bag but no rope or climbing gear.

Near the top of the initial 500m snow slope, I crossed the west-northwest ridge to my left, reached its north flank, and continued up mixed terrain. The angle increased to 65°, but the snow was in good condition and I could climb safely. As the day progressed, the sun reached the west face and the snow began to soften.

At 6,300m, I decided to leave my backpack and attempt the summit that same day. After melting snow to make a liter of water, I continued ascending.

The next snow section was 65° at the start, then steepened to a "wave" that I surmounted on the left (north) to reach gentler slopes (30°–35°), where the snow seemed quite unstable but fortunately did not slide at all.

Above this section, the angle increased, and it became very difficult to make progress. I moved back right to reach the ridge and climbed it over snow and rock (sections up to M4). Eventually, I had to move left (north) to get below the highest point of Kharut II. I had to clean 30cm of soft snow to get each axe placement, and it took me almost an hour and a half to climb approximately 100m. After this, the angle remained similar (45°–50°), but more rock appeared.

A steep snow couloir led to the summit rock tower. I tried to climb the final ten-

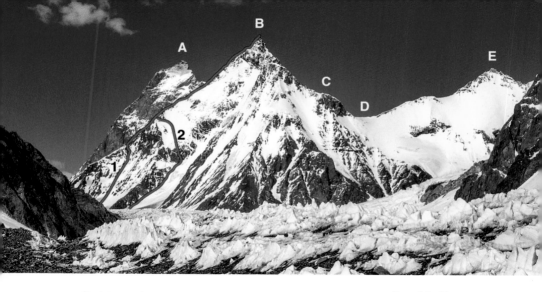

meter wall without gloves, but I broke two handholds and gave up. Then, to my right, I saw a small tongue of snow ending at a block close to the top. I secured myself to the block with a sling and, using aid, made a few moves up the wall overlooking the Kharut Glacier. I hooked the rock on the summit with my axe, pulled up on it until my head was level with the top, and called it good. It was 6 p.m.

Facing in, I downclimbed to 6,300m. Luckily, the shadow cast by K2 helped harden the snow, and at nightfall the temperature dropped, improving conditions further. Unluckily, my gloves froze, and I got mild frostbite on the thumbs of both hands.

Reunited with my pack, I dug into the snow and bivouacked inside the pack and the tent flysheet. During the night there was a snowstorm, and the next day dawned cloudy. Lower down the mountain, I decided to descend a slope to the south of my ascent route. Although it passed under the big serac high on the west face, it avoided the mixed terrain. I arrived at advanced base at 9 a.m. and hugged Vicente, who was waiting for me with open arms. 📷

—Koldo Zubimendi, *Basque Country*

Part of the Kharut Group seen from K2 base camp to the southwest. (A) Kharut I (unclimbed). (B) Kharut II, showing (1) the 2023 route of ascent and (2) the descent route. (C) Peak 6,455m. (D) Sella Pass. (E) Kharut Pyramid (6,420m, unclimbed). *Koldo Zubimendi*

NOTES ON THE KHARUT PEAKS: *The Kharut Peaks lie on the border with China, east of K2, between the Godwin-Austen and Kharut glaciers. Kharut I, the central and highest peak, is 6,928m and remains unclimbed. Kharut II (6,824m) is to the south, and Kharut III, the north peak, is 6,785m and was climbed in 1977 by a team from Japan. On the ridge south of Kharut II lies Sella Pass (6,063m), and south of this is an unclimbed 6,420m peak sometimes called Kharut Pyramid.*

Several teams have aimed to climb Kharut II. In 1974, Japanese climbers went from Sella Pass as far as a rocky shoulder on the southwest ridge of Kharut II, marked on some maps as a peak of 6,455m. A British commercial expedition in 2005 failed to set foot on the mountain due to snow conditions (AAJ 2006), while an American team, which arrived in June 2023, before the Basque pair, gave up due to high avalanche risk.

(H) marks approximate 2023 high point on the southeast ridge of Gasherbrum IV. In center is the unclimbed east face. The right skyline is the 1958 first ascent route (northeast ridge). *Bruce Normand*

GASHERBRUM IV, SOUTHEAST RIDGE, ATTEMPT AND TRAGEDY

In August, Dmitry Golovchenko and Sergey Nilov attempted the unclimbed southeast ridge of Gasherbrum IV (7,925m) in alpine style. Their plan was to descend the original route on the northeast ridge, climbed in 1958 by Walter Bonatti and Carlo Mauri.

The two Russians arrived at Gasherbrum base camp on August 1. From August 8–13, they slowly found a route through the difficult icefall that leads to the glacier plateau between Gasherbrums III and IV. Fierce wind and low temperatures almost produced frostbite, but they were able to reach the plateau, where they stashed gear and food. They arrived back in base camp on the 14th.

I was in touch with Dmitry the next day. With help from one of my friends who is a meteorologist, I agreed to send forecasts to Dmitry's wife, Sasha, who would be keeping in regular contact with her husband.

Dmitry and Sergey left base camp on August 18 for their summit push, and on the 20th they made camp below the southeast ridge at about 7,000m. On the 21st it was windy, and they only managed four pitches, camping at 7,100m. The

following day they were unable to move, but on the 23rd, despite continued strong wind and snowfall, the two climbed 1.5 pitches to a large ledge and a better campsite. Bad weather confined them to the tent the following day.

On the 25th, the weather seemed better, and they climbed another half pitch before rappelling to the tent in a snowstorm. Next day, Sergey climbed a difficult chimney and a second pitch through a series of rocky walls, but the two were then forced to descend to the tent to avoid frostbite. On the 27th, they jumared the four pitches now fixed above the camp, climbed two more pitches, and brought the tent up to a big, snowy ledge at above 7,300m.

On the 28th, they added two more pitches, then, over the next two days, they were able to simul-climb in places as the angle of the ridge eased, and they reported that they could see the final headwall on the ridge. They reached 7,583m by the night of the 30th.

The usual evening satellite phone message did not arrive on the 31st, their 14th day out from base camp. The last tracker location showed them to be at 7,684m, about 240m below the summit (and still below a difficult-looking headwall and sharp final ridge). After a couple of days, during which Dmitry's wife had not received any contact, efforts were made to initiate a rescue. Unfortunately, bad weather and bureaucracy prevented this. Five days later, Nilov arrived in base camp, frostbitten and alone.

A summary of Nilov's account of what had happened was published by Anna Piunova, chief editor of Mountain.ru: On August 31, the two men found a small, sloping shoulder on the ridge, at 7,684m, where they could place the tent. The site needed to be enlarged using stones and snow. Anchoring was difficult, as the rock was shattered and covered in ice.

The tent was secured with the rope, and the two got inside and attached themselves to the rope before making tea and settling in for the night. However, they discovered the tent was slipping. Sergey unclipped from the rope and went out to level the platform. He tied knots in the rope and threw the end inside the tent for Dmitry, who was gathering their equipment so it wouldn't slide out of the tent. Then Sergey heard his partner call, "Sergey, I'm falling!" and saw the tent slide from the platform and down a couloir with Dmitry inside. Only the rope remained.

With no partner and none of his personal equipment, Sergey sat out the night, fighting the cold. Next morning, he made around 15 rappels along the fall line of the tent. He found Dmitry's body on the glacier plateau, wrapped it in the tent, collected what gear he could, and dragged the tent to the middle of the plateau to place it in a crevasse.

Sergey's five-day return to base camp was without food or drink; the stove had been broken in the fall and any remaining food eaten by birds. He spent the nights in snow holes inside two sleeping bags. He was eventually repatriated to Moscow to begin treatment for severely frostbitten feet.

Born in 1983, Golovchenko had climbed new routes on Trango Tower, Kyzyl Asker, Asgard, Jannu, Muztagh Tower, and Thalay Sagar, among other peaks. The two-decade-long Golovchenko-Nilov partnership was one of the most formidable in recent times. [*Victor Gorlov and Natalia Zotova contributed information and translation for this account.*]

—**Federico Bernardi**, *Italy*

KARAKORAM | Masherbrum Range

YERNAMANDU KANGRI, FIRST ASCENT, VIA SOUTHWEST FACE

Martin Sieberer (Austria) and I waited many months for our Pakistan visas, and they only arrived three weeks before departure. Our goal was unclimbed Yernamandu Kangri (7,163m; this is how it is pronounced by the people of Hushe, but other spellings exist, notably Yermanendu on most maps). The approach to our base camp on the Masherbrum Glacier went smoothly. Our camp was at 4,300m, only 20 minutes from the start of the Serac Glacier.

During the first part of July, we twice ventured up the glacier to find a way through the maze of ice walls and crevasses, reaching around 5,300m both times. Snow and rain kept us in base camp the rest of the time.

The weather improved in mid-July, and, wondering if this might be our only chance, we waited one sunny day for the snow to settle and then set out on July 13, despite limited acclimatization. We took

On the final 600-meter southwest face of Yernamandu Kangri. *Simon Messner*

Looking north-northeast over the upper Masherbrum Glacier from high on Cathedral Peak. (A) Mandu Peaks (7,121m and 7,081m). (B) Masherbrum southwest summit (7,806m; the main summit is hidden behind). (C) Yernamandu Kangri (7,163m) with the 2023 route. As far as the plateau below the final steep face, this route coincided with the 1960 American route for the first ascent of Masherbrum. (D) Serac Peak (6,273m, Wala map; behind it lies Broad Peak). (E) Gasherbrum IV. (F) Gasherbrum III. (G) Gasherbrum II. *Irena Mrak*

the minimum of gear so we could move fast, even leaving our rope.

By early morning we had reached 5,400m, where we dug out a north-facing platform in the edge of a crevasse and camped there the rest of the day and following night. On the 14th the weather was fantastic, but we were definitely not used to the altitude, and we sunk into the soft snow with every step. At 6,250m, exhausted, we had to stop and camp below a huge crevasse. We hadn't considered how loud it would be when water dripped on the tent the whole day.

At 4:15 a.m. on July 15, we left the tent and, with nearly empty rucksacks, walked along snow ridges, crossed crevasses, and panted heavily on any snow slopes. This effort brought us to the final southwest face (600m, 60°–70°) of Yernamandu. With only ten meters of cord in our pack, we would have to climb up and down this headwall unprotected. We sat on refrigerator-sized blocks of ice at the base, looking at the face. Then, without any discussion, we stood up and started climbing. If either of us had brought up the subject of turning around, we would have both done so without any argument.

High on the face was an icy section, above which waist-deep snow led to the upper southeast ridge. We traversed granite slabs to a col, from which we saw the summit 100m above us. It was becoming shrouded in cloud.

At 11:15 a.m., exactly seven hours after leaving camp and three weeks after leaving Europe, we reached the top. Our inReach measured 7,185m. We stayed only a few minutes, hammered a piton into a crack a little lower down, then started downclimbing the face. At the bottom, the sun was shining with full force, making progress torturous. Finally, we reached the tent, where we spent a short night before descending all the way to base camp, very tired but happy.

Apart from the 600m headwall, the 3,000m climb had not been technically difficult, but the terrain was complex: many crevasses, exposure to serac fall, and avalanche risk. 📄 📷

—**Simon Messner,** *Italy*

NOTES ON YERNAMANDU KANGRI:
Yernamandu Kangri rises on the southeast ridge of Masherbrum and, before 2023, had seen no known attempt, although in

1981 Volker Stallbohm reached the col at the base of the northwest ridge during an attempt on Masherbrum. The 2023 ascent more or less followed the original route on Masherbrum until the plateau below Yernamandu Kangri's final southwest face (see online report for more details). According to the German chronicler Eberhard Jurgalski, prior to summer 2023, Yernamandu Kangri was the tenth-highest unclimbed summit in the world.

HONBROK, EAST FACE

Previously unreported was the possible first ascent of Honbrok (Honboro, 6,459m) on July 16, 2000, by Satoshi Hatsugai, Mori Hatsuyoshi, and Kumiko Suzuki from Japan.

After acclimatizing on the Deosai Plateau, a high-altitude plain south of Skardu, the trio walked three hours up the Honbrok Valley from Hushe village and camped at around 4,000m, just below the glacier. They left early the next day and headed west along the north bank of the glacier, eventually crossing it and heading for Honbrok's east face. They climbed this snow face to the main summit—a gain of more than 2,000m over eight kilometers—and returned the same way, reaching camp in the evening. [*The slightly lower (6,430m) southwest peak of Honbrok was climbed in 2007.*]

—**Lindsay Griffin**, *with information from the climbers provided by Kaoru Wada*

APOBROK GREAT PYRAMID, ATTEMPT AND TRAGEDY

In August 2023, after attempting Bondit Peak twice in the previous two years, Takayasu Semba and Shinji Tamura made a third visit to the area, this time to attempt a 5,940m peak in the adjacent valley to the northwest. On Jerzy Wala's sketch maps, this peak at 35°21'44.53"N, 76°14'29.49"E is referred to as Apobrok Great Pyramid (Apobrok Peak being an alternative name for Bondit Peak).

Base camp on the North Apobrok Glacier below Apobrok Great Pyramid, showing the 2023 attempted route. The main summit is on the left; the top of the rocky pyramid is 100 meters or less lower. *Ibrahim Koto*

On August 10, Semba and Tamura established Camp 1 at 5,030m, just above the start of the rocky northeast ridge. The next day, the two started up steep snow, then left their crampons and continued up the rock ridge. At 5,400m, they decided to turn back.

At about 2 p.m., during their third rappel, a piton anchor failed and both men fell around 60m. Tamura was badly injured, and, after stabilizing him, Semba urged Tamura not to move, sent an SOS with their inReach, and descended to seek help. A rescue team arrived that evening, but Tamura apparently had tried to descend on his own, and eventually it was determined he must have fallen deep into a crevasse below Camp 1. [*More details are at the AAJ website; see also p.352 for more about Tamura.*]

—**Information from Nathan Dahlberg,** *New Zealand*

Tagas Mountains

DRIFIKA, SOUTH FACE AND SOUTHEAST SPUR

In May, Italians Davide Limongi, Enrico Mosetti, and Giovanni Zaccaria visited the Nangma Valley, where their target was the shapely Drifika (6,447m). The trio identified a new route on the right side of the south face.

The temperature was low as they set off, and Limongi and Mosetti decided to turn back, but Zaccaria continued alone, carrying skis. After nine hours of effort, he reached the summit, having followed the 2004 Slovenian route, White River, for the last 200m. Zaccaria downclimbed the final section (with powder snow over ice) to around 6,250m, then donned his skis and descended to the team's high camp at 5,150m, with one rappel of 20m.

Previously, in early May, the team visited the Passu Glacier in the Batura Muztagh, where they all climbed the north side of Badshani or King's Peak (5,497m). Zaccaria skied their ascent route from the top, while Limongi and Mosetti downclimbed and then skied from a col at around 5,300m. Badshani was first climbed in 1992 via its 1,400m north face, finishing up the northwest ridge, likely the same route climbed by the Italians. 📷

—**Lindsay Griffin,** *AAJ*

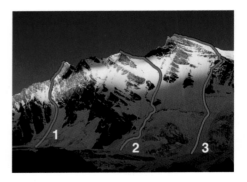

The Korada Peaks, showing (1) the 2021 line, Hot Tang, to Korada North; (2) the 2023 route to the central summit; and (3) the 2004 route to Korada South. *Will Lewallen*

NANGMA VALLEY: KORADA CENTRAL, NURISHAN ATTEMPT, AND OTHER ASCENTS

In August, a Young Alpinist Group supported by the Czech Mountaineering Association reached base camp at 4,300m in the Nangma Valley six days after leaving Prague. We then split into pairs to attempt different projects.

Jakub Kácha and I made the first ascent of Korada Central (at least 6,000m) via the west face. Korada's south top (5,944m) was climbed in 2004 by a team from Slovenia; the north summit (6,146m) was climbed in 2021 by a trio from the U.K. Like the previous Korada teams, we started from a bivouac in the Southeast Drifika Cwm. We climbed the ca 1,000m face at D+ (60°), with one camp at 6,000m on the sharp south ridge, with the tent attached to rock and V-thread anchors.

Kácha also teamed up with Martin Sankot for a valiant attempt on a new route up the west face of Kapura (6,544m), climbing the 1,500m wall with two bivouacs at a grade of M5. They were stopped on the sharp summit ridge, just northwest of the main top, by dangerous,

deep snow. At this point, their GPS registered 6,600m, putting the official altitude of this mountain in question.

Over August 12–13, Sankot and Ondřej Mrklovský tried to climb Nurishan (Peak 148 on the Wala map, ca 6,000m, 35°23'38.71"N, 76°25'26.52"E). After forging a devious route on the right side of the southeast face (VI+ M4+ 70°), Sankot got his hands on top of the northwest ridge, still a long way right of the summit. The GPS said 5,850m.

As he was looking over the far side of the ridge, Sankot released a wet snow slide, which swept down the face and hit Mrklovský, who was still simul-climbing. The latter fell and pulled off Sankot. Fortunately, both of their falls were stopped by a micro-cam, the highest of several pieces of protection between them. The two descended a little and bivouacked with no equipment, as they had intended to complete the climb in a day, then continued down to base camp in the morning.

František Bulička and Anča Šebestíková primarily concentrated on lower-altitude rock routes. As Bulička wrote, "The entire Nangma Valley is a disco with several floors, where you can have fun and dance in various ways. I really liked the middle, rocky floor."

The pair first climbed Bloody Mary on the southwest face of Denbor Brakk (4,800m), established in 2004 by Czechs

Pavel Jonak and Vasek Satava (450m, 14 pitches, IX- A2), and then repeated in 2007 by Anne and John Arran, who climbed a variant to one aid pitch at 5.12c and top-roped a second variant at 5.12d. Bulička and Šebestíková attempted the original pitch five, an offwidth crack through a horizontal roof, and despite repeated attempts could not climb it without a point of aid (free grade estimated at 7c–8a).

The same two free climbed Welcome to Crackistan on the southeast pillar of Zang Brakk (4,800m). This was put up by Anne and John Arran, also in 2007 [*after a previous attempt by Austrians Hannes Mair and Much Mayr*]. The Arrans climbed the route in 17 pitches with difficulties up to 5.12d (British E6/7) and one pitch of A3 on beaks and knifeblades; John Arran estimated it might go at E7 6b (5.13b), but said it might need a couple of protection bolts.

Bulička and Šebestíková climbed the route in 13 pitches, ground-up over two days, largely from 6b/c to 7c. The ninth pitch (A3) was extensively cleaned and then climbed free at 8a without recourse to bolts. 📄 📷

—Standa Mitác, *Czech Republic*

ABOVE: Anča Šebestíková on the second pitch (6c) of Welcome to Crackistan. *Standa Mitác*

TOP LEFT: Martin Sankot during an attempt on the west face of Kapura. *Jakub Kácha*

LOWER LEFT: The complex southeast face of Nurishan (ca 6,000m) and the attempted line in 2023. The lead climber reached the northwest ridge before triggering an avalanche that ended the attempt. *Ondřej Mrklovský*

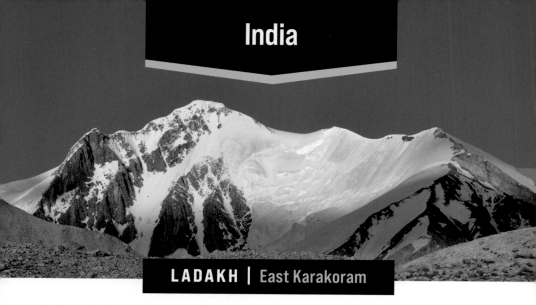

India

LADAKH | East Karakoram

Unclimbed Peak 6,496m in the Saser Muztagh, seen from the northwest during the approach up the Thangman Lungpa. *Divyesh Muni*

SASER MUZTAGH: DZASHEZ KANGRI AND MANLUNG KANGRI

Our expedition, jointly organized by the Himalayan Club and Chakram Hikers, uncovered a hidden treasure of unclimbed peaks in the Thangman Lungpa, located in the Saser Muztagh, the easternmost subrange of the Karakoram. In August, Sudeep Barve, Monesh Devjani, Mahesh Kendurkar, Vineeta Muni, Kamlesh Venugopal, and I visited this unexplored valley, just off the famous Nubra Valley trade route.

From Leh, we crossed the Khardung La into the Nubra, traveled north, then took the military road eastward from Sasoma, over the dramatic Tulum Puti La, and farther up the road leading toward Saser La, before shortly reaching the entrance to the Thangman Lungpa.

Base camp was established at 5,100m (34°54.851'N, 77°37.031'E). From there, we found a route onto the north branch of the Thangman Glacier, where we discovered several unclimbed peaks above 6,000m. High camps were established on the glacier at 5,600m and at 5,800m.

On August 13, Mahesh, Sudeep, Vineeta, and I, along with Phuphu Dorji, Pemba

Sherpa, and Samgyal Sherpa, made the first ascent of Peak 6,075m (34°56'5.92"N, 77°39'26.81"E) via the west face. To mark our friendship on this joint expedition, where some members were climbing together for the first time, we named the mountain Dzashez Kangri (Friendship Peak). Fresh snow from storms that had devastated the region earlier made the climbing difficult. We fixed 100m of rope to secure a safe return over crevasses hidden by the soft snow. On top, we were rewarded with views southeast to the Saser Kangri group, the highest peaks in the region.

A few days later, Sudeep, Samgyal, and Pemba made the first ascent of Peak 6,207m at 34°56'55.33"N, 77°39'9.20"E. Climbing from the south, they fixed 400m of rope to safeguard access to the summit ridge. They named the peak Manlung Kangri, since it overlooks the Manlung Glacier to its north. 📷

—**Divyesh Muni**, *India*

NUBRA VALLEY, NEW ICE ROUTES

Our trip to the Nubra Valley originated through my friendship with the American-Canadian mountaineer Carlos Buhler, who has been visiting Spain for years during his autumn holidays. Carlos told me about his Nubra Valley ice climbs in March 2020 (*see AAJ 2021*) and about Rigzin Tsewang, an enthusiastic Ladakhi mountaineer and driving force behind ice climbing in the area. I contacted Rigzin, and he very kindly invited us to visit. We made a 15-day trip in February 2023, during which we were able to repeat most of the classic falls and contribute five first ascents.

Javier Sánchez climbing the first pitch of Nubra-Spanish Chugyud (WI5) in the Nubra Valley. *Rafa Vadillo*

On February 2, we went to the pretty Chugyud cascade, the bottom of which had already been climbed by Rigzin and his friends. At the top, a narrow corridor continues upward, reaching a wall with three frozen waterfalls. We climbed the steep flow on the left for 50m and then climbed two variations on the 35m second pitch: David Graells and Jordi Vigatà on the right, and Javier Sánchez, Joan Picola, and I to the left. Respecting the local custom of naming ice routes after the valleys and canyons in which they are located, we agreed with Rigzin on the name Nubra-Spanish Chugyud (85m, WI5).

We managed to complete one of the jewels of the valley on February 5: Juniper Tree (85m, WI5+), a delicate fall of ice with a slender upper tube that revealed the great volume of water that runs through its interior. This route was completed by Graells and Vigatà.

Over the next two days, we climbed two new routes in the Changlung valley: Changlung Left (125m, WI3+), climbed by Jesus Almarza, Guillermo Velasco, and Juampi Sabbione; and Changlung Right (180m, WI4+), climbed by Graells, Vigatà, and me.

We descended from all of our routes using Abalakov anchors, leaving nothing behind.

The climactic route was put up by Graells and Vigatà on February 8, creating what could be the longest water-ice route yet climbed in India: The Masri Gyad (480m, WI4+). The two stopped 25m below the top of the ice line after a block of ice hit Graells' face and caused significant injuries, a difficult evacuation down the icefall, and subsequent transfer to a hospital in Leh.

I would like to highlight the kindness and attention of Rigzin and his team, both during the climbing days and in helping with David's accident. We can only say many, many thanks.

—Rafa Vadillo, *Spain*

NYA KANGRI ATTEMPT, K25 RECONNAISSANCE

Nya Kangri (6,480m), at the entrance to the Arganglas Valley, has received multiple attempts, including two from me (*AAJ 2017* and *2023*). In summer 2023, I tried again with Orestis Mitrou-Kintis, approaching the southeast side from Tirit village in the Nubra Valley on July 18.

In two days, we reached a camp at 5,430m on the glacier moraine. We made an attempt starting just after midnight on July 20. We got off-track in the dark and only regained our planned line, the south-southeast spur, at sunrise. (This route was tried by an Indian expedition in 2016; see *AAJ 2017*.) The snow was soft, deep, and avalanche-prone. We turned back at 6,015m, regained camp that day, and the following day descended to Sumar in the Nubra Valley.

We then traveled northwest down the Shyok River valley, then north to Waris village, with the aim of exploring unclimbed K25 (a.k.a. Pastan or Fastan Kangri, 6,520m, 34°54'35"N, 77°08'39"E). The west side of this peak is an almost 2,500m-high rocky triangle, but farther south a gully leads to the south col at 5,500m. We reached this point and saw two possible routes to the summit. The first would be to climb the granite south ridge, which above 6,000m becomes a slope of mixed rock and snow; the second would be to descend the east side of the col to a large glacier and then climb the south-southeast slopes. Both would require about three days from the col, and due to limited time and weather, we attempted neither.

—**Nikolaos Kroupis**, *Greece*

KASHMIR | Sonamarg Valley

THAJIWAS, SECOND ASCENT IN 78 YEARS

Located 80km by road northeast of Srinagar, the hill station of Sonamarg (2,730m) has long been a popular tourist destination, with picturesque alpine meadows and lakes. To the south and east of Sonamarg lies a collection of attractive alpine peaks, culminating in Kolahoi (5,427m). But for many years, this has been a no-go area for foreign visitors due to the Kashmir conflict.

Immediately south of Sonamarg is the Thajiwas Valley and its range of volcanic peaks, rising to a summit of 4,854m:

The Great Couloir on the north face of Thajiwas (4,854m, in back). The highest point is to the right. *Zeeshan Mushtaq*

Thajiwas (formerly Greater Thajiwas, 34°15'40.8"N, 75°15'37.4"E). Until 2023, this mountain had only two recorded ascents. On June 2, 1937, James Waller, along with Pasang Ghekkedi and Mapchi Topgay, climbed the Great Couloir that splits the north side of the mountain, with an average angle of 50°; they reached the summit by an easy rock scramble. The second ascent was in September 1945, when John Buzzard and John Jackson reversed the Waller party's descent route on the east flank.

In July 2023, Indian mountaineer Zeeshan Mushtaq repeated the Great Couloir route. Mushtaq and Faisal Wani climbed about 300m up the couloir together before Wani became fatigued. From that point, Mushtaq continued alone to the top. He returned to his partner and the two continued their descent until Wani was injured in a fall in slushy snow and eventually was rescued.

There is much scope in this area for alpine climbing, but turmoil since the late 1980s has had significant impact on adventure sports in the area, and there are no immediate signs of a resolution. [*More history and information on climbing Thajiwas and other peaks in this area are at the AAJ website.*] 📄 📷

—**Lindsay Griffin**, *with information from Zeeshan Mushtaq, India*

AMAIUR PEAK AND MANY ROCK ROUTES

Our five-member Basque expedition to the Suru and Shafat valleys had eyes for the north face of Shafat Fortress, but on arrival at base camp, those same eyes were immediately drawn to a beautiful rock spire. This peak of about 5,760m is situated on the ridge extending north from Rungofarka (6,495m, climbed in 2017 by Americans Alan Rousseau and Tino Villanueva; see *AAJ 2018*); it lies south of the main Suru Valley at 34°2'50.78"N, 76°6'2.94"E.

Amaiur Peak from the east-northeast. The right skyline ridge was the route of the first ascent in 2023; the lower part of the route is hidden by a foreground ridge. In cloud to the left lie the north flanks of Rungofarka. *Ekaitz Maiz*

After climbing a few rock routes, Joseba Iztueta and I decided to attempt the northeast ridge of the unclimbed spire, which, as far as we could see, would be largely a snow and ice ascent, with a few small rock sections. We set off thinking we were well prepared with some rock gear, a 60m 8mm rope, and six ice screws. On finally reaching the base of the peak, we were surprised to find we would have to climb a 300m rock wall to reach the northeast ridge, and the lower section of the ridge, which we had not previously been able to see, appeared difficult.

We left our tent at 4 a.m. on July 16. Fortunately, the rock was better than expected and presented no major difficulties (V+). Above, a snowfield (50°–60°) led to a shoulder below the ridge. We sank below our knees in the unconsolidated snow.

At around 5,300m, we started up the main ridge, and it soon became clear we would have to fight for every meter. The granite was good and offered protection, but any slab was covered with unconsolidated snow. A section of M6 was followed by more mixed terrain at M3–M5. We climbed to a small shoulder, from where it appeared the difficulties would decrease. In fact, it was the opposite. I was now thinking of the descent, which would certainly be as complex as the ascent, and for which we might barely have enough anchor material. These thoughts were a backpack that became heavier the higher we climbed.

We reached a point where we had two options: a vertical wall leading to a roof or a slab covered with loose snow. I opted for the slab and, after placing a good piton, tiptoed out right. This

Mikel Ezkurdia on the fourth pitch (7a+) of Nassau Errepublika on the north side of the Suru Valley. *Ekaitz Maiz*

routes in the Suru and Shafat valleys, including climbs on the southwest face of Shafat Peak, the south face of Askatasunaren Dorrea, the Shafat Wall, and the central tower of the Pilares de la Tierra on the north side of the Suru Valley. In all, we achieved 17 new routes. Descriptions and topos are at the AAJ website. 📖📷

—**Ekaitz Maiz, *Basque Country***

PUNTA GUILLEM APARICIO, FIRST ASCENT VIA SOUTHWEST FACE; SHAFAT PEAK, LA GENT QUE ESTIMO; SHAFAT WALL, PORS DE GOS

In August 2022, a team of friends traveled to the Shafat Valley, where several of us opened new rock routes.

Marc Toralles and I made the first ascent of a 5,700m peak we named Punta Guillem Aparicio in memory of a good friend who was killed in 2011 while ice climbing. This peak lies at 34°00'17"N, 76°11'42"E in a small side valley that runs west into the Shafat and is a southern outlier of Shafat Peak (5,900m; immediately north of Shafat Peak and at a lower altitude is the well-known Shafat Fortress).

After a long day's approach from base camp, we reached the foot of the access couloir. We started up our proposed line on August 14, loaded with bivouac gear, as we were planning to climb the face over two days. After ten pitches up to 6c+, we reached a narrow ledge, where we spent a terrible night. A storm with lightning, hail, and rain lasted all night, and we survived the best we could using a thermal blanket for protection. It was one of those nights you will never forget.

Next morning, very tired, very wet, and with a dubious forecast, we retreated and returned to base camp.

On August 23, we came back for a second try. Our plan this time was to go fast and light, hoping to climb to the summit and descend in one day. As we already knew the first half of the route, we reached pitch

proved to be the crux pitch (M6), though the next lead also was M6, involving a roof exit on an ice-covered wall protected with screws. Above that, a rib led to the snow-covered summit dome. Despite scratching everywhere with my axes, I couldn't make the final moves up the dome, so I stayed put at the last exposed rock. The GPS registered 5,760m.

Various hang-ups on the descent and a block cutting the rope six meters from one end meant we arrived back at the 5,300m shoulder at dark. After more careful rappelling of the initial wall, we stumbled into camp at 10:30 p.m., drank some tea, and fell asleep.

Our 750m route (V+ M6) had about 1,500m of climbing. We named the mountain Amaiur Peak—it was one of the most intense and beautiful ascents I've done.

Our group also put up many new rock

ten early in the day. Seven more pitches, with several at 6c+ and a crux of 7a+, saw us on the summit. It was now snowing, and we had only a few hours of daylight remaining. Our rappel descent was to climber's left of our ascent, so that we avoided the access couloir. After around 17 rappels from nuts and pitons, we arrived at our tent 20 hours after leaving. Our new route, Txoria Txori (740m of climbing, 7a+), was climbed entirely clean, using only nuts and cams for protection and belays.

Between these two attempts, on August 19, Jordi Mons and I climbed the southwest face of Shafat Peak (34°00'48"N, 76°11'48"E). On July 1, Oriol Baró and Guillem Sancho had climbed this aspect of the mountain via Tukcheche (500m, 6c), following one of the rock pillars that characterize this face and which they had called Wild East Pillar. After another long approach east up a side valley from the main Shafat, we climbed the same pillar but via a line slightly farther right.

After an initial pitch of 4+, five sustained pitches from 6a to 6c, with a little A1+, followed by another pitch of 4+, brought us to the final 100m–150m of straightforward mixed terrain. Heading up right, we reached the summit and then rappelled the wall, the anchors not always coinciding with the line of ascent. We named the route La Gent que Estimo.

The other new route opened in the Shafat Valley was Pors de Gos (130m, 6a A3), put up by Adrià Fidalgo, Núria Garcia, and Guim Llort on the Shafat Wall. This face lies near the entrance to the Shafat Valley and has many existing routes. The three-pitch Pors de Gos is to the right of Los Asfixiados and begins with a laborious pitch of aid on pitons and Peckers, before continuing above in a conspicuous dihedral. 📷

—Tasio Martin Elorrieta, *Basque Country*

TOP: Tasio Martin Elorrieta on the 14th pitch (6c+) of Txoria Txori on Punta Guillem Aparicio. *Marc Toralles*

ABOVE: The southwest face of Punta Guillem Aparicio with the line of Txoria Txori (17 pitches). A rappel descent was made down the wall to the left to avoid the approach couloir. *Tasio Martin Elorrieta*

Jamyang Ri (5,800m) from the southwest, showing the approximate line of Nelim Lam. The first four pitches are shared with the 2017 route Cunka (Dusic-Jost, 2017), which then moves right to climb the southwest ridge. Little Jamyang Ri is the lower subsidiary top on the left, with its very steep northwest face in profile (see photo on next page for routes). *Stefan Plank*

JAMYANG RI, WEST FACE AND NORTHWEST ARÊTE

Editor's Note: This report and the following two cover the activities of a single expedition from South Tyrol in Italy. They are reported separately for clarity.

The Rangtik Tokpo is surrounded by towering granite walls that can be reached in one to three hours' walk from base camp. Moritz Sigmund and I, together with five friends from the Dolomites, followed the call of these rock faces to explore their potential during a five-week trip.

We established our base at 4,900m accompanied by three Tungri locals, having spent the night in their village; they acted not only as our guides but also cooks, taking great pride in providing us with culinary delights. We thoroughly enjoyed the tranquility of base camp, shielded from the hustle and bustle of the world, and engaged in board games, literature, art, and just thinking.

Our main objective was to climb the northwest face of Jamyang Ri (5,800m, 33°27'58.67"N, 76°44'46.29"E), rising over the top of a subsidiary summit that was named Torre Fanni (ca 5,600m) by the 2017 expedition that made the first ascent. [*Little Jamyang Ri would be a more appropriate name, respecting local language and culture.*] The upper wall, above the Torre summit, shimmered in the evening sun, and its smooth facets and sharp edges earned it the nickname "mountain crystal." The northwest arête, which pointed directly toward the valley, provided a fascinating daily vision and made us dream of climbing it.

Our proposed line to reach the summit of Little Jamyang Ri (and thus the upper arête) via the ca 500m northwest face was far more difficult than expected, and we were forced to abandon it after three days, having climbed six pitches up to VIII+ A2. We changed plans, choosing to skirt the tower and reach the northwest arête via the steep west face of Jamyang Ri itself.

We set off from base camp at 4 a.m. on July 21, taking only minimal equipment but a lot of motivation, hope, and confidence. After an 80-minute approach, we started up the west face, following very similar ground to the first four pitches of the 2017 route Cunka (*AAJ 2018*). Where this route makes a long traverse right, we followed previously unclimbed terrain up to the left. Around 11 a.m., having covered about 400m (10 pitches), we were level with the top of Little Jamyang Ri at around 5,600m, just below the "crystal edge."

Once on the northwest arête, we found to our delight that the cracks we had seen from base camp were some of the most beautiful we had ever climbed. When the crack system ended, we made a bold rightward traverse. We only had two bolts and a hand drill, carried in case of a forced retreat, so we made the traverse without protection (and we wouldn't blame any party that wanted to add extra protection to this traverse). This brought us onto the west face, which turned orange in the sun and gifted us with an incredibly beautiful climb.

After some excellent free pitches and a pendulum, we finally reached the summit, full of emotion. While climbing the upper wall, we were pleased to see our friends Elisabeth Lardschneider and Markus Ranalter reach the top of Little Jamyang Ri after spending six days working on its northwest face (*see report below*).

Despite the happiness we felt, we were aware we still had a long descent. Since we knew little about the Slovenian rappel route in the center of the west face, we did not always find their anchors and were forced to drill one bolt. Nevertheless, after 18 hours we reached base camp, exhausted but infinitely happy. We named the route Nelim Lam ("Crystal Route," 700m-plus of climbing, 19 pitches, VIII+/5.12 A0).

Our time in this mountain paradise taught us profound lessons. The cheerfulness and gratitude of the Tungri people left an indelible impression. The "mountain crystal" will forever remind us that truly precious treasures can only be stored in our memories. 🗎 📷 🔍

—**Patrick Tirler,** *Italy*

LITTLE JAMYANG RI (A.K.A. TORRE FANNI), NORTHWEST FACE, NORBU DUK LAM

Our arrival at base camp in the Rangtik Tokpo was followed by three days of heavy snowfall. When this cleared, an obvious choice was the northwest face of Little Jamyang Ri (a.k.a. Torre Fanni, ca 5,600m), which had stayed dry due to its steepness.

On July 11, Elisabeth (Lisi) Lardschneider and I made our first attempt, aiming for a diagonal crack 100m above the ground. This crack line snaked all the way to the summit. We only managed three pitches over the first two days, mainly due to our inexperience at

The northwest face of Little Jamyang Ri (a.k.a. Torre Fanni), showing (1) Sigmund-Tirler attempt, (2) Norbu Duk Lam, and (3) Lam Thuk Khamzang (to southwest arête). All three climbs were in 2023. *Patrick Tirler*

opening new routes. On the fourth pitch, a compact slab separated us from the eagerly awaited crack. Laboriously, we placed a few bolts with a hand drill, but after several attempts we still couldn't free the pitch. On our fourth day we reached the crack, climbed one pitch, and returned to camp.

On the 17th, we returned to our high point with a portaledge. Next day we were highly motivated to climb the beautiful crack above our heads. We made good progress, and the crack was easily protected with natural gear, but the rock never lay back, and we ran out of energy just before meeting the ridge. The following day we returned to base camp to recharge our own batteries.

On the 21st, Lisi and I were back at the base of the wall, ready for one last attempt. Our initial plan had been to reclimb every pitch, but it had rained overnight, so we jumared to the portaledge. Except for a few short sections, we then free climbed to our high point. One more pitch got us to the ridge, from where the summit was visible. Success seemed imminent, and we danced along the crest for three pitches until we were shouting with joy and relief. All the hard work had finally paid off. As the route created many precious memories, we named it Norbu Duk Lam, which means "Very Precious Line" (560m of climbing, 18 pitches, VIII A1).

—**Markus Ranalter,** *Italy*

CHANRASRIK RI, ATTEMPT AND TRAGEDY: *On July 27, soon after completing the route described above, the same two climbers set off to repeat the 2018 route on Peak 6,080m (H2, as designated on the Sakamoto sketch maps). The 2018 team named this rock peak Chareze Ri (see AAJ 2020), but locals state the peak is correctly called Chanrasrik Ri. The start of the route on the east-northeast ridge is reached by ascending a steep snow slope. While climbing this slope, Elisabeth Lardschneider slipped, fell around 150m, and died instantly. She was a member of the Italian National Sport Climbing Team and had led her first 8b when only 14 years of age.*

LITTLE JAMYANG RI (A.K.A. TORRE FANNI), LAM THUK KHAMZANG; SHAWA KANGRI, NORTHEAST FACE, PARTIAL NEW ROUTE

As with the other members of our expedition from South Tyrol (*see reports above*), heavy snowfall immediately after our arrival at base camp in the Rangtik Tokpo prompted Hannes Niederwolfsgruber and me to choose the steep, dry northwest face of Little Jamyang Ri (a.k.a. Torre Fanni, ca 5,600m) for our first climb. We opted for the farthest right of three potential lines.

The first two pitches on our line were precarious, then we reached a wonderful layback crack. Hannes climbed this crack until he encountered a loose flake, followed by a seemingly blank section and an overhang. We retreated; however, the next day, Elisabeth Lardschneider and

Markus Ranalter found a way through a seemingly impassable section more to the left. Their breakthrough would allow us to continue with our route.

We returned to the wall with Patrick Tirler and ascended the pitches climbed by Elisabeth and Markus to a point where our proposed line headed up right. Patrick led a new pitch to a big ledge and then we all descended. Due to time constraints and frequent rain showers, we decided to equip these challenging lower pitches with fixed rope for future attempts.

A few days later, we ascended the ropes, Hannes led another free and aid pitch to a comfortable belay, then I embarked on a precarious, demanding crack with loose flakes. At this point, we saw no future in the line and decided to descend and remove all the ropes. However, in base camp we had a change of heart and decided we had to give it one more try.

On July 28, we found ourselves back on the challenging section with loose flakes. Persevering, we reached more manageable terrain, and three fine pitches of around VII took us to a big shoulder on

the southwest arête of Little Jamyang Ri, basking in the last rays of sunlight. Opting to skip the remaining three pitches to the summit—in order to allow for some daylight on the descent—we began rappelling our line.

We named the new route Lam Thuk Khamzang (370m of climbing, 13 pitches, the first five of which are in common with Norbu Duk Lam, VIII A2). The name comes from a Ladakhi proverb conveying good wishes to a friend embarking on a journey; *khamzang* captures the idea that paths may diverge, but in the end, individuals reunite to continue their shared journey.

During time off from the northwest face, Hannes Sullmann and I tried a direct route up the northeast face of Shawa Kangri (5,728m, 33°27'46"N, 76°44'07"E). Starting from base camp at 4:30 a.m. on July 14 and reaching the foot of the mountain at 8 a.m., we first climbed 65° ice to the base of the steep granite wall, then five engaging pitches in perfect cracks. The cruxes, including one wet section, were short; the pitches were graded VII+, VII, VII, VII+, and VII.

A few meters before a ledge at around three-quarters height, and where the 2008 route Rolling Stones (Pellissa-Ricart) comes in from the left, we made the difficult decision to descend, due to snow on the route and unsafe conditions. We hoped to return after predicted hot weather had melted the snow. Unfortunately, Elisabeth's tragic accident, described above, prevented us from doing so. 📷

—Stefan Plank, *Italy*

ABOVE: Stefan Plank climbing the first pitch (VII+/5.11) on the attempted new route up the northeast face of Shawa Kangri. *Hannes Niederwolfsgruber*

OPPOSITE PAGE: The northeast face of Shawa Kangri (5,728m) with (1) Rolling Stones (2008) and (2) attempt by Stefan Plank and Hannes Sullmann that almost reached the junction with Rolling Stones. *Stefan Plank*

This unnamed peak of about 6,100 meters on the Nateo-Miyar watershed was attempted in 2023 by the left (east-northeast) ridge. *Takaaki Furuhata*

RARU VALLEY, EXPLORATION AND ATTEMPT ON UNNAMED 6,100M PEAK

An exceptionally heavy monsoon washed away many of the roads and bridges leading to the Kullu-Spiti area, where Takaaki Furuhata, Toshihiro Ueda, and Yasushi Yamanoi had hoped to make a first ascent on one of the Dibibokri peaks. A quick change of plan led them to the Raru Valley, accompanied by liaison officer Sartaj Ghuman.

In its upper section, the Raru Valley has three main offshoots: the Tetleh, Nateo, and Katkar nalas (from west to east). The Nateo drainage is steep-sided with several hanging valleys, each holding a debris-covered glacier. It rises southwest to an amphitheater of gleaming glaciers, rimmed by an arc of mountains.

While parties have climbed peaks from the Tetleh and Katkar nalas, including summits on the watersheds with the Nateo, there is no record of peaks being attempted from within the Nateo Nala.

In 2009, Japanese explorer Kimikazu Sakamoto visited the Nateo Nala, taking photos and making a sketch map, but did not attempt any of the mountains. [*Peaks at the head of the Nateo valley also lie on the watershed with the Miyar Valley to the southwest, specifically the Jangpar and Dali glaciers, and several may have been climbed from that side in the 1980s.*]

We drove from Leh via Kargil, then over the Pensi La and past Pandum to the village of Raru on the Tsarap River. From there, on September 13, we walked seven hours to the start of the Nateo Nala. The next day, we crossed the Nateo River and made base camp at an ideal site on its south side at 4,350m.

A ten-hour reconnaissance walk up the valley and onto the glacier gave glimpses of the peak that would become the team's objective. Situated at 33°7'31.98"N, 76°51'11.25"E, it is probably peak R22 on Sakamoto's sketch map. Google Maps showed the peak to be about 5,800m, but our reconnaissance made us believe it might be higher.

On the 19th, we went back up the glacier and established an advanced base on the central moraine at 4,910m. After reconnaissance of a route up our proposed peak the next day, we all headed back to base camp.

On the 26th, Furuhata, Ueda, and Yamanoi started out from advanced base at 4:30 a.m. with a small tent. After ascending the glacier to the left, they came back right and reached the crest of the east-northeast ridge via snow slopes on the north flank. At 9:50 a.m. they were at 5,600m, their intended bivouac spot. After a rest, since it was still early in the day and they felt good, they decided to go for the summit.

The climbing was steeper than it had looked, with 15cm of soft snow over hard ice. As the team carried only two ice screws, the climbing was slow and rather scary. Mixed snow and rock, interspersed with two long traverses, took them to a shoulder on the ridge, where more difficult climbing gained the top of the shoulder, at

Looking south at an impressive unnamed peak seen during an attempt on a ca 6,100-meter peak at the head of the Nateo Nala. *Yasushi Yamanoi*

a measured height of 5,950m.

Although from below the ridge had looked continuous, they now found their way barred by a rocky gap around 150m wide and 40m deep, with overhanging, loose rock walls. With only a single 70m rope, there was no way they could cross the gap and return safely. They turned around and descended all the way to advanced base camp, which they reached at 8 p.m.

They estimated the summit of the unnamed peak to be 200m above their high point, making its elevation closer to 6,100m. Surrounding peaks, marked between 5,800m and 6,100m on various maps, also seemed higher. Some would make very interesting objectives for future expeditions. 📷🔍

—**Sartaj Ghuman**, *India, and* **Yasushi Yamanoi**, *Japan*

LADAKH | Pologongka Range

PEAKS 6,050M AND 6,205M

In July, massive rainfall and flooding in Himachal Pradesh caused widespread loss of life and destruction of roads, properties, and livelihood. My wife, Vineeta, and

I were to visit the Miyar Valley, but at the suggestion of a friend in Manali, we made alternative plans to explore the Pologongka Range in Ladakh. This massif lies north of the road over the Pologongka La; the highest summit, Pologongka, is 6,632m (see *AAJ 2021*).

We hired essential support staff in Manali and drove to Thukje village (4,500m), next to Tsokar Lake on the Manali–Leh Highway. We acclimatized here for a day, then drove east to the Pologongka La (5,000m), where we set up base camp. Our high camp was at 5,800m, northeast of the pass.

On July 24, Hemraj (one of our Manali staff), Vineeta, and I climbed a peak of 6,050m (33°17'12.86"N, 78°14'16.05"E) east of camp. It was an easy walk to the base of the summit pyramid, followed by a scramble over loose rock and boulders. There were no indications of any previous ascent.

The following day, Hemraj and I scrambled up Peak 6,205m (33°17'36.88"N, 78°12'41.68"E), northwest of camp. We discovered old prayer flags on the summit.

Peaks in this area are all non-technical, but the views over the surrounding high-altitude lakes are fantastic, and there is potential for further exploration.

—**Divyesh Muni**, *India*

Himachal Pradesh

BAIHALI JOT GROUP, NOMENCLATURE AND HISTORICAL REVISIONS

A report at the *AAJ* website updates the naming and climbing history of peaks in the Baihali Jot group, of which the high point is 6,279m Baihali Jot, which likely has been climbed only once. Nearby peaks discussed in this article include Duphao Jot, Malkutu Jot, Baihali Jot Northwest (a.k.a. Baihali Jot North), and Baihali Jot South (a.k.a. Jatbam Jot). 📄📷

—**Damien Gildea and Lindsay Griffin**, *AAJ*

ABOVE: Seen from the south, Mont Maudit (about 5,800m) is on the far left. In the center is the 5,400-meter pillar and the approximate line climbed in 2023 up the golden southeast face. To the far right is the upper Takdung Glacier. *Alessandro Baù*

LEFT: Wind of Silence on the southeast face of Neverseen Tower. On the left are the steep east-facing walls of Lotus Peak. *Alessandro Baù*

MIYAR VALLEY: NEVERSEEN TOWER, WIND OF SILENCE, AND OTHER NEW ROUTES

Italian climbers Alessandro Baù, Lorenzo D'Addario, Jerome Perruquet, and Francesco Ratti arrived at base camp at about 4,000m in the Miyar Valley during the middle of a high-pressure system in September. This was an opportunity not to be missed, and as their plan was to inspect the unclimbed south-southeast face of Neverseen Tower (ca 5,750m), they left the next day for an eight-hour walk up the Takdung Glacier to establish an advanced base close to the wall. Conditions were good, and they spotted a possible line, but first they needed to acclimatize.

For this they chose the next peak to the north, Grandfather Enzo Peak, first climbed in 1992 from the opposite side (Chhudong Glacier) via the south face and upper southeast ridge. (The full south-southeast ridge was climbed by another Italian team in 2005.) In 2023, the four climbers made the first ascent of the straightforward east ridge, reached by an ascending traverse of the southeast face. After another night at advanced base, they descended to base camp for a rest.

After a week of unsettled conditions, they received a forecast for a few days of stable weather. On their return to advanced base, a different scene awaited them: The freezing level had plummeted by 1,000m and the wall was encrusted in ice. To see if an ascent was feasible, they climbed to the col separating Neverseen from Lotus Peak, where they found old fixed rope from a team that had approached from the Chhudong Glacier but climbed only one pitch up the southeast face. The four Italians decided to start a little lower and to the right, an aspect that would ensure the snow and ice melted faster.

That first day, they climbed a few pitches and left their ropes fixed. Next morning, September 21, the sky was clear. Returning toward the col, they ascended the ropes and continued upward, finding "really nice granite, always fun and never too difficult." They reached the summit at 2 p.m., naming their line Wind of Silence

(500m, 6b+). Although they had identified a good bivouac site two pitches below the snowy summit ridge, it was not needed and they regained their camp just before dark. Only pitons and removable protection were used.

During reconnaissance, they had spotted a potential second objective lower down the Takdung Glacier: a southeast-facing pillar rising to around 5,400m on Mont Maudit (ca 5,800m, 33°3'30.92"N, 76°53'6.82"E).

The four began their ascent on September 25. The freezing level was now at 3,500m, so starting a rock climb at around 5,000m was unpleasant. They spent two days climbing the face. On the first they were hampered by light sleet and a cold wind; they returned to their tents below the pillar that night. The next day, they began under a beautiful starry sky and climbed the entire route—Super Thuraya (8 pitches, 6c)—finding exceptional granite. They placed bolted anchors to rappel. 🖻

—Lindsay Griffin, *with information from Alessandro Baù, Italy*

On the first ascent of Super Thuraya on a 5,400-meter pillar of Mont Maudit. Behind, across the lower Takdung Glacier, are peaks south of the Ogre group. *Alessandro Baù*

MULKILA GLACIER AREA, SKI DESCENTS

On May 4, the team of Giovanni Fortunato, Anna Fridlyanskaya, Leo Fridlyanskaya, Wyatt Jobe, Lillian Llacer, and Luke Smithwick established a base camp at about 3,350m near the mouth of the Mulkila Valley. From here they made five ski descents in long, steep couloirs on northeast and northwest aspects of peaks above the glacier. The climbs from base camp averaged 1,500m to 2,100m, reaching a high point during one long day of about 5,430m in the southernmost couloir they skied, about 60m below an unnamed summit. More information and photos are at the *AAJ* website. 🖹🖻

—**Information from Wyatt Jobe,** *USA*

ABOVE: Rathan Thadi Dome (4,600m). See the route lines at the *AAJ* website. *Suraj Kushwaha*

LEFT: Suraj Kushwaha leading the final corner on Fissure in Time, Rathan Thadi. *Nikhil Bhandari*

RATHAN THADI DOME, NEW ROUTES

Supported by an AAC Live Your Dream Grant, Suraj Kushwaha from Vermont and Nikhil Bhandari from Hyderabad, India, explored a granite dome above Sethan village, east of Manali. Back in May, Kushwaha had attempted a route on the 4,600-meter formation, which locals call Rathan Thadi, but melting snow soaked the rock and halted the effort.

Kushwaha returned with Bhandari in October and climbed two routes: Rathan Thadi Direct (6 pitches, 5.11-) and Fissure in Time (6 pitches, 5.10 A2 M2). Kushwaha said the latter would go free at about 5.12-. The two also found some quality bouldering in the valley, the highlight of which was Tehelka ("Chaos," V6). The full report is at the *AAJ* website. 📄📷

—**Suraj Kushwaha,** *USA*

DEBSA VALLEY, EXPLORATION, AND RATIRUNI TIBBA, NORTHEAST RIDGE

In July, Hugh Reynolds and I (Ireland) visited the Debsa Valley in Spiti. Our aim was the first ascent of Peak 6,130m at the head of the Bauli Valley, on the Kullu-Spiti divide. However, very bad weather over four days ruled this out.

Instead, we decided to attempt a first crossing of both upper tributaries of the Debsa, starting in the west upper tributary, continuing to its head, then crossing one of two unknown cols to the east upper tributary, before descending this glacial valley and returning to our 4,340m base camp at the Debsa confluence. (This is marked Thwak Debsa on some maps—approximately 31°58'49.21"N, 77°50'44.48"E—accessed from the east via the Pin Valley.) This would be a circuit of approximately 30km.

We set off with six days of food and fuel. Initially, it was hard going, scrambling over the moraine waste, and we soon found it got worse on the glacier, where we were post-holing up to our knees. We slowly and tediously worked our way up the west upper Debsa, reaching the valley head on the 17th.

Early the next morning, we climbed unroped up the snow slopes of the headwall to gain one of the cols at 5,629m

(31°54.9033'N, 77°49.6130'E). The view into the east upper Debsa included several unclimbed 6,000ers, each technical and magnificent. There were many adjoining smaller peaks, all in a gloriously remote white amphitheater. We descended the east upper Debsa over three days and crossed the hazardous Debsa River to return to base camp.

After two days' rest, we decided to attempt the first ascent of a 5,570m snow pyramid (31°57.7375'N, 77°46.7013'E) that we had spotted on the west side of the west upper Debsa during our ascent of that valley. Over the next two days, we reached a high camp on the glacier at around 5,100m. Our peak stood on the watershed between the Debsa and Ratiruni valleys, and was connected by a ridge to the higher peak of 5,655m to its northeast. (On certain online maps, Peak 5,655m is erroneously labeled Ratiruni Pyramid, but this is a mountain of 5,852m elsewhere in the Ratiruni Valley, first ascended by Kenneth Snelson in 1952. Peak 5,655m, which looked even less of a pyramid than our objective, is also unclimbed.)

We left high camp at 4:30 a.m. on the 26th and headed up snow slopes onto a long, left-trending ramp that took us to the basin east of Peak 5,570m. The snow quality was not good, and we had to resort to the now familiar method of stamping each foot into it, up to the ankle, to gain compression beneath.

Dawn broke as we reached the basin, where we cut right to a col on the northeast ridge. The summit was no more than 200m distant, but my big toes were in trouble. On examination, I found them frostnipped and swollen by infection. There was only one thing for it: return to the tent and warm them. Thankfully, Hugh was able to press on and reach the summit. We named the peak Ratiruni Tibba and graded the ascent PD.

—**Gerry Galligan, *Ireland***

TOP: Unclimbed Peak 6,110m (center) at the head of the east upper Debsa Valley. *Gerry Galligan*

BOTTOM: The view up an eastern side branch of the east upper Debsa Valley to unclimbed Peak 6,080m. *Gerry Galligan*

WESTERN GARHWAL | Gangotri

MERU SOUTH

FIRST ASCENT OF THE COVETED SOUTHEAST FACE

By Lindsay Griffin, *with information from Roger Schäli, Switzerland*

On May 13, the team of Simon Gietl (Italy), Mathieu Maynadier (France), and Roger Schäli (Switzerland) completed the first ascent of the southeast face of Meru Peak. Their route, which ended on a minor summit on the long, gently inclined ridgeline of Meru South (ca 6,600m), was climbed in alpine style at M6+ A1. They completed an objective that had been attempted by expeditions in 1985 (British), 1988 (Japanese), 1989 (British, to 6,300m), 1998 (British, also to 6,300m), and 2001 (Basque).

This was Maynadier and Schäli's second attempt, having climbed to within 200m to 300m of the top in the fall of 2019 with Seán Villanueva O'Driscoll (Belgium). Continuous snowstorms forced them down.

The 2023 expedition also seemed to be under a bad star, with persistently adverse weather. The numerous snowstorms had one advantage: The team was able to use touring skis on the lower mountain and thus saved a lot of energy. However, fresh snowfall also meant the ascent from Camp 1 to Camp 2, which was effectively the team's advanced base camp, became increasingly prone to avalanches, and the approach to the col at the base of the east-southeast spur, directly below Camp 2, was made tricky by a heavily melted glacier, with challenging route-finding through a labyrinth of crevasses.

On the final push, the three left Tapovan base camp (4,300m) on May 10 and climbed directly to Camp 2 (5,800m). This was particularly exhausting for Maynadier, who was fighting health issues.

ABOVE: A) Meru South. (B) Meru Central. (C) Meru North. (D) Meru West. (1) Southeast ridge (1980). (2) Southeast face (Goldfish, 2023). (3) Northeast face direct (2008). (4) Shark's Fin (2011). (5) Northeast face (Babanov route, 2001; other lines not shown). (6) East face (Kundalini, 1994). (7) Aurora (1988). (8) Broken Wing (1988). (9) Northeast face and north ridge (1980). *Daniel Hug*

During the next day, Gietl and Schäli moved climbing equipment up to the first rock band, making a track through the steep snowfield. After depositing some gear, they returned to Maynadier, who had used the day to recover.

On the 12th, all three left camp at 3 a.m., and by 11 p.m. they had reached an exposed snow mushroom at around 6,400m, where they bivouacked. After a short and far from comfortable night in a two-man tent, they set off for the top. They found the remaining climbing intense and time-consuming, at times having to clear the rock of half a meter of fresh snow before placing protection. There was no usable ice for screws, and they had to contend with the usual dangers, including falling cornices. In addition, they knew their weather window would be brief.

TOP: Roger Schäli leads the crux pitch of Goldfish, climbing through the first rock band on the southeast face of Meru South. *Daniel Hug*

BOTTOM: Simon Gietl entering the crucial tunnel near the summit ridge. *Mathieu Maynadier*

A little below the north-northwest ridge, they were halted by steep rock but discovered a route through it via a unique ice tunnel. Three spectacular pitches, climbed in icy wind, led to the ridge, from where another 200 vertical meters over steep snow and ice took them southward to their high point, which they reached at around 9 a.m.

This point, to be precise, was the previously unclimbed central top between the main summit of Meru South (ca 6,660m, first climbed by a Japanese team in 1980 via the south-southeast ridge) and the north top of Meru South on the long and almost horizontal summit ridge (first climbed by a Korean team in 2008 after an ascent of the northeast face).

By downclimbing and rappelling the route, the 2023 team was back in base camp the same day. Their route gained 800m above Camp 2. They called the route Goldfish, a tongue-in-cheek reference to the nearby and famed Shark's Fin route on Meru Central. 🄾

The northeast ridge Sara Peak (5,878m), climbed in 2023, is the right skyline. *Tom Davis-Merry*

summit northwest of Dhairya, by the west ridge at PD. This was named Thoda Peak.

On the 18th, the team left base camp five days earlier than planned due to persistent rain, which caused major flooding throughout the region. 📷 🔍

—Lindsay Griffin, *with information from Tom Davis-Merry, U.K.*

SIKKIM | Brumkhangse Group

THREE FIRST ASCENTS

Brumkhangse (5,635m, several known ascents) is one of Sikkim's Open Alpine Peaks, accessed from the Lachung Valley to the east. It is surrounded by eight peaks, which, prior to 2023, were thought to be unclimbed. Several of these are higher than Brumkhangse, and in October they were the goal of a six-member multi-national team, comprising Tom Davis-Merry and Thomas Simpson (U.K.), Kasia Piatek and Ula Stopka-Farooqui (Poland/U.K.), Elie Jaumin (Italy), and Samuele Poletti (Switzerland).

The expedition approached by road via Gangtok, Lachung, and Yumthang to a 4,000m base camp at Shiv Mandir, arriving there on October 2. They moved west toward the Brumkhangse Glacier, made an intermediary camp by a small lake at 4,500m, and established an advanced base on the glacier at 5,100m. The weather was unstable throughout their stay, typically with snowfall in the afternoon.

On October 14, Davis-Merry, Simpson, Piatek, and Stopka-Farooqui climbed Peak 5,543m (provisionally named Dhairya, with a recorded altitude of 5,597m, 27°50'32.67"N, 88°38'54.52"E) via the southwest face (PD). The same day, having previously established a higher camp at 5,200m, Jaumin and Poletti climbed Peak 5,878m (provisionally Sara Peak and recorded at 5,844m, 27°50'32.25"N, 88°38'6.13"E) via the northeast ridge: Cloudy Dreams (300m, D+ M5).

The following day, Davis-Merry and Simpson climbed Peak 5,604m, a small

West Bengal

BANSA HILL CLIMBS

New rock routes have been established on the granite dome known as Bansa Hill (about 280m high, 23°21'59.19"N, 85°55'35.89"E) near the village of Tulin in eastern India. The first long routes here were climbed by Sandeep Maity and Sudipto Pal (India) in late 2021. They climbed Padmasambhaba (270m, 6a) and Bodhisatya (220m, 6c+/7a) on the eastern aspect. Sport climbs and boulder problems also have been developed at the base.

In January 2023, we traveled to Tulin and joined Indian climbing legend Mohit Oberoi. On the southwest aspect of the dome, Mohit and friends established Welcome to Bansa (240m, 5.8), while we established The Lounging Langurs (260m, 5.7+) and The Soaring Kite (260m, 5.8). All routes are bolt-protected.

There are dozens of similar formations in the area, and if permission were granted to climb on more domes, the region could be a slab climber's paradise. 📷 🔍

—Donette and Todd Swain, *USA*

Bansa Hill from the southwest and the approximate line of The Lounging Langurs. *Todd Swain*

2   1

NEPAL | Api Himal

WILDEST NEPAL
THE FIRST ASCENT OF SURMA SAROVAR AND OTHER EXPLORATION

By Paul Ramsden, U.K.

For me, adventure in the high mountains can only be found by climbing alpine style, ideally somewhere remote and rarely visited. These were the ingredients that drew four of us to the rarely visited Salimor Khola (valley), in Far Western Nepal.

Although expeditions have been trying to visit this area for 50 years, information is hard to come by. In 1974, a British team approached up the Seti Khola, then tried to follow the Salimor Khola, but soon were stopped by an "impassable gorge." At that point they headed up a side valley

and unsuccessfully attempted a peak they called Nampa South, later misidentifying it as Rokapi (Kap Chuli, 6,468m), a summit not accessible from that valley.

We also understood that in 1978 a Japanese expedition had passed the "impassable gorge" before making the first ascent of Jethi Bahurani (6,850m). However, though pictures exist from this expedition, we were not able to ascertain how they passed the gorge section of the approach.

Since the Japanese visit, several British and American teams had entered

ABOVE: Surmo Sarovar from the north. (1) The line of ascent up the 2,000-meter northwest face (partially hidden). (2) The descent along the northeast ridge; the climbers continued off-picture to the left and eventually down a rock ridge to the valley. *Hamish Frost*

ABOVE: The exposed section of a shepherds' path on the east side of the gorge guarding entry to the Salimor Khola. *Hamish Frost*

RIGHT: Matt Glenn near the high point on the south ridge of Peak 6,390m, about 300m below the summit. *Hamish Frost*

the valley: All failed to pass the gorge guarding the lower section of the Salimor Khola. Google Earth indicated there were interesting peaks hidden beyond the gorge, particularly Bobaye Chuli (6,808m, first climbed by Tomaž Humar from the opposite side) and Surma Sarovar (6,564m, 29°51'1.88"N, 81°5'17.14"E). There seemed to be only one way to find out more, and that was to go and have a look.

In September, Hamish Frost, Matt Glenn, Tim Miller, and I (all from the U.K.) arrived in Kathmandu. After obtaining permits, we made one internal flight, drove several days, and trekked through jungle and alpine terrain, negotiating river crossings, several earthquakes, and detention by police. Eventually, the porters declared they weren't going any further. We could not argue with them, as the next section of the valley was the "impassable gorge." We decided to make base camp and explore from that point on our own.

The gorge blocking access to the upper Salimor Khola indeed looked formidable, but after careful exploration we discovered a wild and exposed shepherds' track that climbed along the gorge's east side. (It was not a path suitable for porters.) Packing a week's food, we set off to explore and, hopefully, find suitable climbing objectives.

After many days of moraine traversing,

epic river crossings, and storms, we fully understood the size and wildness of this area. Located on the divide between desert-like terrain and areas of dense forest, there was a great variety of climates and terrain within one valley. Nonetheless, Tim and I had found an objective: the northwest face of Surma Sarovar. Matt and Hamish also explored the upper valley, with a view to attempting Bobaye, but the hoped-for route on the north face looked exposed to seracs, so they decided to go back and look at some interesting peaks directly above our base camp, below the gorge.

The northwest face of unclimbed Surma Sarovar looked huge—over 2,000m high—but there seemed to be a safe descent via the northeast ridge. Our main concern was a steep rock band that appeared to block the upper part of the northwest face, with no obvious way through.

After a short rest at base camp, Tim and I left on October 21 and walked for two full days, with two river crossings, to reach the start of our route. Once on the face, the first day was mostly on snow, but one steep mixed step might have been the hardest pitch of the route. The second day was again moderately angled but predominantly on exhausting, bulletproof ice. We bivouacked for the second night of the climb at the foot of the big rock band at a little over 6,000m. Our bivouacs were all on ledges cut into the ice or using a snow hammock.

We now discovered that a steep corner cut through the upper part of the rock band to reach the peak's upper slopes. We spent the next day climbing about 300m of mixed terrain and steep rock, then bivouacked again just above the exit. The next day, October 26, we climbed to the summit, where our GPS recorded an altitude of 6,605m.

Sadly, after many days of good weather, the top was in a whiteout, so we were forced to bivouac there, hoping for improved visibility on the descent—which we could see was going to be longer and more complex than expected. That night it snowed heavily. With the fresh snow, our descent to the northeast was slow and worrying. We threaded a line between seracs and avalanche-prone slopes, abseiling most of the way before downclimbing a long rock ridge that led us to the valley. Exhausted, on day eight we arrived at base camp late in the evening.

Tim Miller above 6,000m on the northwest face of Surma Sarovar, climbing through the rock band that formed the crux of the route. *Paul Ramsden*

Matt and Hamish were freshly back too, though unfortunately had failed to summit on their projects. The two had explored the Gaisar Khola (as named on the HMG-Finn map), southwest of base camp, and had initially tried the very impressive northwest face of Point 6,054m (29°49'33.94"N, 81°8'14.06"E). Bad weather, thin ice, and poor protection resulted in a retreat to base camp after just a few days.

Still keen to climb something, they attempted the south ridge of Peak 6,390m in the same valley (29°49'48.38"N, 81°5'20.74"E). After crossing a subsidiary top of 6,290m, they found avalanche-prone slopes up high, leading to a retreat about 300m below the summit. Interestingly, on this route they found evidence of very old fixed rope, which we presumed was left behind by the 1974 British Expedition, on what they believed to be Rokapi.

The porters had arrived the same day as we did for our return journey, and a tight schedule meant we had to leave for home early the following morning. Over the six-week trip, we had almost no rest days. 📷

ABOVE: West of the upper Nin Khola, these dramatic spires rise to around 5,642m and are very likely unclimbed. *Matt Powell*

ABOVE LEFT: Chandi Himal (6,142m) from the upper Nin Khola to the south. The 2023 ascent finished up the right skyline ridge. *Matt Powell*

CHANDI HIMAL, FIRST ASCENT VIA SOUTHEAST RIDGE

Kevin Bialy (USA), Jaime Iranzo (Spain), and I arrived in Kathmandu on April 29 and reached Simikot on May 5. Our objective was unclimbed Chandi Himal (6,142m, 30°21'31.67"N, 81°56'57.59"E).

Apart from my own efforts, there have only been two expeditions—both British—planning to attempt Chandi Himal. The 2013 expedition managed to climb Peak 6,024m at the far western end of the Chandi Himal range before early season snowfall forced a premature departure. The 2022 team was unluckier, only able to establish their advanced base camp before the arrival of a huge storm. While we were more fortunate, our expedition was unable to evade Nepal's coldest, snowiest spring in 30 years.

We enjoyed a leisurely nine-day trek up the Chuwa Khola and Nin Khola valleys before establishing base camp on May 14 at 4,815m. Deep snow prevented the pack mules from traveling any higher.

After a rest day, Kevin, Jaime, Pemba Sherpa, Kinga Sherpa, and a porter left at 9:15 a.m. on a bluebird day and established advanced base at 5,365m. I had reached this point on a previous attempt in the fall of 2021 (the trip was aborted due to dysentery), and then it lay on bare ground; now it was under two meters of snow.

The following day dawned clear and calm, and Kevin, Jaime, and Pemba went about 200m higher, to a point where they were able to determine that the southeast ridge of Chandi Himal was feasible.

On the 18th, Kinga and two porters went to advanced base camp, and the two porters continued with Jaime to establish a high camp, with Pemba following shortly after. Kevin, who had been experiencing headaches, descended to base camp with Kinga.

Jaime radioed us at 12:15 p.m. with the news that high camp had been established at 5,740m and a summit attempt was planned for the next day.

After a climb of about four and a half hours the next day, an excited Pemba radioed that he and Jaime were on the summit, in very high winds. They had initially climbed the east face and accessed the southeast ridge just above a cliff band. They then followed the ridge to the summit. Jaime assessed the difficulty at F+. The two spent around an hour on the summit, their GPS units giving readings of 6,143m and 6,153m. At 11:30 a.m., they were back in high camp. 📷

—**Matt Powell**, *USA*

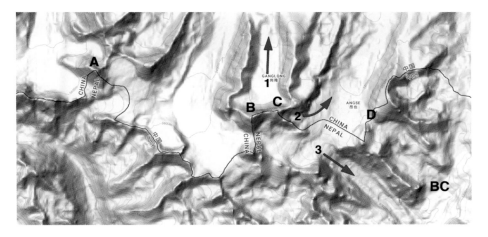

GANGLUNG KANGRI II, FIRST ASCENT AND GEOGRAPHIC SLEUTHING

The approximate sources of the Brahmaputra and Sutlej rivers have been known for 150 years, the main protagonists in their identification being explorers Edmund Smyth, Sven Hedin, and Swami Pranavananda in the 19th and 20th centuries. These rivers, along with the Indus and Karnali, rise near Mt. Kailash, the holy mountain on the Tibetan Plateau, north of Nepal's far northwest frontier.

Hedin identified the Kubi glaciers as the approximate source of the Brahmaputra, and this remained the status quo until the mid-1930s, when the Indian holy man Pranavananda suggested that the river emanated from the Chemayungdung Glacier farther west. This is nearer to today's accepted source.

From 2007 to 2019, I made many journeys to the mountains of Western Nepal, in part to investigate which might be farthest from the snout of the Kubi and Chemayungdung glacier systems. Meanwhile, in 2011, researchers from the Chinese Academy of Sciences (CAS) completed a study of the sources, length, and drainage of the Brahmaputra (known as the Yarlung Tsangpo in Tibet) and the Indus, using remote-sensing images and data from several expeditions to the Tibetan Plateau.

The CAS placed the Brahmaputra's source on the Angsi Glacier (a.k.a. Nanser Glacier), which drains northeast from the Ganglung Kangri massif. (The Chemayungdung, earlier thought to be the source, is the next glacier to the east.)

I decided in 2019 to attempt Ganglung Kangri (6,256m) and, more importantly, Ganglung Kangri II (6,182m). The latter is the furthest peak up the Angsi Glacier from its terminus and therefore, in my reckoning, the source point of the Brahmaputra. The mountain's north ridge, stretching into Tibet, divides the Brahmaputra's Angsi Glacier from the Sutlej's Ganglung Glacier. From this one ridge, waters end up on either side of the Indian

The border area of the Chandi Himal. (A) Chandi Himal (6,142m). (B) Ganglung Kangri (6,256m). (C) Ganglung Kangri II (6,182m). (D) The pass used to access the Angsi Glacier. (BC) Base camp for Ganglung Kangri team.

The sources of three major rivers are in this area. (1) The Ganglung Glacier drains into the Tage Chu, which leads to the Sutlej River and eventually to the Arabian Sea. (2) The Angsi Glacier drains to the Brahmaputra (Yarlung Tsangpo), which reaches the Bay of Bengal. (3) The glacier southeast of Ganglung Kangri drains into the Chuwa Khola and the Karnali River, eventually meeting the Ganges River. *Google Maps*

The upper Angsi Glacier basin from the 5,615-meter frontier pass. On the right are Ganglung Kangri I (left, 6,256m) and II (6,182m). (The summit of the latter is not quite visible.) The 2023 route up Ganglung Kangri II climbed a hidden snow ramp between I and II. The three peaks in center are unclimbed: 6,119 m, 6,085m, and 6,171m (left to right). On the far left is Peak 6,013m, also unclimbed. *Julian Freeman-Attwood*

subcontinent: the Sutlej to Karachi in the Arabian Sea and the Brahmaputra to Calcutta in the Bay of Bengal.

Access to the Angsi Glacier from Tibet is politically impossible, so I decided to find a way to it from the Nepal side, first in 2019 with Nick Colton and Skip Novak. From Simikot, we traveled eight days following the Chuwa Khola to a 5,000m base camp just below Changla pass on the frontier with Tibet. We found a way up the moraine of an unnamed glacier flowing in from the west and put an advanced base at 5,400m. From here we discovered a hidden glacier col at 5,615m on the Tibet border. Crossing this, we were the first onto the Angsi Glacier, which is surrounded by nine peaks above 6,000m, five of which are unnamed. Without snowshoes, we thought it unfeasible to cross the upper plateau toward the Ganglung peaks.

In 2022, I went to the west side of the Ganglung massif, this time with Colton and Ed Douglas. Although we were able to see an approach to Ganglung Kangri from this direction, we were completely thwarted by the worst post-monsoon snowfall for decades. [*In the spring of 2023, the first ascent of Chandi Peak was made from this expedition's ABC; see p.304.*]

In the fall of 2023, Colton and I went back to our 2019 base camp east of the Ganglung massif. This time we were joined by Jim Fotheringham and Jim Lowther. Retracing our 2019 route to the border col, the two Jims pushed across the upper basin of the Angsi in very cold conditions, using snowshoes. On October 16, they made the first ascent of Ganglung Kangri II via a south-facing ramp line (AD).

Only Ganglung Kangri II drains into the Brahmaputra, but both Ganglung Kangri I and II drain west onto the Ganglung Glacier. The outflow from this glacier is known as the Tage Chu until it enters Lake Manasarovar, south of Kailash. This is the infant Sutlej. Thus, in making the first visit to the geographical source of the Brahmaputra, our 2023 expedition also made the first visit to one of the sources of the Sutlej.

—**Jim Freeman-Attwood**, *U.K.*

NEPAL | Mukot Himal

PHURBA KANG AND RIGSUM GOMPO TRAVERSE

In the autumn, I led an expedition to the Hidden Valley, north of Dhaulagiri, to attempt the standard route up the north ridge of 6,920m Tukuche. However, very low temperatures and wind at altitude forced us to abandon our ascent. On the opposite (north) side of the valley, east of the main peaks of the Mukot and Hongde Himals, lies a collection of smaller, little-known, and unnamed mountains. (Some of these likely have had unrecorded ascents.) This small massif is worth a visit, and its snow cover at the end of the autumn would make it very suitable for skiing. We completed an aesthetic six-day crossing.

After placing Camp 1 on the north side of the valley, Anil Rai, Jan De Cooman, Isabelle Guillaume, Bernard Meurin, Kin Mimouni, Dipen Nupa, Sonam Sherpa, Hugues de Varax, and I climbed north on October 12 to reach a 6,339m summit that we named Sanu Phurba (28°49'43.47"N, 83°30'57.56"E). Our Camp 2 was atop this summit.

On the south ridge of Phurba Kang, looking back at the foreground peak of Sanu Phurba; the team's Camp 2 was on its summit. Behind in center is the large north face of Dhaulagiri. To right is part of Sita Chuchura. *Paulo Grobel*

The next day, in excellent weather, Sonam and Kin, Dipen and Jan, and Isabelle and I headed north to a 6,263m col, from which we ascended the south ridge of the beautiful snow pyramid of Peak 6,419m (28°50'17.05"N, 83°30'51.19"E), which we named Phurba Kang. We returned to Camp 2 to spend the night.

On the morning of the 14th, Kin and Sonam, and Isabelle and I set off with a single tent to traverse peaks to the east, which we collectively called Rigsum Gompo. We first headed north, then east, to reach Peak 6,292m, named Chenresig. This was not straightforward and took longer than expected, but the continuation east involved crossing only large snow domes. We traversed Manjushri (6,264m), climbed a couple of years earlier by Isabelle and Dipen, then reached a pass before the last summit, where we made Camp 3. The next day, we crossed over Peak 6,072m and then made our way south down snow slopes to Hidden Valley and base camp. 🔍 📷

—**Paulo Grobel,** *France*

NEPAL | Damodar Himal

PURBUNG, SOUTHWEST RIDGE; PURKUNG TRAVERSE

Contrary to a report published in *AAJ 2022*, Purbung (6,500m, 28°48'4.48"N, 84°1'4.41"E) had been climbed at least once before the reported ascent of the west face and northwest ridge in 2021. In 2017, after one prior attempt from the southeast, a party reached the glacier plateau west of Purbung, crossed this to the southeast, gained the crest of the southwest ridge, and followed it to the summit. The same party then made a northwest-to-southeast traverse of Purkung (6,128m). More details and good photos of this area are at the *AAJ* website. 📄 📷

—**Lindsay Griffin,** *AAJ*

Peak ca 5,735m from the approach above advanced base. The 2023 route gained the right skyline and followed it back left, via a two-pitch summit buttress, to the top. *Richard Goodey*

PEAK 5,735M, PROBABLE FIRST ASCENT

Sarah Allard, Maria Dixon, Richard Goodey, and I spent three days trekking to Nar, with support from the excellent Nepal Nirvana Trails trekking agency. We picked up further supplies and donkeys to help carry the loads, and set off for the Labse Khola.

After two days of trekking up this valley (*useful details are at the AAJ website*), we set our base camp at around 4,800m, 6km before the Teri La.

We spent the next two days reconnoitering routes both west and south of base camp. To the west, we found loose ground with potential landslide risk. To the south-southwest, the approach to Peak 5,810m looked more challenging than we'd hoped. Slightly further east, we identified a promising line up a peak of about 5,735m at 28°46'14.7"N, 84°05'25.9"E, on the watershed ridge between the Labse and Chhubche kholas. To its northeast lay a good site for an advanced base camp, at around 5,150m.

Leaving ABC at 4:30 a.m. on November 10, Richard and I climbed up snow and scree to around 5,400m, then followed a glacier southwest, leading up to a plateau between our summit and Peak 5,810m to its northwest. We then ascended two easy pitches up the summit buttress on a mixture of snow and rock, enjoying stunning views. We judged the route to be around PD.

The ridge connecting our peak and Jinjan (a.k.a. Genjang, 6,111m) offers opportunities for new routes, and the group of peaks a few kilometers southeast of Amotsang (6,393m) looks to have interesting mixed and rocky ridges. 📄📷

—**Mike Ferguson,** *U.K*

NEPAL | Peri Himal

UPCHE DADA AND HULANG GO, FIRST ASCENTS; RATNA CHULI, SKI DESCENT

The project was born one year earlier after Bastien Levy and I met in guides' class; with diplomas in hand, we thought about doing a high-altitude expedition together. At first, we considered skiing an 8,000m summit, but the image of a base camp teeming with mountaineers and the normal routes fixed with ropes did not inspire us. A 7,000m peak in Nepal? Enticing!

We invited two other friends from our class, Firmin Fontaine and Damien Coelho-Mandès, and met fellow guides Jean Annequin and Paulo Grobel for ideas. Jean told us about Ratna Chuli (7,035m, 28°51'57.30"N, 84°22'30.03"E), and how

Looking generally northeast from the Nagoru group at (A) Hulang Go, (B) Peak 6,662m, (C) Seto Chuli (the ascent route climbs the snow ridge just left of the steep rock), and (D) Ratna Chuli. Upche Dada and Camps 1 and 2 are off picture to the right. *Wolfgang Drexler*

this little-visited region on the Tibetan border would lend itself to high-altitude skiing. Coincidentally, Maud Vanpoulle and Victor Colombie had the same objective. We decided to join forces and share costs.

We met up in Kathmandu on October 6, then traveled by bus and jeep to Koto to start the two-day trek to Phu. It was a dream for us to see summits almost twice as big as those in the Alps.

Our base camp was at 4,700m in the Phu Khola valley, northeast of the village. We were the only team in the area. What a privilege!

We headed up the valley that branches to the north, and on the 13th set up Camp 1 at 5,600m. We made several trips to stock it, then made our Camp 2 at 6,000m, on a huge glacial plateau beneath the icefall giving access to Ratna Chuli's normal route up the west ridge (first climbed in 1996 by a joint Nepalese-Japanese team). The weather was mild, the snow conditions were optimal, and the team worked harmoniously.

During our acclimatization, we climbed two new peaks. From Camp 1, all except Bastien, who was suffering from the altitude, made the first known ascent of Upche Dada (6,150m, 28°50'6.83"N, 84°22'13.09"E) on October 15. We reached the summit on skis via the north-northeast ridge: mostly 30°, with two sections of 40° near the top. The team descended all the way to base camp the same day.

On the 22nd, we all left Camp 2 at 7 a.m., gained the upper Hulang Glacier, then climbed the left side of the southwest face of Hulang Go (6,687m, 28°52'22.24"N, 84°20'37.91"E). At first we were on skis, but we changed to crampons for the last ca 300m (45°–50°), with good ice at the top. We were on the summit at

Starting the descent of the west face of Hulang Go. The glacier arm above the lower skier is in Tibet, the frontier being the lefthand ridge. At the head of this glacier arm is Chako (6,704m). The higher summit just visible beyond is Lugula (6,899m). *Maud Vanpoulle*

noon. To descend, we found a line further west, which gave better snow and allowed us to ski down.

Returning to Camp 2 on the 27th, we followed our previous tracks through the icefall, using crampons and axes higher up. Reaching the top of the icefall at sunrise, we then climbed over Seto Chuli (Ratna Chuli's west top, 6,604m) and descended around 200m to the col at the start of the west-southwest ridge of Ratna Chuli, where we left an emergency tent and stove. We continued on skis to the rimaye, then carried them as we cramponed up the last 400m (45°), arriving on the summit at 10:30 a.m. With a few variants, we skied down the same line. We dismantled our Camps 1 and 2 and reached base camp at 7 p.m. on the same day.

We were happy with our expedition, which was more exploratory and adventurous than all about steep skiing. The bonds that have been forged between us are those special to climbers who live through a timeless adventure at the end of the world. 📷

—**Aurélia Lanoe,** *France*

NEPAL | Manaslu Himal

JARKYA, ATTEMPT

In the spring, an eight-member Japanese expedition led by Daijo Saito attempted unclimbed Jarkya (6,473m). Situated at 28°44'30.56"N, 84°31'28.72"E on the Nepal-Tibet border, about 5km northeast of Panbari, Jarkya was opened to climbing in 2014.

Approaching via the Buri Gandaki and Samdo to reach the Hindu Glacier, the expedition reached base camp at 4,570m on April 15. They first attempted the south ridge of the east top, with a high point of 6,257m, and then the southwest ridge, reaching 5,700m. More details are at the AAJ website. 📄

—**Lindsay Griffin,** *with help from* **Rodolphe Popier,** *Himalayan Database*

NEPAL | Langtang / Jugal

DRAGPOCHE, SOUTHEAST FACE; GANCHEMPO, COLD THERAPY

From October 22 to November 5, Oswaldo "Ossy" Freire and I, both IFMGA guides from Ecuador, were based at Kyanjin Gompa in the Langtang Valley. The weather was good, and we were able to complete two ascents.

Our first goal was Dragpoche (a.k.a. Yansa Tsenji, 6,575m). We established a camp at 5,100m on the south side of the mountain, below the Yala Glacier, which descends between Dragpoche and Yala Peak. The next day, we explored the glacier, breaking trail up to 5,400m at the base of the southeast face of Dragpoche, where we left a cache of equipment below the bergschrund.

At 11 p.m. on October 28, we left camp and reascended our tracks from the previous day. We then climbed the obvious couloir in the middle of the face. The first third was mixed terrain with difficulties up to M4+. Several sections of 90° ice in the constrictions of the gully were WI5. Once through this mixed ground, we progressed via less-inclined snow ramps up to 6,000m, where we turned right and headed directly for the summit. This last third of the face comprised alpine ice up to 70°. We reached the top at 7 p.m.

We descended the same line, downclimbing some sections and making 20 rappels. After almost 30 hours on the go, we regained our camp. On the following day we descended to Kyanjin Gompa. We named the route Between Fairies and Unicorns (around 1,100m, ED M4+ WI5), after a personal experience lived during the rappels.

We had two days' rest and then headed east in the main valley toward Ganchempo (6,378m) in the Jugal Himal. We followed a secondary valley, the Nyangutse Chu, located between Ganchempo and Pongen

Dokpu, and made camp at 4,600m on the west side of Ganchempo. The following day we gained more altitude to reach the start of the glacier that falls from the north side of the peak. We made a second camp 5,200m.

On November 3, we left the tent at 1 a.m., crossed the base of the glacier, and reached the fluted northwest face of Ganchempo. After surmounting the bergschrund at 5,600m, we climbed a couloir leading directly to the summit. There were short passages of 90°, but the average inclination was 55°. After 13 hours we reached the summit and then rappelled the route. We skipped passing the night at our top camp and continued down to 4,600m, arriving after 20 hours of action. We named our route Cold Therapy (ca 700m, AI4+) due to the low temperatures experienced during the climb. 📷

—**Joshua Jarrín**, *Ecuador*

ABOVE LEFT: Between Fairies and Unicorns, the 2023 route up the southeast face of Dragpoche for the first recorded ascent of the peak. *Joshua Jarrín*

ABOVE: Ossy Freire on the upper ramps of the southeast face of Dragpoche. *Joshua Jarrín*

HISTORICAL NOTES ON DRAGPOCHE AND GANCHEMPO:

Peaks far up the Langtang Valley were well-known in former days as targets for unauthorized ascents. However, there is no recorded ascent of Dragpoche. It was brought onto the official list of permitted peaks in 2003, when it was attempted by a commercially organized expedition that reached just over 6,100m on the east ridge. In 2010, two Japanese alpinists attempted the peak via the south face of the west-southwest ridge, reaching 5,800m before retreating. In 2022, Joshua Jarrín and friends made the first ascent of Peak 6,192m at the end of Dragpoche's west-southwest ridge (see AAJ 2023).

Bill Tilman attempted Ganchempo in 1949. The earliest known complete ascent was by an American party in 1971 from the southeast. Several teams have climbed lines on the northwest face, though most have not been direct. Three Italian climbers claim to have climbed the face in 2010 following a very similar line to the Ecuadorians.

LEFT: Jeong Ji-hoon climbing the first pitch of steep ice at around 6,100m on the northwest face of Goldum. *Korean Goldum Expedition*

ABOVE: Looking east up a side glacier from the Langtang Glacier, showing the approximate approach to Goldum followed by the 2023 expedition. (A) Goldum (6,632m). (B) Point 6,395m (HMG-Finn map). Hagen's Col is off picture to the left. *Korean Goldum Expedition*

GOLDUM, FIRST KNOWN ASCENT, VIA NORTH-NORTHEAST RIDGE

Also known as Pangri Goldumba, Goldum (6,632m, 28°19'44.10"N, 85°43'25.08"E) is situated toward the head of the Langtang Glacier, on the border with Tibet, directly opposite Xixabangma. The only known prior attempt took place in 1962, when a British party explored the Langtang, and four of the team tried to climb Goldum. The quartet reached around 6,100m on the north-northeast ridge before retreating in appalling snow conditions. The mountain was not brought onto the permitted list until 2014.

In the spring of 2023, an expedition led by Bok Jin-young reached the Langtang Valley with the aim of climbing Goldum. The team included Jeong Ji-hoon, Kim Dae-il, Park Joung-yong, Park So-jeong, and Son Ho-seong. Park Joung-yong had received information on this peak from the late Kim Chang-ho, with whom he had been on several expeditions.

On March 14, two days above Kyanjin Gompa (3,870m), the team established base camp on the Langtang Glacier at 4,750m. Beyond this, technical skills are needed to advance. Due to the distance of about 20km between base camp and the peak, two advanced camps were established, at 4,815m and 5,050m. Jeong, Kim, and Park Joung-yong reached the upper camp on the 18th and explored possible routes on the north side of Goldum.

After some time at base camp, Jeong, Kim, Park Joung-yong, and Son moved up the mountain and established Camp 1 at 5,648m on the 27th and Camp 2 at 5,898m the next day. On the 29th, all four climbed toward the north-northeast ridge (the same ridge attempted in 1962). At one point, Kim fell 30m on steep snow before being arrested, and he returned to camp. The other three reached the ridge, where their progress was stopped by a large crevasse at 6,100m. After this, the expedition spent five days resting in Kyanjin Gompa.

Base camp was regained on April 5, and Jeong, Kim, Park Joung-yong, and Son headed up again, arriving at Camp 2 on the 9th. Next day, taking a different line from their previous foray, they climbed seven long snow and ice pitches to 6,350m on the north-northeast ridge, where they made Camp 3. (The first of these, comprised of hard ice, was nearly vertical.) On summit day, the 11th, Kim felt exhausted and elected to stay in camp while the other three climbed to the top, which they reached at 12:30 p.m. 📄📷🔍

—Oh Young-hoon, *Korea*

HISTORICAL CLIMBS AT THE HEAD OF LANGTANG VALLEY

In the latter years of the 20th century, the Langtang Valley had a certain reputation among some mountaineers as a venue for unauthorized climbing. Despite an arduous approach over loose moraine, various unrecorded activity surreptitiously took place from the hidden upper reaches of the Langtang Glacier. Certainly, there have been attempts and ascents of the southwest face of Xixabangma (Shishapangma, 8,027m) by parties approaching up the Langtang and illegally crossing Hagen's Col into Tibet.

The author was in the Langtang Valley in late November 1987 and, about half a day above Kyanjin Gompa, met two Polish men walking out. They looked extremely weather-beaten, carried enormous packs with poorly concealed ice climbing equipment, had trekking permits that were already three weeks out of date, and sported huge smiles. Who knows what they might have climbed farther up the valley?

European exploration of the upper Langtang began nearly 75 years ago. In 1949, Peter Lloyd and Bill Tilman reached a col on the western rim that now bears Tilman's name. This ca 5,750m col, not to be confused with the far more frequented and lower Tilman's Col, which leads from the Langtang to the Jugal Himal, lies at the foot of the southwest ridge of Langtang Ri and is technically in Tibet, the official border running a little to the east. Lloyd and Tilman surveyed the immediate area but did no climbing.

In 1952, the Swiss geologist and explorer Toni Hagen crossed a col of about 6,000m on the eastern rim (the frontier ridge) near the head of the glacier. From there he had clear views of the upper Nyanang Phu Glacier (Fuqu Glacier in Chinese) and the huge southwest face of Xixabangma directly opposite.

The tallest peak at the head of the glacier is Langtang Ri (7,205m), which has received around 10 attempts, all by the southwest ridge above Tilman's Col. Only four have been successful

Peaks above the upper Langtang Glacier (ULG) and Nyanang Phu Glacier (NPG, a.k.a. Fuqu Glacier). The Nepal-Tibet frontier arcs around the upper Langtang, following the ridge crests in the left and center of the map. The approach to (G) Goldum, climbed in 2023, is shown. (A) Peri. (D) Dragmorpa Ri. (K) Kyungka Ri. (L) Langtang Ri. (M) "Marie Ri". (C) Chumsundo. (T) Tilman's Col. (P) Pungpa Ri. (R) Risum (Fuqu in Chinese). (H) Hagen's Col. (S) Peak 6,102m. (X) Xixabangma (a.k.a Shishapangma), with the huge southwest face prominent. *Google Earth*

Tilman's Col seen from Peak 6,102m on the east side of the upper Langtang Glacier. Left of the col stands Chumsundo (6,581m; the summit is in Tibet). To the right is part of the southwest ridge of Langtang Ri. *Victor Saunders*

and none since the 1989 expedition from Korea that made the first winter ascent. The peak was first climbed by a Japanese expedition in December 1981.

To the southeast of Langtang Ri, and with its summit in Tibet, a little east of the frontier ridge, is Risum (a.k.a. Fuqu, 7,133m). It was climbed in 1997 by a Japanese expedition via the east ridge, approaching from the glacier plateau northwest of Xixabangma. There is no known attempt from the Nepalese side.

Farther south along the frontier ridge is Peri (6,174m), a little north of Hagen's Col. While probably climbed in the last century, this peak was only put on the permitted list in 2014 and was climbed on December 6, 2016, by Werner Frei (Italy), Pasang Sherpa, and Sandesh Sherpa. They followed the glacier leading to Hagen's Col and climbed to the summit from the southwest.

South of Hagen's Col lies unnamed Peak 6,102m and then Goldum (*see report of first recorded ascent above*). Peak 6,102m has a nice west-southwest ridge, which was climbed in December 2001 by Andy Parkin and Victor Saunders (U.K.), and possibly by another party, earlier, in warmer weather. Parkin and Saunders were able to benefit from the winter temperatures by having perfectly flat campsites each night, pitching their tent on frozen glacier pools and securing the guy lines with screws. Parkin, a noted artist, was able to attach his canvas to the ice while painting. 📷

—Lindsay Griffin, *AAJ*

JUGAL V, FIRST ASCENT, VIA SOUTHWEST RIDGE

Nepalese guides and brothers Nima Gyalzen Sherpa and Pemba Dorje Sherpa, along with their nephew Tenzing Jangbu Sherpa (grandson of Ang Rita Sherpa and currently living in the USA), led two clients, Jaime Salinas (Mexico) and the Nepalese singer Sajja Chaulagain, on the first known ascent of the recently named Jugal V. This indistinct summit (5,922m, 28°8'48.26"N, 85°51'17.10") lies on the southwest ridge of Yangri's northwest peak, an unnamed mountain of about 6,300m. Chaulagain is reportedly attempting unclimbed peaks in Nepal to promote women in the arts.

The little-visited Jugal Glacier (see *AAJ 2020*) is being promoted by local tourism officials, and in 2021 guide Tul Singhi Gurung (who in 2019 made the first ascent of Gyalsten, above the east side of the Jugal Glacier) was employed to make a via ferrata up a rock buttress giving access to the glacier. The Jugal V team established base camp above the 130m via ferrata at Nyang Kharka (4,724m). From there, on October 24, they reached the southwest ridge of Jugal V from the south and followed it to the summit. 📷

—Lindsay Griffin, *AAJ*

PHURBI TXIKI, FIRST ASCENT, VIA WEST-NORTHWEST RIDGE; PHURBI CHHYACHU, SOUTHEAST RIDGE ATTEMPT

Iker Madoz, Juan Vallejo, and Mikel Zabalza from Spain planned to climb a new route on Phurbi Chhyachu (6,637m), a remote border peak that has only seen one ascent. In the spring of 1982, a 19-member joint Nepalese-Japanese team, led by Ichiro Yasuda, fixed around 2,000m of rope on the west-southwest ridge, the only line on the mountain they deemed feasible, and many climbers reached the summit.

On October 1, the three Spanish climbers reached base camp at 3,700m via

the Nyanya Masal Khola. The last section needed the help of a local shepherd, who not only showed them the trail but also reopened it using a kukri knife. On most days there was mist and rain.

The team first climbed the 6,125m peak on the frontier ridge immediately southeast of Phurbi Chhyachu. On October 5, they reached a bivouac at 4,900m below the west flank of the mountain, and next day climbed to 5,400m on the west-southwest ridge. On the 7th, they climbed to the summit, which was so thin they couldn't all stand there at the same time. The same day they descended to base camp.

The three had climbed largely unroped, negotiating snow and ice up to 70°, with a few mixed sections. They mostly downclimbed the route, with four or five rappels, and named the peak Phurbi Txiki.

The trio's main goal was the central pillar on the southwest face of Phurbi Chhyachu, but access proved to be unpleasant, with objective risks. The route also favored a capsule-style approach, whereas the team wanted to climb in alpine style. They switched to the unclimbed southeast ridge, of which they'd had a good view from Phurbi Txiki.

From mid- to late October, they made two attempts on this ridge, reaching about 6,200m in three days on the first attempt and then 6,570m, above the most difficult climbing, in very cold and snowy weather, on their second try. They retreated after climbing 1,500m (TD+) because of poor visibility and impending nightfall. 📄 📷

—**Lindsay Griffin, *with information from Rodolphe Popier, Himalayan Database, and Mikel Zabalza, Spain***

TOP: Iker Madoz during the attempt on the southeast ridge of Phurbi Chhyachu, with Phurbi Txiki immediately behind. The latter was climbed by the steep, snow and ice ridge dropping to the right from the summit. In the background are Menlungtse, Gaurishankar, and the Rolwaling peaks. *Mikel Zabalza*

ABOVE: The west-northwest face of Phurbi Txiki (6,125m) with the route of ascent. *Mikel Zabalza*

A

B

ROLWALING KANG SHAR, FIRST ASCENT, VIA SOUTHEAST RIDGE

My friend and former trainer Aleksandr Pogorelov once let me have a look at his dissertation, which studied how the level of risk in mountaineering relates to motives and to the overall synergy of the expedition. He used the expeditions of well-known mountaineers as examples. The lowest risk was found in expeditions with good synergy and a well-thought-out idea, even if the ascent was extremely difficult. Good motives included a keen interest in the project and, in the process of climbing, integration with one's surroundings and intense concentration, without irrelevant, mundane thoughts. Inconsistent and inadequate motives and preparation, and especially doubts, can lead to accidents and even tragedy.

What attracts me to mountaineering most of all is the feeling of presence that comes with high-risk situations, and the escape from a trivial, discursive way of thinking created by iterations of the "algorithm's" tired thought-forms.

Of course, with whom you go to the mountain is also very important. Aleksei Lonchinsky and I had already made the first ascent of Phungi (6,538m; *AAJ 2018*). He's a good, dependable friend on the mountain. Our motives were similar: We climb because of our interest in new discoveries.

The idea of climbing the southeast buttress of Rolwaling Kang Shar (6,645m; 27°53'53.57"N, 86°31'29.51"E) had come to me a long time ago. I knew from *AAJ 2018* that a Japanese team had previously climbed Rolwaling Kang (6,664m), the west (main) summit, in 2016, by its south face.

The entire expedition took 20 days, with a challenging approach across several Himalayan glaciers, followed by the ascent along the southeast buttress. Alpine style and free climbing were our top priorities. We had a careful look at the buttress in advance, mapped out our proposed bivouac spots, and put together a tactical plan that we managed to follow to the letter.

We started from base camp on October 19 with everything we needed for advanced base and the route above, and crossed the Drolambo Glacier in eight hours. On the 20th, we overcame a rocky barrier on the lower part of the Rolwaling Glacier, then found a way through some crevasses and started ascending steep snow to the foot of the ridge. We made Camp 1 that evening. The next two days were difficult but interesting. Aleksei led

on rock and mixed terrain, I on the ice and snowy arêtes. The rock was loose and broken, but generally frozen together. We didn't fix lines or use ascenders, and we were able to free climb the entire route.

On October 22, we bivouacked at 6,550m in a cave below an ice column on a snow arête. The next morning, we reached the summit of Rolwaling Kang Shar after following a sharp, mushroom-shaped arête of untrustworthy snow. The final ridge leading to the summit was curved like a samurai sword.

We had two choices for the descent. Plan A was to follow the route of ascent; plan B was to traverse the ridge to the west summit and go down the Japanese route. The latter turned out to be really bad right away: narrow with overhanging cornices on both sides. It would have been easy to fall off the ridge, and after crossing the initial section we turned back and started down the southeast ridge instead, at first along the line of ascent, then more to the right. We reached advanced base camp that evening. The route had given around 1,800m of climbing with difficulties of 5/5+ M5.

After a great ascent that has kept you in the flow, feeling all the ups and downs, and if your mind has not yet dried out from high-altitude dementia, new thoughts always appear on what is most important. In fact, these are more like sensations, such as when you no longer need an explanation of a sacred text but learn to understand it instinctively. A kind of highly concentrated spiritual practice.

In *Rose of the World*, drafted in a Soviet prison in the mid-20th century, Daniil Andreev writes, "Snow-covered mountain ranges, lifeless, inhospitable, and barren in their sterile magnificence, represent but one of two hemispheres, or one of two closely integrated planes. The other plane...is a land of embodied spirits of stunning majesty, the monarchs of snowy peaks. This plane is called Orliontana. It is Orliontana radiating through the three-dimensional rock and ice that evokes the feeling of august calm, power, and resplendence. Snow-covered mountains evoke these feelings in all who are even slightly susceptible...."

It is the beauty and cosmic magnitude of the worlds described by Andreev that help our perception to expand, and the primordial "unshadowed" aspect of our consciousness to appear. 📄 📷

—**Yuri Koshelenko,** *Russia, translated by Kat Tancock*

OPPOSITE PAGE:
(A) Rolwaling Kang (6,664m) from the southeast. The 2016 first-ascent route climbed the south face (off picture) to the short southwest ridge (left skyline). **(B) Rolwaling Kang Shar (6,645m),** showing the upper part of the 2023 route up the southeast ridge. *Yasuhiro Hanatani*

TOP: On the southeast ridge of Rolwaling Kang Shar. *Aleksei Lonchinsky*

BOTTOM: Yuri Koshelenko on the summit of Rolwaling Kang Shar. Behind and left is the northeast face of Chobutse. *Aleksi Lonchinsky*

LEFT: Marek Disman on the west face of Tengi Ragi Tau with the Drolambo Glacier below and the peaks northwest of the Likhu Chuli group behind. *Jakub Vlček*

ABOVE: The west face of Tengi Ragi Tau with (1) Honzova Cesta (2023), (2) Trinité (2019), and (3) part of Release the Kraken (2019). *Marek Disman*

TENGI RAGI TAU, WEST FACE, HONZOVA CESTA

Jan Kreisinger, Jakub Vlček, and I travelled to Nepal in the post-monsoon season, planning to climb a new route on the west face of Tengi Ragi Tau (6,938m). Kreisinger and Karel Roudnicky had already attempted our proposed line in 2021 but descended from around half-height, after two bivouacs, due to adverse weather.

From October 29 to 31, Vlček and I climbed and descended the line in alpine style, with one bivouac on the ascent and one on the descent. Kreisinger was forced to turn around at the start of the face due to insufficient acclimatization. We later named our line Honzova Cesta ("Johnny's Route," 1,300m, M5 80°) as a tribute to him. It climbs the middle of the west face, left of the 2019 route, Trinité, established by Silvan Schüpbach and Symon Welfringer (*AAJ 2020*).

We first established base camp at 5,300m in the Thame Khola (valley) on the east side of the peak, and then, carrying all our gear, an advanced base on the Drolambo Glacier at 5,400m, below our proposed line. This involved a crossing of the Tashi Lapcha pass (5,753m).

We progressed well during our first day on the face, climbing a fine mixed pitch of M5, then 60° snow/ice slopes spiced with a few mixed sections. The angle increased to 80° as we approached the prominent serac high on the face, which we bypassed via an icy couloir on the left.

Having climbed 1,000m and reached an altitude of about 6,400m, we found a cozy bivouac spot in the upper part of the huge serac. The following day we climbed 300m of flutes at 60°–70° to finish on one of the subsummits (6,772m, approximately 27°51'46.69"N, 86°33'12.38"E) along the north ridge.

Slowed by altitude and the previous long day, we had to bivouac at the same spot on the serac during the descent. On October 31, using mostly Abalakov anchors and slings on rock spikes, we rappelled the remaining face to the Drolambo Glacier. 📷

—**Marek Disman,** *Czech Republic*

CHOLATSE, WEST FACE

Radoslav Groh and I planned to climb a new route on the west face of Cholatse (6,423m). As part of a larger group of Czech climbers, we first acclimatized on Lobuche, then tackled Cholatse's normal route on the southwest ridge (Clevenger-O'Connor-Roskelley–Rowell, 1982). However, on October 25, one of our members, Jan "Honza" Ross, died in a long fall from the ridge. After this, the expedition returned to Kathmandu. After consulting with family and friends, Radoslav and I decided to return to the mountain to see if we could find Honza's camera, which his family wanted, and hopefully attempt our new route.

On November 1, we bivouacked 200m above Cholatse's base camp at 4,900m. Studying the west face, it is obvious the objective danger is significant. There is icefall on the lower part of the face, rockfall from the middle, and just below the summit a guillotine of overhanging seracs. There seemed only one solution: We would split the ascent into two days and seek a safe place to shelter during the heat of the day.

Early on the 2nd, we climbed three pitches of steep ice and mixed at WI4+ M5. Above, four pitches of easier terrain led to an ice cave at 5,400m on top of a prominent serac. We reached this point at 10 a.m. and then sat out the rest of the day, protected from overhead danger.

Starting again at 2 a.m. on the 3rd, we made a single push to the summit. The route was almost entirely difficult ice (60°–90°), although at around half-height there was a single pitch of poor vertical rock (M4/M5). (There would be no safe place to bivouac on

TOP: Radoslav Groh belays beneath a serac barrier early on summit day on the west face of Cholatse. *Zdeněk Hák*

BOTTOM: Looking east at Makalu (left) and Cholatse, showing (1) the northwest ridge (1988), (2) Just One Solution (2023), (3) the west rib (1988), and (4) southwest ridge (1982). *Zdeněk Hák*

the upper face.) After 14 hours, we reached the crest of the southwest ridge, left our packs, and climbed for 30 minutes to the summit.

We descended quickly along the southwest ridge, hoping to get as low as possible that night. At the site of Camp 2, a guide made us tea and offered a place in the tent for the night. We thanked him for the tea but decided to continue, helped by fixed ropes.

At around 5,900m, we passed the spot where Honza fell. I checked the anchors he would have been clipped into at the time, and they were intact. Tired, I nearly made a mistake myself while rappelling. Eventually, we arrived at Camp 1 (5,600m), which was empty. We pitched our small tent and immediately fell asleep.

Next day, we searched the area where we had previously recovered Honza's body, and Radoslav found his camera. After a short remembrance, we continued down to the village of Phortse. We named our route Just One Solution (1,200m, ED WI4+ M5). [*Editor's Note: To the right of the line climbed by Groh and Hak is the west rib, which was climbed to the southwest ridge (but not quite to the summit) in 1988 by Americans Greg Collins, Andy Selters, and Tom Walter, and has been repeated several times. The left edge of the face is formed by the northwest ridge, a 37-pitch, stegosaurus-like crest also first climbed by the 1988 expedition (see AAJ 1989).*] 📷

—**Zdeněk Hák,** *Czech Republic*

MELANPHULAN, NORTHWEST RIDGE, ATTEMPT

Prakash Sherpa, Riten Sherpa (both IFMGA guides), Luigi Santini (Italy), and I attempted the unclimbed northwest ridge of Melanphulan (6,573m) in early November. With porter assistance, we established a high camp at 5,100m on the moraine north of the mountain, where global warming has dramatically changed the condition and size of the Nare Glacier.

We climbed the slope up to the

Melanphulan from Camp 1 on Ama Dablam. The attempted route on the northwest ridge is marked. On the left is the north face, which has received several attempts, one stopping just 50m below the summit ridge (Kurtyka-Loretan, 2000). On the right is the west face, where the first known ascent of the peak was made in 2000. *Jay Mathers*

northwest ridge of Melanphulan and made our Camp 1 at 5,800m, just below and right of the col at the base of the ridge. Up to this point, the climbing was mostly easy 5th class, with some mixed ground on low-angled, unconsolidated snow. The rock was loose, but around 120m below the camp there was one pitch of 5.9 where the rock was sounder.

Our summit bid began at 10 p.m. on November 3. We climbed 100m up to the crest of the ridge, then descended it southeast to the col. Above, the ground was steeper, with 60°–70° snow slopes, mixed in consistency. The rock encountered was loose. At 4 a.m. on the 4th, having reached 6,200m, we turned around due to the bad snow and rock. Retracing our route back to Camp 1 involved downclimbing and a few rappels; from there we made nine rappels. We regained our high camp in 20 hours from our high point.

Melanphulan has received a number of attempts from various directions, and some of these have come very close to the summit. However, perhaps only one party has ever reached the top, via the west face (*see AAJ 2001*). 📷

—**Jay Mathers,** *USA*

Marek Holeček starting up the rock barrier on day two on Hongku's west face in deteriorating weather. After only two pitches, the climbers were forced to suspend their tent on a 70° ice slope for a bivouac. *Matěj Bernát*

HONGKU, WEST FACE

When in the high mountains, you might think your eyes could embrace only one beauty and focus on one goal. My eyes are restless and unfaithful, and even while acclimatizing in 2021 for an ascent of Baruntse's west face (*AAJ 2022*), I was eagerly scanning the surrounding area.

Over the next two years, the image of a fine pyramid rising steeply above a glacier would return to my mind. I eventually searched my photo archive, browsed magazines and the internet, and asked questions, and I found that the rascal was called Sura Peak (better known as Hongku or Hongku Chuli Nup, 6,764m).

Before reaching base camp in the Hinku Valley on May 13, Matěj Bernát and I roamed the central Himalaya for two weeks to train our lungs and legs. It was quickly obvious there was little snow this season, and the spring was unusually cold. Whether this would be good for the climb remained to be seen.

Our ascent of the west face of Hongku began on May 20, after spending the previous night in a comfortable camp below the face at around 5,500m. Taking a line toward the left side, almost directly

below the summit, we were able to move together, gaining height quickly. The sun hit us at around 10 a.m., and shortly after midday we arrived at the big serac barrier that guards the upper half of the face. We passed through this via steep blue ice, with a few vertical sections. Progress slowed, and the afternoon sun was drifting quickly westward when I stumbled upon a natural ice cave. At 6,000m, it was a bivouac sent from heaven.

Up to this point the weather had been fine, and the next morning the sun smiled for a short, joyful moment before clouds moved in. We climbed 150m of ice flutes

The west face of Hongku (6,764m), showing the 2023 route Simply Beautiful, which gained about 900m above the bergschrund. *Marek Holeček*

Traversing away from the second bivouac on the west face of Hongku, with more difficult rock ahead. *Matěj Bernát*

that resembled a quarry. It was snowing when we eventually cleared the rock barrier and Matej took over the lead. After two icy pitches, he found a slot in the face, allowing us to pitch our tent in the middle of a 70° slope.

Next morning, we climbed the remaining 140m of elevation in two hours. We forced our faces to squeeze out smiles, expressing the relief that we no longer had to climb. Baruntse and Chamlang appear close by, provoking an unstoppable wave of emotion as I recalled previous ascents—perhaps I was most moved by the realization that my train was approaching its destination, and in the coming years I would be retiring from Himalayan journeys.

Moving together, we descended the southwest ridge, only reaching the snowline just before dark. Stumbling across rocky ground, we reached Seto Pokhari at 11 p.m., finding our porters already waiting for the homeward journey. We named our route Simply Beautiful (about 900m from the bergschrund, M6 90°). Thank you, Matěj. 📖📷

—**Marek Holeček,** *Czech Republic*

SHERSHON LHO, NORTHWEST FACE

After acclimatizing with a trek to Everest Base Camp, Egon Egger and Benjamin Zörer (Austria) trekked from Num to a base camp (4,564m) located south of the southernmost lake in the Shershon Valley, arriving there on April 20.

Their prime objective was Tutse (a.k.a. Peak 6, 6,758m). The right side of Tutse's serac-torn north face avalanched day and night. The left side appeared safer, but as the face itself was quite dry, they decided to try the east ridge, attempted in 2003 by a Danish team. However, bad weather over the next three weeks hampered their acclimatization, and on May 12, when they launched their attempt, Egger was unable to continue past around 5,500m.

After two days' rest at base camp, Zörer set off for a solo ascent of Shershon Lho

to the rock barrier crossing the upper face. Here was predictable trouble, confirmed by the first few meters where the rock was like gingerbread sprinkled with loose sugar snow. After a lot of effort, I climbed only two rope lengths, with psychological protection, before deteriorating weather indicated we should quickly find a place to sleep. On the 70° slope, we were unable to create a platform and were forced to hang the tent from the belay and then shelter inside. We were two marionettes tied by strings to an inhospitable mountain face, and the awful night took much of our waning strength.

The next day would be key. Descending the terrain we had climbed over the past two days was hard to imagine, and the 80m rock band above us looked like one big overhang. However, every time I feel indecisive, my inner voice whispers, "Just give it a try." The next two pitches took many hours, with feet digging into terrain

(6,112m). On the 14th, he slept beside Shershon Lake at 5,195m. He left camp at 2:30 a.m., reached the foot of the northwest face, and climbed its right side, finishing via the upper section of the west-southwest ridge. He was on the summit a little before 7:30 a.m.

The climb was approximately D, with 12m to 15m of bad ice at WI3/4. The rest of the face was 50°–70° snow slopes, with one short mixed section. Zörer descended the west-southwest ridge, which was relatively easy, with just two sections where he had to downclimb UIAA II/III. [*This was the ridge that Michael Ball and a Sherpa climber used to make the first ascent of the mountain in 1954.*] He was back at the tent by 9:30 a.m. and returned to base camp by noon. 📖📷

—**Information from Benjamin Zörer,**
Austria, and Rodolphe Popier, Himalayan Database

The northwest face of Shershon Lho (6,112m), showing (1) the 2023 ascent on the right side of the face, and (2) the descent via the west-southwest ridge (the route of the first ascent in 1954). *Benjamin Zörer*

HISTORICAL NOTES ON SHERSHON, TUTSE, AND PEAK 5,822M:
On September 3, 1989, Victor Saunders and Stephen Sustad left the lower Makalu Base Camp (ca 4,900m), crossed a ridge to reach the Shershon Valley, and climbed to the summit of Shershon Lho, returning to base camp the same day. Although Saunders believes they climbed the northwest face, the same face climbed by Benjamin Zörer, he is uncertain of the line they followed almost 35 years earlier.

There is no record of an ascent of Tutse, although there are rumors it has been climbed by a party or parties during acclimatization for Makalu. In 2003, the year it was first brought onto the permitted list, a Dutch expedition attempted the east ridge, reaching 5,000m. The Dutch turned their attention to Peak 5,822m, which lies on the ridge running south from Saldim East Peak (6,374m). They climbed through a difficult labyrinth of crevasses on the west flank to reach a col on the north ridge at 5,600m. From here, they followed the steep snow and ice ridge to the summit for a probable first ascent.

NEPAL | Janak Himal

KYABURA, FIRST ASCENT, VIA SOUTH-SOUTHEAST RIDGE

In October, I led a small international team to the Lhonak Glacier, northwest of Kangchenjunga. Kyabura (6,466m), listed as an unclimbed peak by the Ministry of Tourism, is the smaller half of a border massif shared with Dzanye (6,581m), which was climbed by the 1949 Swiss expedition, led by Alfred Sutter, that made the first foray into the region. It lies southwest of Dzanye at 27°53'55.45"N, 88°1'0.42"E and a little northeast of the Chabuk La.

The six-day approach along the Kangchenjunga teahouse

Looking north-northwest to Kyabura from the summit of Peak 6,214m. The ascent route followed the foreground ridge; the summit lies about 500m behind the serac wall in the center. On the right are Dzanye (6,581m, climbed in 1949 by the northwest ridge, crossing into Tibet for the ascent) and then Peak 6,697m, the latter fully in Tibet. At far left is Peak 6,782m, also in Tibet. *Diogo Santos*

trek was uneventful, marked only by the regrettable departure of team member Matt Powell (USA), who was suffering from lingering issues related to a cycling accident. Our base camp was on the eastern moraine of the upper Lhonak Glacier. With no running water behind any of the lateral moraines that we traversed, the only reliable supply was on the glaciers themselves.

All of the hillsides and glaciers were similarly dry, and it was easy to acclimatize by hiking above 6,000m without touching snow. After a week of reconnaissance and shuttling loads alongside the Chabuk Glacier, we moved into a 5,600m camp by a small lake immediately west of Peak 6,214m.

On November 2, all five remaining team members scrambled up steep moraine and slabs to the 5,962m col on the south-southeast ridge of Kyabura. A loose and low-angle rock ridge led to almost 6,200m, where a firm snow crest, followed by 100m of 45° névé, led to the broad summit plateau. The top was reached by Thomas Heidt (Germany), Sarah Marti (Switzerland), Sébastien Moatti (France), Diogo Santos (Portugal), and me (U.K.). Unfortunately, the fine weather of our

first week had been replaced by afternoon snow showers, and we were unable to see anything other than intermittent views of Dzanye in the mist.

Some team members also explored the upper Chabuk and Tsitsima (a.k.a. Tsisima or Chijima) basins, although most climbing ideas were stymied by strong upper-level winds. All the acclimatization peaks between the Chabuk and Tsitsima had reportedly been climbed before, except for Peak 6,170m (27°52'14.73"N, 88°2'37.66"E), which has a relatively steep, snowy west face and a less steep, rocky east face. The latter was climbed in a solo effort by Moatti, who encountered extremely poor rock. 📷

—**Bruce Normand,** *Switzerland*

EASTERN NEPAL, ATTEMPTS ON THREE PEAKS

In the fall, Takahiro Ishikawa, Takahiro Kaneko, and Saki Terada made a spirited attempt on unclimbed Sharphu VI (6,076m) in the Ohmi Kangri Himal. The team approached up the Nupchu Khola from Kangbachen and then climbed southwest to reach the glacier below the north ridge of Tha Nagphu (5,980m, climbed by a Spanish team in 2017). Instead of climbing over this summit, they traversed its eastern flanks to reach the ridge on the far side leading southeast toward Sharphu VI. On their final attempt, they reached around 6,000m on this ridge but were stopped by an apparently impassible section. During the descent, they made a short detour to climb Tha Nagphu (second ascent).

Kazu Amano, Mashu Kawasaki, and Kotaro Miyazu attempted to climb Anidesh Chuli (6,808m), an unclimbed summit in the Kangchenjunga Himal formerly known as White Wave. The first known attempt was in 2013, by a team from New Zealand that tried the east ridge but retreated after a fall. Later attempts on the east ridge and northeast face also failed.

The 2023 team established base camp on September 30, near the base of the Ramtang Glacier at 4,750m. From there, they acclimatized to around 5,800m before attempting the fluted northeast face, which starts at around 6,000m. They retreated from 6,600m, not far short of the upper east ridge.

A pair of Japanese climbers attempted the north face of Phole, one of three summits crossed by the ridge extending west from Jannu as it descends toward the Ghunsa Khola: Sobithongie (6,652m), Phole (6,645m), and Kyabura (6,294m, a different Kyabura than the one in the report above). All were opened in 2002, and all remain officially unclimbed [*rumors that Sobithongie was climbed from the north more than 20 years ago are unconfirmed*].

In the autumn, Hidesuki Taneishi and Daiki Yamamoto attempted the north face of Phole from an advanced base camp beneath the wall at 5,100m. They took a left-rising line over steep ice and mixed ground, aiming toward the col separating Phole from Sobithongie. The 1,400m–1,500m face becomes steeper toward the top, and the two bivouacked three times before reaching a height of around 6,200m. By this point Yamamoto was unwell and the two descended. 🖹 🖸

—**Lindsay Griffin,** *AAJ*

TOP: (A) Jannu, (B) Sobithongie, and (C) Phole from the north, with the route attempted on Phole (6,645m) in autumn 2023. *Stefano Ragazzo*

BOTTOM: The northeast face of Anidesh Chuli and the line attempted in 2023. *Ben Dare*

NEPAL | Kangchenjunga Himal

KABRU SOUTH

A NEW ROUTE UP A 7,318-METER PEAK
ON NEPAL'S EASTERN FRONTIER

By Nives Meroi, *Italy*

The Kabru group lies south of Kangchenjunga on the Nepal-Sikkim border. The south peak of Kabru (7,318m) had received only one confirmed ascent: In 1994, a large Indian Army expedition climbed from Sikkim via the Kabru Glacier, finishing up the north ridge. Kabru South has the distinction of being the most southerly 7,000m peak in the world. Our goal was the unclimbed 2,800m Nepalese (west) face.

On April 18, Romano Benet and I (Italy), Bojan Jan (Slovenia), and Peter Hamor (Slovakia) set up base camp in Ramche (4,610m), close to the last tourist lodge on the Kangchenjunga south-side trek. Next day we walked to Oktang, across the Yalung Glacier from the face, left an offering to the gods, then continued across the glacier to the foot of the mountain.

Our plan had been to complete the line attempted in 2004 by a Serbian team. They started the west face with a difficult rock wall—"the most insecure wall we have ever been on"—climbing a very loose 500m couloir to a camp at around 5,200m. Subsequently, they reached a point a little below 6,000m in an icefall, where unstable weather, avalanche risk, and eventually an accident to the leader forced them to abandon the expedition.

Now we could see that the "icefall" had become a waterfall and the couloir continuously raked by rockfall. We needed creative eyes to find a new line, which requires both experience and talent, and it was Romano and Peter who discovered a feasible route farther left.

In late April and early May, in two forays during poor weather, we established Camp 1 at 5,100m, then moved the tents

a couple of hundred meters higher to a new site and explored the route up to 5,600m.

Early on May 9, we began another attempt. Despite so many days of snow and strong wind, we found our two tents at Camp 1 undamaged. The following day, we climbed above the seracs and made Camp 2 in a safe location at 5,700m.

On the 11th, we continued through a second serac barrier and found a safe spot for our Camp 3 at 6,200m. Although it looked like blizzard conditions on the ridge above, it was calm at this camp and our weather forecast was optimistic. At 4 a.m. on the 12th, we set out for the summit, still 1,100m above us, in windless conditions.

After a dangerous section of crevasses, we reached "The Funnel," where the steepest climbing began. Swept by days of strong winds, the slope was blue ice at 60° or steeper, with a short, mixed section. We finally arrived at "The Balcony," just below the summit rock pyramid, and from there the going became easier, on hard-packed snow.

Peter reached the summit ahead of us, at 4:30 p.m. Once we all were on top, we started down immediately. The descent, from many Abalakov anchors, took many hours. At 1:30 a.m. on the 13th, we decided it would be wise to stop and bivouac, using a huge ice cave at 6,400m. In the light of our torches, the ice around us shone like it was covered in diamonds.

We were away by 5 a.m. and soon regained our tents at Camp 3, where we could get warm, drink, and recover. The following day we descended to base camp.

We felt our line had been logical, and it was climbed in a lightweight style with no fixed ropes, fixed camps, or external assistance. However, in bad snow conditions it would be dangerous. We named the route Diamonds on the Soles of the Shoes (2,800m, D+ 60°). [*The 2023 ascent of Kabru South—only the second—appears to have been the fourth attempt and first successful ascent on any of the Kabru peaks from the Nepalese side. Further notes on the geography and history of this group are at the AAJ website.*] 📄 📷

OPPOSITE PAGE: Diamonds on the Soles of the Shoes on the previously unclimbed west face of Kabru South. The line attempted by Serbian climbers in 2004 topped out on the left side of the lower icefall. Kabru's main summit (7,412m) is off-picture to the left. The peak to the right is Rathong (6,682m). *Peter Hamor*

ABOVE: Romano Benet and Nives Moroi on the ice face above the Funnel, high on the west face of Kabru South (7,318m). *Peter Hamor*

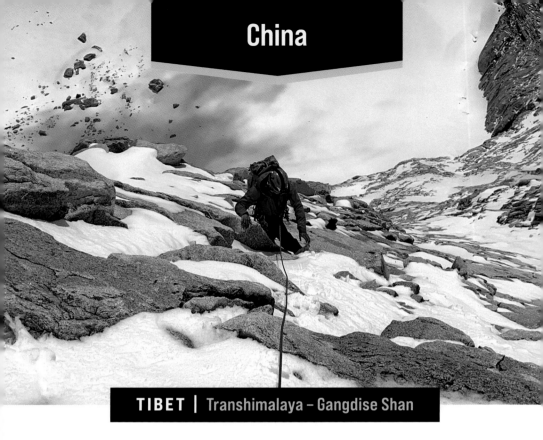

TIBET | Transhimalaya – Gangdise Shan

LOINBO KANGRI, SOUTH FACE; PHOLA KYUNG, SOUTHEAST FACE

Liu Junfu and Zhou Song climbed two new routes in the Loinbo Kangri massif, about 400km west of Shigatse, during a 15-day trip to Tibet in September. The massif's highest summit, Loinbo Kangri (7,095m), is the high point of the Gangdise Range and had two prior routes: the northeast ridge (first ascent of the peak, in 1996) and the north-northwest face, climbed in 2016. Liu and Zhou approached the peak from the south side.

On September 12, they left their base camp at 5,500m and, after picking up previously cached gear, reached the glacier below the unclimbed south face of Loinbo Kangri, where they camped at 5,750m.

Next morning, they set off at 6 a.m. At 6,000m, above the initial snow slopes, they entered mixed terrain where they could simul-climb with solid intermediate protection. However, as the day warmed, the two were subjected to rockfall from the spur above and to their left. They headed up right to reach a névé slope, then climbed a direct line between the rockfall-threatened area to the left and seracs high to the right.

When they reached around 6,800m, the sun dropped behind the spur to the left and the temperature plummeted. They crested the spur, leveled a bivouac site, and spent the night at close to 7,000m. Hoping to get up and down the route in a day, they had not brought a tent but did have a stove and a thin sleeping bag as well as down clothing. It was a miserably cold, shivering night.

The two got on the move again once the morning sun had hit the ridge. Deep, soft snow made the traverse avalanche-prone, and the two belayed in such a way that if the leader fell down one side, the second would be able to jump to the other. They were at the summit at 9 a.m.

Returning to the point where they had reached the spur, they made one rappel from a snow anchor, then downclimbed 18 pitches, reaching the bottom of the face at 3 p.m. and base camp at midnight. The 1,300m route was graded WI3 M4 70° snow.

On September 15, Liu and Zhou drove to Shigatse to recuperate and wait for the next weather window.

Returning to base camp on the 18th, they set off the following morning toward the elegant pyramidal Phola Kyung (6,530m) and reached the bottom of the southeast face quite quickly. They planned to follow a couloir directly toward the summit. [*The peak's first ascensionists, in 2006, climbed a couloir on the far right of the southeast face to reach the east ridge, then a further four pitches up the crest to the top.*]

The couloir was pronounced in its upper section, and as Liu and Zhou were reaching this point, at around 6,150m, they experienced some rockfall. Unable to place a screw in the thin ice, they traversed right to a rock spur. They belayed one pitch, then simul-climbed over snow-covered slabs. The penultimate pitch proved to be the crux: a strenuous thin crack in a dihedral.

After reaching the summit at 4 p.m., they began their descent of the same route immediately. They made seven rappels and regained the glacier at 6,000m, reaching base camp at 9 p.m. The 500m route had maximum difficulties of 5.9+.

—Xia Zhongming, *Germany*

OPPOSITE PAGE: On the upper southeast face of Phola Kyung during the 2023 ascent. *Liu Junfu and Zhou Song*

ABOVE: The south face of Loinbo Kangri (7,095m) with the new route climbed in September 2023. A cold open bivouac was made at the point where the route exits onto the summit ridge. The original route (in 1996 by a joint Chinese-Korean expedition) followed the ridge on the right. *Erik Monasterio*

Camp 2 on the glacier east of Ama Drime and the routes to (A) Ama Drime I (6,669m) and (B) Ama Drime East (6,580m). *Hou Zhao (Gu Niaoniao)*

AMA DRIME I AND AMA DRIME EAST, PROBABLE FIRST ASCENTS

In mid-August, Li Bo, Zhong Wanghong, and I made first ascents of both Ama Drime I (6,669m, 28°5'9.69"N, 87°36'25.89"E) and Ama Drime East (6,580m). These peaks are situated on the border between Tingri County and Dinggye County in the Tibet Autonomous Region. They are part of the Nyonno Ri–Ama Drime subrange, which, unusually for the Greater Himalaya, runs in a north–south direction. The subrange is around 80km long and 40km across and includes dozens of 6,000m peaks, the highest of which are Nyonno Ri (6,730m), Ama Drime I, and Ama Drime East. Before this year, none had recorded ascents. [*The 1933 and 1935 Everest expeditions, the latter led by Eric Shipton, visited the Nyonno Ri subrange, where they climbed three peaks but apparently never attempted the main summits.*]

We left Lhasa on August 12 and drove 500km to Zong Co lake. Here, we could see the north side of Ama Drime, but the approach appeared difficult, so we followed the road farther south toward the village of Riwu, from which we could see a shorter route.

On the 14th, we left the car at 5,000m and, after a walk of 2.5 hours, arrived at Ama Zhibucuo lake (5,500m), east-

northeast of the mountain. From here we could see that the glacier flowing east from Ama Drime splits into two tongues, the left of which was barred by a steep rock cliff. We pitched camp at 5,650m, below the right glacier tongue, which began with a gentle slope and then steepened.

The next day, we climbed seven pitches up the glacier and, passing numerous crevasses, eventually placed Camp 2 (6,150m) in the cwm above. We started our summit push at 9:30 a.m. on the 16th. Gaining elevation slowly on the seemingly endless eastern slope of Ama Drime I, we reached the summit at 1:10 p.m., calling our 1,500m ascent Climbing Community (AI2 55° snow). We returned to Camp 2 later that afternoon; it had been a long, exhausting day.

Despite our fatigue, the next day, August 17, Li and I climbed a direct line from Camp 2 up the southwest face of Ama Drime East. The route started with loose mixed terrain, and we only found seven points of protection in four pitches. Moving together up the final 150m snow slope, Li and I reached the summit. Due to a feeling of complete exhaustion, we named the route Burnt Out (550m, 5.7 R 60° snow). We descended safely and reached our vehicle in the early hours of the following morning.

—**Hou Zhao (a.k.a. Gu Niaoniao),** *China, translated by He Lang*

SEJONG, NORTH-NORTHWEST COULOIR AND NORTH RIDGE

During a reconnaissance of the northwest end of the Chola Shan Range, south of the town of Zhuqing, Fu Yongpeng noticed the unclimbed peak of Sejong (5,816m, 32°2'40.57"N, 98°49'3.07"E) and neighboring Peak 5,680m. Sejong was labeled Nobyugya on Chinese maps, but this was a mistake, subsequently confirmed by the local survey office.

In August, Fu returned with Cao Xinyue and approached the west side of these peaks via the Yehualing Valley, west of Zhuqing. They established a 4,850m camp at the base of the east fork of the glacier and on August 31 set off for the west face of Peak 5,680m. The upper section of the glacier was badly crevassed.

After a pitch of AI3 to get established on the ice face, the two climbed four or five pitches before meeting a wide crevasse that seemed endless in both directions and only crossed by fragile snow bridges. They flew a drone to see if there was a feasible way through but found none and retreated to camp and Zhuqing.

On September 3, they headed back to the 4,850m camp, this time with Sejong as their goal. The next day, they reached the far left side of the west face of Sejong and started up rocky terrain that was loose, with a section of 5.10. They descended and instead went straight up a north-northwest-facing ice couloir to the left. As it was near the end of the rainy season, the ice was thin and poor, but after 300m the angle eased. At 4:30 p.m., they were hit by a strong hailstorm. The two continued until Cao found a crevasse for a sheltered but uncomfortable bivouac. The following morning, after two hours of climbing through mist, they reached the exposed summit ridge and continued along the steep flanks and over a subsidiary top to the main summit.

To descend, they retraced their steps a short distance along the ridge and then dropped directly down the west face in a snow/ice couloir. Eleven rappels, with some sections exposed to rockfall due to the strong afternoon sunshine, took them to the upper glacier. They regained camp a little before dark.

Their ascent to the summit ridge had involved around 900m of climbing at AI3 60° snow.

—**Xia Zhongming**, *Germany*

YINHAIZI, FIRST ASCENT VIA SOUTH SPUR

The large rock peak of Yinhaizi (5,388m, 29°52'25.77"N, 101°52'12.18"E) is located due north of Xiao Gongga and Melcyr Shan, but on the opposite side of the main Riwoche Valley. From the usual trekking route along the Riwoche, the mountain is hidden by foreground peaks. While climbing Reddomain, Chinese climber Hua Feng saw Yinhaizi and noted its broad south face. Later, he learned that the mountain had been attempted in 2008 from the southeast, but the party had given up at 5,050m due to lack of suitable equipment.

On September 10, Hua Feng, his wife, Sun Jing, and photographer Xia Ti arrived in Kangding, to the north of the range, and over two days of acclimatization they used a drone to pinpoint the best position for a camp below Yinhaizi's south face. A good weather window was predicted from the 13th to the 15th, so they hiked toward the mountain and established a camp at 4,550m.

Next day, the 14th, they ascended scree to the foot of the broad south spur at 4,750m. Above rose three groove lines, and they chose the one on the left, first climbing three straightforward pitches (5.7/5.8) and then another eight pitches that were fairly sustained at around 5.10a/b, with a crux of 5.11a. They

Yinhaizi from the southeast, showing the first ascent by the south spur. The team rappelled the face to the right of the ascent line. *Xia Ti*

The Pot Carrier on the west face of Peak 5,800m, the first ascent of the mountain. The snowy summit to the right is Peak 5,804m. *He Lang*

bivouacked on a scree ledge at 5,000m.

In the morning, two slabby pitches of 5.10b/c, followed by a couple of easier rope lengths, brought them to a snow patch where they were able to replenish their water supply. The seventh pitch that day was 5.11a. After that, they were hit by a hailstorm. Hua slipped twice on a pitch that in dry conditions would probably be 5.9. They bivouacked at 5,250m.

It snowed heavily that night, but the next day was better. The team progressed up wet, snowy rock in sunshine, making slow progress. After four pitches, with a crux of 5.11a, and four hours of climbing, they were on top.

To descend, the three chose to rappel straight down the southeast face. After 11 rappels to the scree, two hours of walking took them down to camp. The 600m route (800m of climbing or 25 pitches) was graded TD 5.11a 70°.

—**Xia Zhongming,** *Germany*

MINYA KONKA RANGE, PEAK 5,800M, WEST FACE

In August, Liu Yang, Song Yuancheng, and I made the first ascent of an unnamed peak of 5,800m at 29°48'19.10"N, 101°54'18.88"E. It is a northwestern extension of the Ueba Group, situated northeast across the Tshiburongi Glacier from Xiao Gongga (Little Konka).

We spent two days hiking southeast up the Tshiburongi Glacier to place Camp 1 at 4,860m. The next day we scoped the route and acclimatized.

Setting off on the morning of August 8, we moved mostly unroped or simul-climbing up the first half of the west face. Despite being slowed by a rain and snow storm, we reached 5,700m and bivouacked on a rock ledge. While cooking, Yang accidentally dropped the pot down the wall, and from then on we had to climb without water. For this reason, the team eventually named the route The Pot Carrier (Chinese slang for "scapegoat").

The first pitch after the bivouac proved to be the crux: Yang took an hour to complete this 30m section, crossing a difficult slab; the nighttime snow had melted and then refrozen to form thin ice over the rock. Two pitches of mixed climbing led to the icefield between Peak 5,800m and Peak 5,804m to its right. We crossed a short snow slope and reached the summit ridge. Traversing the north side of the ridge, we made it to the top at 1 p.m. Our 900m route was graded TD 5.8 M6, and all team members climbed free.

After a short celebration, we descended the route. On the very first rappel, rockfall

Liu Yang overcoming
icy rock to climb the
crux of The Pot Carrier
on the west face of
Peak 5,800m in the
Minya Konka Range.
He Lang

cut part of the rope; we tied the cut sections together with a butterfly knot, but now we had to pass the knot on each rappel. After three pitches of downclimbing and 12 rappels, we reached our camp on the glacier at midnight. It had been a long day's climbing without any water, but the first ascent was well worth it.

—He Lang, *China*

XIAO GONGGA, NORTH AND NORTHEAST FACES, FU YAO

In October 2022, Wang Yongpeng and Zhang Xinyi (China) climbed a new route on the north and northeast faces of Xiao Gongga (a.k.a. Tshiburongi or Little Konka, 5,928m).

The two set up camp at 4,500m, north of the peak, near the entrance to the Xiao Gongga/Tshiburongi Glacier. On October 20, they left this camp at 8:30 a.m. in clear but windy weather. After a couple of hours of approach, they climbed three pitches up the lower section of the north face before turning left toward the northeast face. The climbing involved snow-covered rock, where protection was difficult to place.

After reaching the glacial plateau, Zhang broke trail to the bergschrund, where, at 5 p.m. and at an altitude of 5,450m, the two dug one meter down in deep snow to create a bivouac site.

Next day they began at 6 a.m., climbing a thinly snow-covered ice slope on the steep northeast face. At mid-day they reached the crux at around 5,800m: a rock wall covered with minimal snow or just a few millimeters of ice. It was Wang's lead, and he opted to smoke a cigarette while weighing the options before the scary lead.

One hundred meters from the top of the face, the difficulty eased, though there was arduous work through thigh-deep snow to reach the summit at just after 4 p.m. The two descended the northwest ridge, finally reaching their camp on the glacier at 1 p.m. on the 23rd. They named the route Fu Yao (D M4 AI3 70°).

Xiao Gongga, showing (1) Fu Yao (2023) on the north and northeast faces and (2) Russian Style (2022) on the north face. The northwest ridge, descended in 2023, is the right skyline. *Vittorio Messini*

Before this ascent, Xiao Gongga had probably been climbed around ten times. Between mid-October and late November 2022, there were at least five ascents (of which two were new routes), and in 2023 it was climbed multiple times by guides with clients. In the last few years, there has been a surge of guided ascents in the Minya Konka Range, notably on peaks such as Reddomain, Longemain, and Taishan.

—Lindsay Griffin, *with information from Zhu Leibo and 8264.com*

JIAZI, WEST FACE, REBIRTH

On November 3, Tong Zhanghao and Wang Yongpeng completed a new route toward the left side of the west face of Jiazi (6,540m). They had both tried the route in 2022 but retreated from 5,600m.

Earlier, while climbing nearby Xiao Gongga (Little Konka, 5,928m), they noticed Jiazi had three tops along its summit ridge. Intrigued by this, they investigated reports on the various ascents of Jiazi and found there were two small tops toward the north end of the summit ridge, above the left end of its west face, that had never been reached. This led to their 2022 attempt on the face, left of the Chinese lines Judgment and Liberal Dance and the 1982 American route.

ABOVE: Rebirth, the 2023 route on the left side of the west face of Jiazi. The left skyline is the northwest ridge, attempted to 6,100m in 1981. For other routes on the face, see AAJs 2023 and 2012. *Pascal Trividic*

RIGHT: During the first ascent of Rebirth on the west face of Jiazi. *Tong Zhanghao and Wang Yongpeng*

In 2023, the team arrived in October but had to wait nine days below the face in bad weather before they could start climbing at 6 a.m. on November 1. They immediately found very steep mixed ground, with rock that was often loose.

That first day they reached 5,850m on the large snow/ice field that characterizes the central part of this face. After working for 40 minutes, they managed to excavate a platform 40cm wide for an uncomfortable bivouac, hanging from the ropes while being frequently covered by drifting snow. In this half-seated position, they quickly became wet, and Wang adopted the unusual strategy of sleeping in a kneeling position with his butt in the air, in order to minimize his body's contact with the wet snow.

Next morning, they didn't set off until 10 a.m. That day was mostly alpine ice with just a few sections of mixed. At 6,200m they were able to clear a long platform below a rocky barrier for a bivouac. As there was no spindrift that night, they slept well.

Starting to melt water at 5 a.m., they were away by 7 a.m., slanting up right over alpine ice and through the last rock barrier to the final icefield. The climbers' extremities were now sore from the cold

and continuous ice climbing.

They reached the summit ridge at a little after 1:30 p.m., only to find that the entire north–south ridge of Jiazi was composed of unstable snow mushrooms. They were gingerly positioned on a large mushroom that formed one of the north summits and were so concerned about getting down that they forgot to take a summit selfie. [*Editor's Note: The ascent described here finished on a top of approximately 6,460m near the far north end of Jiazi's long summit ridge. This appears to be farther north than Jiazi's highest point, which generally has been called the north summit; the peak's highest point is actually the southerly of two adjacent tops separated by a difficult saddle.*]

It took seven hours to make 26 rappels down the route. Back in town, sleeping in a hotel, everything seemed so novel and beautiful they felt they had been reborn. The two therefore decided to name their route Rebirth (1,400m, TD+ AI4 M6 70° snow).

The pair was supported by the Chinese equipment manufacturer and retailer Kailas through its China Unclimbed Peaks Plan. This project was launched in 2006, in part to establish a "complete mountain database," and through 2023 the project had supported the ascents of 51 new routes and previously unclimbed peaks.

—**Lindsay Griffin,**
with information from Tong Zhanghao
and Zhu Leibo, China

CORRECTIONS ON 2004 JIAZI-AREA REPORT: A British expedition's report on this area in *AAJ 2005* mistakenly described the team attempting "Xiao Pangwa" and neighboring "Da Pangwa," which in fact were Melcyr Shan and Peak 5,630m. (Neither of the names used by the British team exists on maps.) Confused by the local geography, the team actually climbed a southeast-facing couloir rising to the east-southeast ridge of the much higher Jiazi, reaching around 5,500m before retreating. 📖 📷

—*Information from Zhu Leibo, China*

SICHUAN | Tatsienlu Massif

YIPINGFENG AND ERPINGFENG, FIRST ASCENTS

During the first modern survey of the Tatsienlu Massif, led by Arnold Heim in the 1930s, nine major peaks were named. Prior to 2023, seven had been summited, leaving only Yipingfeng (5,800m, 30°1'3.73"N, 102°2'27.81"E) and neighboring Erpingfeng (5,880m) at the north end of the range. Yipingfeng and Erpingfeng simply mean "first peak" and "second peak." According to the Chinese military map, Erpingfeng is named Bijia Shan—a *bijia* is a traditional stationery item that holds the Chinese brush and is often shaped like a mountain skyline.

Liu Yang, Xia Pei, and I traveled to Kangding city at the end of September, aiming to make first ascents of both Yipingfeng and Erpingfeng. We established base camp alongside a beautiful alpine lake at about 4,200m. From there, we concluded that the west face of Erpingfeng was threatened by seracs, so we decided to climb Yipingfeng

first, then traverse the ridge to Erpingfeng.

On October 1, we hiked to the base of Yipingfeng's west face, where we spent some time searching for a feasible route. The face was either too steep or too dangerous; a detour to the north face might be the only chance. The only knowledge we had of this side of the mountain was a blurry picture that showed less than half the face.

After a sleepless bivouac, where we were nearly hit by rockfall, we crossed a 5,300m col on the northwest ridge, then descended the far side to a small glacier at 5,150m. From here, we tried to traverse to the center of the face. Blocked by cliffs, we were forced to turn back and climb rock nearer to the northwest ridge.

After another sleepless bivouac at 5,420m, we traversed left across the north face to the right edge of the overhanging seracs below the summit. A steep snow and ice gully next to the seracs brought us to the northwest ridge and the summit.

Descending Yipingfeng's south ridge was a real challenge. After three hours, we still could not see the col below, so we made our third bivouac, at around 5,600m on the ridge. That night we slept far better. On the 4th, we continued down the

ridge via rappelling and traversing along the crest, with boulder-problem steps. We arrived at the col around noon. The wind was now so strong that one of our rappel ropes blew over the far side of the col and got stuck—we retrieved only half of it. On the plus side, the cold wind had firmed up the snow on Erpingfeng's north ridge, allowing us to climb 300m to its summit in less than an hour.

Quickly regaining the col, we began to rappel the west face. We tried rappelling with our intact 50m rope, but needed more length. Adding the second rope meant we each had to pass the knot. Pei was hit by rockfall and was fortunate to survive. We finally touched down on the glacier at 10 p.m.

We reached Kangding on the 5th, just before the arrival of heavy rain. What luck! We named our ascent One Last Piece of the Puzzle (total of 1,300m, TD+ 5.9 R AI3 55° snow). Now all nine major peaks of the massif have been climbed. 📷

—He Lang, *China*

SICHUAN | Qonglai Mountains

CHUANSHAN CAVE, FIRST ASCENT VIA SOUTHWEST RIDGE

The Jiesi Valley is a little to the west of the Siguniang Range, and at the head of one of the upper branches stands Peak 5,300m (31°22'10.69"N, 102°41'4.25"E). The southeast ridge is characterized by a large hole through the mountain, giving the peak the local name Chuanshan Cave. In November 2022, Li Zongli, Zhang Yagou, and Zhao Congbiao planned to make the first ascent.

Their intention was to climb an obvious mixed line on the right side of the south face, leading directly to the hole, and then onward to the summit. However, after setting up camp below the south face, they had doubts about passing the hole, so they opted for the southwest ridge, which appeared more straightforward.

Leaving camp just after 4 a.m. on November 6, the three slanted left up the lower south face to gain the ridge, which they found to be exposed and narrow, but reasonably well protected. Higher, the terrain became very loose and more snow covered. Rockfall cut through the rope, leaving it 20m shorter. It took 12 hours to reach the summit, which they measured at 5,296m. The 600m route was graded D+ 5.10a M3 80°.

Fearing rope jams while rappelling the ridge, the team opted to descend the south face, which they accomplished with 12 rappels. They returned to camp 18 hours after setting out. 📷

—**Lindsay Griffin**, *with help from Zhu Leibo, China*

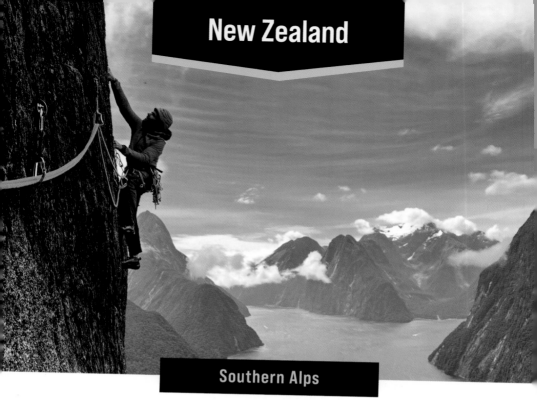

New Zealand

Southern Alps

2023 CLIMBING SUMMARY

The austral summer of 2022/2023 started off with the first ascent of a route 30 years in the making. Situated on a sun-drenched north-facing wall in the Wilkin Valley near Wanaka, The Dark Side of the Moon (305m, 26/5.12c) climbs 13 pitches of compact schist and was climbed free by Rike Andree and Jochen Lenfert. Attempted by Allan Uren and Clinton Bevan in 1992, it sat dormant until 2021, when Uren returned to try it again, this time with support from friends Steven Fortune, Milo Gilmour, Roberto Gomez-Sainz, and Tim Steward. Over the summer of 2021/2022, they cleaned and bolted the route before Andree and Lenfert teamed up to claim the first ascent in October 2022.

Ruari Macfarlane has been one of the most active alpine climbers in the country over recent years, often seeking the paths least traveled, and this year was no exception. Departing from the Lake Marian trailhead in the Hollyford Valley, Macfarlane and Gavin Lang set out to make the first continuous traverse of the Darran Mountains from south to north. Lang had to withdraw on the third day, but Macfarlane continued alone to Martins Bay, having completed the full traverse in ten days. In the process, he reached the summits of all the main peaks in the range, including (but not limited to) Mt. Christina (2,474m), Mt. Crosscut (2,263m), Mt. Patuki (2,246m), Mt. Madeline (2,536m), and Mt. Tutoko (2,723m). Midway through, he met up with Ben Mangan and Quinn Yates to climb a new route on the north ridge of Madeline. Drawbridge Arête (400m, 18/5.10a) climbs from the prominent notch at the base of the ridgeline up to the 2,516m foresummit.

Macfarlane then teamed up with Troy Forsyth to complete the first traverse of the Banks Range from west to east over a four-day period. These peaks are located at the head of the Copland Valley in Westland Tai Poutini National Park, near the Main Divide and Aoraki/Mt. Cook National Park. During this outing, they completed new routes on the west faces of Sibyl Peak (2,411m) and Mt. Unicorn (2,557m). The west face of Sibyl was climbed in ten pitches at 15/5.7, while the west face of Unicorn provided The Secret of the Unicorn, with eight pitches up to 17/5.9.

Moving north again to the Cloudy Peak Range (a small range that runs perpendicular to the Main Divide in the Canterbury region), Grant Piper continued with his recent new route development on the western aspects of Cloudy Peak (2,403m). He teamed up with Kate Bailue, Kevin Barratt, Cliff Ellery, Bernard Frankpitt, and Richard Kimberly to equip and climb Sharp Shooter (350m, 22/5.11c) up the center of the Hourglass Wall, using a mix of gear and bolts. There are a number of existing routes on the wall, and Sharp Shooter is between Unbeliever (McLeod-Dickson, 1992) and Mission Impossible (Beare-Main, 1981).

With the onset of winter, the number of people venturing into the alpine dwindled. But those who persevered with the fickle weather and conditions at the annual Darrans Winter Meet in July were handsomely rewarded. The highlight was a new line on the east face of Flat Top Peak (2,282m), climbed solo by Ben Dare. Apparition (1,100m, 6+, VI) follows the prominent gully line up the center of the face before angling right through the upper headwall to reach the summit just left of Soulfly (Dare, 2021).

Among the lofty summits of Aoraki/Mt. Cook National Park, Sam Smoothy continued with his quest to ski all 24 of New Zealand's 3,000m peaks. Smoothy linked up with Will Rowntree and Jim Ryan on October 20, and the trio claimed the first ski descent of the east face of Malte Brun (3,199m), the sixth-highest peak in the country.

As temperatures rose with the arrival of summer, Daniel Joll returned for his annual pilgrimage to the Airport Wall near Milford Sound in the deep south. He paired up with Llewellyn Murdoch to make the first ascent of Adventure Tourism (405m, 27/5.12d), the third new line established by Joll on the wall in recent years, following Mile High Club (2020) and Dream Liner (2021). Climbed in 14 pitches, Adventure Tourism starts on the first three pitches of Dream Liner before ascending a rising, left-trending traverse for six new pitches to finish up the final five pitches of Mile High Club.

During the same period, farther north, Macfarlane and Keith Riley ventured around to the seldom-visited northern aspects of Mt. Brewster (2,516m) to make the first ascent of the north face via the Central Rib (650m, 16/5.8). About 350m of this was climbed up the rock rib itself, before a further 300m up snowfields and easy scrambling took them to the summit. 📷

—**Ben Dare,** *New Zealand*

TOP: Will Rowntree starts into the first crux on the ski descent of the east face of Malte Brun, a tight choke with heady exposure. *Jasper Gibson*

BOTTOM: Sam Smoothy scopes the spine panel crux on Malte Brun from a lofty perch. *Sam Smoothy*

FACING PAGE: Daniel Joll on Adventure Tourism, a new 14-pitch link-up on the Airport Wall near Milford Sound. *Llewellyn Murdoch*

Many of these tributes have been edited for length. The complete text and additional photos, along with an In Memoriam tribute to David McGivern, are at the AAJ website: *publications.americanalpineclub.org.*

AIMEE BARNES, 1962 – 2023

Losing Aimee Barnes after a long chase by cancer has left a gaping hole in the vast fabric of her friends and family. It's a hole that can't be darned or patched, so we do our best by decorating around the edges and calling into the void to see if there's an echo or her familiar heart-warming cackle coming back. We whisper to her about routes she recommended and beta that panned out, and we struggle against the urge to call her up for advice and encouragement. The climbing and mountain-guide community has lost a titan, a tenacious mentor, and a friend.

Aimee started rock climbing in 1980 and was soon an outdoor trip leader at Idaho State University and the usual winner of the Pocatello Pump. After school, she became a rare female professional guide in the male-dominated worlds of climbing and skiing in the 1980s and 1990s. She started working for Sawtooth Mountain Guides in 1985, and in 1998 she began guiding for Jackson Hole Mountain Guides, where she spent most of her career, ending up as lead guide and director of the Moab branch. Aimee was a member of the 1990 U.S. women's climbing team and also worked for a time for Black Diamond Equipment, initiating their pro purchase program. She had started skiing at age five, which eventually led to work as a backcountry guide at Jackson Hole Mountain Resort as well as guiding heli-skiing in Valdez, Alaska, where she met her husband, Jimbo Collins.

Aimee traveled, climbed, and skied throughout the world, taking part in ski descents in South America, climbs in Asia and South America, and adventures across Bhutan. In Utah and at the City of Rocks, Idaho, she participated in first ascents of dozens of classic routes.

The landscapes that Aimee floated through—the splitter cracks around Moab, the mysterious canyons of the Colorado River, the ridgelines of the Tetons, and the bottomless snow of the Chugach—forged an individual with deep respect for history, the beauty of the natural world, and the ability to work with a significant amount of uncertainty. She called her job "blue collar" and embraced it all with an incredible sense of adventure. Aimee lived out her values and made ample room for her friends, family, colleagues, clients, and so many budding climbers and skiers to thrive.

Aimee grew up with seven sisters of her own and as an adult forged a bond with at least another hundred through what she called the "sisterhood of the rope." Tying

GREG VON DOERSTEN

in with Aimee, physically or emotionally, meant you were guaranteed a friend who was going to be a powerful force in your life. In her own under-the-radar way, Aimee carved a path for so many, connecting us to one another for a climb or a job, sharing beta for an adventure, calling just to catch up or answering the phone when we needed advice, or even through giving us a flat parking spot to sleep for a night, a week, or maybe an entire season. Aimee's generous spirit built a road for us all to travel a little bit easier, and in gratitude.

Scores of Aimee's friends attended a memorial in Jackson, Wyoming, where this apt poem by Rupi Kaur was shared: "i stand / on the sacrifices / of a million women before me / thinking / *what can i do / to make this mountain taller / so the women after me / can see farther.*"

—**Eve Tallman and Izzy Lazarus**

THOMAS F. HORNBEIN, 1930 – 2023

I grew up in Ohio, where there are no mountains, but my parents made the mistake of subscribing to *National Geographic*. There were a number of things in that publication that piqued my ten-year-old mind, one of which was the mountains of the world. I clearly remember reading about the 1960–61 Silver Hut Expedition in Nepal, which studied the physiology of acclimatization, and the 1963 American expedition to Everest.

Tom Hornbein also grew up in the Midwest, in St. Louis. There were no mountains, just the family rooftop and trees in his yard. But Tom's parents made the mistake of sending him as a teenager to a summer camp in Estes Park, Colorado, where he became obsessed with mountains.

Little did our parents know how those boyhood exposures would shape our lives.

I am not going to recount Tom's personal, academic, or mountaineering life in detail. It has been eloquently described in a number of tributes and biographies. In some ways, Tom's life became a legend as he lived it.

Suffice it to say that Tom's mountaineering history grew from Estes Park, where, as a scrawny teenager and with great passion, he scaled challenging new routes on the surrounding crags and in Rocky Mountain National Park. Without losing a beat in his climbing, he switched his studies from geology at the University of Colorado in Boulder to medicine at Washington University in St. Louis, where he became immersed in the field of anesthesiology. In his spare time, he went to Masherbrum in 1960 (the expedition made the first ascent) and then, in 1963, finagled an early exit from the Navy to join the American Everest expedition, during which he and Willi Unsoeld sauntered up the West Ridge—a climb for the ages.

That climb defined Tom, who in the meantime was pursuing an academic medical career. He did not want to be known as the "doctor who climbed Everest," but he was. Over the years he eventually surrendered and carried the banner well, always downplaying the historic ascent but actually having pride in the event. He ascended to the chairmanship of the Department of Anesthesiology at the University of Washington and developed one of the premier departments in the country. I had read Tom's book about the Everest climb when I was in medical school in New York, and I became a passionate climber myself at the Shawangunks, but our paths didn't intersect until I started a residency and fellowship at the University of Washington, where I ended up spending most of my career.

When Tom and I met, he seemed to want to put me on belay. He mentored me in the neurophysiology of breathing, and we taught the respiratory physiology course side by side for 25 years. We eventually co-edited a 968-page book on altitude physiology: *High Altitude: An Exploration of Human Adaptation*. He would always bail me out when an astute medical student would ask a difficult question. In our free time, with a few friends and my kids, we spent as much time as possible in the mountains, scampering up climbs in the Cascades and joining two adventures in Yunnan Province in China in the late 1980s with Nick Clinch, Pete Schoening, and others, hoping to climb the highest peak in the Kang Karpo (Meili Xueshan) range.

In his legendary annual lecture to the second-year medical students, which I heard many times, Tom would spend the first hour teaching high-altitude physiology, and in the second hour he'd recount the 1963 West Ridge climb. Many graduates seemed to remember only one lecture throughout their entire medical school career—Tom's.

Yet I never felt in those talks that he was talking about himself. The Everest climb transcended him and all the climbers on that trip and dealt with more ethereal topics: (1) risk in the mountains, medicine, and life; (2) uncertainty as a motivating force to achieve vision and commitment; (3) focus on the simplicity of the goals to achieve success; and (4) the fellowship that generates a force bigger than its parts. The concept of "on belay" was never spoken but was always understood and present.

There are too many instances where Tom kept me on belay in my academic,

personal, and mountaineering lives to recount. He always listened, supported without reserve, but never directed. I and—I am sure—a multitude of friends, trainees, colleagues, and co-climbers felt the support of his rope that did not tether but allowed one to learn to lead in their own way.

Given who Tom was, should I have been in awe? Should I have wondered why he wanted to hang out with me? Maybe he took vicarious pleasure in my foibles and follies. Regardless of the answers, I never took our friendship for granted, and I felt lucky, but I also knew he would always be there, not asking anything in return, knowing that we always had each other on belay.

I was told that Tom had mellowed from his earlier days, but his insistence on excellence in writing that I did with him, in scientific goals, and in teaching never waned. Part of his mellowing may have come from the good fortune of marrying someone smarter than he was, Kathy Mikesell, a pediatrician, who was an elegant counterbalance to Tom's intensity. They raised a daughter, Melissa, now a successful environmental attorney with elements of both of them steering her life. They blended well with Tom's five older kids from his first wife, Gene Swartz.

The last few years, Tom was obsessed with his "not going to be here much longer." Although he was right, I just told him to be quiet because he was going to outlive me, and that he just needed to keep hiking up to wedding meadow (where his daughter Melissa got married), behind his house near Lumpy Ridge in Estes Park, in order to keep in shape. Although his mind stayed fit, he had a hard time accepting that his body wasn't keeping up.

As I write this, Tom has only been gone a short while, but I realize how much space in my mind he has occupied for more than 45 years, and that now I can't just call him to discuss, cajole, and laugh. When all is said and done, Tom was all of the things that his legend has engendered, but to me he was just Tom, my colleague, belay buddy, and friend.

—**Robert "Brownie" Schoene**

THE WEST RIDGE

AN APPRECIATION

By Sam Lowry

Here's what one most often hears about Tom Hornbein's book *Everest: The West Ridge*: (1) I read it when I was young, (2) it got me into climbing, (3) I've reread it multiple times, (4) I've tried to emulate its philosophy, and (5) it is one of the best mountaineering books ever written.

Like Salinger and Lee—names not chosen lightly in this context—Tom Hornbein left us with one great book. He did not aspire to literary achievement, was possibly a reluctant, conscripted author. But it was Hornbein's *mazel* to have been lead collaborator in not one but two World Heritage–level achievements: the daring 1963 West Ridge climb and the book.

Jon Krakauer (who read *West Ridge* at age 11) cites its prominence in his foreword to the 2013 edition. Hornbein's friend Jake Norton (who read it at 12) tells of his love for *West Ridge* in "The Passing of a Hero." My climbing partner Jeff told me on our last trip that *West Ridge* was his favorite climbing book—and it has always been mine. Since youth I've clung to Hornbein's book, with its photos, aphorisms, and that elegant font, as a storytelling icon, its language crystallizing experiences magnificent, beautiful, and deeply human. Asked what a writer's goal should be, a famous literary agent put it this way: "The quality of the work. The kind of ineffable beauty of something extremely well expressed."

Genetically, or in some St. Louis classroom, Hornbein got that memo. Hear the music in his passages: "May 1. Fresh eggs, chicken, even a can of beer that had somehow escaped prior consumption, then a bucket of warm water for a piecemeal bath in the morning sunshine..." ("Our Turn"); "As we traveled eastward across the grain of the country, blisters healed, muscles hardened, and even the sunburnt red of my balding brow took on a pain-free tan..." ("Wilderness"). Delighting in vocabulary, Hornbein introduced me to *bouldering, blusterous, brinkmanship, balaclava, bowline,* and *brunt.* I believe the respect he showed readers in his willingness to use expressive words and complex sentences is part of what captivated the youthful ones.

Three other things always stayed with me: his extensive use of dialogue, making each scene so actual; his reference to each climbing porter by name, never as "a Sherpa," so humanizing them; and a comparable fleshing out of the expedition's climbing scientists, lending gravitas, drama, and sometimes humor.

Count me finally among the fanboys who tracked Hornbein down to bask in his warm attention. I first tried, unsuccessfully, in 1971. (I'd fallen for his book the year before, at age 12.) When in 1998 I initiated an email correspondence, he blessed me: "You have the perseverance of a high-altitude mountaineer." In later emails, calls on May 22 and November 6 (his birthday), and in a personal visit to Estes Park in 2018, he appreciated hearing of his book's influence, chuckling that everything he'd written since seemed to be an obituary. He loved hearing that Jeff, my climbing partner, and I had finally realized in the eastern Sierra that we shared a youthful love for *The West Ridge.* Jeff, before he died, also in 2023, got to read Tom's words on the matter: "What a sweet update of wanderings of two preciously bonded wanderers, growing older. It resonates."

Tom, apostle of companionship, taught me to write. I will always say so.

LINDA CHAPLINSKY MCMILLAN, 1949 – 2023

Linda McMillan, loving wife and mother, and advocate for mountain preservation and primitive mountain recreation, passed away peacefully on May 14. Her last days were in Moab, Utah, surrounded by family, after a decade-long courageous battle against Alzheimer's disease. Throughout those challenging years, Linda maintained her cheerful, generous nature.

Linda was born and raised in Houston and graduated from the University of California, Berkeley, in 1972 with a B.A. in Latin American studies. She received an MBA from San Francisco State University in 1988. Linda loved adventure and was a gifted athlete. She was a surfer, sailor, and horseback rider during her youth, and in her mid-30s she became interested in rock climbing. The simple act of learning to climb in Yosemite Valley led her to devote the rest of her life to advocating for preserving the beauty of the mountains. She had a lasting impact on organizations and places she served, including the American Alpine Club (AAC), the International Mountaineering and Climbing Federation (UIAA), the International Union for Conservation of Nature (IUCN) WCPA Mountains Biome, the California Recreation Resource Advisory Committee, and various communities in the Sierra Nevada, Nepal, and elsewhere.

In her advocacy role, Linda worked to bring land managers, local communities, and climbers together to promote mountain stewardship. She was an internationally respected speaker on sustainable mountain practices and public partnerships. Her lifetime commitment to mountain advocacy was recognized with honors from the U.S. National Park Service, the National Parks Conservation Association, and the AAC, from which she received an Angelo Heilprin Citation for exemplary service in March 2003.

In 1997, when disastrous Yosemite

floods prompted National Park officials to consider relocating employee and visitor housing in a plan that would dramatically impact Camp 4, Linda was vice president of the AAC, and she played a pivotal role among a coalition of mountaineering and environmental groups that filed suit in federal court. Climbers rallied around their scruffy but historic patch of earth, and under Linda's wise leadership, "contention gave way to collaboration," as she later noted. In 2003, Camp 4 was placed on the National Register of Historic Places.

Linda was president of the Mountain Protection Commission of the UIAA from 2008 to 2016 (only the third woman to be president of a UIAA commission). She was instrumental in the creation of the Mountain Protection Award, which has become the UIAA's lighthouse project in sustainability and has made a significant difference in supporting climate- and conservation-led initiatives worldwide. Linda's work with the UIAA came with the additional benefit of allowing her to climb with international friends in Japan, Sweden, and South Africa.

Linda is survived by her loving husband of 35 years, Thomas Ian McMillan, who accompanied her on climbs in the U.S., the European Alps, northern Wales, Asia, and South America, as well as her son and daughter and two grandchildren.

—**Thomas I. McMillan**

THOMAS I. MCMILLAN

AMMON MCNEELY, 1970 – 2023

"**I would rather live** 40 years of excitement and fun and exhilarating and just *WOO* full volume than 80 years of la-di-da-di-da. You know...boring," Ammon McNeely said in 2006 while filming *El Cap Pirate*. "Why not get out there and live it?"

Loved by many for being rowdy, charming, encouraging, and a modern pirate, Ammon passed away on February 18, 2023, in Moab, Utah. With over 75 ascents of El Capitan, nearly two dozen speed records on big-wall routes in Yosemite Valley and in Zion National Park, and first ascents of hard aid climbs across the United States, Ammon made a huge impact on wall climbing. In addition to his innate boldness—and an extensive BASE jumping résumé—Ammon's friends and family remember the nearly six-foot man with the earrings, the narrow face, and the wide grin for his kindness, his support, and his ability to authentically and unapologetically be himself. Ammon lived a life of volume.

Ammon was the third of five kids and grew up in Saint George, Utah. "He almost killed himself every year of his life," said his older brother, Gabe. He started climbing young, scrambling up 5.6 routes in nearby Snow Canyon. Ammon's parents divorced when he was in high school, and he moved with his mother to Huntington Beach, California. He explored the climbing at Tahquitz, Suicide, and other crags of Southern California, largely teaching himself using John Long's how-to books. He bought a rope and shoes in 1995 and decided to become fully invested in the sport.

"He went up on the NA with nothing," Ammon's friend Kurt Arend said of Ammon's ten-day solo ascent of the North America Wall (VI 5.8 A2) in 1996. "I think he just had a couple sets of cams and a ton of pins. He didn't have a clue. He was just going for it." After summiting El Capitan, Ammon met the big-wall guru Chongo Chuck, who, in exchange for some Olde English and indica, taught him about hauling systems. Ammon moved into a tent in the woods behind Camp 4 and began raging the granite seas of Yosemite. He quickly became known as the El Cap Pirate, climbing routes that others had bailed on and flying his skull and crossbones on the side of El Cap.

"I wanted to hit El Capitan with all the force I could muster," Ammon wrote in *Alpinist* of an unmatched season of Yosemite wall climbing in 2004. "In all, I climbed 11 El Cap routes in five months, nine of them in record time, five as first one-day ascents."

"I can't say I ever saw him get scared," says Chris McNamara, one of Ammon's big-wall partners. "He's also just one of the biggest-hearted, nicest people." On Rodeo Queen (5.10 A4), Chris had a meltdown in the middle of the night, wanting to bail on a pitch. "You're going to feel a lot better if you finish this," Ammon said, aiming to help his friend make it through the difficulties.

Ammon started BASE jumping in January 2007, and he jumped many times off El Capitan, often narrowly escaping the rangers upon landing in the meadow below. Once, he got tased by rangers after jumping. Unfortunately, Ammon suffered a few accidents while BASE jumping, most seriously in September 2017, when he struck a wall in Moab. Among many injuries, Ammon severely damaged his right leg, resulting in amputation below the knee and a prosthetic leg. He continued to jump with a crew in Moab, climbing towers and jumping off.

Ammon worked many jobs over the years, including rigging, tandem BASE guiding, and working for Moab-area ballooning and zip-line companies. He continued to climb and put up new routes.

On February 18, Ammon, his partner, Sarah Watson, and a friend hiked to Hurrah Pass near Moab to watch the sunset. Watson stepped down onto a stone diving board, which had a 200-foot drop. As the sun dipped toward the horizon, Ammon tried to join her. Weighting his prosthetic incorrectly, Ammon lost his balance and fell to his death. He was 52.

—James Lucas

WILLIAM A. READ, 1936 – 2024

William "Al" Read, a.k.a. "The Great Yak" of Moose, Wyoming, passed away peacefully on January 15, 2024, in San Francisco from lung disease. His wife, Susan, and daughter, Kristen, were by his side. He was 87.

Al's childhood years were spent in Albuquerque, New Mexico, and he had many stories about traveling on horseback to the Navajo Reservation of northern New Mexico with his father, a respected paleobotanist and geologist who worked for the U.S. Geological Survey. After his parents divorced, he moved with his mother and stepfather to Denver. His years in Colorado introduced him to climbing and skiing. He graduated from the University of Colorado in Boulder and went on to graduate summa cum laude from Georgetown University with a master's degree in political science and international affairs.

In 1953 he was introduced to the Tetons on a road trip, and by 1958 he was working for Grand Teton National Park as a seasonal ranger and sharing a campsite with Bob "Chief" Dunnagan. Camp was not far from Guides' Hill, where Al met many of

the Exum guides. The following year, he joined Willi Unsoeld, Barry Corbet, Jake Breitenbach, Bob French, Ed Exum, and Sterling Neale as a guide. He eventually earned the title of chief guide, and years later, in 1978, Al, Peter Lev, Rod Newcomb, and Dean Moore purchased the guide concession and continued the Glenn Exum legacy, employing some of climbing's most well-known and accomplished mountaineers. He was president of the renowned company for 20 years.

Exum guide Armando Menocal articulated Al's philosophy: "He loved and cared about Exum, the guides, and the staff. He managed to instill that attitude and respect in each of us, the idea being, 'It's your client's day of climbing, not yours. You climb what clients will enjoy, not routes you think are more fun or want to try.'"

In 1963, along with Lev, Newcomb, and Fred Wright, Al drove from Jackson Hole to Alaska to join Jed Williamson and Warren Blesser for the first ascent of the East Buttress of Denali. He also achieved numerous first ascents in the Tetons, most notably perhaps the Enclosure Ice Couloir on the Grand Teton.

Al was a ski instructor at Badger Pass near Yosemite in the winter of 1967 and the following year joined the ski patrol at Vail in Colorado. Summers were spent guiding and climbing in the Tetons and gaining the skills and experience to pursue climbing expeditions in far-flung ranges such as the Himalaya.

When Boyd Everett Jr. organized the 1969 American Dhaulagiri expedition, Al was named deputy leader. They attempted the difficult southeast ridge, and high on the mountain, at 15,000 feet, Al suffered from serious altitude sickness. Jim Morrissey, the team doctor and a lifelong friend, initiated emergency care, including having Al carried to lower elevation, which saved his life and, in an odd twist of fate, Jim's life as well. Seven of the expedition members forged on, and an avalanche swept all but one of them, Lou Reichardt, off the mountain.

Pursuing his lifelong passion for foreign affairs, Al chose to be a Foreign Service Officer and was accepted to the elite ranks in 1970. He was extremely proud to have graduated second in the CIA's Career Training Program. In June 1971, in Moose, Wyoming, Al married Jennifer Thomas, whom he had met in Kathmandu before departing for Dhaulagiri. The agency then posted him to Calcutta, India, and later to Kathmandu, Nepal, which would become home for 13 years. He stayed with the embassy there for three years, but eventually quit the Foreign Service so he could keep returning to the Tetons during the summers.

Al became the managing director of Mountain Travel Nepal, developing trekking, tourism, and expedition support, as well as creating the first river rafting company in Nepal, Himalayan River Expeditions (HRE), with Mike Yager, a friend from Jackson Hole.

Kristen Annapurna Read was born in December of 1974 in Kathmandu. The Read house served as a staging area for many expeditions, with Al acting as deputy leader or base camp manager for several of them. He also organized some of the first trips by foreigners to Tibet, and in 1986 served as base camp manager for an expedition to Everest's north ridge.

In 1982, Al helped to establish InnerAsia, a San Francisco–based travel company that later became Geographic Expeditions, a.k.a. GeoEx. His unique experience and zest for adventure helped Al craft exotic itineraries to far-flung destinations the world over, including repeating Shackleton's crossing of South Georgia Island and early tourist trips to Bhutan, China, Tibet, Pakistan, Russia, Mongolia, Turkmenistan, and Patagonia, to name only a few.

Al and Jennifer separated in 1984, and three years later, he married Susan Grossnickle, with whom he shared life for 37 years. In his later years, they were the envy of many by somehow managing to split time between Jackson Hole, Wyoming; Chamonix, France; Bariloche, Argentina; and Marin, California.

Al will be most fondly remembered as a leader and a mentor. He enjoyed supporting colleagues to reach their highest potential. He loved sharing his passion for mountains and adventure with all, and his cabin door was always open during the summer months at Lupine Meadows. Now, Al is among good company in the halls of Valhalla and is no doubt raising a glass with great friends and legends, telling tales of exploration and adventure in the remote mountains of the world.

—**Kristen (Read) Tripp**

AUDREY SALKELD, 1936 – 2023

Less than a year before the 100th anniversary of the legendary Everest expedition of Mallory and Irvine, the passing of mountaineering historian Audrey Salkeld severed a vital link with the pioneer climbers.

Born in London in 1936, she could still recall visiting a lecture by Frank Smythe, another luminary from the pre–World War II Everest expeditions, as a teen, and "falling in love with the blonde mountaineer." Later she became acquainted like no other with the files of the Mount Everest Committee at the Royal Geographical Society, the main trove of information about the first

within reach

attempts on the mountain. She became friends with the last two surviving British members of the 1924 expedition, Noel Odell and Captain John Noel, and preserved many of their recollections in her books and on film.

Audrey's research became the foundation for Walt Unsworth's seminal *Everest: The Mountaineering History*, and she put the everlasting enigma of Mallory and Irvine's disappearance back into the public eye with her own book, *The Mystery of Mallory and Irvine*, co-authored with American researcher Tom Holzel. The two were also behind the first organized search for Mallory and Irvine, in 1986, which, although unsuccessful, allowed Audrey to realize her dream of visiting Everest, climbing as high as advanced base camp at 21,000 feet. She had previously gained some rock climbing experience as a member of the informal "Tuesday Climbing Club" in London and remained an avid mountain traveler, later summiting Kilimanjaro.

Her prime motivation as a writer was the human side of mountaineering—why are people drawn to the mountains? What do they experience? How are they shaped by the experience? Her approach, paired with a natural and infectious curiosity, provided Audrey with an inside and outside view of climbers, reflected by the broad scope of subjects in her regular "People" column for *Mountain*

magazine. In addition to writing her own books, including the 1996 winner of the Boardman Tasker Award, *A Portrait of Leni Riefenstahl*, she edited a highly readable compendium of mountain fiction, translated books by Reinhold Messner and Kurt Diemberger, scripted films for Leo Dickinson, and assisted novelist Jeffrey Archer with his fictional account of Mallory's life, *Paths of Glory*.

Audrey's work on Everest and Mallory also would change my life.

I read *The Mystery of Mallory and Irvine* as a 16-year-old in late 1987, and I was hooked immediately, irrevocably. Audrey was among the first to answer the many questions that came up in my own Everest research. Her second book, *People in High Places*, an insightful travelogue of her journeys to Everest and Mustang, became almost a blueprint for my own way to Everest with the 1999 Mallory and Irvine research expedition [*during which Mallory's body was discovered at 26,760 feet on Everest*]. In the challenging times before and after that ultimate encounter with Everest history, Audrey remained a calming voice of reason, staying mostly above any controversies and providing comfort, support, and advice.

In the years that followed, my wife, Sandra, and I visited Audrey and her beloved husband, Peter, a couple of times at their beautiful cottage near Penrith, on the edge of England's Lake District. I last met her at the Alpine Club in London for the 25th anniversary of the 1988 Kangshung Face climb, and it was comforting to see her so welcomed and respected even among climbers of younger generations. I felt sad when I saw her extensive library going up for sale a few years ago—a sure sign that Audrey's health was in decline—and I like to think that some of her spirit gets redistributed with her books across the world.

With Audrey's passing, it feels as if an era in Everest history is about to die out—and with it, perhaps, a certain quality of climbing journalism. In a time when historical amnesia has become widespread, when the need for new "firsts" and records has led to subconscious or even deliberate ignorance of past achievements, someone with an encyclopedic knowledge like hers will be sorely missed. But for me, and I would guess many others, her dedication as a journalist and historian, and above all her kindness, generosity, and integrity as a person, will never be forgotten and will remain an inspiration.

—**Jochen Hemmleb**

ALLEN STECK, 1926 – 2023

Allen Steck was one of the most accomplished and influential American climbers of the 20th century. His long, visionary, and diverse career spanned all types of terrain, literature, and equipment and business innovations. Most American climbers (including the more famous Yosemite figures who followed) benefited from the foundation he built.

A lifelong resident of California's Bay Area, Steck enjoyed his first peak, climbing the east ridge of Mt. Maclure in Yosemite National Park, with his older brother, George. Learning climbing techniques with the Berkeley section of the Sierra Club, Steck spent two formative seasons in Yosemite before visiting Europe in the summer of 1949. There his horizons broadened by climbing classic routes with Karl Lugmayer in the Dolomites, including likely the first American ascent of the north face of the Cima Grande.

Steck returned to California for a marquee 1950 season, starting with the first ascent of Castle Rock Spire in Sequoia National Park, then the oft-tried north face of Sentinel Rock in Yosemite Valley with John Salathé. This notable climb took four days and is still a testpiece of chimneys and offwidths for aspiring Yosemite climbers.

Steck's aspirations transcended pure rock faces and drew him to classic lines on big mountains. An avid skier, he survived an avalanche near Lake Tahoe

and completed the first winter ascent of Clyde Minaret near Mammoth Lakes. Five weeks after completing the Steck-Salathé, he traveled to Canada's Mt. Waddington and nearby peaks, where he participated in several first ascents. In Peru's Cordillera Blanca, in 1952, he checked off several long routes, most notably an alpine-style first ascent of Huandoy East.

After this auspicious beginning, Steck stayed close to home, busy with his 1952 marriage to Cyla and the arrival of two children, Lee and Sara. He signed on as manager of the Ski Hut shop in Berkeley, which became a center of the nascent climbing community in the 1950s. Here he designed sleeping bag and shell clothing innovations for the Trailwise brand and hired Steve Roper, future climbing partner and editor on literary projects.

Around 1963, the mountains beckoned again. The trio of Steck, Dick Long, and John Evans completed the first ascent of the Grand Traverse in the Tetons in a day from south to north, setting the stage for their next great objective, the Hummingbird Ridge on Canada's Mt. Logan. In 1965, a party of six, led by Long and Steck, launched up the huge ridge, which stretched six miles and gained 14,000 feet in elevation. Their most important climbing tool was a drilled-out steel shovel that allowed them to excavate steps quickly and traverse the corniced, narrow spine connecting to Mt. Logan's main mass. They hunkered down at Camp 2 for a week, with the cornice they camped on collapsing the day after they left. After 37 days, their topographic commitment and commitment to one another won the summit. Hummingbird Ridge, the largest route in the Western Hemisphere, has never been repeated in its original form.

The desperate undertaking only whetted Steck's appetite for adventure. He followed Hummingbird with the third ascent (and the first non-Robbins ascent) of the Salathé Wall, in 1966, with Long and Roper. Long lugged up a Super 8 movie camera, and the ensuing film is a priceless piece of climbing history. It shows Roper laybacking the Hollow Flake, with no protection for 40 feet, wearing stiff Spider Kletterschuhe boots.

The same year, Steck and Roper approached David Brower of the Sierra Club about publishing a literary journal dedicated to the art of climbing, as opposed to pitch-by-pitch accounts. Brower eventually agreed and *Ascent* was born. It became arguably the world's most highly respected climbing publication, prompting climber writers to plumb the intensity of their experiences for literary craft. The journal evolved for over 30 years until 1999, when Steck and Roper relinquished editorial oversight.

In 1968, Steck and Leo Le Bon started Mountain Travel, America's first adventure travel company. A citizen of the world, Steck guided Illiniza, Cotopaxi, and Chimborazo in Ecuador and Aconcagua in Argentina. Subsequent Mountain Travel trips took him to China, Tibet, Nepal, Greece, and various other foreign destinations. Other expeditions on his résumé include a 1954 expedition to Makalu, a 1976 trip with the Pakistani army up Paiju Peak in Pakistan, and a 1974 ascent of Peak Lenin in the USSR, where an avalanche buried Steck. His compatriots exhumed him, once again.

His contemporaries took notice of his accomplishments. Jointly with Norman Clyde, he was the first recipient of the Sierra Club's Francis P. Farquhar Mountaineering Award in 1970.

In 1978, a watershed year, Steck sold his interest in Mountain Travel and divorced. He devoted time to writing and editing *Fifty Classic Climbs of North America*, co-authored with Steve Roper and published by Sierra Club Books. When asked years later if he would change any of the climbs, he said, "If anyone complains about them, they can pick their own 50. I hope they do." In 1995, Steck and Roper won the AAC's Literary Award.

Never interested in esoteric climbing debates or personal aggrandizement, Steck joyfully spent his years in the mountains focusing on the climbing. For example, on the Paiju Peak expedition, Steck served in an advisory capacity to the Pakistani team and insisted they summit the peak before him and receive credit for the first ascent.

After retiring, Steck continued to pursue adventurous trips, such as an 82-day expedition through the Grand Canyon with his brother George in 1983. He was the ringleader of a series of climbing trips affectionately called "Golden Gatherings." Including the usual suspects such as Roper, Joe Kelsey, Joe Fitschen, John Thackray, Chris Jones, Eric Beck, and assorted hangers-on, the tribe of elders converged for a week at locations such as Joshua Tree or Owens River Gorge. Evenings were filled with grilling steaks on the fire, embellishing tall tales, and, of course, drinking red wine.

He continued to climb at a high level into his 80s, traveling to exotic locales such as Algeria. He repeated the Steck-Salathé route on Sentinel Rock at least four times, making his 50th-anniversary ascent in 2000, at the age of 74, with Andy Selters, a writer, guide, and frequent Golden Gathering rope gun.

Not a prolific writer or chronicler of ascents, Steck had been urged by Roper and others to record his diverse life. It wasn't until 2009, when his daughter, Sara, asked him to put something on paper to share with his grandson, that

Steck became motivated to write his autobiography. *A Mountaineer's Life*, a comprehensive and highly recommended book describing his long, well-lived life, was published by Patagonia Works in 2017.

His last few years were spent in Bishop at his daughter's home. Friends from all over the world came to pay their respects to this renaissance man, who dabbled in music, photography, and pottery, and read Goethe in the original German, in addition to climbing, raising a family, and starting a business.

Following his death in February, two celebrations of Steck's 96 years were held in summer 2023, in Berkeley and Bishop. The program closed with his advice: "Follow your bliss slowly and carefully. Always be sure you have the necessary skills before undertaking your climbing adventures. And make sure your personal and climbing lives are adequately meshed." Words to live by.

—Sally Moser, with Andy Selters

CONTRIBUTORS

The following climbers who passed away in 2023 wrote many reports and articles for the *American Alpine Journal* over the years. Here, we offer brief tributes to these friends and contributors.

DMITRY GOLOVCHENKO from Russia wrote eight articles for the *AAJ*, describing new routes on Thalay Sagar, Jannu, Muztagh Tower, Trango Tower, and other giants of the Greater Ranges. He died at age 40 in a fall from high on Gasherbrum IV while attempting a new route with longtime partner Sergey Nilov (*see p.276*).

AARON LIVINGSTON, 32, died in September in a solo climbing fall in Northern California. A native of Utah, he was a wide-ranging and multi-talented climber whose most significant report for the *AAJ* covered the first ascent of The Optimist on Mt. Hooker in Wyoming, a route that was itself a tribute to a fallen friend, Nolan Smythe.

NADYA OLENEVA, 38, was a star of modern Russian climbing, with difficult first ascents in Siberia and Kyrgyzstan, from which she reported two climbs in the *AAJ*: the first ascent of a beautiful rock spire called Pik Ostryi, with an all-women team (*AAJ 2022*), and a new route on Pik Korolyova (*AAJ 2023*). She fell while attempting Dhaulagiri in Nepal.

DMITRY PAVLENKO and his wife, Svetlana, and two clients disappeared during an attempt on Pobeda in Kyrgyzstan. He was a key member of two large Russian teams that climbed big-wall-style routes up the west face of Makalu and the north face of Jannu. His last *AAJ* report was in 2023, describing a new route, climbed with Svetlana, up the north face of Free Korea Peak in Kyrgyzstan.

ERMANNO SALVATERRA, 68, a legend of Patagonian climbing, died in a fall while guiding at home in Italy. Among his many accomplishments, the climbs of Cerro Torre stand out: the first winter ascent and new routes on the east, south, and north faces. His feature articles describing these climbs in the *AAJ* spanned two decades, from 1986 to 2006.

JUAN SEÑORET, one of the prolific "Señoret brothers" from Chile, was killed in an avalanche while attempting to ski Volcán Puntiagudo in Chile, along with Christophe Henry from France, who also perished. Juan and his brothers reported numerous new routes in the *AAJ*, most recently the north face of Cerro Catedral in the Torres del Paine, climbed in January 2022 with his brother Cristóbal.

LUIS STITZINGER, 54, a guide and high-altitude climber and skier from Germany, died on Kangchenjunga in Nepal, after reaching the summit alone. He had climbed and skied many 8,000-meter peaks, including descents on Gasherbrum II, Nanga Parbat, and K2. He reported on his solo attempt on Hongku in Nepal in *AAJ 2023*.

SHINJI TAMURA, a Japanese mountain guide based in Zermatt, Switzerland, for decades, wrote about a 2021 attempt on Bondit Peak in the Karakoram for the 2022 *AAJ*. He returned to the same area for the next two years, and in 2023, during an attempt on Apobrok Great Pyramid, a rappelling accident cost him his life (*see p.279*).

KACPER TEKIELI, 38, from Poland, filed *AAJ* reports about new routes in Norway and his home mountains, the High Tatras, where he had climbed hundreds of routes. A veteran of difficult link-ups (including the summer speed record and first winter completion of The Expander link-up in the Tatras, reported in *AAJ 2022*), he died in May as a result of an avalanche in Switzerland, while attempting to enchain all 82 of the Alpine 4,000-meter peaks.

NECROLOGY

In addition, we remember the following AAC members who passed away in 2023.

DONALD ANDERSON
LAUREN BENISHEK
RICHARD BLISS
LINDA BURDET
BRIAN CAREY
MARK CLIFTON

RYAN DAWES
LISA FLEISCHMAN
BRUCE FRANK
LORENTZ HANSEN
R. LEHMAN
GEORGE RIPPLINGER

RICHARD SCOTT
ALEXANDER THOMSON
LEVI WILKINS
BRIAN WILLIAMS
RYAN WONG

BOOK REVIEWS

Edited by David Stevenson

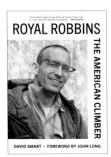

ROYAL ROBBINS: THE AMERICAN CLIMBER
By David Smart. Foreword by John Long. (Mountaineers Books, 2023.) Paperback, 256 pages, $22.95.

David Smart has done it again. His succession of biographies began with a memoir, followed by thorough treatments of Paul Preuss and Emilio Comici. Now, with *Royal Robbins: The American Climber,* Smart demonstrates a mastery of the form.

Most of us know about Robbins: his Golden Age first ascents, eponymous clothing company, his practical and philosophical *Rockcraft* how-to books, his clean climbing environmental ethos, and his sometimes contentious definition of what constitutes fair play. Thanks to Smart, we not only get to know more of all that, but we also get a picture of the human behind the legend.

Smart describes how, in the late 1940s, Robbins—a 12-year-old latchkey kid in Los Angeles—was sent to juvenile hall for burglary. More than simple thrill-seeking, it was part of a bumpy road to climbing, as he needed money for a YMCA summer camp. His crimes led Robbins to the Boy Scouts and, as Smart recounts, "Royal wrote that scouting (which led to rock climbing) kept him 'from drowning in a sea of anarchy and aimlessness.'"

The next era of Robbins' life is more familiar. A few short years after taking up climbing, Robbins would establish historic landmarks like Open Book at Tahquitz Rock—his first free ascent in 1952 was then perhaps the most difficult (5.9) multi-pitch route in the country. In 1957, with Jerry Gallwas and Mike Sherrick, he climbed the Northwest Face of Half Dome. This was the first Grade VI climb in America. What followed was a steady stream of significant routes in Yosemite, the western U.S., and elsewhere that continued into the 1970s. (Smart lists 160 "Notable First Ascents" at the book's end.)

Robbins' first continuous ascent of The Nose on El Capitan, with Joe Fitschen, Tom Frost, and Chuck Pratt in 1960, one-upped the siege style used by Warren Harding, et al, on the first ascent. A year later, on the first ascent of the Salathé Wall, he minimized the use of fixed rope, partnered again with Frost and Pratt. In 1963, Robbins, along with Layton Kor, Jim McCarthy, and Dick McCracken, made the first ascent of the southeast face of Proboscis in Canada's Northwest Territories. This leap into the unknown ushered in a new era of remote big-wall climbing.

As Robbins's style evolved, it influenced the direction of American—and to some extent global—climbing. The routes he authored were evidence of what could be done. Along with articles, lectures, books, and—in the case of The Wall of Early Morning Light—his actions, Robbins pointed out how things *should* be done. Smart observes, "I write from the partisan point of view that Royal's choices and beliefs were significant because his climbs were significant. It's a perspective I believe he would share."

To Robbins, style was not merely a set of rules to which one must adhere, but also meaningful principles that extended beyond personal climbing style. His adaptation and popularization of clean climbing is but one example of how one's choices could influence the wider world. Free climbing, limiting the use of bolts, and minimizing the application of fixed ropes were all gestures towards maintaining the uncertainty that is necessary for adventure.

Smart allows Robbins to tell much of his own story through quotes and passages from personal letters, articles, books, and unpublished material. He fills in gaps left by Robbins' unfinished autobiography—Robbins completed only three of a prospective seven volumes before passing away—and by Pat Ament's 1992 biography of his friend and climbing partner.

Throughout *The American Climber*, Smart portrays the complexities of a man pulled between middle-class values and the freedom offered by the vertical world. He weaves this interior drama with Robbins' progression from a juvenile delinquent to master climber, to a father and devoted husband, a world-class kayaker, and founder of the outdoor company that still bears his name. Throughout much of his life, Robbins was known as focused, outwardly dour, and almost machine-like in performance and persona. Smart reveals something of the inner human without resorting to caricature: "Some of the Royal's acquaintances described him as a man worthy of Hadley Richardson's description of Hemingway with 'so many sides to him, he defies geometry.'"

What's perhaps most engaging about *The American Climber* are the small vignettes: the partnerships that succeeded and disappointed; the complex romantic entanglements set against the sexual and countercultural revolution of the '60s; the squabbles and petty egos unleashed in an era in which pioneering ascents were readily available to the bold. Fascinating characters in Robbins's life emerge in finer detail in *The American Climber,* including his wife, Liz—a pioneer in both climbing and business—Yvon Chouinard, Doug Tompkins, Tom Frost, Warren Harding, and others. Read it for yourself. It's destined to be a classic.

—**Pete Takeda**

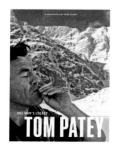

TOM PATEY: ONE MAN'S LEGACY
By Mike Dixon (Scottish Mountaineering Press, 2022). Hardcover, 464 pages, £30.

In the mid-1970s, when I was new to climbing, none of my circle was buying hardcover books. Yet all of us knew the anecdote about Royal Robbins' comment to Tom Patey on how to recognize a good crack climber's hands, or about Patey and Don Whillans' famed retreat off the north face of the Eiger. We repeated these stories gleefully, as if they were our own. And at some point we read all of Patey's *One Man's Mountains* and said to ourselves, "This is the stuff."

Now, a half-century later, Mike Dixon has lifted the veil—much of it anyway—on the man behind the words with *Tom Patey: One Man's Legacy*. The biography is an elegant tome of nearly 500 pages, meticulously researched and beautifully presented.

Patey began climbing in the era of Tricouni-nailed boots and cutting steps on steep ice. He roped up with the most famous names of his era in British climbing: Hamish MacInnes, Joe Brown, Don Whillans, and Chris Bonington, among many others. He made an astonishing number of climbs in the 20 years before he died in a rappelling accident in 1970 at the age of 38: over 200 first ascents in Scotland, including the Cuillin Ridge in winter, as well as the Karakoram plums of Muztagh Tower and Rakaposhi. Dixon notes that his most difficult climb in the Alps was likely the northwest face of the Aiguille Sans Nom.

This sort of list is neither at the heart of the man nor this book. Rather it's Patey's style, both on and off the mountain, for which he was well-known. As a climber, Dixon notes certain strengths: "off-vertical, suspect rock, lacquered in moisture and vegetation, with scanty protection." An early climb is described as having a "crux of double overhangs, coated in a mean slick of verglas, on which he deployed the adhesive properties of...woolly gloves."

Patey was famous for his "cavalier preparation" and often showed up for a climb with "a packet of sausages, a bottle of whisky, and his accordion." Bonington, who despite being parodied in Patey's "Onward Christian Bonington" ("He has climbed the Eigerwand, he has climbed the Dru/For a mere ten thousand francs, he will climb with you"), seems to have enjoyed a lasting friendship with Patey, noted that "it was a problem persuading him to tie in at all, on anything up to HVS [5.9] he preferred soloing. When he did lead, he hardly ever put any protection in, and when he did, it was badly placed. He was not remotely interested in gear."

What he was interested in, and famous for, in addition to going hard in the mountains, was what today we would call "partying." In his case: drinking, storytelling, singing, playing music to all hours—a classic "hail fellow, well met."

In his foreword, Mick Fowler nicely summarizes Dixon's work: "a picture of a driven man who was fired by an irrepressible desire to explore, climb, and serve his patients well." And by all accounts, as a rural family doctor, Patey steadfastly served patients with great dedication and efficacy. True to form, his medical practice also was observed to be *unconventional*: "He [Patey] carried on smoking as he proceeded his examination, occasionally flicking ash in the patient's belly button, in which he would slot the filter end of the fag when requiring both hands free." Fowler calls this a "warts and all" biography.

Dixon in his intro mentions the reluctance of a potential interviewee because they didn't want "the myth to be pierced." He claims he attempted to write a balanced account of Patey's life, rather than a "hagiographic nostalgia trip." However, I couldn't help noting that Patey's wife is essentially absent here. One wonders if, and suspects, this is because Patey was largely absent from her life. Dixon seemed to stop well short of piercing the myth.

At close to 500 pages, you would expect a full treatment of a life, and it is definitely a full treatment of Patey's life as a climber. The hard-drinking raconteur, the up-all-night musician and poet who poured his soul into *One Man's Mountains* is on nearly full display here. It's a compelling, fascinating portrait, brilliantly researched. I couldn't have kept up with Patey in the mountains, but I would have loved to have kept company with him during a night in the pub (where, undoubtedly, I also would have been unable to keep up). I just wouldn't have wanted one of my sisters to have married him.

—David Stevenson

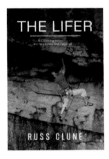

THE LIFER: ROCK CLIMBING ADVENTURES IN THE GUNKS AND BEYOND
By Russ Clune (Di Angelo Publications, 2023). Paperback, 274 pages, $25.

Many of us dream of dropping everything and heading to the crags to climb full-time. Few of us ultimately do. Russ Clune's 2023 memoir *The Lifer* is a purist's take on that dream and follows one man's dedication as he becomes deeply entwined with the history and evolution of the sport. In vivid accounts and often harrowing scenes, Clune brings the reader on adrenaline-pumped adventures across the globe, where he pushes himself and the boundaries of climbing itself.

In 2019, a short film by the same name preceded the book. At 13 minutes, it's a welcoming primer for the book. The film captures Clune's personality and voice, and gives a broader picture of just how long Clune has been climbing in New York's Shawangunks. In the film, his friend and climbing partner Lynn Hill says, "He had a real foothold in the Gunks, and I think still today. He knows more about the Gunks and has probably done more routes than anyone."

The book covers a period starting with Clune's introduction to rock climbing in college in 1977 and ending when he got married in 1991. His obsession with climbing is mirrored by his prose, as he focuses much of the story on the technical features of routes, their difficulty, and the popular climbing style of the day, along with the roster of people he climbed alongside. In that regard, the book resembles a guidebook merged with historical text.

The book comes alive when the scenes turn more personal: when Clune and his partner were harassed by swarms of wasps as they hung precariously from a multi-pitch climb, or when a new partner came to stay at his mom's house, with no apparent social graces, comedically expecting a free ride. There is the infamous tale of climbers eating ten-cent cat food to survive. In one episode while climbing in the United Kingdom, Clune traveled impulsively to Czechoslovakia to meet friends, only to be stood up. Exhibiting his adventuresome spirit, he turned the whole trip around by making friends with East German climbers who didn't speak English.

As Clune traveled across the globe—climbing in far-flung locales from Europe to Asia, and on road trips across the United States—he linked up with the best climbers of his generation and built friendships that became more meaningful than the sport itself. In a climactic scene where he tests his grit and dedication to the climbing life, Clune attempts to free solo Supercrack, a 5.12+ up a 60-foot pinnacle of orange quartz conglomerate in his beloved Gunks. The solo "marked the hardest climb I would ever do without a rope and...a retirement of sorts, at least from full-time climbing."

Wrapping up the book with a cursory tour through his professional life after grad school, Clune details the bankruptcy and sale of his employer, Chouinard Equipment, to an employee-led coalition that became Black Diamond, where he worked for the next 25 years. An ethos emerges from the story: "Climbing is not so much about the routes we climb but instead about the kinships and love created by sharing a rope with friends." His words are a fitting summation of his memoir, and a metaphor for what his life has come to stand for. *The Lifer* is not only a chronicle of Clune's own story, it's also a treatise on why we climb, told by one of the sport's ever-present yet often unsung heroes.

—**Lance Garland**

THE ZEN OF CLIMBING

By Francis Sanzaro (Saraband, 2023). Paperback, 216 pages, $14.95.

Near the middle of *The Zen of Climbing*, Francis Sanzaro offers a succinct and gripping account of finding himself perched precariously on a ledge and staring down into the abyss. It's a moment he refers to as "*the ask.*" He was young and inexperienced. "It was the first time in my life," he writes, "when I saw myself dying." We've all been there. In Sanzaro's case, it forced his mind into "places it hadn't gone before"—and it changed the course of his life. "It was my first Zen experience." Ultimately, this led to the writing of *The Zen of Climbing*.

The title is perhaps a bit misleading. Sanzaro has comparatively little to say about "Zen." For that we must be grateful, as what is there to say about a spiritual practice that aims for a realm beyond words? No book is small enough to do that. Fortunately, *The Zen of Climbing* is mostly about climbing—or rather, Sanzaro's philosophical reflections on the sport of climbing. He is well-credentialed for such a project. With more than three decades of climbing experience under his belt, he is the author of two previous books and served as editor in chief of multiple climbing magazines. On top of that, he has a Ph.D. in religious studies. He writes with admirable clarity and precision, anchoring his more rarefied thoughts in felicitous prose. Given the compact size of this paperback volume, you might even be tempted to throw it into the gear bag for those times when you're waiting to climb at a busy crag.

The Zen of Climbing is replete with sage counsel for the climber less concerned with upping physical strength than with improving mental acuity. Indeed, Sanzaro's most pertinent advice can be summed up in a familiar phrase: *Pay attention!* "That sounds so simple," one is tempted to say, "a three-year-old could understand it." "Ah yes," says many a venerable teacher, "the three-year-old easily understands, but a person of 80 years is still unable to practice it." Sanzaro himself draws upon a variegated array of sources—including philosophy, social science, and religious studies—to make the same point. To pay attention is to open a new window on the world: "For climbers, you may discover you climb for all the wrong reasons and that your friends do as well. You have to recalibrate." Part two of the book consists of a series of mini-essays—bearing such titles as "Routes. Moves"; "Mistake Management"; and "The Myth of Mental Toughness"—each of which investigates from distinct angles this notion of "recalibration."

Sanzaro returns frequently to a notion popularized by Suzuki Roshi in his book *Zen Mind, Beginner's Mind*—namely, a contrast between two styles of consciousness. According to Suzuki: "If your mind is related to something outside itself, that mind is a small mind,

a limited mind. If your mind is not related to anything else, then there is no dualistic understanding.... Big mind experiences everything within itself." Baffling as these words may seem, it gets even trickier. As both Suzuki Roshi and Francis Sanzaro will tell you, these two styles of consciousness are actually one and the same. No difference. So what's the big deal, then? Ah, but this is where the Real Climbing begins. Or as Sanzaro aptly sends it: "If you digest what is in these pages, you will appreciate your climbing more...have more fun, complain less, develop better technique and...become a better athlete."

—**John P. O'Grady**

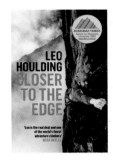

CLOSER TO THE EDGE: CLIMBING TO THE ENDS OF THE EARTH

By Leo Houlding (Headline Press, U.K., 2023). Paperback, 368 pages, £12.99.

A friend and frequent climbing partner has complained to me about the narrowness of climbing literature: "I tried to climb it, almost died, didn't die, and summited." I think what my friend is reacting to is an essential lack of real introspection in much of the narrative, which is another of way of saying that most climbers are not really writers.

This is all preamble to a review of Leo Houlding's *Closer to the Edge* that I do not much relish writing. Houlding might be best known to many Americans as Sandy Irvine to Conrad Anker's Mallory during their filmed re-creation of the 1924 Everest expedition. His first ascents include bold routes on Baffin Island and Antarctica, but even more striking is Houlding's personality, which is on bright display in films like *The Asgard Project*. Houlding likes to party, likes to laugh, likes to take risks. He is likable. I like him. You probably like him, too. He's out on the town, partying away, and then is somehow ready for an alpine start.

Closer to the Edge is Houlding's memoir of climbing, but one is reminded that even memoirs—perhaps especially memoirs—need a purpose. Houlding follows the progression of his climbs, but there's little to suggest there's anything happening behind those moments on the rock. What is Houlding's driving force? What is the mania? One would hope for a book that incorporates some of Houlding's intensity and exuberance, but alas, in print, his story is of climbs completed or left incomplete with his actual living *self* left between the lines.

At one point he relates the story of a fall in Patagonia. Houlding and his partners are attempting Cerro Torre when Houlding's foot blows while negotiating a rock-over. His talus is shattered so completely that doctors will discuss amputation as a possibility. Against the odds, Houlding recovers, and one hopes for some introspection in the aftermath, but he mostly narrates his boredom, filling the time with the decision to buy a house and to begin dating the woman who would become his wife. (They now have two children.) The next chapter has him BASE jumping with Dean Potter, as if the accident had never happened, as if nothing was learned.

It is, of course, a fallacy to review a book for what it is not rather than what it is, but I can't help but imagine what Houlding might have done with an insistent and talented (and funny) co-author, and here I'm not thinking of fellow climbers but of actual *writers*. What might have become of his narrative with someone to coax his exuberance onto the page? What might this book have been with someone like Jonathan Ames in the co-pilot's seat?

One can hardly fault Houlding, for we are enmeshed in a sport where every climber of great note is pushed to write a book. The drama of what we do is the draw, of course, but as a reader (and a writer), I'm still searching for some compelling reason for the narrative. In other words, *why* does this book need to be written? Does Houlding have something unique to add to climbing? He probably does, but it's not particularly apparent in his memoir. Compared with other climbers, and indeed other climbing memoirs, one has to ask: closer to the edge of what?

—**Christian Kiefer**

A FINE LINE: SEARCHING FOR BALANCE AMONG MOUNTAINS
By Graham Zimmerman (Mountaineers Books, 2023). Paperback, 224 pages, $19.95.

Seventy pages into Graham Zimmerman's memoir *A Fine Line*, the author and his partners, who are forging a new route in the Waddington Range, take a break from the hard climbing in front of them to stare out across the Tiedemann Glacier and the Waddington-Combatant col. The once-straightforward icefall is riven with collapsing crevasses; the Tiedemann is a skinny, withering version of its former self. For a moment, Zimmerman weighs what he sees against his team's presence here: "I thought of the helicopter we had used to access the range, one of the least carbon-efficient modes of transportation available. *We are part of the problem*." It's not long before he turns his attention back to the climbing in front of him.

During the first third of *A Fine Line*, these hyper-focused moves on rock, ice, and snow indeed drive the narrative, as Zimmerman quickly ascends the ranks of exploratory alpinism to become one of its foremost practitioners. Like most alpinists of his generation, the young

Zimmerman is steeped in the light-and-fast, "no future" ethos of Mark Twight. Jobs, marriage, and normalcy can only hinder this mission. He bounces between gigs: Yosemite Search and Rescue, a geophysics crew. He returns home only when injured or out of money. He climbs—a lot. Zimmerman's youthful, rowdy psyche sometimes gets him into trouble or hurt, but each lesson informs the climbing that follows.

Life, love, and the stark, mountain-melting reality of climate change trickle slowly into the book. This gentle layering—and how it mirrors the way most of us reconcile with these topics as we age or gain reference points through experience—was my favorite part of *A Fine Line*. Zimmerman slips paragraphs like his Waddington realization between tales of risk, partnership, and adventure, and gradually these themes cascade into major elements of the story.

So, it's no accident that some of the most introspective passages of *A Fine Line* occur toward the end. By this point, Zimmerman has weathered the deaths of close friends and companions, worked through the triumphs and challenges of a serious romantic partnership, and ramped up his climate advocacy work with Protect Our Winters, the grassroots environmental advocacy group founded by snowboarder Jeremy Jones. He climbs, but doing so responsibly now matters as much as the moves themselves.

At the culmination of Zimmerman's 2020 ascent of Link Sar in Pakistan—along with Mark Richey, Steve Swenson, and Chris Wright—the summit has not come easily. Zimmerman is shaken from a big fall. He extols his seasoned companions to make no mistakes on the way down. He wants to survive. For a quick moment on top, though, the author casts his gaze across the expanse of the Karakoram, where "rays of dusk illuminated thin crests of ridges: first gold, then pink and violet" and at "ripples of light and shadow." He soaks in the view

with a wizened perspective that is hard won. I am glad he has shared it with the rest of us.

—**Michael Wejchert**

In Brief

More: Life on the Edge of Adventure and Motherhood, by Majka Burhardt (Pegasus Books, $27.95). Burhardt follows up on her two Ethiopia books with an epistolary memoir exploring the pursuit of risk in the face of responsibility for new children (twins!).

Take the Lead: Hanging On, Letting Go, and Conquering Life's Hardest Climbs, by Sasha DeGiulian (St. Martin's, $29). After "coming of age under the scrutiny of social media" and "navigating a male-dominated sport," DiGiuilan describes her battles with body dysmorphia and her rise to the upper echelons of rock climbing.

Mechanical Advantage: Tools for the Wild Vertical, Volumes 1 & 2, by big-wall climber and gear designer John Middendorf, collected from a popular series of Substack essays. "The story of rock climbing from the enhanced tools perspective."

Mont-Blanc Lines, by Alex Buisse (Vertebrate Publishing, £40). This large-format coffee-table book features portraits of the great mountains of the Alps with climbing routes overlaid topo-style. Buisse generously offers free downloads of his route posters, available at alexbuisse.com.

Mountain Guru: The Life of Doug Scott, by Catherine Moorehead (Birlinn Ltd., £25). The legendary U.K. mountaineer receives full biographical treatment, covering five decades of cutting-edge climbs.

INDEX

COMPILED BY EVE TALLMAN & RALPH FERRARA

Mountains are listed by common and official names. Ranges, geographic locations, and maps are also indexed. Indexed photographs are in bold type. Unnamed peaks (e.g. Peak 2,340m) are listed under P.

100th Anniversary of Russian Alpinism (Russia) **261**

A

Abbey, Michael 151-2
Abercrombie (AK) 104-**5**
Adad Medni (Morocco) 235
Aeschliman, Gabe 118
Airport Wall (NZ) 339
Ak Sar (PAK) 269
Ak-Su Valley (KYRG) 247-8
Alaska 34-43, 94-111
Alaska Range (AK) 34-43, 99-102
Albert, Jason 80-91
Alberta (CAN) 169-70
Alcorn, Josh 182-3
Alice (CO) 154-**5**
Alpinist, Pik (KYRG) **254**-5
Alpomish (Uzbekistan) **243**-4
Ama Drime East (Tibet) **330**
Ama Drime I (Tibet) **330**
Amaiur Pk. (India) **285**-6
Anco Collo (Bolivia) **201**
Andes (Argentina/Chile) 205-21
Andrea, Ross 158-9
Angola 234-5
Anidesh Chuli (Nepal) **325**
Antarctic Peninsula 222
Antarctica 222-3
Anti-Atlas (Morocco) 235
Aoraki/Mt. Cook Natl. Park (NZ) 339
Api Himal (Nepal) 301-6
Apobrok Great Pyramid ("Bondit Pk.")(PAK) **279**
Apolobamba, Cordillera (Peru) 197
Apusiajik Island (Greenland) 182-3
Argentina 205-15
Arjuna Spires (CAN) **160**-1
Asgard (CAN) 170-**1**
Askatasunaren Dorrea (India) 286
Assolari, Daniele 198-200
Astorga, Chantel 148-50
Ataatap Tower (Greenland) 177-82, **179**
Atardecer (Chile) 207
Augustin Pk. (AK) 94-**5**
Aurora Pk. 180-2
Ausangate, Nevado (Peru) 194-6, **195**
Auyuittuq Natl. Park (CAN) 170-2

Aysén Region (Chile) 207-11
Azul, Cerro (Chile) 209-10

B

Badriashvili, Archil 239, 241-2
Baffin Island (CAN) 170-3
Baguet, Paul 176
Baintha Brakk II (PAK) 272
Baintha Kabata (PAK) 271-3, **272**
Baltoro Muztagh (PAK) 273-7
Banks Rg. (NZ) 338-9
Bansa Hill (India) **300**
Barabar Sar (PAK) *See* Koh-e-Brobar
Barnes, Aimee *obit* 340-1
Baró, Oriol 44-9, 210
Barsik (KYRG) 257-8
Barun (Nepal) 321-3
Batura Muztagh (PAK) 270
Baù, Alessandro 294-5
Bearhat (Montana) **145**-6
Bearpaw Dome (CA) 135
Bear's Face (Montana) 147-**50**
Beartooth Mts. (Montana) 147-51
Belgica Glacier (Greenland) 176
Belotserkovskiy, Kirill 259
Bengal, West (India) 300
Berkeland, Ethan 103
Berman, Ethan 161-3, 169-70
Bernardi, Federico 276-7
Berneline (KYRG) 256-7
Bernese Alps (Switzerland) 50-7
Besen, Noah 171-2
Biarchedi (PAK) 273-**4**
Bighorn Basin (WY) 152-3
Bihaili Jot Group (India) 293
Billon, Lise 213-4
Biois, Aguja Val (PAT) 215
Black, Christian 66-73
Blanca, Cordillera (Peru) 190-2
Boe Sar Southeast (PAK) 268
Boisum ("Boisam," "Boesam") (PAK) **267**-9
Bok Jin-young 312
Bolivia 198-201
Bonanza Pk. (WA) **116**-7
Bondit Pk. (PAK) *See* Aprobrok Great Pyramid
Book Reviews 353-9
Closer to the Edge: Climbing to the Ends of the

Earth by Leo Houlding 357-8
A Fine Line: Searching for Balance Among Mountains by Graham Zimmerman 358-9
The Lifer: Rock Climbing Adventures in the Gunks and Beyond by Russ Clune 355-6
Royal Robbins: The American Climber by David Smart 353-4
Tom Patey: One Man's Legacy by Mike Dixon 354-5
The Zen of Climbing by Francis Sanzaro 356-7
Boswell, Greg 224-5
Boyce, Sam 113-4, 139-40
Brazil 202-4
Breeze ("P. 4431m.") (Ak-Su Valley, KYRG) **247**
Breitenbach (ID) 143-**4**
Brewster (NZ) 339
Bridgman (Antarctica) 222
Briggs, Bill 80-91
British Columbia (CAN) 160-8
Brown, Nathan 156-7
Brumkhangse (India) 300
Burrell, Jere 115
Buryatia Republic (Russia) 260-1

C

Cahill, Nathan 234-5
Caldwell, Tommy 111
California 126-37
Callaghan, Matt 109
Canada 160-73
Capicua, Cerro (Chile) 205-**7**
Carey, Dallin 145-6
Cascade Rg. (WA) 120-2
Cathedral Spires (AK) 96-7
Caucasus Mts. (Georgia) 239-42
Cemetery Spire (AK) 97-**8**
Chaltén Massif (PAT) 211-6
Chaltén, Cerro ("Fitz Roy")(PAT) 215
Chambe (Malawi) 236-8
Chandi Himal (Nepal) **304**-6; *map* 305
Chanrasrik Ri ("H2," "Chareze Ri") (India) 290
Chanshan Cave (China) 337
Chapko, Lani 187-8
Chareze Ri (India) *See* Chanrasrik Ri 290
Chastity Tower (Greenland) 179-80
Chaupi Orco (Bolivia) 200
Chaupi Orco Norte (Peru) **197**
Chiefs Head **156**-7
Chile 44-9, 205-21
China 74-9, 249-51, 328-37
Chitistone (AK) 106-8
Chola Shan Rg. (China) 331
Cholatse (Nepal) **319**-20
Chugach Mts. (AK) 104-6
Citadel (AK) **96**-7
Clark, Whitney 166
Cloudy Peak Rg. (NZ) 339

Cloudy Pk. (NZ) 339
Coast Mts. (AK) 108-11
Coast Mts. (CAN) 160-7
Cochamó (Chile) 205-7
Colorado 154-8
Concord Tower (WA) 118
Coricampana (Bolivia) **201**
Cornell, Matt 34-43
Coronation Glacier Area (CAN) 171-2
Costa, Adrien 147-8, 150-1
Councell, Andrew 160-1
Crison, Jonathan 204
Cruz Rodríguez, Juan 192
Cutbirth, Wilson 170-1
Cutthroat Pk. (WA) **115**-6
Cyclades Islands (Greece) 230-1

D

Da Pangwa (China) 336
Damocles (Greenland) 182
Damodar Himal (Nepal) 307-8
Dare, Ben 338-9
Dark Side Wall (CO) **157**-8
Darran Mts. (NZ) 338
Davis-Merry, Tom 300
Daxue Shan (China) 331-6
Debsa Valley (India) 296-7
Denali (AK) 102
Devils Leap (WY) 152-**3**
Devils Thumb Massif (AK) 111
Dhairya (India) 300
Dickey (AK) 34-43, **36**
Diran (PAK) 270-1
Disman, Marek 318
Djangart Rg. (KYRG) 256-8
Dolmans, Joda 226-7
Dragon (KYRG) **258**
Dragpoche (Nepal) 310-**1**
Drifika(PAK) 279-80
Dvorak, Michelle 179-80
Dyer, Jacob 269
Dzashez Kangri ("Friendship Pk.")(India) 282

E

Eiger (Switzerland) 50-7, **52**
Elephant's Perch (ID) 142-3
Elías, Martín 44
Elliott, Christopher 246
Ellsworth Mts. (Antarctica) 222-3
Emperador Guillermo Norte, Cerro (Chile) 209-10
Emperador Guillermo, Cordillera (Chile) 207-10
Erpingfeng (China) 336-7
Espada, La (PAT) 217-**8**
Espírto Santo (Brazil) 202-4
Extra, Aiguille (CA) **137**

F

Fabrikant, Adam 80-91
Fanni, Torre (India) *See* Little Jamyang Ri
Fastan-Kangri (India) *See* K25
Faust, Charlie 157-8
Feistl, Martin 177-8
Fergana Rg. (KYRG) 248
Ferguson, Mike 308
Finklaire, Pete 65
Fischel, Josh 201
Fitz Roy (PAT) *See* Chaltén
Flat Top (India) 58-65, **60**
Flat Top Pk. (NZ) 339
Fowler, Mick 245
Fox Jaw Cirque (Greenland) 184
Franzen, August 106
Freeman-Attwood, Julian 305-6
Frez-Albrecht, Simon 104-5
Friendship Pk. (India) *See* Dzashez Kangri
Frontal, Cordillera (ARG) 205
Fugleholmene (Greenland) 183

G

Galligan, Gerry 296-7
Ganchempo (Nepal) 310-1
Ganga Tower ("Squid")(Greenland) 177-8, **179**
Ganglung Kangri II (Nepal) 305-6
Gangotri (India) 298-9
Garcia, Juliana 183
Garhwal, Western (India) 298-9
Gasherbrum IV (PAK) **276**-7
Georgia (Europe) 239-42
Ghamubar Zom V (PAK) 262-5, **263**
Ghujerab (PAK) 266-9
Ghuman, Sartaj 292-3
Gilbertson, Eric 112, 243-4
Girard, Antoine 270-1
Girls Mt. (AK) 106
Gissar Rg. (Uzbekistan) 243-4
Glacier Natl. Park (Montana) 145-6
Gladsheim (CAN) **168**-9
Glazunov, Evgeny 260-1
Goldbetter, Alan 232-3
Goldum (Nepal) **312**
Golovchenko, Dmitry *obit.* 351
Grand Teton (WY) 80-91
Grand Teton Natl. Park (WY) 80-91, 151-2
Grande, Cerro (PAT) 215
Gray, Spencer 124-5
Great Rapids Ridge (Russia) 261
Greece 230-1
Greenland 174-85
Gribi, Matthias 58-65
Grinnell Glacier Area (CAN) 172-3
Grobel, Paulo 306-7
Gronky (KYRG) **252**
Grundtvigskirken (Greenland) 176

Gu Niaoniao 330
Guillaumet (PAT) 215
Guillem Aparicio, Punta (India) 286-7
Gulba (Georgia) **240**
Gunj-e-Dur (PAK) 269

H

H2 ("Chareze Ri")(India) *See* Chanrasrik Ri
Habrich (CAN) **166**
Hadley, Nathan 120-2
Hák, Zdeněk 319-20
Half Dome (CA) 130-**1**
Hanselman, Marc 143-4
Hard Mox (WA) **112**
Harrison, Lee 267-8
Hart, Ky 172-3
Hayes Rg. (AK) 103
He Lang 332-4, 336-7
Heald, Nathan "Nate" 193, 197
Hearth Mt. (AK) 103-**4**
Heritage Rg. (Antarctica) 222-3
Herrin (Antarctica) 222-3
Herry, Julien 273-4
Heyburn (ID) **140**-1
Hidden Tower (Greenland) 180-2
Himachal Pradesh (India) 293-7
Himalaya (Nepal) 10-23
Himalaya-Nyonno Ri Rg. (Tibet) 330
Hindu Kush (PAK) 24-33, 266
Hindu Raj (PAK) 262-5
Hispar Muztagh (PAK) 270
Höbenreich, Christoph 223
Holeček, Marek 321-2
Honbrok (PAK) 279
Hongku (Nepal) **321**-2
Honnold, Alex 111
Hornbein, Tom *obit* 341-3
Huallatani (Bolivia) **201**
Huallomen (Bolivia) **199**
Huasteca, La (Mexico) 188-9
Huayhuash, Cordillera (Peru) 192
Huayna Cuno Collo (Bolivia) **201**
Huayna Illampu (Bolivia) **198**
Hueco Tanks State Pk. (TX) 158-9
Huila Plateau (Angola) 234-5
Hulang Go (Nepal) **308**-10
Hunter (AK) **102**
Huntington (AK) 99-101, **100**

I

Idaho 140-4
Ile-Alatau (Kazakhstan) 259
Index (WA) 120-2, **121**
India 58-73, 282-300
Inflation Tower (AK) 103
Itabira, Pico do (Brazil) **202**-4

J

Jacha Cuna Collo (Bolivia) **201**
Jamieson, Hayden 205-7
Jamyang Ri (India) **288**-9
Janak Himal (Nepal) 323-5
Jannu ("Kumbhakarna") (Nepal) 10-23, **13**
Jarkya (Nepal) 310
Jarrín, Joshua 310-1
Jasper Natl. Park (CAN) 169-70
Jebel Rum (Jordan) 232
Jebel Sham (Oman) 232-3
Jiazi (China) 334-6, **335**
Jiptik Valley (KYRG) 246
Jobe, Wyatt 295
Jordan 232
Juanillo, Punta (Greenland) **182**
Jugal V (Nepal) 314
Junkar, Christian 190-1

K

K25 ("Pastan," "Fastan-Kangri") (India) 284
Kabru South (Nepal) **326**-7
Kalamos (Greece) **230**-1
Kangchenjunga Himal (Nepal) 326-7
Kangertitivatsiaq Fjord (Greenland) 177-82
Karakoman Glacier (KYRG) 248
Karakoram (India/Pakistan) 266-9, 271-9, 282-4
Kashmir (India) 284
Katya Repina (Russia) 260-1
Kazakhstan 259
Kegreiss, Sebastian 258
Kenai Mts. (AK) 103-4
Kharut II (PAK) 274-**5**
Kharut Pks. (PAK) 274-5
Khergani (KYRG) **246**
Khor Ash-Sham (Oman) 232-3
Khumbu (Nepal) 319-20
Kichatna Mts. (AK) 94-8
Kishtwar (India) 58-65
Kishtwar Shivling (India) 66-73
Kjerag (Norway) 229
Klattasine (CAN) **164**-5
Kleslo, Michal 245
Klokktinden (Norway) **227**-9
Knott, Paul 252-3
Kochubey, Oksana 249-51
Koh-e-Brobar ("Barabar Sar") (PAK) **268**
Kolyma Mts. (Russia) 261
Korada Central (PAK) 280-1
Korada Pks. (PAK) **280**-1
Korsun (KYRG) 252-**3**
Koshelenko, Yuri 316-7
Kovacic, Will 168
Krajnc, Luka 211-2
Kraken (Antarctica) 223
Kroupis, Nikolaos 283-4
Kuenzle, Jack 102

Kuilu Rg. (KYRG) 258
Kulusuk (Greenland) 182-3
Kumbhakarna (Nepal) See Jannu
Kushwaha, Suraj 296
Kyabura (Nepal) 323-**4**
Kyrgyzstan 246-58
Kyzyl Asker (KYRG) 249-**51**

L

Ladakh (India) 282-93
Lake Ann Buttress (WA) 115
Lanius-Pascuzzi, Alessandro 166-7
Langtang Valley (Nepal) 313-4
Langtang/Jugal (Nepal) 310-5
Lanoe, Aurélia 308-10
Lappblad (Norway) 227
Lardschneider, Elisabeth 289-90
Latok Thumb (PAK) 272-**3**
Leah, Gareth 202-4
Leba, Serra de (Angola) 234-5
Liard Island (Antarctica) 222
Lillooet Rg. (CAN) 166-7
Limongi, Davide 279-80
Lisle, Sally 188-9
Little Jamyang Ri ("Torre Fanni")(India) **289**-90
Little Slide Canyon (CA) 126-7
Livingston, Aaron *obit.* 351
Lofoten (Norway) 227-9
Loinbo Kangri (Tibet) 328-**9**
López, Joan 266
Lost River Rg. (ID) 143-4
Lovell, Zach Joseph 96-7
Lowry, Sam 343

M

Macfarlane, Ruari 338-9
Madeline (NZ) 338
Madre, La (NV) **138**
Magadan (Russia) 261
Mahalangur Himal (Nepal) 319-23
Maiz, Ekaitz 285-6
Makalu (Nepal) **319**
Malawi 236-8
Malte Brun (NZ) **339**
Manaslu Himal (Nepal) 310
Mandu Pks. (PAK) **278**
Manlung Kangri (India) 282
Marazzi, Paolo 186, 210-1
Marco, Miriam 180-2
Marshall, Drew 186-7
Martin Elorrieta, Tasio 240, 286-7
Marvell, Jackson 10-23
Masherbrum (PAK) **278**
Masherbrum Rg. (PAK) 277-9
Masri Gyad (India) 282-3
Matheny, Trish 126

Mathers, Jay 320
Matterhorn (Wallowa Mts., OR) **124**-5
Maudit, Mont (India) **294**-5
McEleney, Ian 133
McMillan, Linda *obit.* 344
McNeely, Ammon *obit.* 345-6
Meder, Steve 193
Medialuna, Aguja de la (PAT) 215
Melanphulan (Nepal) **320**
Melcyr Shan (China) 336
Mendenhall Towers (AK) **110**-1
Mendoza, Rodrigo 197
Meroi, Nives 326-7
Merrill, Tucker 118-9
Meru (India) **298**-9
Meru South (India) **298**-9
Mesa, Cerro (Chile) 207-9
Messner, Simon 277-8
Mexico 186-9
Mierda, Torre de (CA) 133
Milford Sound (NZ) 339
Military Topographers Pk. (China) *See*
Voennyh Topografov
Miller, Dylan 108-11
Miller, Punta (Chile) 210
Milluni, Pico (Bolivia) 200
Minafierro Oeste, Nevado (Peru) 193
Minas Gerais (Brazil) 201
Mindzhar Valley (KYRG) 248
Minya Konka Rg. (China) 332-4
Mirador, Cerro (Chile) 207-9
Mirror Wall (Greenland) 175-**6**
Mitac, Standa 280-1
Miyar Valley (India) 294-5
Moby Dick (Antarctica) 223
Mocho, El (PAT) 215
Molodaya Gvardiya (Kazakhstan) **259**
Monasterio, Erik 200
Montana 145-51
Monument Pk. (NV) 139-40
Moran (WY) 80-91
Moro Rock (CA) 134-5
Morocco 235
Morrison (CA) 132-**3**
Muchu Chhhish (PAK) 270
Mukot Himal (Nepal) 306-7
Mulanje Massif (Malawi) 236-8
Mulkila Glacier (India) 295
Muni, Divyesh 282, 293
Murphy, Peter 135
Mururata (Bolivia) **200**
Muryn-Tau (Kazakhstan) 259
Musandam (Oman) 232-3
Mushtaq, Zeeshan 284
Musiyenko, Vitaliy 132-3
Muya Rg. (Russia) 260-1
Muysky Giant (Russia) **260**-1

Muz Tok (KYRG) **246**
Mythics Cirque (Greenland) **177**-82

N
Nakajima, Kenro 24-33
Nakula Spire (CAN) **160**-1
Nalivkin (KYRG) 252-3
Nangma Valley (PAK) 280-1
Nateo Nala (India) 292-3
Negro, Pico (Mexico) **188**-9
Nenana (AK) 103
Nepal 10-23, 301-27
Nevada 138-40
Nevada I, Aguja (Peru) 190-1
Neverseen Tower (India) **294**-5
New Zealand 338-9
Nochnoi Motyl (KYRG) 251
Nora Oeste, Cerro (Chile) **210**-1
Nordland (Norway) 224-9
Normand, Bruce 323-4
North Cascades (CAN) 168
North Cascades (WA) 112-9
Norway 224-9
Nubra Valley (India) 282-3
Nuevo León (Mexico) 186-9
Nunavut (CAN) 170-3
Nurishan (PAK) 280-**1**
Nya Kangri (India) 283-4
Nyholm, Joe 103-4
Nyonno Ri Rg. (Tibet) 330

O
O'Donoghue, Tristan 106-8
Oldhorn (CAN) 169-**70**
Oleneva, Nadya *obit.* 351
Oman 232-3
Oqatssut Wall (Greenland) 174-**5**
Oregon 124-5
Oroy Valley (KYRG) 258
Owen (WY) 80-91, 151-**2**

P
P. 620m. (Qianarteq Island, Greenland) 184
P. 830m. (Apusiajik Island, Greenland) 182-3
P. 4300m. (Ak-Su Valley, KYRG) **247**-8
P. 4643m. (Gissar Rg., Uzbekistan) 243-**4**
P. 5217m. (Western Kokshaal-too, KYRG) 252-**3**
P. 5625m. (Boisum Glacier, PAK) 268
P. 5630m (Daxue Shan, China) 336
P. 5735m. (Damodar Himal, Nepal) 308
P. 5800m. (Minya Konka Rg., China) **332**-4
P. 5822m. (Mahalangur Himal, Nepal) 323
P. 5860m. (Mindzhar Valley, KYRG) 248
P. 5914m. (Mindzhar Valley, KYRG) **248**
P. 6050m. (Pologongka Rg., India) 293
P. 6080m. (Debsa Valley, India) 296-**7**
P. 6100m. (Raru Valley, India) **292**-3

P. 6110m. (Debsa Valley, India) 296-**7**
P. 6205m. (Pologongka Rg., India) 293
P. 6662m. (Peri Himal, Nepal) **308**-10
Paine, Central Tower (PAT) 218-9
Paine, Torres del (PAT) 216-21
Pakistan 24-33, 262-81
Pamir (KYRG) 248
Pamir (Tajikistan) 245
Pamir Alai (KYRG) 246-8
Panmah Muztagh (PAK) 271-3
Papi, Gendarme de (Greenland) 177-8
Parfyonov, Alexander 74-9
Parkes (CAN) 168
Pastan (India) *See* K25
Patagonia 44-9, 205-21
Patkhor (Tajikistan) **245**
Pavlenko, Dmitry *obit.* 351
Peanut Wall (Greenland) **184**
Pelletti, Seba 216-8
Penguin Tower (Greenland) 176
Peri Himal (Nepal) 308-10
Perseverance (KYRG) 258
Peru 190-7
Petra (KYRG) **257**-8
Phola Kyung (Tibet) 328-9
Phole (Nepal) 325
Phurba Kang (Nepal) 306-7
Phurbi Chhyachu (Nepal) 314-5
Phurbi Txiki (Nepal) 314-**5**
Piper, Grant 339
Plank, Stefan 290-1
Poblete, Marco 207-9
Poincenot (PAT) 211-**2**, 215-6
Pologongka Rg. (India) 293
Ponce, Manuel 247-8
Popa, La (Mexico) 186-7
Potrero Chico, El (Mexico) 187-8
Pou, Eneko 191-2
Pou, Iker 191-2
Powell, Matt 304
Prince, Brian 134
Principal, Cuerno (PAT) **216**-7
Prusik Pk. (WA) 123
Purbung (Nepal) 307
Putnam, Roger 126-7

Q
Qarn Sham (Oman) 232-3
Qianarteq Island (Greenland) 184
Qonglai Mts. (China) 337
Queen Maud Land (Antarctica) 223
Quimsa Cruz, Cordillera (Bolivia) 201

R
Radovsky, Marek 190
Ragazzo, Stefano 97-8
Rakaposhi Mts. (PAK) 270-1

Ramsden, Paul 301-3
Ranalter, Markus 289-90
Rangtik Topko (India) 288-9
Ranrapalca (Peru) **191**-2
Raru Valley (India) 292-3
Rasac Oeste (Peru) **192**
Rathan Thadi Dome (India) **296**
Ratiruni Tibba (India) 296-7
Ratna Chuli (Nepal) **308**-10
Read, William "Al" *obit.* 346-7
Real, Cordillera (Bolivia) 198-200
Red Rock Canyons (NV) 138-40
Regge Pole (Sierra Mts., CA) 126-**7**
Renland (Greenland) 175-6
Richey, Mark 236-8
Rigsum Gompo (Nepal) 306-7
Rincón, Punta (Chile) 207-**9**
Riscada, Pedra (Brazil) **204**
Ritschergipfel (Antarctica) 223
Rocky Mtn. Natl. Park (CO) 154-7
Rogaland (Norway) 229
Rolwaling Himal (Nepal) 316-8
Rolwaling Kang Shar (Nepal) **316**-7
Rossidis, Kyriakos 230-1
Rossman (Antarctica) 223
Rotten Monolith (ID) **141**-2
Rudney (KYRG) 252-3
Rulten (Norway) 227-9
Rushan Castle (Tajikistan) 245
Rushan Rg. (Tajikistan) 245
Russia 260-1
Ruth Gorge (AK) 34-43

S
Sabor (KYRG) *See* Zabor
Sahadeva Spire (CAN) 160-1
Salkeld, Audrey *obit.* 347-8
Salvaterra, Ermanno *obit.* 352
Samet, Matt 232
San Juan Mts. (CO) 157-8
San Valentín (Chile) 44-9, **48**; *map* 47
Santa Clara, Cerro (ARG) 205
Sara Pk. (India) **300**
Saraghrar (PAK) **266**
Saraghrar Northwest II (PAK) 266
Saser Muztagh (India) **282**
Satoshi Hatsugai 279
Sawtooth Mts. (ID) 140-3
Schäli, Roger 298-9
Schüpbach, Silvan 50-7, 271-2
Schurovsky (KYRG) **246**
Schweizerland (Greenland) 182-5
Scrivner, Rob 154-5
Seahpo Pk. (WA) **113**-4
Segla (Norway) 224-**5**
Sejong (China) 331
Selkirk Mts. (CAN) 168-9

Senja Island (Norway) 224-5
Señoret, Juan *obit.* 352
Sequoia Natl. Park (CA) 134-5
Serra do Caparaó (Brazil) 202-4
Serra Pks. (CAN) 161-3, **162**
Seto Chuli (Nepal) **308**-10
Shafat (India) 285-93
Shar Izat Pk. (PAK) 266-7
Shark's Fin (Antarctica) 223
Shark's Tooth (AK) 108-**9**
Sharphu VI (Nepal) 324-5
Shawa Kangri (India) **290**-1
Shershon Lho (Nepal) 322-**3**
Shkhara (Georgia) 241-**2**
Shpodeen (PAK) **268**
Shuksan (WA) **113**-4
Sibyl (NZ) 338-9
Sichuan (China) 331-7
Sierra Nevada Rg. (CA) 126-37
Sikkim (India) 300
Silin, Oleg 248
Silver Run (Montana) 150-1
Siren Tower (Greenland) 177-8, **179**
Sister Spire (AK) **106**
Skihist (CAN) 166-7
Slesse Massif (CAN) 168
Sloan Pk. (WA) **118**-9
Smith, Cam 137
Smoothy, Sam 339
Sobithongie (Nepal) **325**
Sonamarg Valley (India) 284
Southern Alps (NZ) 338-9
Spiti (India) 296-7
Squamish Area (CAN) 166
Squid (Greenland) *See* Ganja Tower
Stanhope, Will 164-5
Štebe, Nejc 257-8
Steck, Allen *obit.* 349-51
Stetind (Norway) **226**-7
Stewart, Grant 102
Stitzinger, Luis *obit.* 352
Stuart Rg. (WA) 123
Subriana, Marc 272-3
Surma Sarovar (Nepal) **301**-3, 326-7
Suru (India) 285-93
Suys, Christian 256-7
Suzuki, Yudai 194-6, 262-5
Svaneti (Georgia) 239-42
Swain, Donette 300
Swain, Todd 300
Swineford (AK) **111**
Switzerland 50-7

T

Tagas Mts. (PAK) 279-81
Tajikistan 245
Takayasu Semba 279-80

Tamura, Shinji *obit.* 352
Tanuki Ridge (WA) **113**-4
Tasiilaq Fjord (Greenland) 184
Tatsienlu Massif (China) 336-7
Teewinot (WY) 80-91
Tekieli, Kacper *obit.* 352
Telstad, Michael 94-5
Tengi Ragi Tau (Nepal) **318**
Tetnuldi (Georgia) **239**
Teton Rg. (WY) 80-91, 151-2
Texas 158-9
Thajiwas (India) **284**
Thalay Sagar (India) **298**
Thangman Lungpa (India) 282
Thiel Pk. (AK) 109
Thing (Sierra Nevada Rg., CA) **126**
Thoda Pk. (India) 300
Thompson, Peter 266-7
Tibet 328-30
Tien Shan (China) 74-9
Tien Shan (Kazakhstan) 259
Tien Shan (KYRG) 248, 256-8
Tierra, Pilares de la (India) 286
Timpano, Seth 254-5
Tinke, Nevado (Peru) 197
Tirich Mir (Pakistan) 24-33, **27**, **29**, **31**
Tirier, Patrick 288-9
Tomaszewski, Marcin 174-5
Toro, El (Mexico) **187**-8
Torre, Cerro (PAT) 213-5
Trans Alai (KYRG) 248
Transhimalaya-Gangdise Shan (Tibet) 328-9
Trener (KYRG) **256**-7
Trivor (PAK) **270**
Troms (Norway) 224-9
Tuctubamba, Nevado (Peru) **190**
Tuki Sar (PAK) **269**
Tundavala, Fenda da (Angola) 234-5
Turgen (Kazakhstan) **259**
Turkestan (KYRG) **246**
Tutse (Nepal) 323

U

Ulun (KYRG) 249-51, **250**
Unicorn (NZ) 338-9
Urioste, Danny 138-9
Upche Dada (Nepal) 308-10
Urubamba, Cordillera (Peru) 193
Ushba (Georgia) **241**
Uummannaq (Greenland) 174-5
Uzbekistan 243-4

V

Vadillo, Rafa 282-3
Valhalla Prov. Park (CAN) 168-9
Vanhee, Siebe 207
Vanoni, Adrian 123

Venturosa, Cordillera (Peru) 193
Veronica, Nevado (Peru) **193**
Vikol, Lydiane 184
Vilcanota, Cordillera (Peru) 194-7
Villanueva O'Driscoll, Seán 175-6, 220-1
Voennyh Topografov ("Military Topographers
Pk.") China 74-9, **77**

W
Waddington Rg. (CAN) 161-3
Wadi Rum (Jordan) 232
Wallowa Mts. (OR) 124-5
Ward, Matt 140-2
Washington 112-23
Wehrly, Eric 116-7
Westerberg, Mark 128
Western Kokshaal-too (KYRG) 249-55
Westland Tai Poutini Natl. Park (NZ) 338-9
Whimster, Nick 252
White Sapphire (India) **66**-73
Whitney (CA) 135-7, **136**
Whitney Massif (CA) 135-8
Wickens, Phil 222
Wild Basin (CO) 154-5
Wilkin Valley (NZ) 338
Willis, Justin 115-6, 152-3
Wilson (NV) 138-**9**
Wolf (KYRG) 258
Wolf, Tobias 130-1

Wollant, Benj 142-3
Wolverine Pk. (Antarctica) 223
Wrangell Mts. (AK) 106-8
Wright, Chris 227-9
Wyoming 80-91, 151-3

X
Xiao Gongga (China) **334**
Xiao Pangwa (China) 336

Y
Yang, Fan 135-7
Yasinski, Sasha 168-9
Yasushi Yamanoi 292-3
Yates, Simon 245
Yernamandu Kangri (PAK) 277-9, **278**
Yinhaizi (China) 331-**2**
Yipingfeng (China) **336**-7
Yosemite (CA) 128-31
Yudai Suzuki 262-5
Yuzhny (KYRG) **246**

Z
Zabalza, Mikel 314-5
Zabor ("Sabor")(KYRG) 252
Zanskar (India) 285-93
Zemleprohodtsev, Chokko (KYRG) **246**
Zörer, Benjamin 322-3
Zubimendi, Koldo 274-5

AAJ

INTERNATIONAL GRADE COMPARISON CHART

SERIOUSNESS RATINGS

These often modify technical grades when protection is difficult

PG-13: Difficult or insecure protection or loose rock, with some injury potential

R: Poor protection with high potential for injury

X: A fall would likely result in serious injury or death

YDS=Yosemite Decimal System **UIAA**=Union Internationale des Associations D'Alpinisme **FR**=France/Sport **AUS**=Australia **SAX**=Saxony **CIS**=Commonwealth of Independent States/ Russia **SCA**=Scandinavia **BRA**=Brazil **UK**=United Kingdom

Note: *All conversions are approximate. Search "International Grade Comparison Chart" at the AAJ website for further explanation of commitment grades and waterfall ice/mixed grades.*

YDS	UIAA	FR	AUS	SAX	CIS	SCA	BRA	UK	
5.2	II	1	10	II	III	3			D
5.3	III	2	11	III	III+	3+			
5.4	IV- / IV	3	12		IV-	4			VD
5.5	IV+		13		IV	4+			S
5.6	V-	4	14		IV+	5-		4a	HS
5.7	V / V+		15	VIIa		5		4b	VS
5.8	VI-	5a	16	VIIb	V-	5+	4 / 4+	4c	HVS
5.9	VI	5b	17	VIIc			5 / 5+	5a	E1
5.10a	VI+	5c	18	VIIIa	V	6- / 6	6a	5b	
5.10b		6a							E2
5.10c	VII-	6a+	19	VIIIb		6+	6b		
5.10d	VII	6b	20	VIIIc	V+		6c		E3
5.11a	VII+	6b+		IXa		7-	7a	5c	
5.11b		6c	21	IXb		7	7b		
5.11c	VIII-	6c+	22		VI-	7+	7c		E4
5.11d		7a	23	IXc				6a	
5.12a	VIII	7a+	24				8a		E5
5.12b	VIII+	7b	25	Xa	VI	8-	8b		
5.12c	IX-	7b+	26	Xb		8 / 8+	8c		
5.12d	IX	7c	27				9a	6b	E6
5.13a		7c+	28	Xc		9-	9b		
5.13b	IX+	8a	29				9c		
5.13c	X-	8a+	30			9	10a		E7
5.13d	X	8b	31	XIa	VI+		10b		
5.14a		8b+	32	XIb		9+	10c	7a	E8
5.14b	X+	8c	33				11a		
5.14c	XI-	8c+	34	XIc			11b	7b	E9
5.14d	XI	9a	35				11c		E10
5.15a	XI+	9a+	36	XIIa		10	12a		
5.15b	XII-	9b	37		VII		12b		E11
5.15c	XII	9b+	38	XIIb			12c		
5.15d	XII+	9c	39						